Running company meetings

Running company meetings

ANDREW HAMER AND ANDREW ROBERTSON

ICSA Publishing
The Official Publishing Company of
The Institute of Chartered Secretaries and Administrators

First published 1997 by
ICSA Publishing Limited
Campus 400, Maylands Avenue
Hemel Hempstead
Hertfordshire, HP2 7EZ

Typeset in 9.75/12pt Galliard by
Hands Fotoset, Ratby, Leicester

Printed and bound in Great Britain by
Hartnolls Limited, Bodmin, Cornwall

British Library Cataloguing in Publication Data

A catalogue record for this book is available from
the British Library

ISBN 1-87-286059-1

1 2 3 4 5   01 00 99 98 97

Contents

Table of cases

Table of statutes

Table of statutory instruments

CHAPTER ONE

Introduction

This book deals with meetings of companies incorporated under the UK Companies Acts. It is intended as a guide for those involved with the management and administration of companies. Accordingly, it does not cover meetings in insolvency.

Unless otherwise indicated:

- all statutory references are to the relevant section number of the Companies Act 1985 as amended up to the end of April 1997 (e.g. 's. 379A' refers to a section of the Companies Act 1985 which was inserted by the Companies Act 1989 and which has subsequently been amended by statutory instrument);
- all references to regulations (e.g. reg. 72) are to the 1985 Table A which is contained in the Companies (Table A–F) Regulations 1995 (see para. 1.4.3).

1.1   SOLE TRADERS AND PARTNERSHIPS

Anyone may set up a business as a sole trader. Doing so enables an individual to make decisions informally without reference to anyone else. There is no need to hold a meeting or to keep a record of decisions taken. Even though a sole trader may trade under a business name, the business does not have separate legal person personality. Anyone who deals with it, deals with the sole trader in his or her personal capacity. The sole trader is personally liable for all the debts of the business and has unlimited liability.

Where two or more people carry on a business or profession together with a view to sharing any profits, they are deemed to have formed a partnership, unless they set up the business as a company. All the partners have a right to participate in the management of the business unless they agree otherwise [s. 20, Partnership Act 1890]. Each partner is deemed to be an agent of the firm and can enter into binding agreements on its behalf with third parties unless the partnership agreement specifies otherwise [s. 5, Partnership Act 1890]. Each partner is also separately and personally liable for all the debts of the business or profession in which the firm engages [s. 9,

1

Partnership Act 1890]. This is the case even for a partner who does not participate in the management of the firm.

1.2   CORPORATE STATUS

The basic difference between a company and sole traders or a partnership is that a company has separate legal personality from its owners. This enables it to own property, enter into contracts, sue and be sued in its own name. It is also the foundation of the principle of limited liability.

The limited liability company as we now know it was developed in the nineteenth century to cater for businesses which required large amounts of capital from outside investors. Before then it had been possible to obtain corporate status by applying for a Charter or by sponsoring an Act of Parliament. However, both methods were prohibitively expensive, and most businesses were established as unincorporated associations similar in nature to a partnership. Despite the fact that their liability was unlimited, investors were normally content to leave the management of the business to professional managers or directors. In practice, it was very difficult for creditors to sue the members for the debts of the business. They had to serve the writ on all the members which was difficult where the membership was large and fluctuating. Shares in these unincorporated associations were traded by brokers even though this had been outlawed by the Bubble Act 1720. This legislation had been largely ignored for over 80 years, but in 1807 and 1808 several successful prosecutions were brought against unincorporated associations which stimulated pressure for a cheaper and less formal method of incorporation. This was achieved by the Joint Stock Companies Act 1844 which introduced the simple concept of registration. However, that Act specifically preserved the liability of the members for the debts of the company which made it even less attractive than the unincorporated association which provided a measure of protection by default. It was not until Parliament passed the Joint Stock Companies Act 1856 that limited liability companies could be formed with relatively little formality.

The 1856 Act allowed a company to be formed by submitting certain documents to a government agent known as the Registrar. Investors became members of the company by subscribing for shares in it. They were entitled to share in any profits of the company distributed as dividends and any proceeds that remained after all other debts had been paid on winding up in proportion to their shareholding. Their liability was limited to the amount they had agreed to invest in the company by taking those shares. Creditors had to sue the company for any money they were owed. Although several important changes have been made to company law by successive Companies Acts, these basic principles still hold true today.

1.3   COMPANIES ACT 1985

The main body of company law is now contained in the Companies Act 1985 ('the Act' or 'the 1985 Act'). This Act has been amended significantly since 1985 (most notably by the Companies Act 1989, but also by numerous statutory instruments). So much so, that it would now be dangerous to rely on an original copy of the Act. Fortunately, a number of legal publishers produce amended versions of the Act from time to time. The provisions of the Act (as amended up to April 1997) which are relevant to company meetings are set out at **Appendix A**. Anyone involved in running company meetings or in the general administration of companies should ensure that they have an up-to-date edition of one of these books at all times.

The Act generally prohibits the formation of a partnership with more than 20 partners, except for categories of trades or professions which may be prescribed by the Secretary of State, e.g. auditors, solicitors and various other professions. Any other business or profession with more than 20 members must therefore be established as a company.

The expression 'the Companies Acts' includes the Companies Act 1985, the Companies Consolidation Consequential Provisions Act 1985 and the insider dealing provisions of the Criminal Justice Act 1993 [s. 744]. Only the first of these is particularly relevant for the purposes of this book.

1.3.1   Registration under the Act

In order to establish a company with separate legal personality it is necessary to register it in accordance with the requirements of the Act. This is done by submitting the following documents to the Registrar of Companies together with a fee of £20:

- a copy of the company's memorandum of association (see para. 1.4);
- Form 10: a statement showing the names and details of the first director(s) and secretary and the intended address of the company's registered office [s. 10];
- Form 12: a statutory declaration by a solicitor involved in the formation of the company or a person named as a director or secretary in Form 10 that the requirements of the Act have been complied with [s. 12].

If the Registrar is satisfied that everything is in order, he will register the company, allocate a unique company number and issue a certificate of incorporation. The certificate shows the name of the company, its number and the date of incorporation. The Registrar will not register a company with a name which is identical or too similar to one that has already been registered. Nor will he register a company with a name which includes certain prescribed words without evidence that permission has been obtained from the appropriate authority [ss. 26 and 29].

Types of company

Several different types of company can be formed under the Companies Act 1985.

Private company limited by shares
A private company limited by shares can be formed with one or more members. The liability of the members is limited to the amount (if any) unpaid on shares

respectively held by them. Private limited companies are normally small to medium-sized businesses, although there are no restrictions as to size, the number of members, turnover, etc. A private company cannot offer its shares to the public and cannot therefore be listed on a stock exchange. It must have at least one director and a secretary (a person who is a sole director may not be the secretary). There are no requirements regarding minimum paid up capital. The company's name must have 'Limited' or 'Ltd' (or the Welsh equivalent) as its last word. It may commence trading from the date of its incorporation.

Private company limited by guarantee

In this case, the liability of the members is limited to the amount they have undertaken to contribute to the assets of the company in the event of it being wound up. This amount is determined by the memorandum. It is unusual for it to exceed £10. As the members do not contribute any capital on formation, this type of company is not ideally suited for business start-ups. It is mainly used by charities and other 'not-for-profit' organisations which do not require any initial capital. The constitutional documents of such organisations usually prohibit the distribution of profits or any proceeds on winding up to the members. A private company limited by guarantee may be formed with only one member. It may commence trading immediately on incorporation. It need only have one director and one secretary (a person who is a sole director may not be the secretary). The company's name must have 'Limited' or 'Ltd' (or the Welsh equivalent) as its last word unless it has been given permission to omit this under s. 30.

Public limited company

A public company must have a minimum of two members and a minimum share capital of £50,000 of which at least 25 per cent must be paid up. It may offer its shares to the public and may therefore be listed on a stock exchange. It must have at least two directors and a secretary (one of the directors may act as secretary, although the directors have a duty to appoint as secretary a person they consider capable of performing the functions of secretary). The requirements of the Act are more onerous for public companies. A public company must submit an additional statutory declaration signed by a director or secretary that it has complied with requirements of the Act regarding the minimum paid up capital of public companies and may not commence trading until the Registrar of Companies has issued a certificate authorising it to do so. The name of the company must end with the words 'public limited company' or 'plc' (or their Welsh equivalent).

Unlimited private company

An unlimited company is one whose memorandum of association states that the liability of its members shall be unlimited. This type of company is used to gain the benefit of corporate personality where, perhaps, professional rules dictate that the owners of the business must trade with unlimited liability. The requirements of the Act are less onerous for unlimited companies. Many of the requirements are stated to apply only to companies limited by shares or by guarantee.

1.4   MEMORANDUM AND ARTICLES OF ASSOCIATION

The memorandum and articles of association are the constitutional documents of the company. A copy of the memorandum of association must be submitted to the Registrar with the application for registration. It sets out fundamental information about the company which determines which provisions of the Act apply.

The articles of association contain the regulations which govern the relationship between the company and its members and directors. A company limited by shares need not submit articles of association with its application for registration. If it does not do so, it will be deemed to have adopted a model set of articles prescribed by the Secretary of State, known as Table A. A company limited by guarantee must submit articles of association with its application for registration.

The memorandum and articles, when registered, bind the company and its members to the same extent as if they had been signed and sealed by each member, and contained covenants on the part of each member to observe all the provisions of the memorandum and articles [s. 14]. This provision creates a contract (known as the 'section 14 contract') between the company and its members, the terms of which are contained in the memorandum and articles. The company can enforce the contract against its members (*Hickman's Case* [1915] 1 Ch. 881) and the members can enforce it against each other (*Rayfield* v. *Hands* [1960] Ch. 1). The members can also enforce the contract against the company, but only in limited circumstances (see para. 18.2). Section 14 is made subject to other provisions of the Act. So provisions in the memorandum or articles which conflict with the requirements of the Act will not be enforceable by the members or the company.

The section 14 contract differs in a number of ways from normal contracts. Provision is made in the Act for its terms to be altered by a special majority [see ss. 4 and 9 on the alteration of the memorandum and articles by special resolution]. The consent of all the parties is required to vary normal contracts. And although the courts regard articles as commercial documents which should be construed so as to give them reasonable business efficacy (*Holmes* v. *Keyes* [1959] Ch. 199, 215, per Jenkins LJ), the Court of Appeal has held that terms cannot be implied into the articles in order to do so (*Bratton Seymour Service Co. Ltd* v. *Oxborough* [1992] B.C.L.C. 693).

1.4.1   Memorandum of association

The memorandum of association must state:

- the name of the company;
- whether the registered office of the company is to be situated in England and Wales, or in Scotland;
- the objects of the company, i.e. the purpose for which it is formed;
- whether it is a public or private company, limited by shares or guarantee or unlimited;
- in the case of a company limited by shares, the amount of share capital with which

the company proposes to be registered and the division of the share capital into shares of a fixed amount, e.g. the share capital of the company is £100 divided into 100 shares of £1 each.

The memorandum may include other provisions. However, no provision contained in the memorandum can be altered unless express provision is made by the Act allowing it to be altered and the formalities prescribed by the Act for that purpose have been complied with:

- the company's name can be changed by special resolution [s. 28];
- the objects clause may be changed by special resolution, but minority share-holders may apply to the court to have the change declared invalid [ss. 4 & 5];
- a company may re-register as a different type of company provided certain formalities have been followed [ss. 43 to 55]; and
- a company may alter its share capital by ordinary resolution [s. 121].

It can be seen from the above list that it is possible to alter everything that is required to be in the memorandum except the country in which the registered office is situated. Provisions not required by s. 2 to be contained in the memorandum, may not be changed if the memorandum prohibits their alteration. If it provides a procedure for their alteration, that procedure must be followed, otherwise such provisions can be changed by special resolution but the alteration may be challenged by minority shareholders in the same way as for a change in objects [s. 17].

The memorandum must be signed by each subscriber in the presence of one witness who must attest the signature. The subscribers to the memorandum are deemed to have agreed to become members of the company and on its registration should be entered as such in its register of members [s. 22(1)].

1.4.2   Articles of association

The articles of association ('articles') usually contain detailed provisions which govern the conduct of both general meetings and meetings of directors. Some of these provisions may be contained in the memorandum of association and this possibility should be borne in mind whenever reference is made to the articles. The main difference between the articles and the memorandum is that a company may alter any of its articles by special resolution unless its memorandum provides otherwise [s. 9].

In the case of a company limited by guarantee, articles of association signed by the subscribers to the memorandum must be submitted to the Registrar with the application for registration [s. 7(1)]. A company limited by shares need not do so. However, if it does not, it will be deemed to have adopted as its articles the regulations prescribed by the Secretary of State known as Table A.

Companies which are listed on the London Stock Exchange usually adopt articles which exclude Table A in its entirety. However, most private companies adopt 'short form' articles which state that the company has adopted Table A subject to a number of express exclusions, modifications or additions. In such circumstances, it is often helpful to produce a marked up copy of Table A showing which regulations do not apply and any relevant modifications or additions. However, it should always be remembered that it is the 'short form' articles and not the new consolidated version that are registered as the company's articles.

Articles must be printed, divided into paragraphs numbered consecutively and signed by each subscriber of the memorandum in the presence of at least one witness who must attest the signature(s) [s. 7(3)].

1.4.3 Table A

Table A is a model set of articles (suitable for public and private companies) which a company will be deemed to have adopted unless it registers articles which exclude its provisions in whole or in part. Even if it registers its own articles, Table A will apply in so far as its own articles do not exclude or modify it. The version of Table A which a company is deemed to adopt is the version that is in force at the date of its registration [s. 8(2)]. If Table A is altered, the alteration does not affect a company registered before the alteration takes effect.

Several versions of Table A exist and the relevant version is therefore the one which was in force when the company was incorporated. The current version can be found in the Companies (Tables A to F) Regulations 1985. It is reproduced in full at **Appendix B**. Any reference to 'Table A' or to regulations (e.g. reg. 34) in this book are to this version of Table A unless otherwise indicated. **Appendix C** contains an index to the 1985 Table A.

For companies incorporated under the Companies Act 1948, the relevant version of Table A is the one contained in that Act ('the 1948 Table A'), which is specifically preserved by the Companies Consolidation (Consequential Provisions) Act 1985, s. 31(8). Part I of the 1948 Table A applies (subject to the savings set out in the Companies Act 1980, s. 88(4)) in relation to private companies limited by shares as it applies in relation to public companies so limited [Companies Act 1980, Schedule 3, para. 36(1)]. It is slightly different in many important respects to the 1985 Table A and these differences are highlighted throughout this book.

Some companies still exist which were formed while previous versions of Table A were in force. However, they are so few in number that it is not considered necessary to refer to the position under these versions.

1.4.4 Relationship between Companies Acts and articles

One of the most difficult aspects of company meetings is the complicated hierarchy of rules and procedures. Company meetings are governed by a combination of formal statutory rules, common law rules developed by the courts, and the company's own constitution (primarily its articles of association).

Where articles refer to 'the Act', reference should be made to the article containing the definitions of terms used (usually the first article) which will normally include the following or a similarly worded definition: 'the Act means the Companies Act 1985 including any statutory modification or re-enactment thereof for the time being in force'. For the present this means the Companies Act 1985 as amended.

In the case of the 1948 Table A, 'the Act' is defined as the Companies Act 1948. However, this and all references to section numbers in the 1948 Table A are deemed by virtue of s. 17(2) of the Interpretation Act 1978 to refer to the Companies Act 1985 and its equivalent provisions.

The Companies Act 1985 includes provisions which specify the procedures at company meetings. Generally speaking, these requirements override any provisions contained in the articles of association and must therefore be followed. Articles are usually drafted to ensure that no conflicts exist at the time of drafting. However, conflicts can arise subsequently as a result of amendments to the Act or, indeed, as a result of amendments made to the articles in ignorance of the statutory requirements.

The position is further complicated by the fact that some of the provisions of the Act only apply if the articles do not make alternative provision (e.g. s. 370), while others invalidate the effect of articles not in accordance with certain minimum standards (e.g. s. 372(5) on the lodging of proxies). It is advisable to have any proposed amendments to the articles checked by a solicitor before they are made to ensure that they are consistent with the requirements of the Act.

1.5   COMMON LAW AND PRECEDENT

The common law is the body of rules developed by the courts over many hundreds of years to decide the competing merits of litigants. Provisions contained in Acts of Parliament usually override the common law. Similarly, a company may exclude the operation of common law rules by making provision to the contrary in its memorandum or articles.

Despite this relatively lowly position in the legal hierarchy, the common law is still important in many areas of company meetings. The Act does not provide a comprehensive set of rules, and where the articles do not provide any guidance, it will be necessary to look to the common law of meetings for the answer. The best example of this can be found in relation to the notice required in respect of meetings of directors. No provision is made in the Companies Act in this regard. Consequently, the common law rules regarding notice of meetings will apply subject to anything prescribed by the articles. Most articles specify that notice need not be given in writing but do not specify the length of notice. This must therefore be decided according to the common law rules which provide, somewhat unhelpfully, that the notice given must be reasonable in the circumstances.

The courts are often called upon to rule on the interpretation and application of the Act and the precise effect of provisions contained in a company's articles. Decisions in these cases provide precedents which are useful in clarifying the law. Most cases concerning company law are heard initially in the Chancery Division of the High Court. Appeals can be made to the Court of Appeal and, ultimately, to the House of Lords whose decisions are more influential. Where the point at issue is the interpretation of a European Directive, the case may be referred to the European Court of Justice.

Decisions of the courts which have a bearing on the law of meeting are referred to in this book by their case names and reference. The reference is to the law report in which the case was reported. For example, *Byng* v. *London Life Association Ltd* [1989] 1 All E.R. 560 refers to a case which was reported in the first volume of the All England Law Reports in 1989 on page 560. A table of cases referred to in the text can be found on pp. xiii–xviii.

1.6 STOCK EXCHANGE RULES

Public companies which are listed on the London Stock Exchange ('the Exchange') must also comply with the Listing Rules issued by the Exchange (commonly known as the 'Yellow Book'). Although failure to comply with these rules will not affect the validity of the meeting, the Exchange may take action against the company which could ultimately lead to its listing being withdrawn or suspended. The additional rules imposed by the Exchange are sometimes referred to as the 'continuing obligations'. The primary purpose of the continuing obligations is to protect the interests of investors.

1.7 CODES OF PRACTICE

Although codes of practice by their nature do not have any legal effect, they may be of persuasive authority in court proceedings and, in any case, may be enforceable by other means. The most important examples of codes of practice which are relevant for our purposes are the Cadbury Code on corporate governance and the Greenbury Code on directors' remuneration. The London Stock Exchange requires listed companies to report on their compliance with these codes in their annual reports. Other bodies issue guidelines which influence companies' behaviour, e.g. the Association of British Insurers and the National Association of Pension Funds. These bodies have considerable influence over listed companies as their members normally own or control a large proportion of their shares.

1.8 EUROPEAN LEGISLATION

A number of European Directives have had some influence on the law of meetings, e.g. the 12th Company Law Directive which requires Member States to allow private companies to be formed with only one member. However, as these Directives must be applied by national legislation in each Member State, they are not referred to specifically in the text. For example, the 12th Directive was implemented in the UK by the Companies (Single Member Private Limited Companies) Regulations 1992 which amended the Companies Act 1985.

1.9   WHY MEETINGS ARE NECESSARY

The overriding purpose of the law of meetings is to ensure that a company is actually able to make business decisions and that all those entitled to participate in making those decisions are given a reasonable and fair opportunity to do so. Although a company is deemed to have legal personality, it does not have a mind of its own and cannot act without the intervention of human beings. Indeed, it cannot even survive on its own for long. The Registrar of Companies will eventually dissolve it if certain forms and annual accounts are not delivered to him. Someone must act on behalf of the company. Who may do so and how will depend largely on the company's memorandum and articles of association (its constitution), but also the Companies Acts and the general law of meetings.

Logically, it is the people who own the company (i.e. the members) who should decide what it should and should not do. It is they who represent the mind of the company. The problem is that they may not all be of the same mind. What is to be done if they do not all agree? And how can one find out what they think? The obvious answer is to allow decisions to be taken by a majority at a meeting. If unanimity was required on every matter, the company might never be able to make any decisions at all. And although the views of members could be ascertained by a postal ballot, this method would not allow them to debate the issues before making decisions or give the minority an opportunity to put its case. The only way to ensure that this happens is to require decisions to be taken at formal meetings and, generally speaking, this is what the law requires. Members of private companies may some-times act without holding a meeting, but only if they unanimously approve a particular transaction.

It would be difficult to manage a company if every decision had to be approved by the members in a general meeting. Accordingly, it is usual for the members to delegate wide powers of management to one or more directors appointed to manage the company on their behalf. This is done in the articles of association, one of the constitutional documents of the company which governs the relationship between the company, its members and its directors. The directors must act as a body (usually at a formal meeting) in order to exercise their delegated powers, although most articles allow them to sub-delegate their powers to committees of directors, individual executive directors and other employees and agents. The Companies Act 1985 reserves certain powers to the members and the directors' powers will always be limited by these provisions. For example, the Act gives the members a statutory right to remove directors.

1.10   DULY CONVENED AND CONSTITUTED MEETING

In order to ensure that those entitled to participate in the decision-making process are given a reasonable and fair opportunity to do so, certain procedures must be followed. In short, meetings must be properly convened and constituted. This means that they must be called, held and conducted in accordance with the articles, the Companies Acts and the general law of meetings. The procedural requirements for general meetings of the members are generally more onerous than for meetings of directors. However, the essential components for both are as follows:

- the meeting must be called by someone with authority to do so and in the correct manner;
- notice of the meeting and the business to be transacted must be given in the correct manner to those entitled to receive it (generally those entitled to vote at the meeting);
- a quorum must be present (i.e. the minimum number of persons necessary to transact business);
- those entitled to attend and vote must be allowed to do so;
- a chairman must be elected or appointed;
- the business raised must be within the notice of the meeting;
- the meeting must be conducted properly, particularly in respect of voting;
- the decisions at the meeting should be recorded in a minute book.

If these procedures are not followed, the validity of the meeting and any business transacted at it may be challenged.

1.11   DISPENSING WITH MEETINGS

Until recently, it was necessary for every company to hold general meetings to comply with the requirements of the Companies Act 1985. However, in 1989 amendments to the Act were made which enable private companies to make decisions without holding formal meetings. If all the members agree, private companies may now dispense with the requirement to hold an annual general meeting and several of the formalities associated with it (see Chapter 24). Members of a private company may also act by a written resolution signed by all its members (see Chapter 23). Articles of association usually allow the directors to pass resolutions in a similar manner (see para. 27.9) and it is theoretically possible to manage a private company without holding formal meetings of the members or the directors. This is particularly useful for small owner-managed companies and wholly owned subsidiaries. However, all of these methods require unanimity on the part of the members or the directors. Even if only one person objects, it will be necessary to resort to the more traditional means of decision-making which entail holding formal meetings.

General meetings

A general meeting is a meeting of the members of the company. The term embraces both annual general meetings and extraordinary general meetings. General meetings are sometimes referred to as company meetings or shareholders' meetings.

Articles usually provide that all general meetings other than the annual general meeting shall be called extraordinary general meetings (e.g. reg. 36 of Table A). The same convention is used throughout this book, and the phrase 'general meetings' is used to refer to both annual general meetings and extraordinary general meetings.

Many of the rules and procedures applicable to general meetings also apply to class meetings, meetings of debenture holders and meetings in insolvency. Class meetings are covered separately in Chapter 4. However, meetings in insolvency are outside the scope of this book.

CHAPTER TWO

Annual general meetings

2.1 SUMMARY

The main purpose of the annual general meeting is to enable the members:

- to question the directors face to face and thereby hold them accountable for their management of the company;
- to put forward resolutions for consideration by the company without having to requisition a meeting (the conditions which a member must satisfy to propose a resolution at the annual general meeting (see para. 6.10) are less onerous than those for requisitioning an extraordinary general meeting to propose such a resolution (see para. 5.6));
- to vote on resolutions which the directors are obliged under the articles or the Act to put to the members in general meeting.

Until recently, all companies were required to hold an annual general meeting each year. However, the Act was amended in 1989 to allow private companies to dispense with holding annual general meetings and some of the associated formalities, such as the laying of the report and accounts and the annual appointment of auditors. In order to take advantage of these dispensations, a private company must pass a unanimous resolution of all its members (see further Chapter 24).

All public companies and all private companies which have not passed an elective resolution to dispense with annual general meetings must hold an annual general meeting once every calendar year and not more than 15 months after the date of the last annual general meeting (see para. 2.2). Special rules apply to the first annual general meeting (see para. 2.2.1).

Companies usually use the annual general meeting to deal with business which must be put to a general meeting some time during the year, e.g. laying the accounts and reports before the members, reappointing auditors or any other business which requires shareholder approval (see para. 2.3). In order to do this, it will be necessary to hold the annual general meeting on a suitable date each year (see para. 2.4).

15

2.2   REQUIREMENT TO HOLD ANNUAL GENERAL MEETING
[CA 1985, s. 366]

Every public limited company (plc) must in each calendar year hold an annual general meeting. A private company (Ltd) must also comply with this requirement unless it has elected to dispense with annual general meetings by passing an elective resolution to that effect in accordance with s. 379A (see further para. 24.3). A calendar year starts on 1 January and ends on 31 December and is not calculated by reference either to the date of formation or to the accounting reference date.

Not more than 15 months should elapse between the date of one annual general meeting and the next [s. 366(3)]. A month means a calendar month, i.e. the period expiring on the corresponding day in the following month. If there is no corresponding day in that month, the period expires at the end of that month, e.g. fifteen months after 31 March is 30 June in the following year.

If a company fails to comply with any of the above requirements, its officers (i.e. its directors and secretary) and the company itself are liable to a fine of up to £5,000. If a company fails to hold a meeting in a particular calendar year and more than 15 months has elapsed since the last AGM, two separate offences are committed, each of which may result in a separate fine.

2.2.1   First annual general meeting

A newly registered company must hold its first annual general meeting within 18 months of incorporation. As long as it complies with this requirement, it need not hold an annual general meeting in its year of incorporation or the following year, e.g. a company formed on 20 July 1996 would not need to hold its first AGM until 19 January 1998 (i.e. it need not hold one in 1996 or 1997).

2.2.2   Notice

The above requirements are not satisfied by holding an extraordinary general meeting during the period in question, even if the business at that extraordinary general meeting is the same as that which would normally be dealt with at the annual general meeting. This is because s. 366 requires the notice which must be sent to members before the annual general meeting to specify that the meeting will be held as the annual general meeting.

2.2.3   More than one annual general meeting

Problems can arise with respect to the date of the annual general meeting when a company changes its accounting reference date. For example, following a change in its accounting reference date (year end), a company which routinely holds its annual general meeting in January might wish to move it to a date in August so that it can continue to lay its report and accounts at the annual general meeting. It would not be possible to postpone the annual general meeting until August without breaching the 15-month rule. The simple solution might seem to be to hold an annual general meeting in both January and August in the relevant year. However, most commentators agree that s. 366 does not allow more than one annual general meeting to be held in any one year. If this interpretation is correct (it has never been tested in the courts), then the second annual general meeting would not be valid as an annual general meeting. It would therefore follow that the annual general meeting held in August of the following year would be in breach of the 15-month rule.

Much the safest course of action in these circumstances, is to stagger the change, e.g. in the first year to hold the AGM in April and in the second to hold it in July, only moving to August in the third year. This should not pose insuperable problems in any of those years as long as the accounts can be finalised earlier than normal during the transition period.

2.3   BUSINESS OF THE AGM

The Companies Act does not specify the business of the annual general meeting. However, unless an elective resolution is in force, all companies must at some stage:

- lay the report and accounts before the members at a general meeting [s. 241] (see paras. 2.4.1 and 20.2);
- appoint or reappoint auditors at that meeting [s. 385(2)] (see para. 20.3); and
- fix the auditors' remuneration [s. 390A] (see para. 20.6).

Although these matters need not be dealt with at the annual general meeting, it is plainly sensible to do so in order to avoid having to hold an additional general meeting.

It is also common to deal with the following matters at the annual general meeting:

- appointment of directors (see para. 20.8);
- reappointment of directors retiring by rotation (see para. 20.10);
- approval of dividend recommended by the board (see para. 20.7);
- renewal of directors' authority to allot shares in accordance with s. 80 (if required);
- special resolution to disapply pre-emption rights in accordance with s. 95 (if required);
- special resolutions to amend memorandum or articles of association (if required);
- other business required by the articles to be conducted at the AGM;
- any other business which needs shareholder approval and which it is convenient to deal with at the time; and
- resolutions validly proposed by the members (see para. 6.10).

2.3.1   No business to be transacted

If the accounts are not ready to be laid at the annual general meeting, the only business to be conducted could be the reappointment of directors retiring by rotation in accordance with the articles of association. If the articles make no such provision or none of the directors are subject to retirement by rotation, there may be no business to transact at the annual general meeting. Nevertheless, a meeting must still be held and notice of that meeting must be sent to members (indicating that no business is to be proposed). It may be difficult to obtain a quorum for such a meeting in which case it will be necessary to comply with the articles governing adjournment in these circumstances (see para. 17.4).

2.4   CHOOSING A DATE

Before choosing a date for the annual general meeting, it is necessary to calculate the last date on which the meeting must be held. The first annual general meeting must be held within 18 months of incorporation. Thereafter an annual general meeting must be held once every calendar year on a date not more than 15 months after the last annual general meeting [s. 366].

Having calculated the last possible date, it is possible to select a preferred date within the remaining period. It is normal to aim for a date which allows the report and accounts to be laid before the meeting and it may be advisable to delay the meeting in order to do so (if that is possible in view of the above requirements).

2.4.1   Laying of accounts

Private companies must lay their accounts before the members in general meeting within ten months after the year end and public companies must do so within seven months [s. 244]. Although it is sensible to hold the annual general meeting on a date within that period, it should be borne in mind that the date chosen will also affect the timing of the meeting in the following year.

Example
A private company with a 31 March year end has until 31 January in the following year (i.e. ten months) to lay and deliver its report and accounts. If the last annual general meeting was held in December the previous year, the last available date would be 31 December in the current year because of the requirement that a meeting must be held at least once every calendar year. If it is not possible to finalise the accounts in time to lay them at this meeting, an extraordinary general meeting will also need to be held in January.

However, if the last annual general meeting was held on, say, 20 January in the current year, the next meeting could be held as late as 20 June in the following year (in accordance with the 15-month rule). It might be preferable in these circumstances to opt for a date on or before 31 January to enable the report and accounts to be laid at the meeting.

The existence of other companies within the group with the same or similar accounting reference periods may influence the choice of date. It may be desirable to hold the annual general meetings of all subsidiary companies on the same day, particularly if the membership of each company is similar. The annual general meeting cycle for such subsidiaries could be brought forward to coincide with that of the parent, although consideration should be given to dispensing with the requirement to lay the accounts and hold annual general meetings for wholly owned subsidiaries (see Chapter 24).

Finally, it should not be forgotten that 21 clear days' notice of the meeting must be given unless the consent of all the members to shorter notice can be obtained (see further para. 6.8). If the accounts which are to be laid at the meeting are sent out less than 21 days before the meeting, separate consent will also be required [s. 238(4)] (see para. 20.2).

Table 2.1 Dates by which accounts must be laid and filed with Registrar

Year end	31 March		31 July		30 September		31 December	
	plc	Ltd	plc	Ltd	plc	Ltd	plc	Ltd
Accounts laid by	31 Oct.	31 Jan.	28/29 Feb.	31 May	30 Apr.	31 July	31 July	31 Oct.

2.5   DISPLAY DOCUMENTS

2.5.1   Register of directors' interests in shares or debentures

Companies are required to maintain a register of directors' interests in shares or debentures of the company [s. 325]. The register must be made available at the annual general meeting for inspection by any person attending the meeting [para. 29 of Schedule 13 of the Companies Act 1985].

2.5.2   Directors' service contracts

The London Stock Exchange requires listed companies to make copies of directors' service contracts available for inspection by any person at the place of the annual general meeting for at least 15 minutes prior to and during the meeting [Listing Rules, para. 16.9]. Where one directors' service contract covers both directors and executive officers, the company may make available for inspection a memorandum of the terms of the contract which relate to the directors only [Listing Rules, para. 16.10].

Directors' service contracts available for inspection must disclose or have attached to them the following information:

- the name of the employing company;
- the date of the contract, the unexpired term and details of any notice periods;
- full particulars of the director's remuneration including salary and other benefits;

- any commission or profit sharing arrangements;
- any provision for compensation payable upon early termination of the contract; and
- details of any other arrangements which are necessary to enable investors to estimate the possible liability of the company on early termination of the contract [Listing Rules, para. 16.11].

The Listing Rules (para. 14.20) used to require the notice convening the annual general meeting to contain a note that copies of directors' service contracts will be available for inspection at the locations and times stipulated in para. 16.9, or that there are no such contracts. This requirement was deleted in June 1996.

CHAPTER THREE

Extraordinary general meetings

3.1 SUMMARY

This chapter provides a brief summary of the procedures which apply to extraordinary general meetings. Articles usually specify that all general meetings other than annual general meetings shall be called extraordinary general meetings. The phrase 'general meeting' embraces both annual general meetings and extraordinary general meetings.

3.2 PURPOSE OF EXTRAORDINARY GENERAL MEETINGS

It may be necessary throughout the year to call an extraordinary general meeting of the company to approve certain resolutions which cannot wait until the next annual general meeting. A private company which has elected to dispense with holding annual general meetings under the elective regime (see Chapter 24) may need to call an extraordinary general meeting to deal with any business which needs shareholder approval, although this could also be done at an annual general meeting if one has been demanded by a member under special procedures which apply when such an election is in force.

It is not necessary to lay the accounts, reappoint auditors or fix their remuneration at the annual general meeting. The Act simply requires accounts to be laid at a general meeting and the auditors to be reappointed at that meeting. In other words, this can be done at an extraordinary general meeting.

The members may requisition an extraordinary general meeting (see para. 5.6) and require the directors to circulate a statement in connection with any business to be proposed at any extraordinary general meeting (see para. 6.10).

3.3 NOTICE

The Act requires 14 days' notice to be given to the members of any extraordinary general meeting other than one called for the passing of a special resolution, in which case 21 clear days' notice is required. It also requires 21 days' notice to be given of ordinary resolutions requiring special notice and elective resolutions (see para. 6.2 and **Precedent 6.5B**). Shorter notice may be given with the consent of a majority in number of the members entitled to vote at the meeting holding together not less than 95 per cent in nominal value of the shares giving the right to vote (see para. 6.8). It is usual for the notice to specify the meeting as an extraordinary general meeting, although it is sufficient for it to refer to it as a 'meeting' or a 'general meeting' of the company (see para. 6.5).

3.4   RESOLUTIONS

Not all resolutions passed at extraordinary general meetings must be passed as extraordinary resolutions. The type of resolution required to approve a particular item of business is determined by the Act and the company's articles of association (see Chapter 7).

The members cannot force the directors to include resolutions on the agenda for an extraordinary general meeting called by the directors. They may only do this in respect of annual general meetings (see para. 6.10). In order to propose resolutions at an extraordinary general meeting, the members must requisition the meeting themselves (see para. 5.6).

3.5   PROCEEDINGS

Subject to the above, the rules governing the proceedings at extraordinary general meetings are exactly the same as for annual general meetings.

CHAPTER FOUR

Class meetings

4.1 SUMMARY

The memorandum or, more usually, the articles, normally provide that the company may divide its capital into shares of more than one class (e.g. reg. 2 of Table A). This means that the company can issue shares which give their holders different rights from the holders of other shares. Shares which give their holders the same rights are deemed to be shares of the same class. Class meetings are meetings of the holders of a class of shares.

A class meeting may be required where a company has more than one class of shares and proposes to vary the rights attached to a particular class or where the articles provide that a transaction requires the separate consent of a meeting of the holders of a certain class of shares. The procedures which must be followed to vary class rights under s. 125 differ according to the manner in which those rights are conferred and whether the memorandum or articles make specific provision for variation of those rights (see para. 4.3).

4.2 CLASSES OF SHARES

If the memorandum or articles allow, a company may issue different classes of shares which may give their holders different rights with regard to dividends, voting at general meetings, participation in capital and surplus assets on winding up, or any other matter. If no such provision is made in the memorandum or the articles, the company may only issue one class of shares, i.e. its ordinary shares. The members may, however, authorise the company to issue more than one class by amending the articles. The combined total nominal value of the various classes of shares issued must not exceed the authorised share capital (as stated in the memorandum).

Different classes of shares are usually given different designations (e.g. 'A' shares, 'B' shares, preference shares, etc.) in order to distinguish them from other shares with different rights. However, this will not always be the case and shareholders holding shares of the same name may have different rights. This may arise as a result of a separate shareholders' agreement under which the shareholders agree to modify the rights of the respective shareholders.

The rights attached to shares are usually specified in the memorandum or articles. If they are contained in the memorandum, it is more difficult to vary them. It is therefore more common for them to be set out in the articles. The rights may, however, be set out in some other document, such as a shareholders' agreement. Articles sometimes allow the directors to determine the rights attached to shares, in which case the rights will be set out in the relevant board minute.

The holders of all classes of shares are members of the company. They are therefore entitled to receive notice of general meetings of the company and to attend and vote at such meetings unless those rights are withdrawn or restricted.

4.2.1   Ordinary shares

The ordinary shares are the basic shares of the company which carry the right to vote at general meetings, to receive dividends and to participate in any surplus when the company is wound up. Where a company has only one class of shares, these will be the ordinary shares.

4.2.2   'A' and 'B' shares

A company may have more than one class of ordinary shares. This is common in joint venture companies where each partner will hold a separate class of shares which give them the right to appoint one or more directors but which otherwise have the same rights. Having two categories of ordinary shares may also be used to give a minority shareholder (often the founder) certain entrenched rights, e.g. by giving him enhanced voting rights on any resolution to remove him as a director (see *Bushell* v. *Faith* [1970] A.C. 1099 which is discussed at para. 20.11).

4.2.3   Non-voting shares

These are usually issued to ensure that the founder shareholders retain control. They usually have the same rights as the ordinary shareholders to receive dividends, etc. However, they do not have the right to vote at general meetings. Holders of non-voting shares will, however, be entitled to vote at any meeting of the non-voting shareholders held to approve a variation of their rights, e.g. to authorise the terms of their conversion into voting shares.

4.2.4   Preference shares

Preference shares are shares which carry preferential dividend rights, usually a fixed percentage of their nominal value, which must be paid out of profits available for distribution before dividends are paid to the ordinary shareholders. These rights are often cumulative, which means that any dividends payable to the preference shareholders which are in arrears must be paid before the ordinary shareholders are paid a dividend. The articles usually give preference shareholders the right to vote at general meetings if their dividends are more than six months in arrears, but not otherwise. If the company is wound up, preference shareholders will usually have the right to have their capital returned before the ordinary shareholders but are not usually entitled to share in any surplus.

4.3 VARIATION OF CLASS RIGHTS

The rights of different classes of shares may only be varied in accordance with the relevant provisions of the memorandum or articles and s. 125 of the Act which provides safeguards to ensure that the interests of one class of shareholders are not prejudiced by another. The section applies to any variation of the rights attached to any class of shares in a company. It does not apply to the variation of the rights of different classes of members of a company limited by guarantee.

The procedures which must be followed to vary class rights under s. 125 differ according to the manner in which those rights are conferred and the existence in the memorandum or articles of provision for variation. Any alteration of a provision contained in a company's articles for the variation of the rights attached to a class of shares, or the insertion of any such provision into the articles, is itself to be treated as a variation of those rights [s. 125(7)]. For the purposes of s. 125 and any provision for the variation of class rights contained in a company's memorandum or articles, references to the variation of those rights are to be read as including references to their abrogation (i.e. cancellation) [s. 125(8)].

4.3.1 Rights not set out in memorandum and no provision in articles regarding variation

Where the rights are attached to a class of shares otherwise than by the company's memorandum, and the company's articles do not contain provision with respect to the variation of the rights, section 125 (2) provides that those rights may be varied if, but only if:

(a) the holders of three-quarters in nominal value of the issued shares of that class consent in writing to the variation; or
(b) an extraordinary resolution passed at a separate general meeting of the holders of that class sanctions the variation;

and any requirement (howsoever expressed) in relation to the variation of those rights is complied with to the extent that it is not comprised in paras. (a) and (b) above.

The holders of not less in aggregate than 15 per cent of the issued shares of the class in question (being persons who did not vote in favour of the variation) may apply to the court to have a variation passed under s. 125(2) cancelled, and if such application is made, the variation has no effect unless or until it is confirmed by the court [s. 127].

4.3.2   Provision for variation made in the memorandum or articles but variation concerns s. 80 authority or reduction in capital

Where the memorandum or articles contain provision for the variation of rights attached to a class of shares and the variation of those rights is connected with the giving, variation, revocation or renewal of an authority for allotment under section 80 or with a reduction of the company's share capital under section 135, section 125(3) provides that those rights shall not be varied unless:

(a) the holders of three-quarters in nominal value of the issued shares of that class consent in writing to the variation; or
(b) an extraordinary resolution passed at a separate general meeting of the holders of that class sanctions the variation;

and any requirement of the memorandum or articles in relation to the variation of rights of that class is complied with to the extent that it is not comprised in that condition.

4.3.3   Provision for variation made in the memorandum or articles and variation concerns other matters

Where the variation is not connected with the authority of the directors to allot shares under s. 80 or a reduction in capital in accordance with s. 135 and:

(a) the rights are attached to a class of shares in the company by the memorandum and the articles contain provision with respect to their variation which had been included in the articles at the time of the company's original incorporation; or
(b) the rights are attached to a class of shares by some other means and the articles provide for their variation (whenever first so included),

section 125(4) provides that those rights may only be varied in accordance with that provision of the articles.

The holders of not less in aggregate than 15 per cent of the issued shares of the class in question (being persons who did not consent to or vote in favour of the variation) may apply to the court to have the variation cancelled where the memorandum or articles authorise variation of class rights subject to the consent of a specified proportion of the holders or a resolution at a meeting of that class, and if such application is made, the variation has no effect unless or until it is confirmed by the court (s. 127).

4.3.4   Rights attached by memorandum and no provision for variation in memorandum or articles

Where the rights are attached to a class of shares by the memorandum, and the memorandum and articles do not contain provision with respect to the variation of those rights, section 125(5) provides that those rights may only be varied if all the members of the company agree to the variation.

4.4   PROCEEDINGS AT CLASS MEETINGS

4.4.1   Special provisions as to quorum and a demand for a poll

Section 125(6) provides that at any class meeting held to consider (amongst other things) the variation of the rights attached to that class of shares the quorum shall be two persons holding or representing by proxy at least one-third in nominal value of the issued shares of the class in question, and that at an adjournment of such a meeting the quorum shall be one person holding shares of the class in question or his proxy.

Section 125(6) also provides that any holder of shares of the class in question present in person or by proxy may demand a poll.

Subject to the above requirements, section 125(6) provides that the following provisions shall apply (so far as they are capable of applying) in relation to any class meeting held to consider the variation of the rights attached to a class of shares:

- section 369 (length of notice for calling company meetings);
- section 370 (general provisions as to meetings and votes);
- sections 376 and 377 (circulation of members' resolutions); and
- the provisions of the company's articles relating to general meetings.

4.4.2   Notice

Section 369 requires a company to give at least fourteen days' notice in writing of any meeting of the holders of a class of shares (see **Precedent 4.4**) or, in the case of an unlimited company, at least seven days' notice in writing. By virtue of s. 369(3) a majority in number of the holders of a class of shares together holding not less than 95 per cent in nominal value of the shares giving a right to attend and vote at the meeting may consent to shorter notice.

As the resolution authorising a variation of rights must be passed as an extraordinary resolution, there are no additional notice requirements in connection with the passing of such a resolution.

Section 370(2) requires notice of a class meeting to be served on every holder of shares of that class in the manner in which notices are required to be served under Table A. This provision only applies in so far as the articles of the company do not make other provision. For example the articles will usually specify the manner in which notices must be served and may restrict the right to receive notice (see para. 6.6).

4.4.3   Right to call a meeting

Section 370(3) provides that two or more members holding not less than one-tenth of the issued share capital may call a meeting. With the necessary modifications this means that, unless the articles provide otherwise, two or more holders of a class of shares holding not less than one-tenth of the issued share capital of that class may call a meeting of that class of shares.

4.4.4   Appointment of chairman

Section 370(5) provides that any member elected by the members present at a meeting may be chairman. Making the necessary modifications this means that, unless the articles provide otherwise the holders of a class of shares present at a meeting of that class of shares may elect the chairman of that meeting. In fact articles often provide that the chairman of the board of directors or a director nominated by the board shall act as the chairman of any meeting (e.g. reg. 42 of Table A). And, the class members will normally only be able to elect the chairman in default of these provisions.

4.4.5   Voting

Section 370(6) provides that in the case of a company having a share capital, every member has one vote in respect of each share or each £10 of stock held by him. This provision will apply to class meetings, subject to any provisions in the articles. For example, articles usually contain provisions restricting the right to vote in certain circumstances (see para. 16.4).

4.4.6   Attendance

In *Carruth* v. *Imperial Chemical Industries Ltd* [1937] A.C. 707, the directors convened an extraordinary general meeting of the company and two class meetings to approve a reduction of capital. The meetings were held on the same day and at the same venue. As one meeting finished, the next meeting was started and each meeting was attended by the holders of the other classes of shares. The resolution passed at one class meeting was challenged by a member of that class on the basis that people who were not members of that class were present at the meeting. The resolution was held to be valid and Lord Russell said:

> There are many matters relating to the conduct of a meeting which lie entirely in the hands of those persons who are present and constitute the meeting. Thus it rests with the meeting to decide whether notices, resolutions, minutes, accounts, and such like shall be read to the meeting or be taken as read; whether representatives of the Press, or any other persons not qualified to be summoned to the meeting, shall be permitted to be present, or if present, shall be permitted to remain; whether and when discussion shall be terminated and a vote taken; whether the meeting shall be adjourned. In all these matters, and they are only instances, the meeting decides, and if necessary a vote must be taken to ascertain the wishes of the majority. If no objection is taken by any constituent of the meeting, the meeting must be taken to be assenting to the course adopted.

CHAPTER FIVE

Calling general meetings

5.1 SUMMARY

Unless the time and place at which meetings are to be held each year is fixed, someone must be given the power to call meetings, i.e. to direct that a meeting will be held at a certain time and place to consider certain business. A general meeting must be called (convened) by a person or body with appropriate authority otherwise the meeting and any business transacted at it will be invalid (see para. 5.2.1). The articles usually give the board power to convene general meetings (see para. 5.2). However, they usually provide alternative procedures for situations where the board of directors is unable or unwilling to exercise its powers (see para. 5.3). In addition, the Secretary of State (see para. 5.4) and the court (see para. 5.5) have powers under the Act to direct that general meetings be held.

Members who are able to satisfy certain requirements may require the directors to convene an extraordinary general meeting to consider business proposed by them (see para. 5.6). In addition any member of a private company which has dispensed with the holding of annual general meetings may require the directors to convene an annual general meeting (see para. 24.3.1).

5.2 MEETINGS CONVENED BY THE BOARD OF DIRECTORS

Articles usually give the board of directors power to convene general meetings (e.g. reg. 37 of Table A). The directors may exercise such powers whenever they think it appropriate in the interests of the company to do so (*Pergamon Press* v. *Maxwell* [1970] 1 W.L.R. 1167).

Where the articles state that the directors may call general meetings, they must exercise that power collectively at a duly convened and constituted meeting of the board (*Browne* v. *La Trinidad* (1887) 37 Ch.D. 1), although a written resolution of the directors (e.g. under reg. 93 of Table A) will have equivalent effect. This is probably the case, even though the articles provide that the directors may delegate 'any of their powers' to a committee of directors or to individual executive directors. This is because the power to convene general meetings is a special power and not subject to the standard article on delegation. Modern articles attempt to get round this by stating that the power to delegate shall be effective in relation to the powers, duties and discretions of the directors generally, whether or not express reference is made in the articles to powers, duties or discretions being exercised by the directors. Care should therefore be taken to ensure that the power to delegate is applicable and where there is any uncertainty, it is probably safest to assume that it is not.

The directors' resolution should state the date, time and place of the meeting and its purpose (see **Precedent 5.2A** and **Precedent 5.2B**). A draft copy of the notice together with any additional documents which will accompany it should also be approved. The board should authorise someone (usually the secretary) to sign and issue the notice to all those entitled to receive it.

A further board meeting would be needed to approve the addition of any further item of business or to amend the substance of the notice.

5.2.1   Ratification of invalid notice

Notice of a general meeting given by any person without the sanction of the directors or other proper authority will be invalid (*Re Haycroft Gold Reduction Co.* [1900] 2 Ch. 230). This is the case even though it was issued by the secretary in response to a valid requisition by the members under s. 368 (*Re State of Wyoming Syndicate* [1901] 2 Ch. 431). However, a meeting called without proper authority will be valid if it is ratified before the meeting by the body with authority to call the meeting. Thus, a notice issued by a director or the company secretary without the authority of the board, will be valid if it is subsequently ratified prior to the general meeting by the directors at a properly convened and constituted meeting of the board (*Hooper* v. *Kerr Stuart & Co.* (1900) 83 L.T. 729).

A general meeting convened by an irregularly constituted board (e.g. at an inquorate meeting) will be invalid. However, a defect in the appointment of any of the directors may be cured by an article in the form of reg. 92 of Table A which provides that all acts done by any meeting of directors, a committee of directors or by any person acting as a director, notwithstanding that it be afterwards discovered that there was some defect in the appointment of any such director or that they or any of them were disqualified, had vacated office, or were otherwise not entitled to vote, be valid as if every person had been duly appointed, was qualified to be a director and entitled to vote (*Transport Ltd* v. *Schomberg* (1905) 21 T.L.R. 305) (see further para. 31.2).

5.2.2   Practical points on convening annual general meeting

In practice, a proof of the AGM notice is usually tabled at the board meeting held to approve the report and accounts and its contents are used to frame the appropriate board resolution convening the meeting. The board resolution should specify the date, time and place and the business to be transacted. The directors should also authorise the secretary to sign the notice and send copies to all persons entitled to receive it (i.e. the members and the auditors and anyone else specified in the articles) (see **Precedent 5.2B**).

As soon as the proof print of the report and accounts has been approved by the directors, the balance sheet, directors' report and auditors' report should be signed and dated by the appropriate people. A further copy should be prepared with the names of the signatories and the dates on which they signed inserted at the appropriate points. This copy can then be printed together with final copies of the notice and, if necessary, any circular or proxy cards.

The notice usually goes out under the name of the secretary who signs 'by order of the board'. It is usually dated for the day on which it is sent out and this date can be included in the proofs sent to the printers even though the notice may not yet have been physically signed. The secretary can sign and date a master copy of the notice on the appropriate day and this copy should be retained.

If accounts are to be laid at the annual general meeting, copies of the report and accounts must be sent to members not less 21 days before the meeting. As members must be given 21 clear days' notice of the annual general meeting it is sensible to send both in the same envelope. The notice of the meeting can be incorporated in the document containing the annual report and accounts.

5.3   PROBLEMS CONVENING MEETINGS

5.3.1   Number of directors below quorum

Articles usually provide that where the number of directors falls below the number fixed as the quorum, the continuing directors may act for the purposes of calling a general meeting (e.g. reg. 90 of Table A). Regulation 90 also allows the continuing directors to exercise their powers under reg. 79 to appoint a director either to fill a casual vacancy or as an additional director. This type of article can only be invoked where the remaining directors would be unable to fulfil the quorum requirements even if they all attended a board meeting.

5.3.2   Not sufficient directors in United Kingdom

Most articles include a provision similar to reg. 37 of Table A which provides that any director or any member(s) may call a general meeting if there are not sufficient directors in the United Kingdom to do so. Regulation 37 is of no assistance if there are sufficient directors in the United Kingdom even though they are not capable of acting to form a quorum for these purposes, e.g. because of illness. The wording of Table A can be modified to cover such circumstances (see art. 56 of Whitbread plc). However, if the articles have not been so modified, an application may need to be made to the court under s. 371 (see para. 5.5) or to the Secretary of State under s. 367 (see para. 5.4).

5.3.3   Director refuses to attend board meetings

In small companies, it is quite common for one or more of the directors to refuse to attend board meetings in order to prevent the board forming a quorum and transacting business to which they are opposed. Although it may not be their intention to prevent the calling of a general meeting, this is often one of the side effects of such tactics. If they are not opposed to calling a meeting and assuming the articles allow, it might be possible to call the meeting by written resolution (see further para. 27.9). A more dubious method might be to call a board meeting while the directors who refuse to attend are outside the United Kingdom and to call a meeting under reg. 37 of Table A or its equivalent. Reasonable notice of such a board meeting would still need to be given and notice would need to be sent to the directors' usual addresses. The members could requisition a general meeting under s. 368 and, if the directors do not convene a meeting within 21 days, convene a meeting themselves in accordance with s. 368(4) (see para 5.6). If all else fails, an application may need to be made to the court under s. 371 (see para. 5.5) or, in respect of an AGM in default, to the Secretary of State under s. 367 (see para. 5.4).

5.3.4   Directors refuse to call meeting

Where the directors refuse to call a general meeting, the members can requisition one under s. 368 and convene it themselves if the directors fail to do so within 21 days. Any member of the company may request the Secretary of State to call or direct the calling of an annual general meeting in default (see para. 5.4). In addition any director or member may apply to the court for an order in respect of a general meeting (see para. 5.5).

5.4   POWER OF SECRETARY OF STATE TO CALL AGM IN DEFAULT [s. 367]

Where a company is in default of the requirements of s. 366 for holding an annual general meeting, any member may apply to the Secretary of State for an order calling or directing the calling of a general meeting [s. 367].

In making such an order, the Secretary of State may give such ancillary or consequential directions as he thinks fit. These directions may modify or supplement the company's articles in relation to the calling, holding and conduct of meetings and may include a direction that one member present in person or by proxy be a quorum for that meeting.

A meeting called under s. 367 will, subject to any direction to the contrary by the Secretary of State, be deemed to be an annual general meeting of the company. If, as will often be the case, an annual general meeting called on the direction of the Secretary of State is not held in the year in which it became due, it will not be treated as the annual general meeting of the year in which it is held unless at that meeting the company resolves by ordinary resolution that it be so treated [s. 367(4)].

Although the wording of this section is obscure, it is usually taken to mean that the company may resolve that it be treated as the annual general meeting of the year in which it was held as well as the annual general meeting for the year in which it is overdue. As prior notice of any such resolution would be required, this is unlikely to be a common occurrence bearing in mind the circumstances. A copy of any such resolution must be submitted to the Registrar of Companies within 15 days [s. 367(5)].

5.5   POWERS OF THE COURT TO CALL A GENERAL MEETING [s. 371]

If for any reason it is impracticable to call a general meeting, or to conduct the meeting in the manner prescribed by the company's articles or the Act, the court may order a meeting of the company to be called, held and conducted in any manner it thinks fit [s. 371(1)]. The court may make such an order on the application of any member who would be entitled to vote at the meeting or any director. In doing so, the court may give such ancillary or consequential directions as it thinks fit, which may include a direction that one member present in person or by proxy be deemed to constitute a meeting [s. 371(2)]. Any meeting called, held and conducted in accordance with an order of the court made under s. 371 is deemed for all purposes to be a meeting of the company duly called, held and conducted [s. 371(3)].

These powers have been exercised where it was impracticable to hold a meeting with a quorum in accordance with the articles (*Re Edinburgh Workmen's Houses Improvement Co. Ltd* 1934 S. L.T. 513) and where the directors, being minority shareholders, failed to call a general meeting (including an annual general meeting) thus preventing the majority shareholder from exercising his right to remove them (*Re El Sombrero Ltd* [1958] Ch. 900 and *Re H. R. Paul & Son Ltd* [1973] 118 S. J. 166). The court has also used these powers to direct that a vote be taken by postal ballot because previous general meetings had been disrupted by protesters in such a violent manner that it was likely that most ordinary members would not attend any future meetings (*Re British Union for the Abolition of Vivisection* [1995] 2 B.C.L.C. 1).

The court may also convene a meeting under s. 425 where a compromise or arrangement is proposed between the company and its creditors.

5.6   MEMBERS' REQUISITION [s. 368]

A member or members holding one-tenth of the company's paid-up capital carrying the right to vote may require (requisition) the directors to convene an extraordinary general meeting at the company's expense. If the directors fail to call a meeting, the requisitionists may do so themselves and recover their expenses from the company [s. 368]. The members may also requisition a resolution at an annual general meeting under s. 376 with the support of only one-twentieth of the voting shares. However, the company can require the requisitionists to pay its expenses in giving effect to the requisition under s. 376 (see para. 6.10). It may therefore be preferable from the requisitionists' point of view to requisition an extraordinary general meeting under s. 368 if they can muster the necessary support.

5.6.1   Conditions for demand

The directors are required by s. 368 to convene an extraordinary general meeting of the company on receipt of a demand made by members holding at the date of deposit of the requisition not less than one-tenth of the paid-up capital of the company which at that date carries the right to vote at general meetings of the company.

In calculating whether a valid demand has been made, the critical factor is the amount of paid-up capital held by the members rather than the number of votes attached to those shares. Where all the shares are of equal value and carry the same number of votes, this calculation will be simple. However, care should be taken to ensure that shares which confer the right to vote in limited circumstances are included in the calculation if those circumstances operate at the time of the deposit. For example:

> ABC Ltd has a share capital of 5,000 £1 ordinary shares and 2,000 £1 preference shares. The preference shareholders only have a right to vote if their dividends are in arrears. As long as the preference dividends are not in arrears, any ordinary shareholder(s) holding 500 or more shares can requisition a meeting. If the dividends are in arrears, a member(s) holding 700 or more shares (either ordinary shares, preference shares or a combination of the two) would be needed.

It should be noted that articles commonly remove the right to vote when any calls on a share are unpaid (e.g. reg. 57 of Table A). It has also been held that the right to requisition a meeting requires paid-up share capital (*Re Bradford Investments plc* [1990] B.C.C. 740).

In the case of a company not having a share capital (e.g. a company limited by guarantee), the demand must be made by members representing not less than one-tenth of the total voting rights of all members who have at the date of deposit of the requisition a right to vote at general meetings.

Articles cannot impose more stringent conditions than those established under s. 368. They may, however, provide a less stringent regime.

5.6.2   Form of requisition

The requisition must be signed by the requisitionists and deposited at the registered office of the company (see **Precedent 5.6A**). In the case of joint holders, the requisition must be signed by each of them (*Patent Wood Keg Syndicate* v. *Pearse* [1906] W.N. 164). The requisition may consist of several documents in like form each signed by one or more requisitionists [s. 368(3)]. This allows a master document to be prepared and for copies to be circulated to members for signature.

The requisition must state the objects of the meeting and the board cannot refuse to act on the requisition unless the objects cannot be legally be carried into effect (*Isle of Wight Railway Co.* v. *Tahourdin* (1883) 25 Ch.D. 320). The object is very similar to the general nature of the business (see para. 6.5). It does not need to be stated as a specific resolution unless it is required to be proposed as a special or extraordinary resolution (see paras. 7.4 and 7.3).

5.6.3   Directors must duly convene meeting

On receipt of a valid requisition, the directors must convene an extraordinary general meeting of the company in the proper manner [s. 368(1)]. In the case of a requisitioned meeting at which a resolution is to be proposed as a special resolution, the directors are deemed not to have properly convened the meeting if they do not give the minimum statutory notice required for special resolutions [s. 368(7)]. The meeting will also not be duly convened if it is called for a date more than 28 days after the date of the notice convening the meeting [s. 368(8)]. This provision prevents the directors defeating the objects of the requisitionists by delaying the holding of the meeting.

When it convenes the meeting, the board may add other items to the agenda for the requisitioned meeting by giving notice in the normal manner. However, a member cannot raise any other matter at the meeting which was not specified in the requisition. For example, a member may not propose a resolution to remove a director at a requisitioned meeting where that was not one of the objects of the requisitionists (*Ball* v. *Metal Industries Ltd.* 1957 S.L.T. 124).

5.6.4   In default requisitionists may convene meeting

If the directors do not properly convene a meeting within 21 days from the date of deposit of the requisition, the requisitionists (or any of them representing more than one half of their total voting rights) may convene a meeting, which must be held within three months of the date of deposit [s. 368(4)].

The meeting must be convened by the requisitionists in as near to the same manner as possible as it would if the directors had convened it [s. 368(5)] (see **Precedent 5.6B**). Thus, if the articles do not provide for notice to be given by advertisement, the requisitionists are not entitled to give notice in that manner.

The requisitionists are entitled to be repaid any reasonable expenses they incur as a result of the failure of the directors to convene a meeting. These expenses will be payable by the company which must retain an equivalent sum from any fees or other remuneration payable by the company to the defaulting directors in respect of their services [s. 368(6)].

5.7   REQUISITION BY AUDITOR

An auditor may resign his office by giving the company notice in writing to that effect together with a statement of circumstances [ss. 392 and 394]. If the statement is of circumstances which the auditor believes should be brought to the attention of members, he may deposit at the same time a signed requisition calling on the directors of the company to convene an extraordinary general meeting for the purpose of receiving and considering his explanation of the circumstances of his resignation [s. 392A]. The auditor also has a right to have a statement in writing of the circumstances connected with his resignation circulated to the members before any meeting convened on his requisition.

The directors (but not the secretary) are liable to a fine if they do not take reasonable steps within 21 days from the date of the deposit of the requisition to convene a meeting for a day not less than 28 days after the notice convening the meeting is given [s. 392A(5)]. However, the auditor has no right to convene a meeting in default.

CHAPTER SIX

Notice of general meetings

6.1 SUMMARY

The Act makes detailed provision as to the length of notice that must be given to shareholders. Most other aspects are dealt with by the articles or, failing them, by the common law. Thus, the Act requires a minimum of 21 days' notice to be given of annual general meetings and any meeting to pass a special or elective resolution or one which requires special notice to be given. Other meetings may be called by only 14 days' notice (see para. 6.2). Clear days' notice is required unless the articles provide otherwise (see para. 6.2.1). The members may waive some of these requirements, although the majority required means that this is only likely to be possible for closely held private companies and subsidiaries (see para. 6.8).

In addition to the date, time and place, the notice must state the business of the meeting. The exact text or the entire substance of the resolution should be stated for certain types of resolution. However, it is normally sufficient to state the general nature of the business. Circulars and other documents sent with the notice can be used for this purpose and will be read in conjunction with it for the purposes of determining the validity of the notice (see para. 6.5).

All the members are entitled to receive notice of general meetings unless the articles provide otherwise (see para. 6.6). Articles usually provide that the accidental omission to give notice to a member will not invalidate the proceedings (see para. 6.7).

Special notice requirements exist for resolutions to remove a director, appoint a director aged 70 or more or remove or replace the auditors (see para. 6.9). Members who satisfy certain qualifications have a statutory right to require the directors to give notice of resolutions which they wish to propose at an annual general meeting. They may also require the directors to circulate a statement in connection with the business of any general meeting (see para. 6.10).

6.2   LENGTH OF NOTICE

The Act requires not less than 21 days' notice in writing to be given in respect of annual general meetings and not less than 14 days' notice in writing to be given of extraordinary general meetings other than one held for the passing of a special resolution. Any provision in a company's articles will be void in so far as it specifies a shorter time. The articles may, however, specify a longer period of notice [s. 369(1) and (2)]. Unless the members consent to receive short notice (see para. 6.8), meetings called with less than the notice required by the Act or the articles (if they specify a longer period of notice) will be invalid.

Although s. 369 does not itself specify the period of notice required for an extraordinary general meeting called for the passing of a special resolution, it is clear from s. 378(2) that at least 21 days' notice is required (see para. 7.4), unless the members consent to receive shorter notice (see para. 6.8). It is also necessary to give 21 days' notice of an extraordinary general meeting in order to pass an elective resolution [s. 379A(2)] or an ordinary resolution which requires special notice [s. 379(2)], although the members may unanimously consent to receive shorter notice in the case of an elective resolution.

Failure to give at least 21 days' notice of an extraordinary general meeting called for the passing of an elective resolution (without the members' unanimous consent), or of an ordinary resolution requiring special notice, will invalidate those resolutions but not the meeting itself, provided at least 14 days' notice has been given in accordance with s. 369. In other words it would still be possible to pass any ordinary or extraordinary resolutions included in the notice.

The same is probably true for an extraordinary general meeting called for the passing of a special resolution. However, the situation is complicated by the fact that s. 369 deliberately makes an exception to the normal 14 days' notice requirement for 'a meeting for the passing of a special resolution' without specifying a minimum notice period for such a meeting. Section 378 states that a special resolution must be passed at a meeting of which not less than 21 days' notice specifying the intention to propose the resolution as a special resolution has been given, although the members may consent to receive shorter notice in accordance with s. 378(3). It is therefore arguable that unless the members consent to receive short notice, a meeting called at less than 21 days' notice is not 'a meeting for the passing of a special resolution' in the context of s. 369. In other words, the ordinary 14 days' notice rule would apply in default. However, if this is the case, there would seem to be little point in having the exception in s. 369 for meetings for the passing of special resolutions.

Table 6.1 provides a simple guide as to the length of notice required for any combination of the above circumstances.

The ICSA's *Guide to best practice for Annual General Meetings* recommends that notice of annual general meetings should be circulated at least 20 working days before the meeting, i.e. excluding weekends and bank holidays.

Table 6.1   Length of notice

Type of resolution	Type of meeting to be proposed at	Minimum notice, CA 1985
Any resolution	Annual General Meeting	21 days, s. 369(1)
Extraordinary resolution	Extraordinary General Meeting	14 days, s. 369(1)
Ordinary resolution	Extraordinary General Meeting	14 days, s. 369(1)
Elective resolution	Extraordinary General Meeting	21 days, s. 379A(2)
Special resolution	Extraordinary General Meeting	21 days, s. 378(2)
Ordinary resolution for which special notice is required to be given	Extraordinary General Meeting	21 days, s. 379(2)

6.2.1   Clear days

Articles usually provide that the period of notice required shall be clear days (e.g. reg. 38 of Table A). It has been decided in the English courts that unless the articles provide otherwise the number of days' notice required under the Companies Act shall be interpreted as being clear days (*Re Hector Whaling Ltd* [1936] Ch. 208). This is usually taken to mean that the day the notice is deemed to be served and the day of the meeting should not be counted. However, a more recent Scottish case has thrown this interpretation into doubt by deciding that when calculating the period of notice required under the Companies Act the day of service must be excluded, but the day of the meeting may be counted (*Neil McLeod & Sons Ltd, Petitioners* [1967] S.C. 16). Articles sometimes define the meaning of clear days in order to avoid any uncertainty in this regard.

6.3   SERVICE OF NOTICE

Articles usually prescribe the method by which notices must be served. If they are silent on the matter, notice of general meetings must be served in the manner required by the version of Table A in force at that time [s. 370(2)].

6.3.1   Method of service

Notice of general meetings must be given in writing [s. 369 and reg. 111 of Table A]. Under Table A, notices must be served either personally or by post in a prepaid envelope to the member at his registered address [reg. 112]. A notice may be served personally by handing it to the member. Service by post includes ordinary and registered post and by recorded delivery (*Re Thundercrest Ltd* [1995] 1 B.C.L.C. 117 and *TO Supplies (London) Ltd* v. *Jerry Creighton Ltd* [1951] 2 All E.R. 992).

Under Table A members whose registered address is not within the United Kingdom are not entitled to receive notices unless they supply the company with an address in the United Kingdom for that purpose [reg. 112]. The London Stock

Exchange requires listed companies to make such a facility available to overseas members [Listing Rules, para. 19 of Appendix 1 to Chapter 13]. The company must maintain a separate record of the addresses supplied by overseas members for these purposes and their registered address should not be changed unless they specifically request that it be changed. It is open to question whether the company can send other documents to the address supplied by an overseas member for the purposes of receiving notices. For example, s. 238 requires a copy of the report and accounts to be sent to every member but does not specify where it should be sent. The obvious place would be the registered address. However, it may be that the company may send it to the address supplied by an overseas member for the purposes of receiving notices.

The London Stock Exchange requires listed companies to use air mail when sending notices and other documents to members resident in countries outside the European Union [Listing Rules, para. 9.29].

Table A is commonly modified to allow notices to be served by advertisement. This is clearly necessary for companies which allow members to hold shares in bearer form. However, the ability to give notice by advertisement can also be useful in the event of a postal strike. The courts have held that a provision in a company's articles (similar to reg. 115 of Table A) which stated that notices shall be deemed to have been served a certain period after posting did not apply where there was such a disruption to the postal service that placing the letters in a letter-box could not reasonably be expected to result in delivery to members within that time (*Bradman* v. *Trinity Estates plc* [1989] B.C.L.C. 757). Public companies are increasingly taking power in their articles to give notice by advertisement in such circumstances (see arts. 160 and 163 of Whitbread plc). Such articles need to be carefully worded to ensure that they apply where there is only a partial disruption of the postal service. The London Stock Exchange requires notices given by advertisement to be inserted in at least one national newspaper [Listing Rules: para. 18 of Appendix 1 to Chapter 13].

6.3.2   Date of service

A notice which is handed or given to a member personally is deemed to have been served on the day it was given. Most notices are, however, sent by post and Table A provides that such a notice shall be deemed to have been given 48 hours after the envelope containing it was posted (reg. 115). As it makes no distinction between first- and second-class post, there is nothing to be gained from using first-class. Articles sometimes clarify the position, e.g. art. 161 of Whitbread plc provides that notices sent by first-class post shall be deemed to have been served 24 hours after posting and those sent by second class 48 hours after posting.

If a company's articles are silent on the deemed date of service, s. 7 of the Interpretation Act 1978 will apply and a notice which has been properly addressed and posted will be deemed to have been given at the time when the letter would be expected to be delivered 'in the ordinary course of post'. In the case of a letter sent by first-class post, this is the day next after posting, and in the case of second-class post, the day next but one after posting, although in both cases any day on which there is no delivery of post must be excluded. Unless otherwise proved, it will be assumed that second-class post has been used (*Practice Direction* [1968] 3 All E.R. 320).

Notices given by advertisement are deemed to have been served the day after the newspaper is published (*Sneath* v. *Valley Gold Ltd* [1893] 1 Ch. 477) unless the articles provide otherwise (e.g. see art. 161 of Whitbread plc).

6.3.3   Proof of service

The common law provides that a meeting will be invalid unless notice of it is given to all those entitled to receive it. When notices are sent by post, there is, of course, a danger that some may be lost and not delivered. To avoid the possibility of a meeting being invalidated for this reason, articles usually provide that proof that an envelope containing a notice was properly addressed, stamped and posted shall be conclusive evidence that the notice was given (e.g. reg. 115). When sending out notices of meetings, it is advisable to obtain and retain a receipt (proof of posting) from the Post Office for this purpose. For companies with large shareholder registers, this may be impractical and an undertaking by the registrars that the proper procedures were followed will probably be sufficient.

Although it might be possible in theory to calculate the number of notices which should be sent and compare this with the number which were actually sent, it may be impossible in practice to discover the reason why the two figures do not reconcile. In *Re West Canadian Collieries Ltd* [1962] Ch. 370, it was held that a failure to send notices to nine shareholders was accidental where the reason for the omission was that it had been forgotten that the plates for printing their addresses had been separated from the rest because earlier communications had been returned undelivered.

It has been held that articles similar to reg. 115 are effective only where there is uncertainty as to whether a document has been delivered and not where it is clear that it has not been delivered (*Re Thundercrest Ltd* [1995] 1 B.C.L.C. 117). The notice in this case was given in connection with an offer of shares in accordance with ss. 89 and 90. It was sent by recorded delivery (a method which requires the recipient to sign an acknowledgement of receipt). When it was returned to the company by the Post Office, it was therefore obvious that it had not been delivered. Judge Paul Baker said:

> The purpose of deeming provisions [such as reg. 115] in the case of management of companies is clear. In the case of uncertainty as to whether a document has been delivered, with large numbers of shareholders and so forth, there has to be some rule under which those in charge of the management can carry on the business without having to investigate every case where some shareholder comes along and says he has not got the document.

The directors have to proceed and transact the company's business on the basis of the deeming provisions. But in my judgment, all that falls away when you find it is established without any possibility of challenge that the document has not been delivered.

In the normal course of events, notices sent by ordinary post will be delivered whether or not the recipient is in or has gone away. However, it is unlikely that the principle established in *Re Thundercrest* would be applied where a notice sent in this manner was returned undelivered.

6.4   PRACTICAL ISSUES ON TIMING OF NOTICES

The date by which notices should be sent out needs to be calculated carefully in accordance with the above rules to ensure that proper notice is given. If the date of the meeting is already known it is necessary to work backwards from that date to establish the latest date by which the notices should be posted or served. For companies registered in England or Wales, the basic rules are:

- the statutory period of notice commences the day after the notice has been served or is deemed to have been served on the member;
- the meeting must be held after the last day of the period of notice required by statute or, if longer, by the articles.

In Scotland the meeting may be held on the last day of the period of notice required by statute or, if longer, the articles (see para 6.2.1).

To take an example, an English company which has adopted Table A in full must post the notice of its annual general meeting at least 24 days before the date of the meeting. If the notices were posted on the 1 April they would be deemed to have been served 48 hours later, i.e. on 3 April. The period of 21 days' notice would not commence until 4 April, the first clear day, and would expire on 24 April. The earliest date that the meeting could be held would therefore be on 25 April, the first clear day after the notice period has expired. A meeting of a Scottish company could be held on 24 April (see para. 6.2.1).

The same principles would apply to an extraordinary general meeting, and notices would have to be posted a minimum of 17 days before the date of the meeting.

The ICSA has recommended in its *Guide to best practice for Annual General Meetings* that listed companies should circulate the notice of their annual general meetings at least 20 working days before the meeting, excluding weekends and bank holidays. This is so that nominee companies have more time to obtain and submit proxy votes on behalf of their underlying investors. In order to comply with this recommendation for an annual general meeting to be held on 25 April, it would be necessary to issue the notice on 28 March or, if there are any bank holidays, even earlier.

6.5   CONTENTS OF NOTICE

Notices of general meetings should include:

- the name of the company [s. 349(1)(b)];
- the time and place of the meeting;
- the type of meeting (e.g. whether the meeting is the annual general meeting in accordance with s. 366(1) and reg. 38 of Table A) (see Note 1);
- the business to be transacted at the meeting (see para. 6.5.2);
- the full text of any resolution to be proposed as special or extraordinary resolution [s. 378], an elective resolution [s. 379A], or as an ordinary resolution for which special notice is required [s. 379];
- state on whose authority it is issued, e.g. the board, requisitioning members, court, etc. and the name of the person who signed it on their behalf, e.g. the name of the secretary (see, however, *Re Brick and Stone Company* [1878] W.N. 140);
- be dated;
- in the case of a company having a share capital, include with reasonable prominence a statement of a member's right to appoint a proxy or, if a public company, one or more proxies and a statement that a proxy need not be a member of the company [s. 372(3)] (see Note 2);
- a company whose shares have been admitted to CREST, may specify in the notice a time, not more than 48 hours before the time fixed for the meeting, by which a person must be entered on the relevant register of securities in order to have the right to attend and vote at the meeting [Uncertificated Securities Regulations, reg. 34] (see para. 16.2.1).

Notes

1. Although the Act and most articles only require the notice to specify annual general meetings as such, it is plainly sensible to specify extraordinary general meetings as such, although the words 'a meeting of XYZ Limited' would be sufficient for this purpose; the assumption being that it must be an extraordinary general meeting if it is not specified as an annual general meeting. However, it would not be sufficient to use the words 'a meeting of XYZ Limited' for a meeting of the holders of any class of shares of XYZ Limited.
2. The articles of a company not having a share capital may entitle members to appoint a proxy and may require a similar statement to be included.
3. The requirement of the Listing Rules that listed companies include a note that copies of directors' service contracts will be available for inspection was deleted in June 1996.
4. Notices may be required by the Act, the articles or Stock Exchange regulations to be accompanied by statements (see para. 6.10), circulars (see para. 6.5.4), forms of proxy (see para. 14.6.2) and other documents.

A notice will be invalid if it states that the meeting will only be held in certain pre-determined circumstances (e.g. on the passing of a resolution by members of a different class), unless the articles specifically allow such notices to be given (*Alexander* v. *Simpson* (1889) 43 Ch.D. 139 and *Re North of England Steamship Co.* [1905] 2 Ch. 15). However, resolutions may be included in the business of a meeting which are contingent upon other events (see para. 6.5.2).

6.5.1   Signing the notice

At least one copy of the notice should be signed by or on behalf of the person or body under whose authority the notice is issued. In practice, the notice will normally be signed and dated by the secretary or one of the directors above the words 'By order of the board'. The original signed copy should be retained by the company. Copies of the notice sent to shareholders do not need to be signed but should include the name and position of the person who signed it on behalf of the board (see **Precedent 6.5A**). The notice is usually dated for the day on which it is to be posted or the advertisement is to be placed. However, this will not always be possible and is not strictly necessary. It should of course always be dated for the day on which it is actually signed.

6.5.2   Nature of the business

The notice need not give the exact text of the resolutions to be proposed, unless required by the Act, i.e. in relation to special, extraordinary and elective resolutions and ordinary resolutions requiring special notice (see Chapter 7). Doing so does not guarantee, in any case, that the notice will be valid. Under the common law, the notice must also give a 'fair and candid and reasonable explanation' of the purposes for which the meeting is called (*Kaye* v. *Croydon Tramways Co.* [1898] 1 Ch. 358).

Whether a notice is adequate will depend on the particular facts in each case. In *Normandy* v. *Ind, Coope & Co.* [1908] 1 Ch. 84, notice was given of a resolution to consider and, if thought fit, to approve a new set of articles to replace the existing articles. No indication of the content or effect of the new articles was given in the notice although it stated that copies were available for inspection at the company's office. It was held that the notice was defective because it did not properly inform the shareholders of the nature of the business.

The articles may modify this rule, e.g. by specifying certain business as 'ordinary business' (see para. 6.5.3). Where the articles require the notice to specify the 'general nature of the business', the common law rules will apply (e.g. reg. 38 of Table A).

Notices are not construed with excessive strictness. The test the courts apply is what the notice would fairly convey to an ordinary person (*Henderson* v. *Bank of Australasia* (1890) 45 Ch.D. 330). In determining the validity of the notice the courts often apply the absent shareholder test. In *Tiessen* v. *Henderson* [1899] 1 Ch. 861, Kekewich J. said (at p. 886):

> The question is merely whether each shareholder as and when he received notice of the meeting, in which I include the circular of the same date, had fair warning of what was to be submitted to the meeting. A shareholder may

properly and prudently leave matters in which he takes no interest to the decision of the majority. But in that case he is content to be bound by the vote of the majority; because he knows the matter about which the majority are to vote at the meeting. If he does not know that, he has not a fair chance of determining in his own interest whether he ought to attend the meeting, make further inquiries, or leave others to determine the matter for him.

He added (at p. 870):

The man I am protecting is not the dissentient, but the absent shareholder – the man who is absent because having reviewed and with more or less care looked at this circular, he comes to the conclusion that on the whole he will not oppose the scheme, but leave it to the majority. I cannot tell whether he would have left it to the meeting to decide if he had known the real facts. He did not know the real facts; and, therefore, I think the resolution is not binding upon him.

There must be adequate disclosure of all material facts relevant to the question on which members will be asked to vote. In *Kaye* v. *Croydon Tramways Co.* [1898] 1 Ch. 358, a notice which failed to disclose the financial interest of the directors in a proposed reconstruction was held to be invalid. In *Baillie* v. *Oriental Telephone & Electric Co. Ltd* [1915] 1 Ch. 503, notice of a resolution to sanction the remuneration of the directors in connection with services rendered to certain subsidiaries was held to be inadequate because it did not specify the amount of that remuneration.

Business which has not been sufficiently notified or which is substantially different from that notified cannot be validly transacted (*Re Bridport Old Brewery Co.* (1867) 2 Ch. App. 19). However, amendments which are relevant to, and arise fairly out of, an item of business of which notice has been given may be proposed at the meeting (*Re Trench Tubeless Tyre Co.* [1900] 1 Ch. 408). For example, it has been held that a notice 'to elect directors' was sufficient for the meeting to elect directors up to the number permitted by the articles even though the notice only named one director (*Choppington Collieries Ltd.* v. *Johnson* [1944] 1 All E.R. 762). Amendments may not be made to the substance of resolutions proposed as special, extraordinary or elective resolutions or resolutions requiring special notice (see further para. 12.2).

The business actually carried out must substantially correspond to what was included in the notice. If notice is given of a single resolution which contains more than one proposal, it is not possible to adopt only part of it, because it is impossible for the court to know how many shareholders were satisfied with the arrangement as proposed and therefore abstained from attending the meeting (*Clinch* v. *Financial Corporation* (1898) L.R. 5 Eq. 450). Where notice was given of a meeting to consider resolutions for reconstruction and for winding up as incidental thereto, and only a resolution to wind up was passed, it was held to be invalid as it resulted in a position fundamentally different from that contemplated by the notice (*Re Teede and Bishop* (1901) 70 L.J. Ch. 409). However, where the notice specified several separate resolutions and one of those was to wind up the company, that resolution was effective even though the other resolutions which were concerned with the sale of the undertaking and consequent reorganisation, were found to be *ultra vires* and therefore void (*Thomson* v. *Henderson's Transvaal Estates Co.* [1908] 1 Ch. 765). The difference between these two cases is that in the first the notice implied that a resolution to wind up would only be passed as part of a reconstruction. In the second, the notice of the resolution to wind up was capable of standing in its own right. It follows that if it is intended to make a resolution contingent on the passing of another resolution, this should be done either by combining the two proposals in one resolution or clearly stating in the notice that the resolution is (or resolutions are) contingent upon the passing of another resolution(s).

6.5.3   Ordinary and special business

Many companies still have articles similar to the 1948 Table A which distinguishes between ordinary and special business. The articles of listed companies normally distinguish between ordinary and special business (see art. 61 of Whitbread plc) and the Listing Rules are drafted on this assumption (see Listing Rules, para. 9.31 and definition of 'ordinary business' in the Listing Rules).

Special business is defined in reg. 52 of the 1948 Table A as any business

> that is transacted at an extraordinary general meeting, and also all that is transacted at an annual general meeting, with the exception of declaring a dividend, the consideration of the accounts, balance sheets, and the reports of the directors and auditors, and the election of directors in the place of those retiring and the appointment of, and the fixing of the remuneration, of the auditors.

Any resolution which is not special business will be ordinary business.

Reg. 50 of the 1948 Table A states that in the case of special business the notice shall specify 'the general nature of that business'. Thus it must give a 'fair and candid and reasonable explanation' of the business to be transacted and give all material information to enable it to be understood.

No such requirement exists with respect to ordinary business and the effect of such provisions is to enable notice of annual general meetings to be given without setting out the general nature of the ordinary business. The members will be assumed to know what the ordinary business includes by virtue of the articles.

In practice, most listed companies also specify the general nature of ordinary business in notices. Indeed, although their articles may distinguish between ordinary and special business, they may still require the general nature of all business to be specified (e.g. see art. 57 of Whitbread plc). Whether or not this is the case, it would not generally be considered acceptable to do otherwise, not least because the Stock Exchange requires proxy cards sent to members to give them the opportunity to instruct their proxy to vote on all resolutions intended to be proposed at the meeting [Listing Rules, para. 13.28].

6.5.4   Circulars

Where the business is complex or important it is desirable to supplement the notice with an explanatory circular (*Young* v. *South African & Australian Exploration & Development Syndicate* [1896] 2 Ch. 268). Where a circular is sent with the notice, it will normally be read in conjunction with the notice in order to determine whether adequate notice has been given (*Tiessen* v. *Henderson* [1899] 1 Ch. 861). The same is true of the directors' report (*Boschoek Proprietary Co. Ltd* v. *Fuke* [1906] 1 Ch. 148) and presumably of any other document referred to in the notice and sent with it.

Whenever a listed company sends a notice of a meeting which includes any business other than ordinary business at an annual general meeting, the notice must be accompanied by an explanatory circular. If such other business is to be considered on the same day as the annual general meeting, the explanation may be incorporated in the directors' report [Listing Rules, para. 14.17]. A circular in connection with a resolution proposing to approve the adoption or amendment of the memorandum or articles of association, trust deeds, or employee share schemes must satisfy the requirements of Chapter 13 of the Listing Rules.

Paragraph 13.9 of the Listing Rules provides that a circular to shareholders in connection with proposed amendments to the memorandum and articles of association must:

- include an explanation of the effect of the proposed amendments;
- include either the full terms of the proposed amendments, or a statement that the full terms will be available for inspection:
  - (a) from the date of despatch of the circular until the close of the relevant general meeting at a place in or near the City of London or such other place as the Exchange may determine, and
  - (b) at the place of the general meeting for at least 15 minutes prior to and during the meeting;
- comply with the requirements of para. 14.1 (contents of all circulars).

Paragraph 14.1 of the Listing Rules provides that any circular sent by a company to a holder of its listed securities must:

- (a) provide a clear and adequate explanation of its subject matter;
- (b) if voting or other action is required, contain all information necessary to allow the holders of the securities to make a properly informed decision;
- (c) if voting or other action is required, contain a heading drawing attention to the importance of the document and advising holders of the securities who are in any doubt as to what action to take to consult appropriate independent advisers (Note 1);
- (d) where voting is required, contain a recommendation from the directors as to the voting action shareholders should take, indicating whether or not the proposal described in the circular is, in the opinion of the directors, in the best interests of the shareholders as a whole (Note 1);

(e) state that where all the securities have been sold or transferred by the addressee the circular and any other relevant documents should be passed to the person through whom the sale or transfer was effected for transmission to the purchaser or transferee (Note 1);

(f) where new securities are being issued in substitution for existing securities, explain what will happen to existing documents of title;

(g) not include any reference to a specific date which has not been agreed in advance with the Exchange on which listed securities will be marked 'ex' any benefit or entitlement;

(h) where it relates to a transaction in connection with which securities are proposed to be listed, include a statement that application has been or will be made for the securities to be admitted to the Official List and, if known, a statement of the following matters:

   (i) the date dealings are expected to commence;

   (ii) how the new securities will rank for dividend or interest;

   (iii) whether the new securities rank pari passu with any existing listed securities;

   (iv) the nature of the document of title;

   (v) the proposed date of issue; and

   (vi) the treatment of any fractions; and

(i) where a person is named in the circular as having advised the issuer or its directors, a statement that such adviser has given and has not withdrawn its written consent to the inclusion of the reference to the adviser's name in the form and context in which it is included.

Note 1: These items do not apply in the case of a circular or other document convening an annual general meeting.

Circulars which do not fall within the definition in para. 14.5 of the Listing Rules (Circulars of a routine nature) must be submitted to the Listing Department for prior approval. Six copies of every circular in its final form (whether or not it is required to be submitted for approval) must be lodged with the Company Announcements Office of the Exchange at the same time as it is despatched to shareholders [Listing Rules, para. 14.4].

Specific guidance on the content of circulars relating to the following business is also provided in Chapter 14 of the Listing Rules:

- authority to allot shares [para. 14.7];
- disapplication of pre-emption rights [para. 14.8];
- increase in authorised share capital [para. 14.9];
- reduction of capital [para. 14.10];
- capitalisation issue [para. 14.11];
- scrip dividend alternative [paras. 14.12 to 14.14];
- scrip dividend mandate schemes [paras. 14.15 and 14.15A];
- purchase of own securities [para. 14.16];

- early redemption [paras. 14.22 to 14.24]; and
- reminders of conversion rights [paras. 14.25 and 14.26].

6.6 PERSONS ENTITLED TO RECEIVE NOTICE

Notice of meetings must be given to all persons entitled to receive it by virtue of the articles of association. Where the articles are silent on the matter, notice must be given to every member of the company [s. 370(1)]. This would include joint shareholders, members whose calls are in arrears or who are resident abroad, and the holders of all classes of shares whether or not they have a right to attend and vote. Articles usually modify or exclude the rights of these members to receive notice (see para. 6.6.1). Articles usually specify that notice shall be given to the directors (e.g. reg. 38), although the Act makes no such provision.

Auditors have a statutory right to receive notices of meetings and any other communications relating to any general meeting which a member is entitled to receive [s. 390(1)]. An auditor who has been removed under s. 391(4) or who has resigned from office under s. 392A(8) retains the rights conferred by s. 390 in relation to any general meeting at which his term of office would otherwise have expired, or at which it is proposed to fill the vacancy caused by his removal. An auditor who has resigned also retains the rights conferred by s. 390 in relation to any general meeting requisitioned by him [s. 392A(8)].

The right to receive notice is suspended for members who are enemies or who are situated in enemy territories. A meeting will be properly convened if no notice is served on such persons (*Re Anglo-International Bank* [1943] Ch. 233).

Companies whose securities are participants in CREST can set a record date for determining entitlement to receive notice of a meeting (see para. 6.6.2). The London Stock Exchange requires listed companies to ensure that at least in each member state of the EU in which its securities are listed all the necessary facilities and information are available to enable holders of such securities to exercise their rights. In particular it must inform holders of securities of the holding of meetings which they are entitled to attend and enable them to exercise their right to vote, where applicable [Listing Rules, para. 9.24].

6.6.1 Restrictions on right to receive notice

Articles usually specify who is entitled to receive notice of meetings. For example, reg. 38 of Table A provides that, subject to any restrictions imposed on shares, notice shall be given to all the members, all persons entitled to a share in consequence of the death or bankruptcy of a member, the directors, and the auditors.

Other regulations in Table A specify the circumstances in which members are not entitled to receive notice. It should be noted that a person may have a right to receive notice but not a right to attend or vote at the meeting. A person may also have a right to attend and vote at a meeting but not to receive notice of it, e.g. a member whose registered address is outside the United Kingdom. The following restrictions on the right to receive notice of meetings are commonly found in articles:

- *Joint shareholders*

  A notice sent to the joint holder whose name stands first in the register of members in respect of the joint holding shall be sufficient notice to all the joint holders, e.g. reg. 112 of Table A. Companies often allow joint shareholders to split their holding, if it is capable of being split, so that two or more accounts are entered in the register of members each with a different name as the first named holder. By doing so, each joint holder whose name stands first in one of the accounts in the register is assured of receiving notice of any meeting.

- *Address not within the United Kingdom*

  A member whose registered address is not within the United Kingdom may not be entitled to receive notices unless he has given the company an address within the United Kingdom at which notices may be served, e.g. reg. 112 of Table A. This type of article requires the company to keep a separate record of UK addresses notified by such persons as their address in the register of members will still be outside the United Kingdom. (See *Parkstone Ltd* v. *Gulf Guarantee Bank plc* [1990] B.C.L.C. 850 for a case on reg. 113 of the 1948 Table A.)

- *Subsequent purchaser*

  A person who becomes entitled to have his name entered in the register of members as a member shall be bound by any notices given to the person from whom he derives his title, e.g. reg. 114 of Table A.

- *Calls unpaid*

  Articles commonly restrict the rights of members whose calls are in arrears to vote at a general meeting, e.g. reg. 57 of Table A. Such members must still be given notice of that meeting unless the articles specify otherwise. Table A makes no provision in this regard.

- *Preference shareholders*

  It is common for companies with preference share capital to restrict the rights of preference shareholders to receive notice of, attend and vote at general meetings. However, Table A makes no such provision and any company which intends to issue preference shares and which wishes to restrict these rights should amend its articles accordingly. Typically, the preference shareholders might be entitled under the articles to receive notice of any general meeting at which it is proposed to wind up the company or where a resolution is to be proposed that will affect the rights and privileges of the preference shareholders Where the right to receive dividends is cumulative, the preference shareholders will normally be entitled to receive notice of (and to attend and vote at) general meetings if those dividends are in arrears for a specified period (normally six months). Where preference dividends were payable each year out of profits earned in that year only, it was held that dividends were not in arrears for a particular year where there were no profits in that year. Accordingly the preference shareholders had no right to receive notice (*Coulson* v. *Austin Motor Co.* (1927) 43 T.L.R. 493).

- *Non-voting shares*
  Again, Table A makes no provision for non-voting shares and such members must be given notice unless the articles specify otherwise.

6.6.2   Record date

Companies whose securities have been admitted to CREST may set a record date for determining entitlement to receive notice of meetings. The date must not be more than 21 days before the date on which the notices are sent out (i.e. the actual date of posting and not necessarily the date of signing shown on the notice). If a company sets such a record date, only those members whose names have been entered on the relevant register of securities at the close of business on that date will be entitled to receive notice [Uncertificated Securities Regulations 1995, reg. 34 (see Appendix B)]. Boards may set a record date by including in their resolution to approve the notice something on the following lines (although no reference needs to be made in the notice itself to this resolution):

> For the purposes of regulation 34 of the Uncertificated Securities Regulations 1995 the members entitled to receive notice of [description of meeting] shall be those entered on the company's register of [members/other securities] at the close of business on [date].

6.7   FAILURE TO GIVE PROPER NOTICE

Unless all the members actually attend the meeting, the failure to give proper notice to any person entitled to receive it invalidates the meeting (*Smyth* v. *Darley* (1849) 2 H.L.C. 789). However, articles often provide that the accidental omission to give notice of a meeting or the non-receipt by a member of notice of a meeting shall not invalidate the proceedings at that meeting (e.g. reg. 39 of Table A). Such an article was held to validate a meeting for which notice had not been given to several members because the address plates for those members had inadvertently been separated from the rest because their dividends had been returned uncashed (*Re West Canadian Collieries Ltd* [1962] Ch. 370). However, a deliberate failure to send a notice to a member will not be validated even if the company had reason to believe that the notice would not reach the member at his registered address (*Musselwite* v. *C. H. Musselwite* [1962] Ch. 964). Once it is shown that some members were not given notice, the onus lies with those claiming that the meeting was valid to show that the omission was accidental (*POW Services Ltd* v. *Clare* [1995] 2 B.C.L.C. 435).

Some companies have adopted articles which provide that a member shall not be entitled to receive notice if on the three most recent occasions on which they were sent documents by the company, they were returned undelivered, unless they have subsequently confirmed their address or notified a new address.

Articles commonly provide that a member present, either in person or by proxy, at any meeting of the company or of the holders of any class of shares shall be deemed to have received notice of the meeting and of the purposes for which it was called (e.g. reg. 113 of Table A). Even without such a provision a member who was present and voted at a meeting of which irregular notice had been given may be deemed to have acquiesced in the irregularity (*Re British Sugar Refinery Co.* [1857] 26 L.J. Ch. 369).

6.8   CONSENT TO SHORT NOTICE [s. 369]

6.8.1   Annual general meetings

An annual general meeting may be called by notice shorter than the minimum required by s. 369 and will be deemed to have been properly convened if all the members entitled to attend and vote give their consent.

If accounts are to be laid at the annual general meeting, consent will probably need to be given to accept the report and accounts less than 21 days before the meeting (see **Precedent 6.8A**). The consent of all the members is required to do this whether the accounts are to be laid at the annual general meeting or an extraordinary general meeting [s. 238(4)].

6.8.2   Extraordinary general meetings

In the case of any other meeting, consent to short notice need only be given by a majority in number having a right to attend and vote at the meeting holding together not less than 95 per cent in nominal value of the shares conferring that right [ss. 369(3) and (4)] (see **Precedent 6.8B**).

It should be noted that the majority required is calculated by reference to the rights of all the members and not simply by reference to the rights of those who actually attend the meeting. Where a majority of 95 per cent is required, one member cannot form a majority in number and overrule the minority in this regard. However, a sole member would clearly be able to satisfy the requirements for both annual general meetings and extraordinary general meetings.

6.8.3   Separate consent required for special and extraordinary resolutions

If it is intended to propose either a special resolution or an extraordinary resolution at a meeting held at short notice, consent must also be obtained to dispense with the requirements of s. 378 as to notice which must be given to pass such resolutions (see **Precedent 6.8C**). In both cases these requirements can be dispensed with by a majority in number of the members having the right to attend and vote holding together not less than 95 per cent in nominal value of the shares conferring that right [s. 378(3)].

By using this procedure it is also possible to pass a special or extraordinary resolution which was not included in the notice of the meeting. However, it does not override the need for the consent of all the members to be given in relation to short notice of an annual general meeting. Equally, consent to short notice of the intention to propose a special or an extraordinary resolution must be given at a meeting for which consent to short notice has itself been given.

6.8.4   Some notice still required

By consenting to short notice in accordance with the statutory provisions, the members do not consent to receive no notice at all. Some notice (however short) must be given prior to the meeting and that notice must be served in a manner allowed by the articles, unless all the members attend the meeting and, in the case of a special or extraordinary resolution, vote in favour of the resolution.

6.8.5   Elective resolutions

Consent to short notice may now be given in respect of elective resolutions. Previously no such provision was made. However, the Deregulation (Resolutions of Private Companies) Order 1996 inserted a new subsection (2A) in s. 379A which provides that an elective resolution shall be effective notwithstanding the fact that less than 21 days' notice in writing of the meeting is given if all the members entitled to attend and vote at the meeting so agree. Although this is a more onerous requirement than for special and extraordinary resolutions, it should not present any difficulties in practice because elective resolutions must also be approved unanimously by all the members entitled to vote.

6.8.6   When consent cannot be given

The Act makes no provision for consent to short notice of resolutions requiring special notice (e.g. a resolution to remove the auditors or a director). This is logical because the special notice requirements are intended to allow the auditors or the director concerned time to prepare a statement for circulation to the members.

6.8.7   Practical points

In practice, consent to short notice will only be useful to companies with a relatively small number of shareholders, e.g. small private companies and subsidiaries. It is not strictly necessary for the members' consent to be given in writing. A resolution passed by the appropriate majority at the start of the meeting will suffice. It is, however, advisable to obtain the written consent of members prior to the meeting. It may prove to be impossible to obtain the necessary majority at the meeting perhaps because some members do not attend or have not submitted proxies. Consent in writing is also preferable as a method of proving compliance with the requirements of the Act. The form(s) of consent signed by the members should be entered in the minute book for this purpose.

As a final point of detail, notice still needs to be given to any person entitled to receive it who is not entitled to vote at the meeting. This would include the auditors who have a statutory right to receive notice but, having received it, cannot object to the meeting being held at short notice. The articles might also require notice to be given to other classes of member or the directors.

6.8.8   Elective resolution to reduce percentage required to consent

A private company may by elective resolution reduce to 90 per cent the majority required to consent to the holding of an extraordinary general meeting and for the passing of special and extraordinary resolutions at short notice (see further para. 24.7).

6.9   SPECIAL NOTICE [s. 379]

6.9.1   Conditions

Certain resolutions connected with the appointment and removal of directors and auditors cannot validly be proposed at a general meeting unless the requirements of s. 379 as to special notice have been followed, i.e.:

- notice of the intention to propose the resolution has been given by a member(s) to the company at least 28 days before the meeting at which the resolution is to be proposed (see **Precedent 6.9A**); and
- on receipt of such notice, the company gives members at least 21 days' notice of the fact that special notice has been given of the intention to propose the resolution (see **Precedent 6.9B**).

The requirements of s. 379 apply whether a resolution requiring special notice is to be proposed by a dissident member or to be included in the notice of a general meeting at the instigation of the board of directors. If it is to be proposed at the instigation of the board, a director who is also a member may give the necessary notice to the company.

6.9.2   Resolutions requiring special notice

Special notice is required by the Act in relation to the following resolutions:

- to remove a director by ordinary resolution before the expiration of his period of office under s. 303(1) or to appoint somebody instead of a director so removed at a meeting at which he is removed [s. 303(2)];
- to appoint or approve the appointment of a director who has attained the age of 70 [s. 293(5)];
- to fill a casual vacancy in the office of auditor [s. 388(3)(a)];
- to re-appoint as auditor a retiring auditor who was appointed by the directors to fill a casual vacancy [s. 388(3)(b)];

- to remove an auditor before the expiration of his term of office [s. 391A(1)(a)]; and
- to appoint as auditor a person other than a retiring auditor [s. 391A(1)(b)].

6.9.3   Additional requirements

In addition to the requirement to notify the members on receipt of special notice of the intention to move a resolution, the company must also comply with special requirements for each resolution which are set out in the relevant section of the Act (see para. 6.9.2 above). For example, s. 293 requires the company to include in the notice sent to members the age of the director whom it is proposed to appoint. On receipt of notice from a member of his or her intention to propose a resolution to remove a director or auditor, the company must forthwith send a copy of the notice to the person proposed to be removed. In the latter case, the director or auditor concerned then has a right to have a statement circulated with the notice of the meeting.

6.9.4   Company's obligations on receipt of special notice

A company is not obliged to include a resolution for which special notice has been given in the notice of the meeting or give members notice of it in any other manner unless the member also satisfies the conditions of s. 368 (extraordinary general meeting on members' request) or s. 376 (circulation of members' resolutions) (*Pedley* v. *Inland Waterways Association Ltd* [1977] 1 All E.R. 209). This is not immediately apparent from s. 379(2) which states 'The company shall give its members notice of any such resolution . . .'. However, Hoffman J. held in *Pedley* that this phrase is merely intended to confer on the members of a company the right to receive notice of any resolution of which special notice is required and has been duly given which is to form part of the agenda to be dealt with at the relevant meeting. Thus, a member who cannot comply with the conditions of s. 368 or s. 376, cannot force the company to include the resolution in the notice of the meeting or give notice of it in any other manner.

It is important to note, however, that a company may choose to do so if it so wishes, e.g. when a director notifies the company and the resolution is to be proposed at the instigation of the board. If the company gives members 21 days' notice of a resolution requiring special notice even though it was not required to do so under the *Pedley* principles, it must allow the member to propose the resolution because by giving notice it has included the matter on the agenda for the meeting.

If the member who intends to propose the resolution satisfies the above conditions, or the company wishes in any event to include the resolution on the agenda for the meeting, it must give at least 21 days' notice of the resolution at the same time and in the same manner as notice of the meeting is given (see **Precedent 6.9B**). If this is not practicable, the notice must be given either by advertisement in a newspaper having an appropriate circulation or in any other mode allowed by the company's articles [s. 379(2)].

If, after a member has notified the company of his or her intention to propose a resolution which requires special notice, a meeting is called for a date 28 days or less after the notice has been given, the notice shall be deemed to have been properly given to the company [s. 379(3)]. This safeguard is necessary in order to prevent a company avoiding giving notice of an otherwise valid resolution by calling a meeting for a date before the 28 day period required by s. 379(1) has elapsed.

There is nothing in s. 379 which requires a company to convene a meeting to consider a resolution for which special notice has been given. Indeed, a company which has elected to dispense with annual general meetings might never hold a meeting at which such a resolution could be proposed unless the member also gave notice under s. 366A requiring it to hold an annual general meeting or requisitioned an extraordinary general meeting under s. 368.

6.9.5   No consent to short notice

No provision is made in the Act for consent to short notice with respect to a resolution requiring special notice. Therefore, such a resolution cannot be passed at a meeting held at short notice. It should also be noted that 21 days' notice must still be given of a resolution requiring special notice if the resolution is to be validly proposed at an extraordinary general meeting.

6.10   CIRCULATION OF MEMBERS' RESOLUTIONS AND STATEMENTS [s. 376]

In addition to the right to requisition an extraordinary general meeting under s. 368, the members of a company have a statutory right under s. 376 to require the company to give notice of resolutions which they intend to propose at annual general meetings. They also have a right to have statements circulated by the company in connection with any business that is to be dealt with at any general meeting. This includes a statement on any matter pending before an extraordinary general meeting of the company and any business that is to be dealt with at an annual general meeting, including a requisitioned resolution.

6.10.1   Conditions for valid requisition under s. 376

The conditions which a member or members must satisfy for a members' requisition under s. 376 are less onerous than those for requisitioning an extraordinary general meeting under s. 368 (see para. 5.6). This is logical because the company is not required to call an additional meeting but merely to do something in relation to a meeting which must be held. Section 376(2) provides that a valid requisition may be made by:

(a) any number of members (which includes one) holding not less than one-twentieth of the total voting rights of all the members having at the date of the requisition the right to vote at the meeting to which the requisition relates; or

(b) not less than 100 members holding shares in the company on which there has been paid up an average sum, per member, of not less than £100.

It should be noted that under (a) above the validity of the requisition will be determined by reference to the number of members who would have been entitled to vote if the meeting had been held on the date of the requisition. Thus, if preference dividends are in arrears on the date of the requisition and the company's articles give preference shareholders the right to vote in such circumstances, the requirements for a valid requisition will be more onerous (see Table 6.2 below).

In relation to (b) above, the number of shares which members must hold is calculated in relation to the nominal value of the shares. For example, if the nominal value is £1, each member must hold on average 100 fully paid shares. If the nominal value is 25p, each member must hold on average 400 shares.

Table 6.2   Examples of the minimum requirements for members' requisitions

Number of voting shares in issue	Notice of AGM resolution/Circulation of statement		Convene EGM under s. 368
	under s. 376(2)(a)	under s. 376(2)(b)	
100 fully paid £1 ordinary (voting) shares	One or more members holding together 5 shares	N/A	One or more members holding together 10 shares
200,000 fully paid £1 ordinary (voting) shares	One or more members holding together 10,000 shares	100 members holding together 10,000 shares	One or more members holding together 20,000 shares
1 million fully paid £1 ordinary voting shares	One or more members holding together 50,000 shares	100 members holding together at least 10,000 shares	One or more members holding together 100,000 shares
1 million fully paid £1 ordinary voting shares and 500,000 £2 preference shares carrying the right to vote	One or more members holding together 75,000 shares (ordinary or preference)	100 members holding shares (ordinary or preference) on which an average of not less than £100 per member has been paid up	One or more members holding together shares (ordinary or preference) representing £200,000 of the paid up capital

6.10.2   Form of requisition

A copy of the requisition under s. 376 signed by the requisitionists (or two or more copies which between them bear the signatures of all the requisitionists) must be deposited at the company's registered office (see **Precedents 6.10A and B**).

6.10.3   Timing of requisition

The members' requisition must be deposited at the registered office:

- in the case of a requisition requiring the company to give notice of a resolution, not less than 6 weeks before the meeting [s. 377(1)(a)(i)]; and
- in the case of a requisition requiring the company to circulate a statement, not less than one week before the meeting [s. 377(1)(a)(ii)].

A company is not bound to comply with a demand made after the above dates. However, after the requisition has been deposited at its registered office, it cannot avoid its obligations by calling an annual general meeting for a date six weeks or less. In these circumstances, the requisition will be deemed to have been properly deposited [s. 377(2)].

6.10.4   Company's duty

On receipt of a valid requisition, a company has a duty to:

- in the case of a requisition requiring the company to give notice of a resolution, give to the members of the company entitled to receive notice of the next annual general meeting notice of any resolution that may be properly moved and is intended to be moved (by the requisitionists) at that meeting, [s. 376(1)(a)]; or
- in the case of a requisition requiring the company to circulate a statement, circulate to members entitled to have notice of any general meeting sent to them any statement of not more than 1,000 words with respect to the matter referred to in any proposed resolution or the business to be dealt with at that meeting [s. 376(1)(b)].

Although the Act imposes these duties on the company, it will fall to the directors to ensure compliance with them, and it is noteworthy that under s. 376(7) the directors, but not the company, are liable to a fine in default.

Under s. 376(1)(a) the members may require the company to give notice of a proposed resolution only in respect of an annual general meeting. A company is not required to include such a resolution in the notice of an extraordinary general meeting to be held before the next annual general meeting. If the members are not prepared to wait until the next annual general meeting, they should requisition an extraordinary general meeting under s. 368, assuming that they are able to satisfy the more onerous conditions.

The company must give notice of the requisitioned resolution and circulate any requisitioned statement to members of the company who are entitled to have notice of the meeting sent to them by serving a copy of the resolution or statement in any manner permitted for service of notice of the meeting [s. 376(3)] (see **Precedents 6.10C** and **D**). Copies should also be sent to the company's auditors who are entitled to receive all notices of, and other communications relating to, any general meeting which a member of the company is entitled to receive [s. 390(1)] and to any other persons entitled to receive notices under the articles.

Members who are not entitled to have the notice sent to them but who are entitled to receive notice by some other means (e.g. the holders of bearer shares who are entitled to be given notice by advertisement) must be given notice of the general effect of the resolution in any manner permitted for giving such members notice of meetings [s. 376(4)]. It should be noted that this provision does not apply to a requisitioned statement which need only be circulated to members who are entitled to have notice of the meeting sent to them [s. 376(1)(b)].

The copy or notice of the general effect of the resolution must be served or given in the same manner and (where practicable) at the same time as the notice of the meeting or as soon as practicable thereafter [s. 376(5)].

Notwithstanding anything in a company's articles, any business of which notice is given in accordance with the requirements of s. 376 may be dealt with at an annual general meeting and an accidental omission to give notice of a requisitioned resolution to one or more members shall not invalidate the proceedings [s. 376(6)].

6.10.5 Costs

A company need not comply with a requisition unless the requisitionists deposit or tender with it a sum which is reasonably sufficient to meet its expenses in giving effect to the requisition [s. 377(1)(b)]. However, the members may vote by ordinary resolution to release the requisitionists from any obligations they may have to pay the company's costs [s. 376(1)].

It is difficult for the requisitionists to make an accurate assessment of the company's costs and they will normally seek guidance from the company before depositing the requisition. If there is a dispute between the company and the requisitionists as to the sum required, the directors would be well-advised to give effect to the requisition as they could be liable to a fine for failing to comply with the requirements of s. 376 if the court takes the view that the sum deposited or tendered by the requisitionists was in fact reasonably sufficient.

The cost of giving effect to a members' resolution should not be prohibitive if it is deposited in time for inclusion in the notice calling the annual general meeting, although this deadline will often be more than six weeks before the meeting in the case of listed companies. If the company has already printed the notice at the time of the deposit, it should attempt to minimise the cost of giving effect to the requisition by issuing a separate notice of the resolution rather than, for example, having the original notice reprinted, particularly if that notice is embodied in the annual report and accounts.

In practice, the company (i.e. the directors) may sometimes agree to give effect to a requisition without charge to the requisitionists. Section 377(1)(b) does not prevent the company (i.e. the directors) from doing this. It merely provides that the company 'need not' (rather than 'shall not') give effect to a requisition unless the requisitionists have deposited or tendered with it a sum reasonably sufficient to meet the company's costs in giving effect to it. And, in giving effect to the requisition without charge, the directors can be assumed to have waived any liability the requisitionists may have under s. 376(1) to pay the company's costs.

If the directors do not agree to give effect to the requisition without charge, the requisitionists may wish to include in their requisition a proposal that the company bears its own costs in giving effect to the requisition. Requisitionists sometimes achieve this by embodying a proposal regarding costs in their main requisitioned resolution. This has the advantage of ensuring that they will not be required to pay if the resolution is passed. However, it may be preferable from their point of view for the proposal to be drafted as a separate requisitioned resolution, particularly where their main proposal is one which requires a special majority. This is because the resolution regarding costs need only be passed as an ordinary resolution. Even where their main proposal is in the form of an ordinary resolution and it is defeated, the requisitionists may find that the members will approve a separate ordinary resolution regarding costs.

In its *Guide to best practice for Annual General Meetings*, ICSA recommends as a best practice point that unless the company agrees at the outset to absorb all the costs of circulation, shareholder resolutions requisitioned under section 376 of the CA 1985 should automatically be accompanied (in any notice) by another resolution giving shareholders the opportunity to decide whether the company or the requisitionists should bear the relevant costs. If the directors feel that any particular case does not justify the adoption of such a resolution, they should, however, be free to recommend a vote against it. ICSA also says in the *Guide* (but not as a best practice point):

> Where [shareholder] resolutions are not vexatious, frivolous, substantially repetitive or seeking a purpose which will clearly have no legal effect, we support including [them] in the notice without charge. It is not possible, in the context of a best practice guide, to provide an exhaustive list of all the circumstances in which companies should accept/reject shareholder resolutions for circulation. All companies should be willing to enter into a dialogue with shareholders about resolutions submitted, especially giving reasons for rejection where that is the case.

Statements

Although a requisition requiring a statement to be circulated can be deposited after the notice has been sent out, the cost of circulating it at this late stage will obviously be greater. It should also be noted that, unless the directors agree to waive the costs of circulating a statement, the requisitionists will have no choice but to pay them. If, however, the requisitioned statement is deposited at least six weeks before the meeting, the requisitionists could also requisition a resolution proposing that the company bears its own costs in giving effect to the requisition.

It should be noted that as an alternative to requisitioning a statement under s. 376, any member may (on payment of the prescribed fee) demand a copy of the company's register of members [s. 356] and use the names and addresses of the members to circulate a statement to all or part of the members. This may well be cheaper if it is only necessary to target, say, shareholders holding more than 5 per cent of the company's equity.

6.10.6   Abuse of rights under s. 376

If the court is satisfied that the rights conferred by s. 376 are being abused to secure needless publicity for defamatory matter, it may on the application of the company or any other aggrieved person order that the company is not bound to circulate any such statement and that the requisitionists pay the company's costs in making such an application [s. 377(3)]. In an Australian case on a similarly worded provision, it has been held that the applicant must demonstrate that the statement is defamatory *and* that the section is being abused to secure needless publicity (*Re Harbour Lighterage Ltd* (1968) 1 N.S.W.L.R. 438). In the same case, it was held that the court had no power to order the deletion of the defamatory parts of a members' statement. It could only order that the whole statement should not be sent.

6.10.7   Default

In the event of default, every officer of the company who is in default is liable to a fine [s. 376(7)].

6.10.8   DTI consultation

In 1996, the Department of Trade and Industry issued a consultation document on proposals to amend the procedures for members' resolutions and statements under sections 376 and 377 (*Shareholder Communications at the Annual General Meeting*, DTI, April 1996). The consultation document asked whether companies should be required to circulate qualifying resolutions and statements in connection with the annual general meeting without charge if they are deposited within a certain period (say, two months) after the company's year end. Shareholders submitting a resolution after this deadline would still be liable to pay the company's costs and the company would still be bound to comply with a valid demand deposited within the normal deadline of six weeks before the meeting.

The DTI also indicated in the consultation document that it was prepared to consider:

- raising the threshold under which members' resolutions qualify for circulation from 100 members having on average '£100 paid up capital' to the equivalent amount in real terms to £100 in 1948 (about £1,900 in 1996);
- introducing a requirement that each requisitionist must have held the relevant qualifying shares for a minimum specified period of time, e.g. one year;
- introducing a provision which releases the company from its obligation to circulate any resolution which is irrelevant, repetitious or a duplication of a

resolution which has already been accepted for circulation (it is suggested that some sort of appeal mechanism would be required in these circumstances).

The consultation document also asked whether companies should be required to make provision at the annual general meeting for shareholders' questions or whether shareholders should be given a statutory right to ask questions at the annual general meeting (see para. 9.4). At the time of writing, the DTI has not yet published its conclusions regarding these proposals.

CHAPTER SEVEN

Resolutions

7.1 SUMMARY

The type of resolution required to deal with an item of business is determined primarily by the Companies Acts. For each type of resolution, there are different requirements with regard to the notice which must be given and the majority which is needed to pass the resolution. An ordinary resolution can be passed by a simple majority of the members voting at a meeting for which proper notice has been given (see para. 7.2). Extraordinary resolutions require a majority of 75 per cent of the members voting and are generally required in connection with the winding up of companies (see para. 7.3). Special resolutions are far more common and are generally required where it is proposed to alter the rights of members or the constitution of the company. The majority required is the same as for extraordinary resolutions. However, the requirements as to notice are more stringent (see para. 7.4).

Elective resolutions can only be passed by private companies and are used to dispense with various requirements connected with the holding of annual general meetings. All the members of the company must vote in favour of the resolution otherwise it will be invalid (see para. 7.5).

A copy of all special, extraordinary, elective and some ordinary resolutions must be filed at Companies House 15 days after they have been passed and be embodied in or annexed to every copy of the articles issued after the passing of the resolution (see para. 7.6).

7.2 ORDINARY RESOLUTIONS

Unless the Companies Acts or the articles specify otherwise, all business at general meetings may be dealt with by ordinary resolution. Where a provision in the Companies Acts requires a matter to be authorised 'by the company in general meeting' this means by ordinary resolution.

There is no definition of ordinary resolution in the Act. However, it is well established that a resolution will be passed as an ordinary resolution when it is passed

Table 7.1 Matters which may be passed by ordinary resolution under the Act (unless otherwise indicated, the articles may specify a higher majority).

Nature of resolution	Companies Act 1985
Giving authority to directors to allot shares (Note 3)	s. 80
Transfer to public company of non-cash asset in initial period	s. 104
Alteration of share capital	s. 121
Authority for market purchase of own shares (Note 3)	s. 166
Removal of a director (Notes 1 and 2)	s. 303
Approval of payment for loss of office to director	ss. 312 & 313
Director's contract of more than 5 years	s. 319
Approval of substantial property transaction involving directors	s. 320
Resolution to revoke elective resolution (Note 2)	s. 379A
Appointment of auditors by company in general meeting	ss. 385 & 385A
Resolution to fix remuneration of auditors	s. 390A
Removal of auditors (Notes 1 and 2)	s. 391
Making provision for employees on cessation or transfer of business	s. 719

Notes:
1. This resolution requires special notice to be given in accordance with s. 379.
2. Articles cannot exclude the members' right to remove a director by ordinary resolution.
3. Resolution must be filed at Companies House under s. 380.

by a simple majority of the members who are entitled to vote and who actually vote (whether in person or by proxy) at a meeting of which proper notice has been given. An abstention is not considered to be a vote for these purposes. Put quite simply, therefore, an ordinary resolution will be passed if the number of votes in favour exceeds the number against the motion.

Articles often give the chairman of the meeting a casting vote where an equal number of votes are cast for and against a resolution proposed as an ordinary resolution, e.g. reg. 50 of Table A (see para. 16.9).

Listed companies must forward 'without delay' to the Company Announcements Office six copies of any ordinary resolutions passed at a general meeting other than those concerning the ordinary business [Listing Rules, para. 9.31]. Ordinary business for these purposes includes receiving the accounts and reports, reappointing the auditors and fixing their remuneration, and the re-election of directors retiring by rotation [Listing Rules, Definitions].

7.3   EXTRAORDINARY RESOLUTIONS

7.3.1   Majority required

An extraordinary resolution must be passed by a majority of not less than 75 per cent of the members who are entitled to vote and who actually vote (whether in person or by proxy) at a general meeting of which notice specifying the intention to propose the resolution as an extraordinary resolution has been duly given [s. 378(1)].

On a show of hands the majority required is 75 per cent of the members actually voting (including corporate representatives but not proxies unless, unusually, the articles confer on them the right to vote on a show of hands). An abstention is not a valid vote for these purposes. Thus, if 100 members are present at a meeting and 79 actually vote on a show of hands, 60 must vote in favour in order to pass a resolution as an extraordinary resolution (i.e. 75.59 per cent – 59 would be a majority of only 74.68 per cent). An extraordinary resolution will, however, be passed where the majority in favour is exactly 75 per cent, e.g. 75 in favour, 25 against.

On a poll, where each member is entitled to votes in proportion to their holdings, the number of votes required is calculated by reference to the total number of votes cast for and against the resolution. On a show of hands, a member holding 75 per cent of the voting shares will not be able to pass an extraordinary resolution unless no other member votes. However, the same member would be able to on a poll.

7.3.2   Notice

An extraordinary resolution will be invalid if the notice does not specify the intention to propose it as an extraordinary resolution (*MacConnell* v. *E. Prill & Co. Ltd* [1916] 2 Ch. 57) and if it does not state the text or entire substance of the proposals to be submitted (*Re Moorgate Mercantile Holdings Ltd* [1980] 1 All E.R. 40).

There are no specific requirements as to the period of notice which must be given for extraordinary resolutions. Accordingly, the period of notice required will be determined by the requirements for the type of meeting at which the resolution is to be proposed. It also follows that, unlike special resolutions, if consent to short notice is being sought for a meeting, separate consent is not required for an extraordinary resolution which is to be proposed at that meeting.

A copy of every extraordinary resolution passed by a company must be filed with the registrar of companies within 15 days of it being passed [s. 380(1)] and a copy must be annexed or embodied in every copy of the articles issued after the passing of the resolution [s. 380(2)] (see para. 7.6).

Table 7.2   Matters which must be passed by extraordinary resolution

Nature of resolution	Source
Voluntary winding up of a company that cannot continue its business by liabilities	Insolvency Act 1986, s. 84(1)
Members' voluntary winding up, to sanction liquidator's proposals for a compromise with the company's creditors	Insolvency Act 1986, s. 165(2)
Variation of class rights (not attached by memorandum) for which the articles make no alternative provision with respect to variation.	Companies Act 1985, s. 125(2)
Distribution by a liquidator of surplus assets in kind instead of realising them in cash.	Table A, reg. 117

Listed companies must also forward 'without delay' to the Company Announcements Office six copies of any extraordinary resolution passed at a general meeting [Listing Rules, para. 9.31].

7.4 SPECIAL RESOLUTIONS

A resolution will be a special resolution when it has been passed by a majority of not less than 75 per cent of members who are entitled to vote and who actually vote (whether in person or, where proxies are allowed, by proxy) at a general meeting of which not less than 21 days' notice has been given of the intention to propose it as a special resolution [s. 378(2)]. The majority required is calculated in accordance with the principles set out for extraordinary resolutions above.

7.4.1 Notice

At least 21 days' notice must be given of the intention to propose a special resolution at a general meeting. However, consent to short notice may be given in accordance with s. 378(3) which requires the agreement of a *majority in number* of the members having the right to attend and vote at such a meeting, holding not less than 95 per cent in nominal value of the shares giving that right. In the case of a company not having a share capital, the majority required is a majority in number together representing not less than 95 per cent of the voting rights.

The intention to propose a resolution as a special resolution should be clearly stated in the notice calling the meeting. The notice should also specify either the text or the entire substance of the resolution (*Re Moorgate Mercantile Holdings Ltd* [1980] 1 All E.R. 40 (see para. 12.2).

A copy of every special resolution passed by a company must be filed at Companies House within 15 days of it being passed [s. 380(1)] and must be annexed or embodied in every copy of the articles issued after the passing of the resolution [s. 380(2)] (see para. 7.6).

Listed companies must also forward 'without delay' to the Company Announcements Office six copies of any special resolution passed at a general meeting [Listing Rules, para. 9.31].

7.5 ELECTIVE RESOLUTIONS

A private company may elect to dispense with certain formalities by passing an elective resolution (see further para. 24.2). An elective resolution will not be effective unless:

- at least 21 days' notice in writing is given of the meeting, stating that an elective resolution is to be proposed and stating the terms of the resolution;
- the resolution is agreed to at the meeting, in person or by proxy, by all the members entitled to attend and vote at the meeting [s. 379A(2)].

Table 7.3 Matters which must be passed by special resolution under the Companies Act 1985 and the Insolvency Act 1986

Nature of resolution	Companies Act 1985
Change of situation of registered office to Wales in memorandum of association	s. 2(2)
Alteration of objects in memorandum of association	s. 4(1)
Alteration of articles of association	s. 9(1)
Alteration of conditions in memorandum which could lawfully be contained in the articles	s. 17(1)
Change of company name	s. 28(1)
Ratification of (and relief for) action by directors which is outside the capacity of the company	s. 35(3)
Re-registration of private company as public	s. 43(1)
Re-registration of unlimited company as public	s. 48(2)
Re-registration of unlimited company as limited	s. 51
Re-registration of public company as private	s. 53(1)
Disapplication of pre-emption rights	s. 95
Resolution that uncalled share capital shall not be called up except in a winding up	s. 120
Reduction of share capital	s. 135
Financial assistance by private company for acquisition of own shares	s. 155
Resolution authorising terms of off-market purchase of own shares	s. 164
Purchase of own shares under contingent purchase contract	s. 165(2)
Assignment or release of company's right to purchase own shares	s. 167
Purchase of own shares (payment out of capital of private company)	s. 173
Resolution of dormant company not to appoint auditors	s. 250
Resolution making liability of directors unlimited	s. 307
Approval of assignment of office by a director	s. 308

	Insolvency Act 1986
Resolution to wind up voluntarily	s. 84(1)
Authorise liquidator to transfer assets of company to new company in exchange for securities in the new company	s. 110(3)
Resolution to be wound up by court	s. 122(1)

However, less than 21 days' notice in writing of the meeting may be given if all the members entitled to attend and vote at the meeting agree [s. 379A(2A) inserted by the Deregulation (resolutions of Private Companies) Order 1996]. A private company can also avoid the statutory notice requirements by passing an elective resolution as a written resolution (see Chapter 23).

A copy of every elective resolution passed by a private company must be filed at Companies House within 15 days of it being passed [s. 380(1)] and must be annexed or embodied in every copy of the articles issued after the passing of the resolution [s. 380(2)]. A private company should also indicate on its annual return whether an election is in force either to dispense with the holding of annual general meetings or to dispense with the obligation to lay copies of the report and accounts before the company in general meeting.

7.6   FILING OF RESOLUTIONS

The Act requires copies of certain resolutions to be filed with the registrar of companies at Companies House within 15 days of being passed [s. 380] (see **Precedent 7.6**). The resolutions which must be filed include any:

(a) special resolution;
(b) extraordinary resolution;
(c) elective resolution;
(d) a number of ordinary resolutions specified in s. 380(4) (see Table 7.1).

If any of the above are done by written resolution, they must still be filed. In addition, any agreement which has the same effect as a resolution (e.g. a shareholders' agreement which has the effect of modifying the articles) must also be filed under s. 380.

7.6.1   Date resolution is passed

The date of passing a resolution will be the date of the meeting or, if the resolution was passed at an adjourned meeting, the date of the adjourned meeting [s. 381]. However, where the business of a meeting is suspended for the purposes of conducting a poll at a later date, the date of the resolution will be the date of the meeting at which the poll was demanded.

CHAPTER EIGHT

Chairman

8.1 SUMMARY

A general meeting cannot proceed without a chairman for legal and practical reasons. There must be someone to put motions to the meeting, declare the results of voting, and rule on points of order. In view of the importance of the role, it is common for the articles to determine who should chair the meetings rather than allow the members to elect the chairman at each meeting (see para. 8.2).

In common law, the person appointed as the chairman of the meeting is deemed to have been given authority by the meeting to regulate its proceedings. As this is a form of delegated authority, the chairman must still act in accordance with the wishes of the majority at the meeting, unless exercising a power conferred by statute or the company's articles of association or one which the courts have ruled can be exercised by the chairman without reference to the members (e.g. the power to adjourn to restore order).

The chairman has a duty to ensure that the meeting is properly conducted (see para. 8.5), that all shades of opinion are given a fair hearing (see para. 8.6), and that the sense of the meeting is properly ascertained and recorded (see para. 8.7). It is also the chairman's duty to maintain order (see para. 10.4).

8.2 APPOINTMENT OF CHAIRMAN

Articles usually state that the chairman of the board of directors shall chair meetings of the company and make provisions for circumstances in which he or she is not present or is unwilling to act. For example, Table A provides:

> **42.** The chairman, if any, of the board of directors or in his absence some other director nominated by the directors shall preside as chairman of the meeting, but if neither the chairman nor any such other director (if any) be present within fifteen minutes after the time appointed for holding the meeting and willing to act, the directors present shall elect one of their

number to be chairman and, if there is only one director present and willing to act, he shall be chairman.

43. If no director is willing to act as chairman, or if no director is present within fifteen minutes after the time appointed for holding the meeting, the members present and entitled to vote shall choose one of their number to be chairman.

Where there is no director present or willing to chair the meeting, articles like reg. 43 of Table A, appear to require the members to elect another member to act as chairman. However, the word member must include a proxy where the articles say that proxies can be counted in calculating whether there is a quorum and only proxies are present (*Re Bradford Investments plc* [1990] B.C.C. 740). In the same case, it was held that a person who is neither a member, corporate representative or a proxy may take the chair at the start of the meeting to preside over the election of a chairman. However, the rulings of such a person will be liable to challenge in the courts irrespective of anything contained in the articles, e.g. on the validity of any votes tendered in the election process.

A person who has legitimately taken the chair in the absence of the chairman may (but need not) vacate it if the chairman subsequently arrives. Any objection to the appointment of a chairman at a meeting should be made immediately as any irregularity in the nomination may be cured by the acquiescence of those present (*Booth* v. *Arnold* [1985] 1 Q.B. 571).

8.3 REMOVAL OF THE CHAIRMAN

A chairman elected by the meeting, e.g. when no director is present or willing to act in that capacity, may be removed by the meeting (*Cornwall* v. *Woods* (1846) 4 notes of Cases 555). This is normally done by a motion of no confidence in the chair. If such a resolution is proposed, the chairman should step down until the result of the vote is determined.

It is doubtful whether a person who holds office as the chairman by virtue of the articles and his or her position in the company (e.g. as the chairman of the board or as a director) can be removed by the members.

8.4 CHAIRMAN'S DUTIES

The chairman has an overriding duty to act in good faith in the best interests of the company and is responsible for:

- the proper conduct of the meeting (see para. 8.5);
- the preservation of order (see para. 10.4);
- ensuring that all shades of opinion are given a fair hearing (see para. 8.6);
- ensuring that the sense of the meeting is properly ascertained and recorded (see para. 8.7).

8.5 PROPER CONDUCT OF THE MEETING

The chairman must ensure that the meeting is conducted in accordance with the requirements of the Act, the company's articles of association and any applicable common law rules, and will normally be guided in this respect by the company secretary.

The chairman should not open the meeting before the time specified in the notice and should, as far as possible, ensure that the meeting starts on time and that all the business on the agenda is transacted. The start of the meeting can, however, be delayed in certain circumstances. The most obvious is where there is no quorum, in which case the meeting cannot proceed to business in any case. The chairman can also legitimately delay the meeting to allow members who arrived on time to register and gain admittance (see Chairman's Scripts in Chapter 21). As a rule of thumb, it is not advisable to delay the meeting for any longer than 15 to 20 minutes. Problems which take longer than this to sort out should be dealt with by proposing an adjournment immediately after opening the meeting (see Chapter 17).

The chairman may rule on any question raised from the floor relating to the conduct of the meeting (*Re Indian Zoedone Co.* (1884) 26 Ch.D. 70). If his decision is challenged, the matter should be put to the meeting and decided by the majority of those present (*Wandsworth and Putney Gas Light Co.* v. *Wright* (1870) 22 L.T. 404). The following example serves to demonstrate this process:

> At a meeting of a public company, a person begins to ask a question but is interrupted by a member on a point of order. The member informs the chairman that the previous speaker is a proxy and therefore has no right to speak at the meeting, and requests that the chairman make a ruling to that effect. The chairman may think that the proxy should be allowed to speak. However, instead of making a ruling to that effect, he should attempt to gauge the feelings of the members by saying: 'I am minded to allow proxies to speak at this meeting. Does anyone else object to this proposal?' If there is no other opposition from the floor, he may rule that the proxy be allowed to speak. If the member still objects, the chairman should perhaps take a proper vote on the matter. If, however, there is significant opposition from the floor, the chairman would be well advised to drop the proposal or risk being defeated on a vote and losing the confidence of the members. It is rare for such issues to be the subject of a poll, although not impossible.

If the chairman conducts the meeting in a certain way or makes a ruling that is not challenged at the meeting, the members present will be deemed to have acquiesced or consented to that conduct. In *Carruth* v. *Imperial Chemical Industries Ltd* [1937] A.C. 707, the directors convened an extraordinary general meeting of the company and two meetings of different classes of shares to be held on the same day and at the same venue to approve a reduction of capital. As one meeting finished, the next meeting was started and each meeting was attended by each of the different classes of member. The resolution of one class of members was challenged on the ground that people who were not members of that class were present at the meeting. The resolution was held to be valid and Lord Russell said:

> There are many matters relating to the conduct of a meeting which lie entirely in the hands of those persons who are present and constitute the meeting. Thus it rests with the meeting to decide whether notices, resolutions, minutes, accounts, and such like shall be read to the meeting or be taken as read; whether representatives of the Press, or any other persons not qualified to be summoned to the meeting, shall be permitted to be present, or if present, shall be permitted to remain; whether and when discussion shall be terminated and a vote taken; whether the meeting shall be adjourned. In all these matters, and they are only instances, the meeting decides, and if necessary a vote must be taken to ascertain the wishes of the majority. If no objection is taken by any constituent of the meeting, the meeting must be taken to be assenting to the course adopted.

The chairman cannot close the meeting until all the business has been dealt with. In *National Dwelling Society Ltd* v. *Sykes*, the chairman wrongly refused to accept an amendment to a resolution to receive the report and accounts and closed the meeting before all the business had been transacted. The members elected another chairman to transact the unfinished business and adjourned the meeting. It was held that the chairman had acted outside his powers by closing the meeting without its consent before the business had been completed and that the meeting could go on with the business for which it had been convened and appoint another chairman to conduct that business.

See also Chapter 12 on amendments, Chapter 11 on procedural motions, Chapter 17 on adjournment and Chapter 21 for examples of chairman's scripts.

8.6   ENSURING THAT ALL SHADES OF OPINION ARE GIVEN A FAIR HEARING

The chairman should seek to ensure that all members who hold different views on a resolution before the meeting are given a fair hearing. To do otherwise would defeat the object of holding the meeting. In particular, the chairman should not curtail the debate unless the minority have had a reasonable opportunity to put its views (*Wall* v. *London & Northern Assets Corporation Ltd* [1898] 2 Ch. 469).

The amount of time that should be made available for debate will vary depending on the nature of the business and the number of people wishing to speak on it. This does not mean that the discussion should be allowed to go on for ever. Shortly before closing the debate, the chairman should ask members to refrain from speaking unless they have a different point to make. Although it not an easy thing to do without causing offence, the chairman should at this point cut short any speaker who is repeating a point made earlier in the debate in order to ensure that those with different views are given a fair hearing. When the chairman considers that a full range of views have been expressed, he may seek to curtail discussion and put the resolution to a vote. If any member objects, the chairman should seek the consent of the meeting by proposing a formal 'closure' motion, i.e that the question before the meeting be now put to the vote (see further para. 11.2 and, for an example script, para. 21.9).

8.7   ASCERTAINING AND RECORDING THE SENSE OF THE MEETING

8.7.1   Ascertaining the sense of the meeting

In *National Dwelling Society Ltd* v. *Sykes* [1894] 3 Ch. 159, it was held that the chairman has a duty to ensure that 'the sense of the meeting is properly ascertained with regard to any question which is properly before the meeting'. In doing so the chairman should put resolutions to a vote, ensure that the votes are properly counted and declare the results of that vote. In order to prevent issues regarding the precise number of votes cast for and against the resolution being re-opened after the meeting, s. 378(4) provides that, unless a poll is demanded, a chairman's declaration that an extraordinary or special resolution has been carried is conclusive evidence of that fact without proof of the number or proportion of votes. The courts have refused to intervene in several cases where questions have been raised as to the validity of the chairman's declaration and have confirmed that the word conclusive means exactly that (see *Arnot* v. *United African Lands* [1901] 1 Ch. 518; *Re Hadleigh Castle Gold Mines* [1900] 2 Ch. 419; and *Graham's Morocco Co. Ltd, Petitioners*, 1932 S.C. 269). However, the court has intervened in a case where the chairman put a resolution and declared the result in the following fashion: 'Those in favour . . . 6. Those against . . . 23 but there are 200 voting by proxy and I declare the resolution carried as required by Act of Parliament.' Buckley J. refused to hold that the chairman's declaration was conclusive as it was clear from the chairman's declaration that he had acted on a mistaken principle (*Re Caratal (New) Mines Ltd* [1902] 2 Ch. 498).

Articles usually extend the operation of s. 378(4) to other resolutions by stating that a declaration by the chairman that a resolution has been carried or carried unanimously, or by a particular majority, or lost, or not carried by a particular majority and an entry to that effect in the minutes shall be conclusive evidence of that fact without proof of the number or proportion of the votes recorded in favour of or against the resolution (see reg. 47). Although the operation of s. 378(4) is not conditional on an entry having been made in the minutes, the minutes will in any proceedings be *prima facie* evidence of the proceedings and therefore of the nature of the chairman's declaration.

8.7.2   Recording the sense of the meeting

Every company is required to produce and keep minutes of all proceedings of general meetings [s. 382(1)]. The directors can be fined for any default by the company of the provisions of the Act relating to the maintenance of minutes [s. 382(5), s. 383(4) and s. 722(3)]. The chairman can be said to have a special duty in this regard in so far as minutes signed by the chairman of the meeting are *prima facie* evidence of the proceedings [s. 382(2)] (see Chapter 25).

8.8   CHAIRMAN'S POWERS

The chairman will usually have power:
- to adjourn the meeting, e.g. reg. 45 (see para. 10.4.1 and Chapter 17);
- to demand a poll, e.g. reg. 46 (see para. 16.8);
- to rule on the validity of votes at general meetings, e.g. reg. 58 (see para. 16.10);
- to rule on the validity of an amendment (see para. 12.4.4).

CHAPTER NINE

Right to attend and speak

9.1 SUMMARY

Company meetings are private meetings and, as such, the company is bound to admit only those who are legally entitled to attend. The right to attend goes hand in hand with the right to vote. Any member or corporate representative entitled to vote at a meeting has a right to attend the meeting in order to exercise that right. A proxy of such a member also has a statutory right to attend meetings. The company's auditors have a statutory right to attend general meetings. The articles usually give the directors the right to attend (see para. 9.2 and table at Appendix F).

Members entitled to attend and vote at general meetings also have a common law right to speak at the meeting. The Companies Act 1985 gives proxies of members of private companies and all corporate representatives the same rights as members in this regard, but not proxies of members of public companies. Auditors have a statutory right to speak on matters which concern them as auditors. The articles usually give the directors a right to speak even if they are not members (see para. 9.4.1).

The chairman has a duty to ensure that all shades of opinion are given a fair hearing. However, this does not mean that every member must be allowed to speak on a resolution or that they should be allowed to speak for as long as they want (see para. 9.4.2).

Members may ask questions at general meetings, but have no right to receive an answer (see para. 9.4.3).

9.2 RIGHT TO ATTEND

9.2.1 Members and corporate representatives

Voting at general meetings is usually conducted by a show of hands or a poll. Both methods require the presence of the person voting (or their proxy). It follows that in order to exercise their right to vote, the members must also have a right to attend the meeting. However, a member who does not have a right to vote may still have a right to attend the meeting, unless the articles provide otherwise.

Companies whose shares have been admitted to CREST may specify in the notice a time, not more than 48 hours before the time fixed for the meeting, by which a person must be entered on the relevant register of securities in order to have the right to attend and vote at the meeting [Uncertificated Securities Regulations, reg. 34] (see para. 16.2.1).

A member who persistently disrupts the meeting may be ejected (see para. 10.4). However, a member who is wrongfully excluded from a meeting, and thereby prevented from voting, may be able to challenge the validity of the proceedings, e.g. a person cannot be excluded merely because they have disrupted previous meetings.

Care should be taken to ensure that a member's right to attend is not prejudiced by the terms and conditions imposed under the licence to use the venue where the meeting is to be held. For example, it would be unwise to choose a venue which imposes a dress code. Some companies have taken power in their articles which allow them to exclude members who refuse to comply with conditions imposed for the purposes of security, e.g. electronic screening and prohibitions on taking hand baggage into the meeting.

If the meeting room is not big enough to accommodate all the members who wish to attend, the meeting should be adjourned (see para. 17.3.2).

9.2.2   Joint holders

Where shares are registered in the names of joint holders, each of the joint holders is a member of the company and therefore entitled to attend the meeting, unless the articles provide otherwise. Most articles make special provision for voting by joint holders but do not restrict the right to attend (e.g. reg. 55 of Table A).

9.2.3   Death or bankruptcy

Articles commonly provide that a person who becomes entitled to a share in consequence of the death or bankruptcy of a member shall not be entitled to attend or vote at any meeting of the company or at any meeting of the holders of any class of shares until he has been registered as the holder of the share (e.g. reg. 31 of Table A).

9.2.4   Corporate representatives

Corporate representatives are deemed to have the same rights as individual members by virtue of s. 376. Accordingly, they have the same right to attend as an individual member.

9.2.5   Proxies

Proxies have a statutory right to attend on behalf of those who appointed them [s. 372]. If the person who appointed the proxy is not entitled to attend, the proxy will not be entitled to attend. A proxy and the member who appointed the proxy may both attend the meeting. If the member does not vote on a poll, the proxy may do so. If the articles allow members to appoint more than one proxy, each proxy appointed has a right to attend the meeting.

9.2.6 Auditors' right to attend and speak at general meetings

A company's auditors have a statutory right to receive notice of any general meeting of the company and to attend and speak at any such meeting on any part of the business which concerns them as auditors [s. 390].

9.2.7 Directors' right to attend general meetings

Directors have no statutory right to attend general meetings, except where a resolution to remove them is to be proposed under s. 303 [s. 304]. Directors who are members (or a representative or proxy of a member) will be entitled to attend in that capacity.

Articles usually state that directors who are not members shall be entitled to attend and speak at meetings of the company (e.g. reg. 44). There is some doubt as to whether a director who is not a member could enforce such a right as he is not a party to the contract which is deemed to exist between the members and the company by virtue of the articles.

The 1948 Act Table A makes no such provision, presumably because directors were usually required to hold some shares in the company which would give them the right to attend general meetings. A company which proposes to delete an article which imposes a share qualification, should perhaps ensure that it also adopts a provision similar to reg. 44 of the 1985 Table A.

A director who is not a member but who is appointed as the chairman of the meeting in accordance with the articles must be deemed to have a right to attend.

9.2.8 Company secretary

The company secretary has no statutory right to attend general meetings. Articles rarely address the subject. However, in view of the role it would be unusual for the secretary to be excluded from the meeting.

9.2.9 Other classes of member

All members have the right to attend general meetings unless the articles provide otherwise. Where a company has more than one class of shares, it is usual for the articles to specify the rights of each class. For example, preference shareholders are not usually entitled to attend general meetings unless their dividends are in arrears. They will, of course, be entitled to attend meetings of their own class.

9.2.10   Attendance by invitation

The board may invite any other person to attend a meeting of the company. It is normal, for example, for a public company to invite lawyers, specialist advisers, brokers, analysts, press representatives, etc. These invitations are usually issued by the secretary on behalf of the board. The presence at a meeting of persons not entitled to be present or to vote does not invalidate the meeting (*Re Quinn and the National Society's Arbitration* [1921] 2 Ch. 318). However, the meeting and the chairman personally may decide at any time to ask them to leave the meeting. If they refuse, reasonable force may be used to eject them.

Companies should employ some method of ensuring that people attending by invitation cannot vote on any resolution (e.g. by issuing voting cards to the members) or are not counted when a vote is taken (e.g. by placing them in a separate area).

9.3   RECORD OF ATTENDANCE

A record should be kept of the names of the members, proxies and corporate representatives who attend any general meeting (see **Precedent 9.3**). The record is used primarily to ensure that a quorum is present throughout the proceedings. Totals of the members, corporate representatives and proxies present should be calculated and shown in the minutes. The record of attendance can also be useful in helping to reconcile the votes cast on a poll. In theory, no-one should vote on a poll unless they are present either in person or by proxy.

Listed companies usually send each shareholder an attendance card with a unique bar-coding and require them to produce it on arrival at the meeting. The information on the attendance card is scanned using a light pen and fed into a portable computer which holds details of the register of members. The computer is then able to calculate the number of members present in person or by proxy and to print out a list of attendees. This enables the company to identify whether certain shareholders are present, e.g. institutional investors or members who represent pressure groups.

Regulation 100 of Table A requires the minutes to show the names of the directors present at general meetings.

9.4   RIGHT TO SPEAK

The purpose of holding general meetings is to enable the members to reach decisions after debating the issues. If voting was allowed to be conducted without holding a meeting (e.g. by postal ballot) and the members were not unanimously in favour of the proposal, they would have no opportunity to debate the issues and the minority would be deprived of their opportunity to persuade the majority of the merits of its arguments. In practice, the Act does not allow public companies to conduct a ballot of the members without holding a meeting, and only allows private companies to do so if all the members approve the transaction by written resolution. In such circumstances, it is reasonable to assume that no shareholder would wish to make a speech opposing the resolution.

A general meeting is an opportunity for both sides to put their case to the floating voter. Where all or most of the members attend, the debate may have an influence on the final outcome. In practice, the outcome is often determined in advance by the votes given by proxy before the meeting. In the case of listed cornpanies, it is not uncommon for the proxy votes in favour of resolutions proposed by the board to exceed the total number of votes held by all the members actually present at the meeting and the proxy votes cast against the resolution. In other words, even if a speaker persuades everyone at the meeting to oppose a resolution, it can still be carried on a poll called by the chairman. Nevertheless, this does not mean that the chairman would be justified in curtailing debate on the issues. A member who has appointed a proxy may revoke that proxy by attending the meeting in person and voting. It is also possible for a member to issue new voting instructions any time before the vote is taken. These two factors mean that the outcome will not always be a foregone conclusion.

9.4.1 Extent of right to speak

Members entitled to attend and vote at general meetings also have a common law right to speak at the meeting. Whether a member who is entitled to attend but not to vote is entitled to speak is a moot point. This will be relevant where the articles provide that the vote of the senior joint holder shall be accepted to the exclusion of all others but do not restrict the other joint holders' right to attend meetings of the company. The question may also be relevant for a member who has been disenfranchised for some reason (e.g. under art. 78 of Whitbread plc). In practice, most companies allow members who are entitled to attend to speak even though they are not entitled to vote, and this is undoubtedly the safest course of action.

Corporate representatives are deemed to have the same rights as individual members to speak by virtue of s. 375(2).

All proxies have a statutory right to demand or join in a demand for a poll [ss. 373 & 374]. In the case of private companies, proxies appointed by the members to attend and vote on their behalf have the same right to speak as the member who appointed them [s. 372(1)]. No such provision is made with regard to proxies of members of public companies. Accordingly, the articles of public companies may specifically confirm or deny the right of proxies to speak. In the absence of any guidance in the articles, the matter is probably one of those which the chairman should decide in accordance with the principles laid down by Lord Russell in *Carruth* v. *Imperial Chemical Industries Ltd* (see para. 8.5). The DTI has consulted on proposals to give proxies of members of public companies the same right to speak as members of private companies (see *Shareholder Communications at the Annual General Meeting*, April 1996). In its *Guide to best practice for Annual General Meetings*, ICSA recommends that chairmen of listed companies should seek the consent of the meeting to proxies speaking and participating in the debate. However, some listed companies still prefer not to do so because they believe protest groups would abuse the right.

Although it would be unusual to do so, there is nothing to prevent the articles restricting the rights of members who are entitled to attend and vote from speaking at the meeting. The members' right to speak is a common law right and, as such, is capable of modification by the articles, subject to anything to the contrary contained in the Act. In fact, the Act does not preserve the members' right to speak at all. Even proxies of members of private companies only have the same rights as the member who appointed them, and corporate representatives the same rights as the corporation would have if it was an individual member. Accordingly, if the rights of individual members are restricted, then the rights of their proxies or corporate representatives will be similarly restricted.

Directors who are not members or a corporate representative or, in the case of private companies, a proxy do not have a statutory right to speak at meetings, except on a resolution to remove them [s. 304]. Articles usually give directors who are not members the right to speak (e.g. reg. 44). Where they are silent on the matter, it is possible that the meeting could refuse to allow directors to speak if they are not otherwise qualified to do so. Clearly, this is not something which the members would normally wish to do. However, it could cause problems if the director concerned was the chairman. In practice, directors will normally be invited by the chairman to speak as and when necessary, and it should be assumed that they may do so unless the meeting objects.

Auditors have a statutory right to speak on matters which concern them as auditors [s. 390(1)]. This right is preserved in the case of auditors who have been removed before the expiry of their period of office [s. 391]. Resigning auditors have a right to speak at a meeting requisitioned by them to consider the circumstances of their resignation [s. 392A].

9.4.2   Common law restrictions on the right to speak

The members' right to speak will always be subject to any reasonable limitations imposed by the chairman or the meeting itself. Under the common law, the chairman has a duty to ensure that all shades of opinion on a resolution before the meeting are given a fair hearing. In particular, the chairman should seek to ensure that the minority has had a reasonable opportunity to put its views (*Wall* v. *London & Northern Assets Corporation Ltd* [1898] 2 Ch. 469). This does not mean that all those who hold those views must be allowed to speak. It will suffice if members representing the range of views on a resolution have been allowed to do so.

The chairman also has a duty to ensure that all the business before the meeting is conducted. In order to facilitate the conduct of the meeting, the chairman may, if the meeting does not object, apply various rules of debate. The most commonly applied is that speakers must confine themselves to the subject of the resolution before the meeting. This is particularly appropriate where a member is speaking on a matter which will be the subject of a subsequent resolution put to the meeting. From a practical point of view, it is normal for the chairman to inform speakers that they will be given an opportunity to raise these matters at the appropriate time and to ask them to keep to the subject of the resolution. It is not so easy to apply this rule where a member wishes to raise a matter which, strictly speaking, is not on the agenda. Here the chairman ought, perhaps, to allow slightly more leeway, particularly if other members want to speak on the same subject. In reality, it is often difficult for the chairman to rule that an issue raised by a member has no connection with the resolution before the meeting. Experienced speakers will normally be able to manufacture a reason why the point they wish to make is relevant to the business before the meeting and the chairman cannot really decide whether their contribution is relevant without giving them an opportunity to state their case. In such circumstances, it might be advisable for the chairman to allocate time at the end of the meeting to discuss the issues raised.

Another rule of debate which is sometimes applied is that no person other than the proposer of the resolution may speak more than once in connection with it. In the context of general meetings, this may not always be appropriate. For example, members who exercise their right to speak by asking a question ought perhaps to be given an opportunity to comment on any answer given. Ordinarily, there is no reason why a member who has spoken previously should not be allowed to respond to comments made by other speakers, particularly if that member is in the minority. It may, of course, be appropriate to apply this rule where there is only a limited time available for debate and there are still several members who wish to speak. In addition, there will always come a point where a member has had a reasonable opportunity to make his or her point. The chairman need not allow a member to make the same points over and over again or to speak for an inordinate length of time.

The amount of time which should be made available for debate will vary depending on the nature of the business and the number of people wishing to speak on it. This does not mean that the discussion should be allowed to go on for ever or that everyone who wishes to speak must be allowed to do so. Shortly before closing the debate, the chairman should ask members to refrain from speaking unless they have a different point to make. Although it not an easy thing to do without causing offence, the chairman should at this point cut short any speaker who is repeating a point made earlier in the debate in order to ensure that those with different views are given a fair hearing. When the chairman considers that a full range of views have been expressed, he may seek to curtail the discussion and put the resolution to a vote. If any member objects, the chairman should seek the consent of the meeting by proposing a formal 'closure' motion, i.e. that the question before the meeting be now put to the vote (see further para. 11.2 and the example script at para. 21.9). If the resolution is defeated on a show of hands, the chairman could, if the articles so provide, demand a poll on the question and would be justified in casting votes given to him as proxy in favour of the substantive resolution in favour of the formal closure motion.

9.4.3   Shareholder questions

In exercising their right to speak, members may ask the chairman or another director to answer a question. Although the chairman and the directors have no legal obligation to respond, it is usual for them to do so in order to explain their point of view and to persuade the members to support the resolution before the meeting. In answering members' questions, directors of listed companies are constrained by the rules of the Stock Exchange on the release of unpublished price-sensitive information. As a result, members often receive prepared answers which rarely expand upon previously published information.

In a consultation document issued in April 1996, the Department of Trade and Industry (DTI) asked whether shareholders have any difficulties asking questions at annual general meetings and, if so, whether they should be given statutory rights in this regard (*Shareholder communications at the annual general meeting*, DTI, April 1996). It recognised that giving shareholders a statutory right to ask questions would make it impossible for the chairman to curtail the debate until all the members had asked their questions. However, it suggested that companies could be required to set aside time at the annual general meeting for shareholders' questions and debate. Such a proposal would not advance the position of shareholders a great deal. The common law already requires the chairman to give members an opportunity to debate resolutions put to the meeting and to give the minority a fair hearing during that debate. In exercising their right to speak, members may ask questions but have no right to receive an answer, and the DTI's proposal would not affect the members' rights in this regard. If the members were given such a right, the directors might be forced to reveal commercially sensitive or price-sensitive information.

In practice, most companies invite members to ask questions when the meeting considers the report and accounts. Even if the company does not make the accounts the subject of a substantive resolution and simply lays them before the members, the members probably have the same right to speak (and ask questions) because, by doing so, the chairman is putting some business before the meeting upon which there may be a debate. Indeed, it is arguable that the sole purpose of the requirement to lay the accounts at a general meeting, is to enable the members to question the directors on their stewardship of the company. No other purpose is served by doing so. If the directors put a resolution to receive or adopt the accounts and it is lost, the accounts will still be the company's statutory accounts. Questions and debate are usually allowed on a broad range of issues when the report and accounts are laid because it is difficult to define the scope of the meeting at that point. Almost any subject raised by a member could have an impact on the financial performance of the company. The chairman would, however, be justified in refusing to allow discussion on a matter which will be raised formally later in the meeting.

The DTI conceded in its consultation document that the handling of questions at the annual general meeting was probably a matter which should be dealt with by the development of best practice by companies. Accordingly, the Institute of Chartered Secretaries and Administrators, with the encouragement of the DTI, produced a *Guide to best practice for Annual General Meetings* to address this and several other issues raised in the consultative document. On shareholder questions and debate, the *Guide* recommends that:

- Boards should provide adequate time for shareholder questions at AGMs.
- When moving the adoption or receipt of the accounts, the chairman should allow shareholders to raise questions on any item concerning the company's past performance, its results and its intended future performance. However, the directors need not answer questions which are irrelevant to the company or its business or which could result in the release of commercially sensitive information. Nor should they disclose price-sensitive information unless it can be done in compliance with the Stock Exchange Listing Rules and guidance regarding the release of price-sensitive information.
- Before each resolution is put to the vote, the chairman should explain again its purpose and effect. If necessary, he should elaborate on the information previously provided in the explanatory circular which accompanied the notice of the meeting. He should also invite shareholders to speak.
- Where concerns are raised by a shareholder at the AGM and the chairman undertakes to consider them, the shareholder should subsequently be sent a full report of the action taken.

The *Guide* also suggests that when a particular issue has been raised by a shareholder, the chairman may assist the flow of the meeting by inviting other shareholders who wish to speak on the same subject to do so at that time.

Some listed companies include in the documents sent to shareholders prior to the annual general meeting an invitation to submit questions in advance of the meeting. This enables them to select the most common questions and provide an answer for each one at the meeting. Answers can be given orally by the chairman or the relevant director, or they can be distributed to shareholders in the form of a printed question and answer sheet. The latter allows more detailed information to be provided in numerical or graphical form and enables the chairman to refer questioners who raise similar issues at the meeting to the relevant written answer. Although ICSA urged more companies to invite shareholders to submit questions in advance in its *Guide to best practice for Annual General Meetings*, it did not include it as one of its 24 best practice points. It said:

> Of course giving shareholders the opportunity to raise questions in advance of the AGM may not always assuage all their concerns. Questions on broadly the same subject may arrive in 40 or 50 different forms for the company to co-ordinate into a single response. Such a reply may satisfactorily answer most points, but is unlikely to address them all.
>
> We recommend that companies invite shareholders to submit questions in

advance, as this makes structuring the AGM more manageable. We leave it to companies to decide how best to convey the invitation. We stress that inviting questions in advance is not to be deployed by companies as a method of manipulating the AGM by requiring written notice of questions; nor is it intended to replace spontaneity at the AGM, which we regard as one of its greatest attributes.

CHAPTER TEN

Security and disorder

10.1 SUMMARY

Security is not normally a problem for private companies. However, for companies which are in the public eye, it is becoming an increasingly important issue. Pressure groups frequently disrupt meetings of listed companies in order to gain publicity for their cause. In the current political and social environment, companies can no longer discount the possibility of terrorist attack or the possibility that a member or customer with a grudge against the company will behave in a violent manner at the meeting. Many companies now invest a considerable amount of time and money on security measures to counter these threats. Disruption at general meetings is nothing new, and the common law has developed various rules which enable the chairman to deal with it (see para. 10.4). The company's first line of defence is, however, the registration process. Most listed companies still allow members of the public to attend their annual general meetings without an invitation. However, more and more are restricting entry for the purposes of security and require people wishing to gain entry to prove their identity (see para. 10.2.1).

A skilful chairman can sometimes avoid undue disruption by dealing with dissident members firmly, politely and fairly and with good humour. Even if this has no effect on the dissident members, it will probably ensure that the chairman retains the support of the meeting should further action need to be taken. If the dissident members persist in their disorderly conduct to such an extent that the meeting is no longer able to transact the business before it, the chairman may either order the ejection of those who are causing the disorder (see para. 10.4.2) or adjourn the meeting in an attempt to restore order (see para. 10.4.1).

10.2 SECURITY

10.2.1 Proof of identity

A company may refuse to admit members who cannot prove their identity. If it were otherwise, the company could be forced to admit two people claiming to be the same person. Most members will have no difficulty satisfying any reasonable request made by the company. This might include the production of a driving licence or some other document showing their name and address. A company should, perhaps, also accept the confirmation of an individual's identity by someone else who is known to the company. It is also arguable that anyone who is able to furnish accurate information about their holding (e.g. full name, address, size of holding, date of purchase of shares, mandate details, etc.) should also be admitted. In cases of doubt, it is probably wise to err on the side of caution as the exclusion of a person entitled to attend and vote could render the meeting liable to challenge.

If proof of identity is required, security and registration staff should be properly briefed. The procedures which should be followed before refusing entry to a person who would be entitled to attend if able to prove their identity should be approved by the chairman. Indeed, it may be preferable to refer difficult cases to the chairman. In cases of doubt, the person could be admitted but asked to sit in a specially allocated area. If that person's vote would have affected the outcome of a show of hands, the chairman may need to make a ruling on the validity of the person's vote. Alternatively, the chairman could demand a poll (if the articles so allow) in the hope that this will resolve the difficulty. This would also enable the company to take further steps to establish the identity of the person claiming to be a member, etc. If the result of the poll is affected by the disputed votes, the chairman will have to make a ruling on their validity. The courts have endorsed the use by the chairman of a 'conditional' casting vote where the validity of some votes had been in doubt and it was not clear whether or not the vote was tied (see para. 16.9).

10.2.2   Attendance cards

Some companies send shareholders attendance cards and request that they produce them on arrival in order to gain entry to the meeting. The main advantage of this system is that it helps to speed up the registration process. It does, however, have a number of weaknesses. The first of these is that attendance cards actually facilitate impersonation where no other identity checks are made. In addition, a company cannot refuse to admit members merely because they are unable to produce an attendance card, unless the articles specify this as a condition of entry. Members who cannot produce their attendance cards must be allowed to prove their identity in another way.

10.2.3   Security checks

Some listed companies have taken specific powers in their articles to refuse entry to members who refuse to comply with certain conditions of entry (see **Precedent 10.2**). However, it is submitted that even if the articles do not make specific provision, the company can (and perhaps should where it has reason to suspect trouble) take reasonable security measures.

The chairman has a duty to preserve order at meetings. Security procedures such as screening devices and baggage searches are, it is suggested, a legitimate method of ensuring that the meeting is not disrupted. Many listed companies deliberately hold their meetings at venues which have built-in security screening at the point of entry. Anyone wishing to attend must pass through an electronic screening device and have their baggage inspected. It is submitted that a company can exclude a person who refuses to be screened if the purpose of that screening is to ensure the safety of other members present and to prevent disorder at the meeting. Clearly, it would be irresponsible to admit anyone found in possession of explosives. They should be arrested and handed over to the police. On the other hand, it might be considered unreasonable to exclude a person found in possession of a klaxon or whistle. The correct course of action would be to ask the person to hand over these items for the duration of the meeting.

10.3   SECURITY CHECKLIST FOR ANNUAL GENERAL MEETING

The following checklist is based on material produced by company secretaries of companies whose meetings have been disrupted by protesters and demonstrations.

Planning the meeting

- Make someone responsible for security.
- Identify issues which are likely to be controversial, e.g.:
    (a) any company issues likely to lead to demonstrations;
    (b) any staff issues likely to lead to demonstrations;
    (c) any shareholder issues likely to lead to demonstrations;
    (d) any active shareholder protest groups;
    (e) any known agitators likely to attend;
    (f) any historical issues which have arisen at the company's AGM.
- Consider issuing a statement concerning any controversial or difficult issues prior to the AGM to diffuse potential protests.
- Notify the local police of security concerns and request their availability.
- Persuade the chairman to rehearse any complications.
- If cameras and tape recorders are not to be allowed in, the notice to shareholders should include this information.
- Be aware of the possibilities for various forms of protest and take appropriate precautions, e.g.:
    (a) irrelevant questioning;
    (b) mass sit-in;
    (c) storming the platform;
    (d) handcuffing to immovable objects;
    (e) protests outside the AGM venue;
    (f) abseiling from the roof.

The AGM Venue

- Ensure that the company's security staff are involved in selecting the venue.
- Can entry to the venue can be controlled with limited access points.
- Consider which access routes to the meeting hall are to be used.
- Is there a clear route for the directors to the meeting hall from the venue of any pre-meeting get-together? Can they enter and leave the room by a separate exit which is easily accessible from the stage?
- Is physical security satisfactory?
- Are there any areas which are always open to the public?
- Who else has booked conference facilities on the same day?
- Does the venue have adequate security procedures, e.g. to deal with bomb alerts?
- Does it have a security manager or other in-house security staff?
- Has the venue hosted AGMs before?
- What are the normal arrangements for dealing with disturbances?
- Where does the venue boundary meet the public highway?
- Is there a tannoy system?
- Does it have a controlled car parking area?
- Is it possible to erect barriers at the venue entrance and reception areas to control the flow of attendees?
- Is the reception area large enough to accommodate all attendees before entering the meeting hall?
- Are the toilets inside the secure area or will attendees need to go through security checks each time they enter the hall?
- Check availability of discrete exits to remove demonstrators.
- Are the seats fixed?
- Are the hand rails or other fittings removable?
- Are there any balconies or other public areas from which items could be thrown, banners displayed or photographers planted?

Precautions

- Prevent demonstrators erecting banners on the stage by using floral arrangements or guards.
- Thoroughly search the meeting area before commencement of meeting for suspicious objects and then secure until access is opened for the meeting.
- Conduct regular security patrols.
- Consider personal searches, including metal detectors. If detectors or scans are to be used, ensure that trained staff are employed to operate them.
- Consider inspection of baggage and/or barring of baggage from the meeting hall. If baggage is not allowed in, consider providing clear plastic folder for documents.
- Establish a policy on:
  - (a) cameras and videos;
  - (b) recording equipment;

(c) mobile telephones;
(d) access for TV/radio crews.
- Display clear notices detailing the items not allowed in the meeting.
- Arrange for secure storage of items not allowed into the meeting.
- Alert venue staff to any person who may be carrying anything unusual.
- Send out invitation cards which must be presented to gain access to the meeting. In the event of failure to produce invitation, entry to meeting should only be permitted on production of identification, personal verification by a known third party or, for shareholders, identification on the share register.
- Organise a system of security passes for all attendees and staff.
- Rotate the colour of passes each year.
- Prepare a script for the chairman to follow in the event of disruptions, covering ejection of protesters by stewards and/or adjournment of the meeting.
- Use radio mikes to prevent attachment or damage to cables.
- Ensure that radio microphones do not interfere with security radio network and vice versa.
- Use hands-free radios for security guards.
- Have the following equipment available:
  (a) large bolt cutters;
  (b) solvent for superglue;
  (c) smother blankets for smoke bombs;
  (d) tools to remove handrails.
- Bring spare clothes for chairman in case missiles thrown.
- Consider videoing the proceedings.
- Have paramedics (St John's Ambulance) standing by.

Demonstrators

- Identify known activists.
- Review recent purchases of small number of shares, paying particular attention to purchases of one share. Obtain details of purchaser (and, if off-market, the transferor) and obtain background information on them if possible (some registrars have compiled a database of shareholders who are known to be connected with certain groups).
- Alert staff on AGM registration desk of suspects' names.
- Obtain copies of questions if possible.
- Be positive with demonstrators – they will attempt to intimidate or antagonise.
- Consider delaying opening doors to meeting hall until, say, half an hour before the start of the meeting. This may prevent potential agitators obtaining pole positions.
- Consider refusing entry to any press not authorised by the company's PR department.
- Protest groups often pre-warn the press. The company's PR department may be able to find out whether this has happened from its press contacts.

Staffing

- If necessary, engage additional security staff and ensure that the security staff includes a number of women. Use well-trained staff.
- Arrange protection for chairman, directors and senior executives especially during period of mingling with shareholders.
- If there is risk of violence to the chairman or other speakers, access to the rostrum should be restricted by security staff facing the audience.
- Consider the need to have extra security staff available but hidden in the immediate vicinity of the meeting hall.
- Stewards and security staff should be briefed and given a checklist on the arrangements for, and their powers for dealing with, disturbances.
- Place staff on every door leading to the meeting hall and only allow persons with the requisite pass to enter the hall.
- Arrange for venue's own security staff to be present to help in fire or bomb emergencies.
- Consider how security staff (company's own staff, external staff and AGM venue staff) are to be dressed – high or low profile.
- Clearly identify the role of all staff involved.
- Establish with the venue's management that they will deal with the removal if necessary of demonstrators from their property to the public highway boundary.
- If staff demonstrations are anticipated, arrange for an industrial relations manager to be available to meet with staff representatives.
- Use staff as fillers to occupy areas of seating and/or form barriers.

10.4   PRESERVATION OF ORDER

The chairman's primary responsibility is to ensure that all the business before the meeting is properly and fairly transacted. This is unlikely to be achieved if the meeting is constantly disrupted by dissident members. The chairman is therefore responsible for the preservation of order at the meeting and should seek to ensure that the meeting is carried out without undue disruption.

A skilful chairman can sometimes avoid undue disruption by dealing with dissident members firmly, politely and fairly and with good humour. Even if this has no effect on the dissident members, it will probably ensure that the chairman retains the support of the meeting should further action need to be taken.

Where it is known that a group of shareholders is likely to attempt to disrupt the meeting, the chairman may take preventative action before the meeting, e.g. to prevent shareholders entering the hall with klaxons, tape recorders, banners, and any other objects which could be used to disrupt the meeting.

10.4.1   Adjournment to restore order

If there is persistent and violent disorder, the chairman has a right and may even have a duty to adjourn the meeting in order to restore order. In *John* v. *Rees* [1969] 2 W.L.R. 1294, Megarry J. explained this principle as follows:

> The first duty of the chairman of a meeting is to keep order if he can. If there is disorder, his duty, I think, is to make earnest and sustained efforts to restore order, and for this purpose to summon to his aid any officers or others whose assistance is available. If all his efforts are in vain, he should endeavour to put into operation whatever provisions for adjournment there are in the rules, as by obtaining a resolution to adjourn. If this proves impossible, he should exercise his inherent power to adjourn the meeting for a short while, such as 15 minutes, taking due steps to ensure as far as possible that all persons know of this adjournment. If instead of mere disorder there is violence, I think that he should take similar steps, save that the greater the violence the less prolonged should be his efforts to restore order before adjourning. In my judgment, he has not merely a power but a duty to adjourn in this way, in the interests of those who fear for their safety. I am not suggesting that there is a power and a duty to adjourn if the violence consists of no more than a few technical assaults and batteries. Mere pushing and jostling is one thing; it is another when people are put in fear, where there is heavy punching, or the knives are out, so that blood may flow, and there are prospects, or more, of grievous bodily harm. In the latter case the sooner the chairman adjourns the meeting the better. At meetings, as elsewhere, the Queen's Peace must be kept.

> If then, the chairman has this inherent power and duty, what limitations, if any, are there upon its exercise? First, I think that the power and duty must be exercised bona fide for the purpose of forwarding and facilitating the meeting, and not for the purpose of interruption or procrastination. Second I think that the adjournment must be for no longer than the necessities appear to dictate. If the adjournment is merely for such period as the chairman considers to be reasonably necessary for the restoration of order, it would be within his power and his duty; a long adjournment would not. One must remember that to attend a meeting may for some mean travelling far and giving up much leisure. An adjournment to another day when a mere 15 minutes might suffice to restore order may well impose an unjustifiable burden on many; for they must either once more travel far and give up their leisure, or else remain away and lose their chance to speak and vote at the meeting.

10.4.2   Powers of ejection

Members may be expelled from a meeting if they seriously interfere with the business of the meeting. 'The power . . . of suspending a member guilty of obstruction or disorderly conduct during the continuance of [a meeting] is . . . reasonably necessary for the proper exercise of the functions of any . . . assembly' (*Barton* v. *Taylor* (1886) 11 App. Cas. 197, per Lord Selborne at p. 204).

If possible, the chairman should seek the consent of the meeting before ordering that a person be expelled. In practice, it will rarely be possible to take a vote on the matter and the chairman must rely on his innate authority to take action to preserve order at the meeting. Expulsion should only be used as a last resort or in cases of severe disorder. Members should, if possible, be warned of the consequences of their actions. If they continue to disrupt the meeting, they should be given an opportunity to leave the meeting voluntarily. If they refuse to do so, they can be forcibly ejected, although only reasonable force should be used (*Collins* v. *Renison* (1754) 1 Sayer 138). If unnecessary force is used, the person removed will have a cause of action for assault against the persons responsible (*Doyle* v. *Falconer* (1866) L.R. 1 P.C. 328). This may include the chairman as the person who authorised their removal.

CHAPTER ELEVEN

Procedural motions

11.1 SUMMARY

Procedural motions (formal motions) are used to expedite the business of the meeting. The terminology used to describe these motions is old-fashioned and obscure. There is no magic or mystery in the use of this terminology. Provided that the intention of the motion is clear, there is little to be gained from insisting that it be used.

As procedural motions relate to the conduct rather than the business of the meeting, no prior notice is required or, indeed, could be given. The chairman or any member entitled to vote and speak at the meeting may propose a formal motion. The word member includes a joint holder or a corporate representative for these purposes. It is not clear whether proxies can propose formal motions even where they have the right to speak. Should a proxy who has the right to speak attempt to do so, it may be advisable for the chairman to ask whether a member is prepared to propose the motion. If none are prepared to do so, the chairman might be able to persuade the proxy to withdraw the proposal due to lack of support. Failing that, the chairman could propose the motion on the proxy's behalf.

A motion to adjourn is also a procedural or formal motion (see Chapter 17).

11.2 THAT THE QUESTION BE NOW PUT (THE CLOSURE)

A closure motion (traditionally referred to as 'the closure') is a simple way of curtailing the debate. The chairman or any member may simply propose 'that the question be now put' or words to that effect. The motion need not be seconded although it is unlikely that it would be carried if a seconder could not be found. No debate need be allowed on the motion, although it might be difficult to prevent objections from those who still wish to speak on the question before the meeting. The chairman may, it is suggested, refuse to put the motion to the vote on the ground that it is an infringement of the rights of the majority. However, if, acting in good faith, the chairman allows it to be put, the court will not intervene (*Wall* v. *London & Northern Assets Corporation* [1898] 2 Ch. 469). If a closure motion is carried, the question before the meeting must be put to the vote immediately.

11.3 THAT THE MEETING PROCEED TO THE NEXT BUSINESS (NEXT BUSINESS)

The object of this motion is to delay or preclude a decision by the meeting on the main question. It can be put at any time during discussion or during the discussion of an amendment. If the motion is carried, no further discussion or decision on the substantive question before the meeting should be allowed at the meeting (or any adjournment thereof) as its effect is to remove the question from the scope of the meeting. The question can only be considered again if it is proposed at a subsequent meeting. If it is rejected, discussion on the main issue may continue.

11.4 THAT THE QUESTION BE NOT NOW PUT (PREVIOUS QUESTION)

The motion, 'that the question be not now put', differs slightly from a motion 'to proceed to the next business' in that it may be moved only during the discussion on the main question before the meeting and not while an amendment is being considered. Discussion is normally allowed before putting the motion to a vote. If the motion is lost, it is normal to put the question before the meeting to an immediate vote although the chairman could allow debate to continue if it is clear that several members still wish to speak.

This motion is known as the 'previous question' because it gives rise to an issue which must be decided before the main question. It is probably the least common of the formal motions as substantially the same effect can be achieved by a motion to proceed to the next business.

11.5 THAT THE QUESTION LIE ON THE TABLE

The effect of this motion is that the question is put aside for the time being. It can however be restored if the meeting so desires. A more modern form of words might be 'that consideration of the question before the meeting be postponed until such time as the meeting wishes to reopen discussion'.

11.6 THAT THE MATTER BE REFERRED BACK TO . . .

This motion is used to refer back for further investigation or inquiry a matter which has arisen from the recommendations of another body or committee. Psychologically, it is obviously preferable to do this rather than to reject a proposal outright.

CHAPTER TWELVE

Amendments

12.1 SUMMARY

Dealing with amendments is one of the most difficult duties of the chairman. Unless the articles require prior notice of amendments to be given, the chairman will have to decide at the meeting whether to allow the proposed amendment to be put to the meeting. In the case of extraordinary, special and elective resolutions, the answer will normally be no (see para. 12.2). However, for ordinary resolutions, the answer will depend on a variety of factors (see paras. 12.3 and 12.4).

12.2 AMENDMENT OF EXTRAORDINARY, SPECIAL AND ELECTIVE RESOLUTIONS

Extraordinary, special and elective resolutions may only be amended in very limited circumstances. In *Re Moorgate Mercantile Holdings Ltd* [1980] 1 All E.R. 40, Slade J. established the following principles:

1. If a notice of the intention to propose a special resolution is to be a valid notice, it must identify the intended resolution by specifying either the text or the entire substance of the resolution which it is intended to propose. In the case of a notice of intention to propose a special resolution, nothing is achieved by the addition of such words as 'with such amendments and alterations as shall be determined on at such meeting'.
2. If a special resolution is to be validly passed, the resolution as passed must be the same resolution as that identified in the preceding notice; the phrase the resolution in [s. 378(2)] means the aforesaid resolution.
3. A resolution as passed can properly be regarded as 'the resolution' identified in a preceding notice, even though:
    (i) it departs in some respects from the text of a resolution set out in such notice (for example by correcting those grammatical or clerical errors

which can be corrected as a matter of construction, or by reducing the words to more formal language); or

(ii) it is reduced into the form of a new text, which was not included in the notice, provided only that in either case there is no departure from the substance.

4. However, in deciding whether there is complete identity between the substance of a resolution passed and the substance of an intended resolution as notified, there is no room for the court to apply the de minimis principle or a 'limit of tolerance'. The substance must be identical. Otherwise the condition precedent to the validity of a special resolution as passed, which is imposed by [s. 378(2)], namely that notice has been given 'specifying the intention to propose the resolution as a special resolution' is not satisfied.

5. It necessarily follows from the above propositions that an amendment to the previously circulated text of a special resolution can be properly be put to and voted on at a meeting if, but only if, the amendment involves no departure from the substance of the circulated text, in the sense indicated in propositions (3) and (4) above.

6. References to notices in the above propositions are intended to include references to circulars accompanying notices. In those cases where notices are so accompanied, the notices and circulars can and should, in my judgment ordinarily be treated as one document.

7. All the above propositions may be subject to modification where all the members or a class of members, of a company unanimously agree to waive their rights to notice under [s. 378(2)], see *Re Pearce, Duff & Co. Ltd* and *Re Duomatic Ltd* [1969] 1 All E.R. 161.

The Act makes similar provision with regard to the notice required to be given to the members of extraordinary and elective resolutions. The same principles will apply to amendments of such resolutions.

In *Re Willaire Systems* [1987] B.C.L.C. 67, it was held that where a special resolution for the reduction of a company's capital contained an error (the number of shares was said to be 14,926,580 instead of 14,926,583), the court could confirm the reduction on terms which corrected the error provided that it was so insignificant that no one could be thought to be prejudiced by its correction and the way in which it was to be corrected was clear. This case is probably an example of an amendment which could have been made at the meeting in order to rectify a minor clerical error (see also *Re European Home Products plc* [1988] 4 B.C.C. 779).

12.2.1 Articles on amendments

To eliminate any uncertainty with regard to amendments, companies sometimes adopt an article which disallows any amendment of extraordinary and special resolutions (see art. 68 of Whitbread plc).

12.3   RESOLUTIONS REQUIRING SPECIAL NOTICE

It is arguable that the rules on amending extraordinary and special resolutions also apply to resolutions requiring special notice. The wording of s. 379(2) (resolutions requiring special notice) is similar to that of s. 378 (extraordinary and special resolutions) in so far as the company is required to give its members notice of 'any such resolution'. It is submitted therefore that the substance of such resolutions should not be amended and that an amendment should only be accepted to rectify a clerical error (see para. 12.2).

12.4   AMENDMENT OF ORDINARY RESOLUTIONS

An amendment to an ordinary resolution must be put to the vote unless it is:

- outside the scope of the notice of the meeting (see para. 12.4.1);
- irrelevant in so far as it bears no relation to the original motion or subject matter;
- redundant because its effect is simply to negate the resolution or to propose something which has already been resolved by the meeting (see para. 12.4.3);
- incompatible with a decision previously made by the meeting;
- vexatious, i.e. its sole purpose is to obstruct the transaction of business;
- rejected by the chairman under a discretion granted by the articles (see para. 12.4.5).

12.4.1   Outside the scope of the notice

Amendments must be within the scope of the notice of meeting. The meeting may transact any business which is within the 'general nature' of the business set out in the notice. In deciding what the 'general nature' of the business in the notice is, the test is what a reasonable shareholder reading the resolution would consider the business to be. The courts normally adopt a practical approach and, where there is any ambiguity, apply a restrictive interpretation, so as to protect the absent shareholder. A guide endorsed by the courts is that an amendment should not be allowed if it would have affected a member's decision to attend. For example, a resolution authorising the directors to allot shares could be amended to reduce the number they may allot, but not to increase it.

In *Betts & Co. Ltd* v. *MacNaghten* [1910] 1 Ch. 430, it was held that the notice of meeting, which set out the names of the proposed directors, was sufficient to enable unnamed directors to be elected in place of or in addition to the named directors, because on reading the notice a reasonable shareholder would realise that those nominated might not be elected and therefore that others could be put up in their place. In this case the notice stated that the meeting was to consider resolutions 'with such amendments and alterations as shall be determined upon at such meeting'. These words could be considered redundant as it can be assumed that resolutions might be amended at the meeting.

In *Choppington Collieries Ltd* v. *Johnson* [1944] 1 All E.R. 762, the Court of

Appeal held that a notice which referred to the election of directors but which also stated that only one director was retiring and offering himself for re-election was wide enough to permit the election of directors, up to the maximum allowed by the articles. The court's decision was based on the general nature of the phrase in the notice 'to elect directors' which a shareholder might reasonably interpret as contemplating the appointment of more than one director. In this and other cases, the courts have emphasised that the question of the scope of the notice of meeting will turn on the construction of the notice in any given case.

12.4.2   Ordinary and special business

Articles sometimes distinguish between 'ordinary' and 'special' business (e.g. art. 61 of Whitbread plc and reg. 52 of the 1948 Table A). Matters specified in the articles as 'ordinary' business may be considered at an annual general meeting without prior notice having been given. These usually include:

- declaration of a dividend;
- consideration of the report and accounts;
- election of directors in the place of those retiring;
- appointment and remuneration of the auditors.

In effect notice is deemed to have been given of any of these matters. Thus any resolution or amendment to any resolution on these matters will be within the scope of the notice of the annual general meeting. By default, any other business will be deemed to be 'special' business and, as such, the notice must specify the general nature of that business for it to be within the scope of the notice.

The 1985 version of Table A requires the notice of general meetings to specify 'the general nature of the business to be transacted' [reg. 38]. In other words, all business is treated in the same way as special business.

12.4.3   Other reasons for rejecting amendments

An amendment need not be allowed if its effect is to negate the original resolution. The chairman should refuse to put such an amendment and point out that those who support it can achieve the same result by voting against the original resolution. For example, an amendment may be proposed to a resolution authorising the board to fix the remuneration of the auditors which imposes a maximum sum. But if the amendment proposes a limit of 1p, it effectively negates the resolution to authorise the board to fix the remuneration.

The chairman can reject amendments if they seek to re-open business already settled at the meeting or they are incompatible with a previous decision of the meeting. The chairman may sometimes do so where the proposed amendment is either obstructive, vexatious, dilatory or irrelevant. For example, where the proposer is merely attempting to obstruct the conduct of the business by proposing a series of amendments.

12.4.4   Consequences of wrongly refusing to submit

If the chairman wrongly refuses to submit an amendment to the meeting and the original resolution is passed, it will be invalid. It makes no difference whether the mover of the amendment contested the chairman's ruling or left the meeting (*Henderson* v. *Bank of Australasia* (1890) 45 Ch.D. 330). Articles sometimes provide that substantive resolutions shall not be invalidated by any error in good faith on the part of the chairman in ruling an amendment out of order. For example art. 68 of Whitbread plc states:

> *Amendment of resolution*
> 68.   If an amendment shall be proposed to any resolution under consider-
> ation but shall in good faith be ruled out by the Chairman of the meeting the
> proceedings on the substantive resolution shall not be invalidated by any error
> in such ruling. In the case of a resolution duly proposed as a Special or
> Extraordinary resolution no amendment thereto (other than a mere clerical
> amendment to correct a manifest error) may in any event be considered or
> voted upon.

The effect of such articles has not been tested. The courts might not find it too difficult to avoid giving effect to them should the need arise.

12.4.5   Articles may require prior notice of amendment

Some companies have articles which provide that no amendment shall be considered (except at the discretion of the chairman) unless prior notice in writing of the proposed amendment has been given to the company (see art. 68 of Whitbread plc). This enables the chairman to take legal advice before the meeting as to whether the amendment should be accepted.

12.5   AMENDING A RESOLUTION TO APPOINT DIRECTORS

Amendments to resolutions to appoint directors are probably the most common as shareholders often seek to propose a new person as a director, whether in place of or in addition to a nominated director. Unfortunately, this area is beset with diffi-culties. The principles outlined in para. 12.4 in respect of ordinary resolutions apply and the basic question which must be considered is whether the amendment is within the scope of the notice. Before addressing this point, the chairman should, however, check the following points which may prevent the amendment being put.

(a) Articles normally fix (or determine the method of fixing) the maximum number of directors that may be appointed. If that maximum would be exceeded by passing the amendment, it can be rejected.

(b) Articles usually require notice to be given to the company of the intention to propose someone as a director who is not recommended by the board, e.g.

reg. 76 of Table A which requires notice to be given by a member not less than 14 nor more than 35 clear days before the date appointed for the meeting together with the particulars which would, if that person was appointed, be required to be included in the company's register of directors together with notice executed by that person of his willingness to be appointed.

Assuming that the company receives no such notice from a member entitled to vote 14 clear days before the meeting, no-one other than a director retiring at the meeting or a person recommended by the board would be eligible for election as a director at the meeting.

(c) The articles may require prior notice to be given to the company of any amendments to be proposed at the meeting. If no such notice has been given, the chairman may reject the amendment.

12.6   PROCEDURE ON AN AMENDMENT

An amendment may be moved at any time after discussion on the original motion has been invited by the chairman and before the motion has been put to the vote. It is not necessary for an amendment to be seconded unless the articles so provide (*Re Horbury Bridge Coal, Iron & Waggon Co.* (1879) 11 Ch.D. 109).

An amendment may alter the original motion by making deletions, additions or insertions. The proposal must be carefully drafted and, if necessary, the chairman should assist the proposers in giving proper effect to their proposal.

For example, on a resolution 'to appoint ABC as auditors until the next annual general meeting at which accounts are laid and to authorise the directors to fix their remuneration' the following amendment might be proposed: THAT the motion before the meeting be amended by deleting the word 'annual' and adding after the word 'remuneration' the words 'provided that the amount paid as remuneration shall not exceed £25,000'.

12.6.1   Order in which amendments taken

A properly moved amendment must be considered and put to the meeting before the original motion. It is normal for discussion to be restricted to the amendment itself. If it is carried, the chairman should read out the amended motion and invite discussion on it before putting it to the vote. If more than one amendment is proposed to the same motion, each amendment should be considered in the order in which it affects the motion.

For example, on a motion 'to appoint ABC as auditors until the next general meeting at which accounts are laid and to authorise the directors to fix their remuneration' an amendment proposing to delete 'ABC' and to insert 'BCD' should be taken before an amendment proposing to limit the amount that the directors are authorised to pay as remuneration for the auditors.

An amendment to an amendment may be proposed before the principal amendment is put to the vote. In these circumstances, the secondary amendment must be taken first. If it is carried, it must be embodied in the principal amendment which should be read to the meeting before discussion is invited.

CHAPTER THIRTEEN

Quorum

13.1 SUMMARY

The quorum is the minimum number of persons entitled to vote who must be present or represented at a meeting in order for it to transact any business. Articles usually specify the quorum for general meetings. In default, the Act provides that the quorum shall be two members who must be personally present. Special quorum requirements exist for class meetings held to consider a variation of the rights of class members (see para. 4.4).

Corporate representatives are counted in calculating whether a quorum exists. Proxies should not be counted unless the articles provide otherwise. An individual may be counted more than once for the purposes of calculating whether a quorum exists where he or she represents more than one member (see para. 13.2). However, a meeting cannot normally take place with only one person present even if that person represents sufficient members to form a quorum or, indeed, represents all the members (see para. 13.3).

Articles usually provide that a general meeting will be automatically adjourned if a quorum is not present within a specified period after the time appointed for the start of the meeting (see para. 13.4). A quorum must be present throughout the meeting unless the articles provide otherwise (see para. 13.5).

The Act provides that the quorum at meetings of single-member companies shall be one member present in person or by proxy (see para. 13.7).

13.2 WHO MAY BE COUNTED IN THE QUORUM

To be counted in the quorum, a person must first and foremost be eligible to vote (*Young* v. *South African & Australian Exploration & Development Syndicate* [1896] 2 Ch. 268; cf. *Re Greymouth Point Elizabeth Railway and Coal Co. Ltd* [1904] 1 Ch. 32). A member may be ineligible to vote for a variety of reasons (see para. 16.4). For example, because a call is outstanding on his or her shares (reg. 57 of Table A).

Members must also be personally present, unless the articles provide otherwise. Corporate representatives are deemed to be members for these purposes and should always be counted unless they are not eligible to vote (*Re Kelantan Coco Nut Estates Ltd* [1920] W.N. 274). However, members represented by a proxy should not be counted unless the articles allow. Proxies may not be counted under articles like reg. 53 of 1948 Table A which states:

53.   No business shall be transacted at any general meeting unless a quorum of members is present at the time when the meeting proceeds to business; save as herein otherwise provided *three members present in person shall be a quorum.* [The words in italics were substituted by the words 'two members present in person or by proxy shall be a quorum' by the Companies Act 1980, Sch. 3 and these words apply to any company registered on or after 22 December 1980.]

In contrast, reg. 40 of the 1985 Table A explicitly allows members represented by proxy to be counted in the quorum. It provides:

40.   No business shall be transacted at any meeting unless a quorum is present. Two persons entitled to vote upon the business to be transacted, each being a member or a proxy for a member or a duly authorised representative of a corporation, shall be a quorum.

Where the articles allow members represented by proxy to be counted in calculating whether a quorum exists care should be taken to ensure that:

• proxies are not counted when the member who appointed them is also present;
• a member represented by more than one proxy is only counted once.

Table 13.1 shows what combinations would qualify for the purposes of reg. 40 of 1985 Table A.

Table 13.1   Possible combinations for a quorum under reg. 40 of 1985 Table A

First person	Second person
Member	Member
Member	Proxy
Member	Corporate representative
Proxy	Proxy
Proxy	Corporate representative
Corporate representative	Corporate representative

13.3 MORE THAN ONE PERSON

A quorum may exist even though the actual number of persons present is less than the number specified as the quorum by the articles. This is because a person may represent more than one member. For example, in *Neil McLeod & Sons, Petitioners,*

1967 S.C. 16, the quorum specified in the articles was three members personally present. It was held that a quorum was present at a meeting even though there were only two people present at a meeting where one of those members attended in his own capacity and as a trustee.

This rule is subject to the basic common law principle that for a meeting to take place there must be a coming together of at least two people. In *Sharp* v. *Dawes* [1876] 2 Q.B.D. 26, Mellish L.J. said: 'It is clear that, according to the ordinary use of the English language, a meeting could no more be constituted by one person than a meeting could have been constituted if no shareholder at all had attended.'

Thus, a meeting attended by only one member who held proxies for all the other members was held to be invalidly constituted (*Re Sanitary Carbon Co.* [1877] W.N. 233). Similarly, where a company's articles provided that two or more members present in person or by proxy shall be a quorum, one member present in his own capacity and in his capacity as the first named trustee for two trusts and as proxy for another member did not constitute a valid meeting (*Prain & Sons Ltd., Petitioners*, 1947 S.C. 325).

13.3.1   Exceptions to *Sharp* v. *Dawes*

As mentioned previously there are a number of important exceptions to the rule that a meeting cannot take place without at least two persons.

If default is made in holding an annual general meeting, the Secretary of State may call or direct the calling of a general meeting and direct that one member present in person or by proxy be deemed to be a quorum, ss. 367(1) & (2). The court may make a similar direction where it has ordered a general meeting to be called under s. 371.

It has been held in relation to class meetings, that a single person may constitute a meeting where that person holds all the issued shares of a particular class (*East* v. *Bennett Bro. Ltd* [1911] 1 Ch. 163). This principle does not apply where all the shares in a public company fall into the hands of a single member. In these circumstances the correct procedure would be for the member to transfer at least one share into the name of another person (normally a nominee) so that a meeting may be held. If this is not possible, an application should be made to the Secretary of State [s. 367] or the court [s. 371] for an order that a meeting may be held with a quorum of one.

A private company which has only one member may, notwithstanding any provision to the contrary in the articles, hold meetings with a quorum of one by virtue of s. 370A [inserted by the Companies (Single Member Private Limited Companies) Regulations 1992, reg. 2, Schedule, para. 5].

13.4   FAILURE TO OBTAIN A QUORUM

Reg. 41 of the 1985 Table A provides that if a quorum is not present within half an hour from the time appointed for the meeting, the meeting shall stand adjourned to the same day in the next week at the same time and place or such time and place as the directors may determine. Where this article applies, the quorum required for the transaction of business at the adjourned meeting will be the same as for the original meeting. However, it is common for this article to be modified so that if at the adjourned meeting a quorum is not present within a certain time, 'the members present shall be a quorum' (see, for example, reg. 54 of the 1948 Act Table A and art. 63 of Whitbread plc). Thus the normal requirement of, say, eight members present in person or by proxy would be reduced to at least two. If the articles allow proxies to be included, it would seem that the words 'members present' would allow them to be included for this purpose. However, the principle in *Sharp* v. *Dawes* would probably prevent a meeting of one person being allowed in such circumstances even if that person held proxies for other members (see *Daimler Co. Ltd* v. *Continental Tyre & Rubber Co. (Great Britain) Ltd* [1916] 2 A.C. 307).

It is also common for articles to provide that a meeting convened on the requisition of members shall be dissolved if a quorum is not present within the allotted time (see art. 63 of Whitbread plc and reg. 54 of the 1948 Table A). Where such provision is made, the company would be well-advised to ensure that a quorum is present if it has taken the opportunity to propose resolutions at the meeting.

If it is impracticable or impossible to hold a meeting with a quorum in accordance with the articles, application can be made to the court under s. 371 for an order calling a meeting to be held with some other quorum (*Re Edinburgh Workmen's Houses Improvement Co. Ltd* 1934 S. L.T. 513) (see para. 5.5). The Secretary of State has similar powers in relation to annual general meetings (see para. 5.4).

13.5   FAILURE TO MAINTAIN A QUORUM

For companies with articles similar to reg. 40 of the 1985 Act Table A, which provides that no business shall be transacted unless a quorum is present, the quorum must be maintained throughout the meeting. Reg. 41 of the 1985 Table A provides that if during a meeting such a quorum ceases to be present, the meeting shall stand adjourned to the same day in the next week at the same time and place or such time and place as the directors may determine. Strictly speaking, under reg. 41, a meeting will be adjourned automatically if sufficient members leave the meeting and the number remaining is not sufficient to form a quorum, even if those who have left actually return shortly thereafter. Where the number of members present is only just sufficient to form a quorum, the chairman should ask members not to leave the meeting without informing him that they are about to leave. This would allow him to propose a formal motion to adjourn the meeting to a time and place which is agreeable to the members before the member leaves and forces the meeting to be adjourned automatically.

In order to avoid this problem altogether, articles commonly provide that a quorum need only be present 'at the time when the meeting proceeds to business' (e.g. reg. 53 of 1948 Act Table A). If so, the meeting may continue to transact business even though the quorum is not subsequently maintained (*Re Hartley Baird*

[1955] Ch. 143) provided that the number of persons present does not fall below two, in which case the *Sharp* v. *Dawes* principle applies (*Re London Flats Ltd* [1969] 1 W.L.R. 711). This type of article also prevents a dissenting minority obstructing the transaction of business by absenting themselves from the meeting once they realise things are not going their way.

13.6 ABUSE OF QUORUM REQUIREMENTS

If a minority shareholder attempts to frustrate the will of the majority by refusing to attend a meeting and thereby preventing the formation of a quorum, the court may order the holding of a meeting under s. 371 (see further para. 5.5) and direct that the quorum for that meeting shall be less than the number normally required (*Re El Sombrero Ltd* [1958] Ch. 900 and *Re H. R. Paul & Son Ltd* (1973)118 S. J. 166). The court will only do so where the quorum is a fixed number of shareholders and the minority shareholder's ability to prevent the holding of meetings is merely a consequence of the number of shareholders there are at that time. It will not do so where the articles specifically provide that a meeting shall not be quorate without the presence of that shareholder (see para. 13.7 below).

13.7 SPECIAL QUORUM REQUIREMENTS

The quorum requirements can be used to protect the interests of certain shareholders. The articles or a shareholders' agreement may provide that a quorum shall not exist unless a particular member or the holder of particular class of shares is present. These special requirements can be restricted to certain types of business, e.g. the appointment and removal of directors. Such provisions will usually be framed so that they attach special rights to a certain class of shares. The courts have held that where they apply to a named shareholder, that shareholder will be treated as having class rights which may not be modified unless the proper procedures for variation are followed. The Court of Appeal has also held that, where the articles or a shareholder agreement create class rights by requiring the presence of the holder of a certain class of share for meetings to be quorate, it would not be right for the court, on an application under s. 371 (see para. 5.5), to order that a meeting be held with some other quorum requirement (*Harman* v. *BML Group Ltd* [1994] 1 W.L.R. 893). Dillon LJ said: 'it is not right, in my view, to invoke s. 371 to override class rights attached to a class of shares which have been deliberately – in this case by the shareholders' agreement – imposed for the protection of the holders of those shares'.

An article which requires all the members entitled to vote to be present in person or by proxy in order to form a quorum (irrespective of the number of members there is at any particular time) may offer similar protection. However, such an article would not normally be advisable except for companies with very few members.

13.8   SINGLE MEMBER COMPANIES

In 1992, the Companies Act was amended by the Companies (Single Member Private Companies) Regulations 1992 to allow private limited companies to have only one member [s. 1(3A) and s. 24]. Prior to these changes, every company was required to have at least two members. In order to give effect to the Directive, the Regulations also inserted a new s. 370A in the Act which provides that notwithstanding anything to the contrary in the articles of a private company limited by shares or guarantee having only one member, one member present in person or by proxy shall be a quorum at general meetings of the company.

CHAPTER FOURTEEN

Proxies

14.1 SUMMARY

The right to vote at general meetings enables members to influence or control the company. In order to maintain the balance of power, it is essential that members have the right to exercise their votes even though they are not able to attend the meeting in person. The Act achieves this by giving members a statutory right to appoint another person (a proxy) to attend the meeting and vote on their behalf (see para. 14.2).

The Act confers certain rights on proxies which cannot be excluded by a company's articles. The articles may, however, extend those rights (see para. 14.3).

The notice of every general meeting must include a statement explaining to members their right to appoint a proxy (see para. 14.4). The directors may send the members proxy forms at the company's expense. However, they may not invite selected members to appoint a proxy (see para. 14.5).

Articles usually require proxies to be appointed in writing and may prescribe the form which must be used to make the appointment. The Stock Exchange requires listed companies to send shareholders a proxy form which allows them to instruct their proxy how to vote (see para. 14.6). Articles usually require proxy forms to be deposited with the company at least 48 hours before the time appointed for the meeting (see para. 14.7). A proxy deposited in time for the original meeting will also be valid for any adjournment of that meeting (see para. 14.8). Articles usually make special provision for the deposit of proxies in connection with a poll not taken at the meeting (see para. 14.9).

A member may revoke the appointment of a proxy. Articles normally require notice of revocation to be given to the company. However, a member may revoke the appointment of a proxy without giving notice by attending and voting in person at the meeting (see para. 14.10). A member may change his or her voting instructions at any time before the vote is taken (see para. 14.11).

A proxy cannot be forced to attend or vote on behalf of his or her appointer unless there is a contractual relationship between the parties or the proxy has a fiduciary duty to do so. The chairman may have a fiduciary duty to vote in accordance with the instructions of members who have appointed him (see para. 14.14).

Articles usually make special provision with regard to the validity of proxies appointed by joint shareholders (see para. 14.12) and proxies appointed by members who subsequently die or suffer from some mental disorder (see para. 14.13). The chairman is usually given authority by the articles to rule on the validity of proxy votes (see para. 14.15).

The word 'proxy' is commonly used to describe the person appointed by a member, the form for the appointment of proxies sent to members and the votes held by a proxy (e.g. the chairman of the meeting). Only the first of these is strictly correct. A proxy is a person appointed by a member to attend and vote on his or her behalf. To avoid confusion, the instrument of appointment can be referred to as the 'proxy form' and the votes cast by a proxy as 'proxy votes'.

14.2   STATUTORY RIGHT TO APPOINT A PROXY

Every member entitled to attend and vote at a meeting of the company has a statutory right to appoint another person (who need not be a member of the company) to attend and vote on his or her behalf at that meeting, s. 372(1). A person so appointed by a member is known as a proxy.

The ability to appoint someone who is not a member is important as it ensures that a member can find someone who is willing to act. This would not necessarily be the case if the articles required only other members to be appointed.

For members of public companies the right to appoint another 'person' in s. 372(1) is deemed by virtue of s. 6 of the Interpretation Act 1978 to mean one or more persons. A member of a private company is not entitled to appoint more than one proxy to attend the same meeting unless the articles confer that right [s. 372(2)(b)]. This does not prevent a member of a private company appointing an alternate proxy. However, they may not both attend. It should be noted that reg. 59 of Table A allows a member to appoint more than one proxy to attend on the same occasion.

The right to appoint a proxy in the case of companies limited by guarantee will depend on the articles. There is no common law right to vote by proxy (*Harben* v. *Phillips* (1883) 23 Ch. D. 14). The statutory right to appoint a proxy does not apply in the case of a company not having a share capital, e.g. a company limited by guarantee, s. 372(2)(a).

14.3   RIGHTS OF PROXIES

Proxies have a statutory right to attend and vote on behalf of the members who appointed them. The right to attend will, however, be subject to the usual rules on ejection in cases of severe disorder.

A proxy appointed by a member of a private company has the same right as that member to speak at the meeting [s. 372(1)]. The Act makes no such provision with regard to proxies appointed by members of a public company. The articles of public companies sometimes confirm or deny proxies' right to speak. Where they are silent, the question may be determined by the chairman with the consent of the meeting in accordance with the principles laid down in *Carruth* v. *Imperial Chemical Industries Ltd* (see para. 8.5). In its *Guide to best practice for Annual General Meetings*, ICSA recommends that chairmen of listed companies should seek the consent of the meeting to proxies speaking and participating in the debate. However, some listed companies still prefer not to do so because they believe protest groups would abuse the right to speak.

All proxies may demand or join in a demand for a poll [s. 373(2)]. This will be the case even where the articles provide that proxies may not speak. All proxies are entitled to vote on a poll but not on a show of hands unless the articles so provide [s. 372(2)(c)]. Table A does not allow proxies to vote on a show of hands.

Proxies must attend the meeting in person in order to vote. Proxies appointed to attend and vote at the original meeting have a right to attend and vote at any adjournment of that meeting unless the articles provide otherwise (*Scadding* v. *Lorrant* (1851) 3 H.L.C. 418), e.g. they require members to submit a new instrument of proxy for any adjourned meeting. It makes no difference in this regard whether the articles allow members to appoint proxies between the date of the original meeting and the adjourned meeting. In this case, instruments of proxy deposited for the original meeting and those deposited in accordance with the articles for the adjourned meeting will both be valid (see further para. 14.8).

On a poll a member who is entitled to more than one vote need not use all his votes or cast all the votes he uses (whether in person or by proxy) in the same way [s. 374]. There is nothing to prevent a person acting as proxy for more than one member.

A proxy may in certain circumstances act as the chairman of a meeting (*Re Bradford Investments plc* [1990] B.C.C. 740).

14.4   STATEMENT IN THE NOTICE OF THE MEETING

A statement must be included with reasonable prominence in the notice of every general meeting of a company which has a share capital to the effect that a member entitled to attend and vote is entitled to appoint a proxy or, where that is allowed, one or more proxies to attend instead of him and that a proxy need not be a member [s. 372(3)]. If the articles of a private company allow members to appoint more than one proxy, the statement should make this clear. The statement is usually positioned at the end of the notice (see **Precedent 6.5**). If the articles of a company without a share capital allow members to appoint a proxy, they usually require a similar statement to be included in the notice.

14.5   INVITATIONS TO APPOINT A PROXY

Listed companies are required by para. 9.26 of The Listing Rules to send two-way proxy forms with the notice convening the meeting to each person entitled to vote at the meeting. Although other companies are not required by the Act to issue proxy forms, they may do so at the company's expense. Generally, any expenses incurred in good faith in the best interests of the company to secure votes in support of the directors' policy are payable out of the funds of the company. Thus, the directors may send proxy forms made out in their own names to shareholders accompanied by a stamped addressed envelope to encourage a greater response (*Peel* v. *London & North West Ry. Co.* [1907] 1 Ch. 5).

However, invitations to appoint a person (e.g. the chairman) or one of a number of persons may only be issued at the company's expense if they are sent to all the members entitled to receive notice of the meeting. An officer of the company who knowingly or wilfully permits the issue of invitations to selected members is liable to a fine unless the invitation was issued in response to a written request by a member for a form of appointment naming the proxy or a list of persons willing to act as proxy and that form or list was freely available to all other members entitled to vote by proxy at the meeting [s. 372(6)]. For the purposes of s. 372(6), an invitation will include any proxy form with the name of a person already inserted as the proxy or any document, circular or letter inviting members to appoint a particular person or persons as their proxy.

It should be noted that s. 372(6) does not prevent anyone (including the directors) from soliciting proxies at their own expense.

14.6   METHOD OF APPOINTMENT OF A PROXY

The Act does not specify how proxies should be appointed, although it assumes that it will be by a written instrument [s. 372(5)]. The relationship between a member and his or her proxy is one of principal and agent. In the normal course of events, an agent can be appointed either in writing or orally. However, almost without exception, articles provide that proxies must be appointed in writing. For example, reg. 60 of Table A provides that appointments shall be made by depositing with the company an instrument of appointment in writing executed by or on behalf of the appointor.

Older articles sometimes require the instrument appointing a proxy to be attested (i.e. signed in the presence of a witness). An instrument of proxy which does not comply with such a requirement contained in the articles will be invalid (*Harben* v. *Phillips* (1883) 23 Ch.D. 14) and a proxy cannot attest his or her own appointment in such circumstances (*Ex parte Cullen* [1891] 2 Q.B. 151). In the vast majority of cases, and certainly in the case of reg. 60 of Table A, the signature of the member will be sufficient.

A corporation which is a member of a company may execute a proxy under its common seal or by signature in accordance with s. 36A (in England) and s. 36B (in

Scotland). However, articles may allow corporate members to execute proxies under the hand of an authorised officer. This is a requirement of the Listing Rules for listed companies (see para. 14.6.2).

It is not necessary for a named person to be nominated as proxy as long as the person appointed is capable of being identified (*Bombay–Burmah Trading Corporation Ltd* v. *Dorabji Cursetji Shroff* [1905] A.C. 213). Shareholders may, for example, nominate 'the chairman of the meeting' as their proxy.

Articles usually allow the appointment of a proxy to be executed on behalf of a member. In these circumstances, they normally require the authority under which the person executed the instrument of appointment (e.g. a power of attorney) or a copy of it to be deposited by the deadline for deposit of the instrument of proxy, e.g. reg. 62 of Table A. Articles sometimes give the directors the power to dispense with this requirement (see art. 83 of Whitbread plc).

A member may authorise (either in writing or orally) another person to complete the proxy form by filling in the name of the person entitled to vote (*Re Lancaster* (1877) 5 Ch.D. 911). A blank proxy form signed by a member given to a person in connection with a requisitioned meeting together with authority to fill it up was held to be valid for a later requisitioned meeting called for the same purpose after the original requisition had been withdrawn (*Sadgrove* v. *Bryden* [1907] 1 Ch. 318). The secretary has no authority to enter the date in proxies returned without a date unless authorised by the member to do so, although that authority may be implied in some circumstances (*Ernest* v. *Loma Gold Mines* [1897] 1 Ch. 1).

14.6.1   Form of proxy under Table A

Reg. 60 of Table A provides that an instrument appointing a proxy shall either be:

- in the same form as a specimen provided in that regulation (see below) or as close to it as circumstances allow;
- in any other form which is usual; or
- in any other form which the directors approve.

Under Table A, it can be assumed that proxy forms sent to members by the company have been approved by the directors for the purposes of reg. 60. Where proxy forms are not sent to members with the notice of the meeting, as will often be the case in private companies, members should use the specimen contained in reg. 60 or any other form of appointment that is usual. What constitutes a usual form of appointment may depend on the type of company and its previous practice in this regard.

The following form of proxy is prescribed by reg. 60:

XYZ Limited
Form of proxy

I/We, [name of member/names of joint holders], of [address/addresses], being a member/members of the above-named company, hereby appoint [name of proxy] of [address of proxy], or failing him, [name of alternate proxy, if any] of [address], as my/our proxy to vote in my/our name[s] and on my/our behalf at the annual/extraordinary general meeting of the company to be held on [date], and at any adjournment thereof.

Signature(s)   *[Date]*

Although this form of proxy appears to give the person appointed as proxy complete discretion as to how to vote, a member can issue separate voting instructions (see para. 14.14 for a discussion of a proxy's obligation to vote in accordance with instructions).

Reg. 61 of Table A prescribes the following form of proxy which may be used 'where it is desired to afford members an opportunity of instructing the proxy how he should vote':

Plc/Limited

I/We, [name of member/names of joint holders], of [address], being a member/members of the above-named company, hereby appoint [name of proxy] of [address of proxy], or failing him, [name of alternate proxy, if any] of [address], as my/our proxy to vote in my/our name[s] and on my/our behalf at the annual/extraordinary general meeting of the company to be held on [date], and at any adjournment thereof.

This form is to be used in respect of the resolutions mentioned below as follows:

Resolution No. 1 *for *against.
Resolution No. 2 *for *against.
*Strike out whichever is not desired.

Unless otherwise instructed, the proxy may vote as he thinks fit or abstain from voting.

Signed this   day of   19   .

The words 'where it is desired to afford members an opportunity of instructing the proxy how he should vote' in reg. 61 seem to imply that the directors may, where it is not so desired, reject an appointment made in the form prescribed by that regulation (i.e. on a two-way proxy form). In fact, it is submitted that this form of appointment is now so common that it should be accepted under the heading 'or in any other form which is usual' in reg. 60.

14.6.2   Stock Exchange requirements

The London Stock Exchange requires listed companies to send members two-way proxy forms. Para. 9.26 of the Listing Rules requires a proxy form to be sent with the notice convening any meeting of the holders of listed securities to each person entitled to vote at the meeting. The proxy form must comply with the requirements of paras. 13.28 and 13.29 of the Listing Rules which state:

- it must provide for two-way voting on all resolutions intended to be proposed (except that it is not necessary to provide proxy forms with two-way voting on procedural resolutions), para. 13.28(b);

- it must state that a shareholder is entitled to appoint a proxy of his own choice and provide a space for insertion of the name of such proxy, para. 13.28(c);
- it must state that if it is returned without an indication as to how the proxy shall vote on any particular matter, the proxy will exercise his discretion as to whether, and if so how, he votes, para. 13.28(d); and
- if the resolutions to be proposed include the re-election of retiring directors and the number of retiring directors standing for re-election exceeds five, the proxy form may give shareholders the opportunity to vote for or against the re-election of the retiring directors as a whole but must also allow votes to be cast for or against the re-election of the retiring directors individually, para. 13.29.

In addition the articles of a listed company must allow a corporation to execute a form of proxy under the hand of a duly authorised officer [Listing Rules, para. 12 of Appendix 1 to Chapter 13].

Proxy forms which comply with the requirements of Chapter 13 of the Listing Rules and which have no unusual features (see, for example **Precedent 14.6**) do not need to be approved by the Exchange before they are despatched. However, two copies must be lodged with the Exchange (marked for the attention of the Listing Department) no later than the date on which they are despatched to the holders of the relevant securities.

14.7   DEPOSIT OF PROXIES

A company may require instruments appointing proxies (and any document relating to or necessary to show the validity of any such appointment) to be lodged with the company by a specified time before the meeting. This is normally done to allow the validity of the instruments to be checked and the votes for and against the resolution to be counted before the meeting. If no such provision is made in the articles, the company must accept a vote tendered by proxy at the meeting even though the proxy is unable at the meeting to establish his authority (*Re English, Scottish & Australian Bank* [1893] 3 Ch. 385).

Any provision in a company's articles will be void in so far as it requires proxies to be lodged more than 48 hours before the meeting or adjourned meeting [s. 372(5)]. In such circumstances proxy forms delivered any time before the commencement of the meeting will be valid.

Most articles (including reg. 62 of Table A) require proxy forms to be deposited not less than 48 hours before the time for holding the meeting or adjourned meeting either:

- at the company's registered office; or
- at such other place in the United Kingdom as is specified in the notice convening the meeting or in any instrument of proxy sent out by the company in relation to the meeting.

Instruments of proxy are commonly required to be deposited at the offices of the company's registrar and the reverse of the proxy form will normally be in the form of a pre-addressed and pre-paid postcard.

Proxy forms received by the company after the time specified in the articles will not be valid for that meeting. If a meeting is held on a Monday or a Tuesday, it will normally be necessary for someone to be present at the nominated office at the deadline to ensure that proxies delivered after that time are not accepted.

It has been held that a proxy form delivered by fax is valid for the purposes of a creditors' meeting in relation to an individual voluntary arrangement to be entered into pursuant to the Insolvency Act 1986 (*Re a debtor* (No. 2021 of 1995) [1996] 1 B.C.L.C. 538). Although Laddie J. stressed that his ruling in this case did not apply to meetings held under the Companies Act 1985 or, indeed, to other creditors' meetings held in accordance with the Insolvency Act 1986, the case may be of wider significance because it hinged on the question whether the signature on a faxed proxy satisfied the requirements of rule 8.2(3) of the Insolvency Rules 1986 that 'a form of proxy shall be signed by the principal, or by some person authorised by him'. Laddie J. held that it did and, after examining the authorities, said:

> I have come to the conclusion that a proxy form is signed for the purposes of r. 8.2(3) if it bears upon it some distinctive or personal marking which has been placed there by, or with the authority of, the creditor. When a creditor faxes a proxy form to the chairman of the creditors' meeting he transmits two things at the same time, the contents of the form and the signature applied to it. The receiving fax is in effect instructed by the transmitting creditor to reproduce his signature on the proxy form which is itself being created at the receiving station. It follows that, in my view, the received fax is a proxy form signed by the principal or by someone authorised by him.
>
> . . . From the chairman's point of view, there is nothing about a received fax which puts him in a worse position to detect forgeries than when he received through the post or by hand delivery a document signed by hand by a person whose signature he has never seen before or one signed by stamping. The reality is that fax transmission is likely to be a more reliable and certainly is a more speedy method of communication than post.

The validity of faxed proxies in relation to general meetings will depend upon the contruction of the articles. There is certainly nothing in the Act to prevent appointments being made in this manner. Most articles require proxies to be 'executed by or on behalf of the appointor'. Where execution can be effected by signature, it seems that the ruling in *Re a debtor* will be relevant. The only other question would seem to be whether faxing the proxy form would satisfy the requirement in most articles that it be 'deposited at the office'.

14.8   PROXIES AT ADJOURNED MEETINGS

An instrument of proxy deposited prior to the original meeting will also be valid for any adjournment of that meeting, unless the articles provide otherwise (*Cousins* v. *International Brick Co. Ltd* [1931] 2 Ch. 90) (see para. 17.8).

14.9 PROXIES ON A POLL

A proxy delivered after the time specified in the articles will not be valid on the suspension of business for the purposes of taking a poll (*Shaw* v. *Tati Concessions* [1913] 1 Ch. 292) unless the articles expressly allow proxies to be deposited at a specified time before the poll is taken, e.g. reg. 62 of Table A. Reg. 62 provides that in the case of a poll taken more than 48 hours after it is demanded, proxies must be deposited after the poll has been demanded and not less than 24 hours before the time for the taking of the poll. Therefore a proxy deposited after the time allowed for the original meeting but before the poll was actually demanded would still not be valid for these purposes.

Reg. 62 also provides that in the case of a poll taken less than 48 hours after the meeting at which it was demanded, proxies may be delivered at the meeting at which the poll was demanded to the chairman or to the secretary or to any director. In this case, it would seem that all proxies delivered late for the original meeting would be invalid unless they were delivered at the meeting. This provision can cause problems in the case of a member who is represented at the original meeting by a proxy other than the chairman who is unable to attend the poll. The member would not be able to appoint a further proxy and would therefore have to attend the poll in person in order to vote. This problem can best be avoided by nominating the chairman of the meeting as an alternate by using the words 'or failing him, the chairman of the meeting'.

14.10 REVOCATION OF PROXIES

The appointment of a proxy in relation to a share will automatically be revoked (terminated) on the registration of a transfer of that share. The death or insanity of a member automatically revokes any appointment by that person of a proxy unless the articles provide otherwise. Articles commonly provide that a proxy appointed by a member who subsequently dies will be valid unless the company receives notice in writing of the death of that member (see art. 87 of Whitbread plc).

Revocation can be effected by notifying the company that the appointment has been revoked or that the authority under which the instrument of proxy was signed has been revoked, e.g. the revocation of a power of attorney (*R.* v. *Wait* (1823) 11 Price 518). A proxy which is expressed as being irrevocable cannot be revoked.

Articles usually require notice of revocation to be given before the meeting or the time appointed for the taking of a poll. For example, reg. 63 of Table A states:

63. A vote given or poll demanded by proxy or by the duly authorised representative of a corporation shall be valid notwithstanding the previous determination of the authority of the person voting or demanding a poll

unless notice of the determination was received by the company at the office or at such other place at which the instrument of proxy was duly deposited before the commencement of the meeting or adjourned meeting at which the vote is given or the poll demanded or (in the case of a poll taken otherwise than on the same day as the meeting or adjourned meeting) the time appointed for taking the poll.

Notice usually means notice in writing (e.g. reg. 111 of Table A). If, unusually, the articles make no provision as to the notice required, a member may (subject to the above proviso) revoke a proxy by giving notice at the meeting itself. If the articles do not make specific provision in respect of a poll not taken at the meeting, the revocation must be deposited before the meeting at which the poll was demanded.

A proxy may vote on behalf of the member who appointed him even though that member attends the meeting. However, the proxy is impliedly revoked if the member votes in person (*Knight* v. *Bulkley* (1859) 5 Jur. (N.S.) 817). This will be the case even where the articles require notice of revocation to be given to the company a specified period before the meeting (*Cousins* v. *International Brick Co. Ltd* [1931] 2 Ch. 90, C.A.).

The execution and deposit of a second or later instrument of proxy in respect of the same holding within the time allowed for deposit under the articles will act as a revocation of any previous appointment where members are entitled to appoint only one proxy. This may be the case, even though the deadline for appointments has expired. Where more than one appointment is made within the period specified by the articles, the company should accept the form which was signed and dated the latest.

Where members are entitled to appoint more than one proxy, the deposit of a second instrument appointing a different person may not be conclusive evidence of the intention to revoke the original appointment, except, perhaps, where the second appointment is accompanied by new voting instructions.

The ability to appoint more than one proxy allows nominee companies to appoint separate proxies to attend and vote on behalf of the various underlying holders. Several instruments of appointment, each representing different shares within the same registered holding, can be deposited. However, if the sum of the parts exceeds the whole, the company will obviously need to find some way of limiting the number of votes cast. It might inform the various proxy holders in the hope that they are able to come to an arrangement between themselves. If all the proxies attempt to vote, the company must scale down the votes of one or more of the proxies. One way of doing so might be to assume that the last proxy submitted had the effect of revoking (either in whole or in part) one or more of the previously submitted proxies on a first in first out basis.

14.11   CHANGE OF INSTRUCTIONS

Members may change the instructions given to their proxy at any time before a vote is taken. This may cause particular problems for companies which issue two-way proxy forms inviting members to appoint the chairman of the meeting as their proxy. The chairman should act on any change of instructions received in respect of those shares up to the time that the poll is taken.

It is common practice for chairmen to seek to deter members from demanding a poll by stating the number of proxies which they hold for and against the resolution, the implication being that the result is a foregone conclusion. In fact, the chairman can never be certain of the result of a poll until it is actually taken because his authority as a proxy may be revoked by a member voting in person at the meeting and members may alter their instructions at any time prior to the taking of the poll.

14.12   JOINT SHAREHOLDERS

Most companies' articles include a provision similar to reg. 55 of Table A which sets out the voting rights of joint shareholders. This is necessary to prevent each joint shareholder having a vote on a show of hands and to allow the company to determine which of the members' votes it should accept if more than one of them votes on a poll. Reg. 55 of Table A states:

> In the case of joint holders the vote of the senior who tenders a vote, whether in person or by proxy, shall be accepted to the exclusion of the votes of the other joint holders; and the seniority shall be determined by the order in which the names of the holders stand in the register of members.

If the joint holders of a share attend a meeting and vote in different ways on a resolution, only the vote of the most senior should be counted. If the senior does not vote, the vote (if any) of the next most senior should be counted. The same principle applies to votes tendered by proxy.

Companies often insist that proxy forms are signed by or on behalf of all the joint holders. It is however, doubtful whether this practice is correct. Section 372(1) provides that any member of a company entitled to attend and vote at a meeting is entitled to appoint a proxy to attend and vote instead of him. Each of the joint holders are members (see s. 22(2)) and each have a right to attend and (if none of the more senior joint shareholders vote) to vote. They are therefore each entitled to appoint a proxy. Under reg. 55, the vote of a proxy appointed by the senior joint holder (or by the senior and any of the other joint holders) should be counted to the exclusion of any votes tendered by proxies appointed by any of the other joint holders. The vote of the senior tendered by proxy should also be counted to the exclusion of any vote tendered in person by any of the junior joint holders. The vote of a junior holder in these circumstances is not a revocation of the proxy of the senior. This will probably be so even where the proxy was appointed by all the joint holders.

14.13   PERSONAL REPRESENTATIVES

Normally the death or insanity of a member automatically revokes the appointment by that person of a proxy. Articles sometimes provide that any proxy appointed by a member who subsequently dies will be valid unless the company receives notice in writing of the death of that member (see art. 87 of Whitbread plc). A person who becomes entitled to a share in consequence of the death or bankruptcy of a member will not normally be entitled to attend or vote at any meeting of the company until he or she is registered as the holder of the share, see for example reg. 31 of Table A. It follows that such a person will not be entitled to appoint a proxy.

Reg. 56 of Table A deals with the position of a member in respect of whom an order has been made by the court on the ground of mental disorder. A receiver, curator bonis or other person authorised by the court in that regard may appoint a proxy provided that evidence of the authority of the person claiming the right to do so is deposited not less than 48 hours before the meeting at the same place as instruments of proxies must be deposited.

14.14   PROXIES' OBLIGATIONS AND DISCRETIONS

A person who agrees to act as a proxy is considered to be the legally constituted agent of the member who makes the appointment (*Re English, Scottish & Australian Bank* [1893] 3 Ch. 385). However, the relationship of principal and agent 'can only be established by the consent of the principal and the agent' (per Lord Pearson in *Garnac Grain Co. Inc.* v. *HMF Faure & Fairclough Ltd* [1967] 2 All E.R. 353). Thus, a person appointed by a member as his proxy need not act in that capacity unless there is a binding contract between the parties or the proxy has a legal or equitable obligation to do so.

Where there is a contractual agreement to vote in a certain way, the court may enforce that contract by mandatory injunction (*Puddephatt* v. *Leith* [1916] Ch. 200). The member may also be entitled to damages for any loss he incurs as a result of his proxy failing to vote in accordance with instructions in breach of a contractual or fiduciary duty.

Where a proxy is appointed without consideration, a gratuitous agency will exist which gives rise to negative obligations on the part of the agent (e.g. not to vote contrary to the member's instructions, if any) but not positive obligations (e.g. to attend and vote). In *Oliver* v. *Dalgleish* [1963] 1 W.L.R. 1274, several members nominated the same person as their proxy but gave him different instructions as to how to vote on a series of resolutions. The proxy voted in favour of the resolutions without specifying how many votes he was casting. It was held that the chairman had acted improperly in rejecting all the proxy's votes. He should have accepted those for which the proxy had instructions to vote in favour of the resolutions. As the votes of those who had instructed the proxy to vote against the resolution would not have affected the outcome, the court did not rule on the proxy's obligation to vote. However, it was impliedly accepted that the proxy did not have an obligation to use them (see, however, para. 14.14.1 below on the position of the chairman).

Not surprisingly the courts have sought ways to ensure that proxy votes are given effect without tampering with the law of agency. The problem was first identified by

Maugham J. in *Re Dorman Long & Co. Ltd* [1934] Ch. 635 which arose after the court had made an order under a scheme of arrangement calling a meeting and requiring the directors of the company to issue two-way proxies to those entitled to attend and vote. Maugham J. held that as a result of the court's order the directors had a duty to use the proxy votes and the people who gave them were entitled to assume that they would be used. However, he doubted whether directors had a general duty to attend and vote in respect of proxies and he noted that it would be difficult to allow the proxies to have force if none of the directors named as proxy holders attended the meeting. He said: 'In a sense, in all these cases, the dice are loaded in favour of the views of the directors . . . proxy forms are made out in favour of certain named directors and, although it is true that the word "for" or "against" may be inserted in the modern proxy form, the recipients of the circulars very often are in doubt as to whether the persons named as proxies are bound to put in votes by proxy with which they are not in agreement.'

14.14.1   Chairman's obligations

The position of the chairman in relation to proxies is particularly important. Most two-way proxies name 'the chairman of the meeting' as the default proxy. Accordingly, the vast majority of shareholders appoint the chairman as their proxy. By doing so they at least ensure that their nominated proxy attends the meeting. They also secure the added benefit of appointing a person who has a duty to ascertain the sense of the meeting. In *Second Consolidated Trust Ltd* v. *Ceylon Amalgamated Tea & Rubber Estates Ltd* [1943] 2 All E.R. 567, the chairman of a public company failed to call a poll even though he had the power to do so under the company's articles and held sufficient two-way proxies to reverse a decision taken at a meeting on a show of hands. It was held that he had acted in breach of his duty to ascertain the sense of the meeting. Uthwatt J. said:

> It appears to me that the power to demand a poll is a power possessed by the chairman which is to be exercised or not to be exercised according to his decision whether it is necessary to exercise his power in order to ascertain the sense of the meeting upon the matter before them; in other words it is a power directed towards enabling him to carry on the meeting for the purpose for which it was convened. In addition to this duty to demand a poll or to exercise his power to demand a poll . . . he would be under a duty in law to exercise all the proxies which he held as chairman in accordance with the instructions they contained.

It would seem to be irrelevant for these purposes whether or not the chairman of the meeting is a director of the company. And, according to the judgment of Uthwatt J., the duty to vote arises independently of the duty to demand a poll. It will therefore also apply where a poll is demanded by the members.

14.14.2 Proxies' discretion

Where a member uses a form of proxy similar to that contained in reg. 60 of Table A, the proxy has complete discretion as to how to vote on any resolution before the meeting.

Where a member issues voting instructions, the extent of the proxy's discretion will depend on the wording of those instructions and the instrument of appointment. The form of proxy in reg. 61 allows members to instruct their proxy how to vote (two-way proxies) and states that in the absence of any instructions the proxy may vote as he thinks fit or abstain from voting, e.g. reg. 61. This obviously means that the proxy may exercise his discretion on those resolutions of which the member has had notice but has not issued voting instructions. A more difficult question is whether the proxy can also vote on resolutions which come before the meeting of which the member has not had notice, such as amendments, proposals to adjourn, etc. In *Re Waxed Papers Ltd* [1937] 2 All E.R. 481, a meeting was held to approve, with or without modifications, a proposed scheme of arrangement. Various members appointed the chairman of the meeting as their proxy with instructions to vote in favour of the proposed scheme 'either with or without modification as my proxy may approve'. The chairman cast those votes against an amendment which would have deferred consideration of the scheme until the accounts for the current year had been finalised. It was held that he had acted properly. On the wording of the instrument of appointment, the power conferred on the proxy was not limited to voting for or against the proposed scheme and was sufficiently wide to enable him to vote on any incidental matter which might arise before the main question.

In *Re Waxed Papers Ltd*, the chairman exercised his discretion in a manner which was consistent with the voting instructions he had been given. He would not have been able to carry out his instructions properly if he had allowed the amendment to be passed. In addition, it was not clear whether the members would have been in any better position had consideration of the proposed scheme been deferred. It is, however, relatively easy to envisage occasions where it would be more advantageous for members if their proxies did not exercise their discretion in this way. Modern forms of proxy attempt to cater for this by using words such as:

> I/We hereby authorise and instruct the proxy to vote on the resolutions to be proposed at such meeting as indicated in the boxes below. Unless otherwise directed, the proxy will vote or abstain from voting as he or she thinks fit. Should any resolutions, other than those specified, be proposed at the meeting, the proxy may vote thereon as he or she thinks fit.

Where this form of words is used, there can be no doubt that the proxy has complete discretion to vote on amendments, adjournments, etc. Whether, the proxy should follow any guiding principles in determining how to vote on such matters is a difficult question. The answer is probably no where there is no contractual or fiduciary relationship between the proxy and his appointor. However, where such a relationship exists the proxy presumably has a duty to act in the best interests of his appointor. It is arguable that the chairman of the meeting is in such a position, particularly where the company has issued proxy forms inviting members to appoint him as their proxy. The difficulties this can cause can be demonstrated by the chairman's options on a proposal to adjourn.

The approach taken by most chairmen on a proposal from the floor to adjourn is to assume that those members who have given instructions to vote in favour of the remaining resolutions proposed in the notice of meeting approve of the conduct of the business before the meeting at this time, and accordingly, would wish to vote against the proposal to adjourn. The chairman might also cast against the proposal those votes where he has been given discretion how to vote and abstain in relation to those members who have instructed him to vote against any of the remaining resolutions proposed in the notice of meeting. However, the chairman can hardly be expected to follow these guiding principles where he has proposed an adjournment to facilitate the conduct of the meeting. In such circumstances, he will normally assume that those who have instructed him to vote in favour of the resolutions would vote in favour of the adjournment. If the resolution is passed on a show of hands and would, in view of his discretionary votes be passed on a poll, it would appear that he would not be under any obligation to demand a poll.

Likewise, chairmen nearly always assume that those who have issued instructions to vote in favour of a resolution would wish to vote against any amendment to that resolution. This will normally be sufficient to defeat any amendment. However, listed companies commonly require proposals to amend resolutions to be notified in advance of the meeting. This enables the chairman to take legal advice before the meeting on any proposed amendments and, almost certainly, serves to minimise the number of amendments proposed. In view of the fact that the vast majority of votes at meetings of listed companies are cast by proxy and the fact that a proxy has no real way of knowing how his appointor would have voted, this is perhaps a sensible precaution.

14.15   VALIDITY OF PROXIES

All decisions on the validity of proxies fall to the chairman to decide (*Re Indian Zoedone Co.* (1884) 26 Ch.D. 70). The chairman should not reject a properly executed proxy form merely because he believes it has been obtained by misrepresentation (*Holmes* v. *Jackson* (1957) *The Times* 3 April) or because it contains a minor error, e.g. it describes the meeting as an annual general meeting instead of an extraordinary general meeting (*Oliver* v. *Dalgleish* [1963] 1 W.L.R. 1274).

However, in ruling on the validity of proxies, the chairman is effectively ruling on the validity of votes and is therefore protected by any article which provides that the chairman's ruling on any question of the validity of votes shall be final and conclusive (e.g. reg. 58). In *Wall* v. *London and Northern Assets Corporation (No. 2)* [1899] 1 Ch. 550, on a poll one of the two scrutineers raised objections to the validity of certain proxy votes. Despite the fact that his objections appeared to be well-founded and that the disputed votes would have affected the outcome of the meeting, the chairman ruled that they were valid and declared the resolution carried. The company's articles stated that every vote, whether given in person or by proxy, not disallowed at the meeting would be deemed valid for all purposes. North J. held that the scrutineer (who was also a shareholder) could not object after the event unless it could be shown that there had been fraud.

CHAPTER FIFTEEN

Corporate representatives

15.1 SUMMARY

A company which is a shareholder in another company can appoint a proxy to attend and vote on its behalf. However, the rights of proxies are limited in comparison to the rights of members present in person at a meeting. As a company clearly cannot attend and vote in person, it would be at a disadvantage if it were not given special rights of representation. In order to place a corporation on the same footing as individual members, the Act allows a corporation to appoint a person to act as its representative at company meetings (see para. 15.2).

A corporate representative is entitled to exercise the same powers on behalf of the corporation as the corporation could exercise if it was an individual member, creditor or debenture-holder of the company (see para. 15.3).

The Act prescribes the method of appointment, although articles may allow appointments to be made in other ways (see para. 15.4). There is some debate as to whether a company may appoint more than one representative. The DTI has recently proposed that the Act should be clarified to allow companies to appoint more than one representative (see para. 15.5).

15.2 RIGHT TO APPOINT REPRESENTATIVE

In order to place corporations on the same footing as individual members, s. 375(1)(a) allows a corporation which is a member of another company to appoint a person to act as its representative at any meeting of the company or any meeting of any class of members of the company. This right is also extended to meetings of creditors and debenture-holders where the corporation is a creditor or debenture-holder as the case may be [s. 375(2)]. A person so appointed by a company is usually known as a corporate representative.

For the purposes of s. 375, a corporation includes any body which has separate legal personality (including companies incorporated outside Great Britain), but does not include a corporation sole or a Scottish firm [s. 740].

15.3   RIGHTS OF CORPORATE REPRESENTATIVES

A corporate representative is entitled to exercise the same powers on behalf of the corporation as the corporation could exercise if it was an individual member, creditor or debenture-holder of the company [s. 375(2)]. Thus a corporate representative will, for example, be counted as a member for the purposes of calculating whether there is a quorum (*Re Kelantan Coco Nut Estates Ltd* [1920] W.N. 274). Unlike a proxy, a representative may vote on a show of hands and has a right to speak at any meeting. Unless prevented from doing so under the terms of appointment, a corporate representative may also appoint a proxy. Table 15.1 shows a comparison of the rights of proxies and corporate representatives.

Table 15.1   Comparison of the rights of proxies and corporate representatives

Rights		Proxy	Corporate representative
Counted in quorum		Only if articles specify	Yes
Attend		Yes	Yes
Vote on show of hands		Only if articles specify	Yes
Speak at meetings:	Private Co.	Yes	Yes
	Public Co.	Depends on articles	Yes
Appoint a proxy		No	Yes

15.4   APPOINTMENT OF CORPORATE REPRESENTATIVES

A corporation may appoint a person as its representative by a resolution of its board of directors or other governing body [s. 375(1)]. For these purposes a 'corporation' includes any UK or foreign company and the words 'other governing body' can include a liquidator (*Hillman* v. *Crystal Bowl Amusements and Others* [1973] 1 W.L.R. 162, C.A.).

As far as the Act and Table A are concerned, there is no requirement for a corporation to deposit a form of appointment prior to the meeting. The articles of listed companies normally specify that a representative may be required by the company to produce evidence of his or her authority on admission or at any time during the meeting or in connection with the exercise of any right to vote on a poll (e.g. art. 88 of Whitbread plc). Although Table A does not make specific provision in this regard, a company can and should take steps to ensure that those who attend and vote are eligible to do so. For individual shareholders and creditors, proof of identity will be sufficient for these purposes. Clearly this will not be the case with regard to a corporate representative and it will be necessary in addition to obtain evidence of their appointment.

As a resolution of the directors is required, the evidence should be provided in the form of a certified copy of a board minute. The board resolution can be authenticated (certified) by any director, secretary or other authorised officer of the company by virtue of s. 41. However, it is not uncommon for appointments to be made under seal. In these circumstances, it can be assumed that the appointment was properly authorised even though no evidence of a resolution of the directors has been provided.

The appointment of a representative may relate to a specific meeting or, as is commonly the case, may be of more general application (see **Precedent 15.4**).

15.5   ONE OR MORE REPRESENTATIVES

It is open to debate whether a corporate member can appoint more than one person to act as its representative. Section 375 uses the word 'person' in the singular. However, s. 6 of the Interpretation Act 1978 states that in any Act, unless the contrary intention appears, words in the singular include the plural. The intention of s. 375 is clearly to place a corporation in the same position as an individual shareholder and not in a more advantageous position. If a corporation is allowed to appoint more than one representative, each joint representative would, by virtue of s. 375(2), be 'entitled to exercise the same powers on behalf of the corporation which he represents as the corporation could exercise if it was an individual shareholder, creditor or debenture holder'. There is therefore a school of thought that a corporation is entitled to appoint only one representative to attend, speak and vote on the same occasion. Any other interpretation, it is argued, would enable a corporation which owned only one share to appoint as many people as it could muster as its representatives, each having the right to speak at the meeting, join in a demand for a poll and vote on a show of hands. An individual shareholder could not achieve the same result even if entitled to appoint more than one proxy. His proxies would not have the right to vote on a show of hands or, with regard to meetings of public companies, speak at a meeting. If the word 'person' in s. 375 is not intended to include the plural, all these problems are eliminated at a stroke, and it is hardly surprising that this is the view that most companies adopt.

It may be that in order to rebut the basic principle contained in s. 6 of the Interpretation Act the courts would require stronger evidence of a contrary intention. The restrictive interpretation would prevent a corporation appointing different representatives for different blocks of shares which form part of the same holding as well as preventing the appointment of two or more persons as representatives for the same block of shares. It is clear from s. 372(2)(b) (a member of a private company may only appoint one proxy unless the articles otherwise provide) that the parliamentary draftsmen were aware that the word 'person' in s. 372(1) (and presumably in s. 375) was capable of meaning more than one person.

If, contrary to the generally accepted view, a corporation can appoint more than one person to act as its representative for the same holding, it is submitted that it is far from certain whether the consequences are as dire as some might suggest. If the word 'persons' is substituted for the words 'a person' in s. 375(2) and appropriate grammatical changes are made, it would read 'persons so authorised are entitled to exercise the same powers on behalf of the corporation which they represent as the corporation could exercise if it was an individual shareholder, creditor or debenture holder'. This could be interpreted as meaning that the representatives must act jointly in the exercise of the corporation's rights. The corporation, as a member, is still entitled to only one vote on a show of hands. Which of the representatives should cast that vote in practical terms would be a matter for them to decide between themselves. It is only if s. 375(2) is interpreted as conferring on *each* representative the same rights as an individual member that the problem of more than one vote on a show of hands arises. Articles usually provide that each member shall be entitled to one vote on a show of hands but, in the case of joint holders, that the company shall only accept the vote of the senior joint holder who tenders a vote. No precedent exists on the voting rights of joint holders where the articles are silent on this matter. However, it has been held that in the absence of any provision to the contrary in the articles, joint holders should be counted as a single member for the purposes of demanding a poll (*Cory* v. *Reindeer Steamship Co.* (1915) 31 T.L.R. 530). There is no reason to believe that the courts would not adopt a similar approach with regard to corporate representatives by treating them as one member for the purposes of voting.

15.5.1 DTI consultation

The Department of Trade and Industry has recently issued a consultative document (*Shareholder Communications at the Annual General Meeting*, DTI, April 1996) which discusses a proposal that s. 375 should be amended to allow corporate shareholders to appoint more than one representative to attend general meetings. The proposal has been made for the benefit of nominee companies which would like to be able to appoint their underlying shareholders as corporate representatives rather than as proxies.

CHAPTER SIXTEEN

Voting

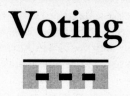

16.1 SUMMARY

Every member of a company has a statutory right to vote unless the articles provide otherwise. Membership is determined by the register of members (see para. 16.3). Articles usually specify the voting rights of members and the circumstances in which those rights are restricted or removed (see paras. 16.4 and 16.5). However, if they are silent on any matter, the presumption must be that the member has the right to vote (see para. 16.2).

Members entitled to attend and vote at general meetings have a statutory right to appoint a proxy to attend and vote in their stead (see Chapter 14). Corporate members have a statutory right to appoint a person as their representative to attend and vote at meetings (see Chapter 15).

Voting is usually conducted by a show of hands, at least initially. On a show of hands, each member and corporate representative is entitled to one vote (see para. 16.6). This method of voting does not reflect the fact that some members may be entitled to more votes than others by virtue of the number of shares they hold. In addition, proxies are not normally entitled to vote on a show of hands. Accordingly, members and proxies are given a statutory right to demand a poll (see para. 16.8). The number of votes each member may cast on a poll, depends on the number and type of shares they hold and the provisions of the articles.

The chairman may be called upon to rule on the validity of votes tendered at the meeting. At common law, the validity of a resolution passed at a general meeting may be challenged if the result would have been different had certain votes not been wrongly counted or excluded. To avoid any uncertainty in this regard, articles usually provide that the chairman's ruling will be final or conclusive (see para. 16.10).

Generally speaking, members are free to exercise their votes as they wish (see para. 16.11).

16.2   RIGHT TO VOTE

The Act provides that every member of a company having a share capital shall have one vote for each share (or each £10 of stock) held and, in the case of a company limited by guarantee, that every member shall have one vote [s. 370(6)]. However, this provision only applies if the articles do not make some other provision. Almost without exception, articles override s. 370(6) by setting out the voting rights of members. This is usually done by an article which sets out members' basic voting rights (e.g. reg. 54 of Table A), which is usually expressed as being subject to other restrictions or enhancements set out in the articles (see paras. 16.4 and 16.5).

16.2.1   Record date for securities admitted to CREST

A company whose shares (or other securities) have been admitted to CREST may specify in the notice a time, not more than 48 hours before the time fixed for the meeting, by which a person must be entered on the relevant register of securities in order to have the right to attend and vote at that meeting (or meeting of the holders of those securities) [Uncertificated Securities Regulations, reg. 34 (see Appendix H)].

Such a provision is necessary because CREST operates on a real-time basis and the dematerialised part of the register could be changing right up to (and even during) the meeting.

As reg. 34 uses the expression 'a time', it is probably safer to give a specific time in the notice rather than to use an expression like 'the close of business' (which could cause some uncertainty if the CREST system is operating unusual hours on that date). Where the meeting is to be held on a Monday or a Tuesday, the notice could specify, say, 11.00 pm on the Sunday preceding the meeting or a time early on Monday morning before any entries will have been made on the register.

It may be preferable to specify a time in the notice which is considerably less than the 48 hour maximum allowed under reg. 34 in order to avoid any problems which could arise if the meeting has to be adjourned for a short time. Provision might also need to be made in the notice for any adjournment which results in the meeting being reconvened more than 48 hours after the time specified in the notice for the original meeting. For a suggested form or wording, see **Precedent 6.5A**.

16.2.2   Statutory restrictions on the right to vote

Where a special resolution is required under s. 174 to make a payment out of capital to redeem shares, the votes attaching to the shares to be redeemed must be ignored. Similarly, when a special resolution is required under s. 164 to confer authority on a company to purchase its own shares in an off-market transaction, the votes attaching to the shares which are to be purchased must be ignored.

The Secretary of State in carrying out an investigation under s. 442 or s. 444 into the ownership of a company's shares may impose voting restrictions on those shares.

He may also do so where a person has been convicted of an offence under s. 210 (disclosure of interests in shares). The court may make a similar order where a person has failed to give the information required following service of a s. 212 notice.

16.3   MEMBERSHIP

The register of members is evidence of membership for the purpose of voting (*Pender* v. *Lushington* (1877) 6 Ch.D. 70). The subscribers to the memorandum of association become members on incorporation and no entry on the register of members is required (*Nichol's Case* (1885) 29 Ch. D 421; see also s. 22(1) of the Companies Act 1985). Every other person who agrees to become a member, and whose name is entered in the register of members, is a member of the company [s. 22(2)]. The holders of preference shares or any other class of shares are members of the company for the purposes of s. 22(2). They will therefore have the same right to vote as the ordinary shareholders unless the articles provide otherwise.

16.3.1   Bearer shares

A bearer share is a share which is evidenced by a certificate which does not show the name of the holder and which can be transferred by the holder to another person by giving up possession. For obvious reasons, the names of the holders of bearer shares are not entered in the register of members. Accordingly, they are not members for the purposes of s. 22 and are not entitled to receive notices of meetings or to vote unless they surrender their certificates and become registered holders before the meeting. The articles of companies which may issue bearer shares usually require notices to be published in national newspapers and provide a simpler procedure to allow the holders of bearer shares to vote at general meetings. This normally involves depositing their certificates at a nominated bank before the meeting.

16.4   RESTRICTIONS ON VOTING IN THE ARTICLES

Companies have considerable discretion in determining who may vote and under what circumstances. The statutory rights of members as stated in s. 370(6) are usually modified by the company's articles. Restrictions on the right to vote can usually be found in articles which deal with the transmission of shares, calls, and the votes of members. The following paragraphs summarise some of the more common examples which may be found in the articles. Other restrictions may be imposed and it will be important to examine the articles carefully in order to ascertain the true position.

16.4.1   Joint holders

Where members are allowed to hold shares jointly, the articles will determine (as between the company and the joint holders) which of the holders shall be entitled to vote in respect of any shares jointly held. Most companies adopt an article similar to reg. 55 of Table A which provides that the vote of the senior who tenders a vote (whether in person or by proxy) shall be accepted to the exclusion of the votes of the other joint holders, seniority being determined by the order in which the names appear in the register of members (see para. 14.12).

Joint holders can circumvent these restrictions by having their holdings split into two or more joint holdings, each having a different person registered as the senior joint holder (*Burns* v. *Siemens Brothers Dynamo Works Ltd* [1919] 1 Ch. 225). By doing so, the joint holders gain an advantage with respect to voting on a show of hands and, in most cases, satisfying the requirements for demanding a poll.

16.4.2   Death and bankruptcy

Most articles restrict the right of a person who becomes entitled to a share in consequence of the death or bankruptcy of a member to attend and vote at any meeting of the company. Under the general law a personal representative is entitled to be registered as the holder of shares in the absence of any provisions to the contrary (*Scott* v. *Frank F. Scott (London) Ltd* [1940] Ch. 794). Reg. 30 of Table A provides that a personal representative or a trustee in bankruptcy may, upon providing satisfactory evidence of appointment, elect to become the holder of the share (by giving notice to that effect) or to have some other person registered as the holder (by executing an instrument of transfer). Reg. 31 further provides that personal representatives or trustees in bankruptcy shall not be entitled to attend or vote until they have been registered as the holders of the share.

If they do not elect to become the holder of the shares or to have them registered in the name of someone else, it is advisable to stop sending them notices of meetings and proxy forms (although it will still be necessary to send copies of the annual report and accounts). If the company continues over a period of time to send notices of meetings and proxy forms to the representatives or trustees, it is possible that it may be estopped from denying their right to attend and vote because it has created a reasonable expectation on their part that they may attend and vote.

Normally the death of a member automatically revokes the appointment by that person of a proxy. However, articles sometimes provide that any proxy appointed by a member who subsequently dies will be valid unless the company receives notice in writing of the death of that member (see art. 87 of Whitbread plc).

Personal representatives are entitled to determine the order in which their names appear on the register of members (*Re Saunders & Co Ltd* [1908] 1 Ch. 415).

A bankrupt who remains registered as a member of the company is entitled to vote at general meetings but must vote in accordance with the directions of his trustee (*Morgan* v. *Gray* [1953] Ch. 83). It should be noted, however, that the company is not bound to ensure that those instructions have been followed.

16.4.3　Mental disorder

Articles usually make provision on the voting rights of members who are suffering from some sort of mental illness. For example, reg. 56 of Table A provides that a member in respect of whom a mental health order has been made by any court having the jurisdiction (whether in the United Kingdom or elsewhere) may vote by his receiver, curator bonis or other person appointed by a court to act in a similar capacity. Evidence of authority must be deposited at the registered office, or at such other place as is specified by the company for the deposit of proxies, not less than 48 hours before the meeting at which the right to vote is to be exercised.

16.4.4　Calls unpaid

Most articles restrict the voting rights of members in respect of shares on which calls or other sums presently payable have not been paid. The scope of the restrictions which can be imposed varies and care should be taken to ensure that the power to disenfranchise is properly exercised. Reg. 65 of the 1948 Table A provides that no *member* shall be entitled to vote at any general meeting unless all calls or other sums presently payable by him in respect of shares have been paid. In other words, a member will be disqualified from voting even if a call on only one of his shares remains unpaid. Article 77 of Whitbread plc imposes similar restrictions but gives the directors discretion not to enforce them. Reg. 57 of the 1985 Table A is far less restrictive in that it merely restricts the right to vote in respect of those shares on which money is still due.

It has been held that where shares in a public company are allotted for consideration other than cash without an independent valuation, the effect of s. 103(6) is to create an immediate liability which, together with an article similar to reg. 65 of the 1948 Table A, has the effect of disenfranchising the allottees (*Re Bradford Investments plc* [1990] B.C.C. 740).

16.4.5　Failure to respond to s. 212 inquiry

Public companies often take power in their articles to disenfranchise shares held by a member who has not replied to a notice served under s. 212 of the Companies Act (c.g. art. 78 of Whitbread plc). The Listing Rules state that where such power is taken in the articles the sanction may not take effect earlier than 14 days after the service of the notice [Listing Rules, para. 13 of Appendix 1 to Chapter 13].

16.4.6　Non-voting or restricted voting shares

Articles usually provide that the company may issue more than one class of shares. Shares will be of a different class if they give their holders different rights from other shares. The rights of the holders are usually set out in the articles. A company may issue shares with restricted or no voting rights. The London Stock Exchange requires listed companies which issue non-voting shares or shares with restricted voting rights to designate them as such [Listing Rules, para. 2 of Appendix 1 to Chapter 13].

16.4.7 Preference shares

Preference shares are perhaps the most common class of shares issued in addition to the ordinary shares. They usually have priority over the ordinary shares with respect to the payment of dividends and repayment of capital on winding up. Articles usually remove the right to vote except where dividends are in arrears. If the shares are listed, the London Stock Exchange requires that they carry voting rights in at least the following circumstances:

- when dividends are more than six months in arrears; and
- on any resolution for the winding up of the company [Listing Rules, para. 4 of Appendix 1 to Chapter 13].

16.5   ENHANCED VOTING RIGHTS

The articles may give members enhanced voting rights in certain circumstances. The most common example is as a protection for a founder member against removal as a director of a private limited company (see **Precedent 16.5**). The method employed in Precedent 16.5 does not create a different class of shares – any member who is a director will be entitled to more votes per share on a resolution to remove him as a director or to amend the article conferring those rights. Normally, the number of extra votes will be sufficient to defeat the other members. If the membership of the company subsequently changes, it may be necessary to amend this type of article to preserve that position. This sort of protection against removal was held to be valid in *Bushell* v. *Faith* [1970] A.C. 1099.

If it is intended to give some but not all members protection against removal as a director, it is necessary to give those members a different class of shares with different voting rights.

16.6   VOTING ON A SHOW OF HANDS

Under the common law, voting is conducted on a show of hands unless there are regulations or enactments to the contrary (*R.* v. *Rector of Birmingham* (1837) 1 Ad. & El. 254). The Act is drafted on the assumption that voting will proceed first by some means other than a poll, and the articles of most companies adopt the common law practice. There is, however, no statutory requirement to do so and a company's articles could provide, for example, that voting shall be conducted by a poll on all substantive resolutions. In the United States, voting at general meetings of listed corporations must be conducted in this way. Some UK listed companies have also adopted this practice recently (e.g. SmithKline Beecham and British Aerospace).

However, most companies adopt provisions similar to reg. 46 of Table A which provides that a resolution put to the vote at a meeting shall be decided on a show of hands unless before, or on, the declaration of the result of the show of hands a poll is duly demanded.

Under the common law, each member present has one vote on a show of hands regardless of any other factors such as the number of shares held (*Re Horbury Bridge Coal, Iron & Waggon Co.* (1879) 11 Ch.D. 109) or the fact that he may be attending in more than one capacity (*Ernest* v. *Loma Gold Mines* [1897] 1 Ch. 1). Articles usually provide that on a show of hands each member or corporate representative shall have one vote (e.g. reg. 54). Articles do not usually allow proxies to vote on a show of hands, particularly where a member may appoint more than one proxy because this would allow a member represented by more than one proxy to cast more votes on a show of hands than a member present in person.

Voting on a show of hands is clearly not a perfect method of ascertaining the sense of the meeting. It does not reflect the different number of votes which members may be entitled to exercise by virtue of their holding, and does not take into account the votes of members who have appointed a proxy. This does not really matter because members and proxies have a statutory right to demand a poll whereupon all these factors are taken into account. The advantage of taking a vote on a show of hands, rather than voting on a poll, is that it is quicker and more convenient. If all the members present support the resolution, there will be little to be gained from calculating the precise number of votes in favour. Even if the vote is not unanimous, it is advantageous to be able to assume that those who oppose it do not have sufficient votes to defeat the resolution on a poll. It is, of course, open to members who oppose the resolution, to demand a poll.

16.7   DECLARATION OF RESULT BY CHAIRMAN

At any meeting at which an extraordinary resolution or a special resolution is submitted to be passed, a declaration by the chairman that the resolution is carried is, unless a poll is demanded, conclusive evidence of the fact without proof of the number or proportion of votes recorded in favour or against the resolution [s. 378(4)]. For the purposes of any legal proceedings, the minutes would be prima facie evidence of the declaration made by the chairman. Other evidence would therefore be admissible to show that they were not an accurate record.

Articles usually extend the operation of s. 378(4) to cover declarations made by the chairman in respect of other types of resolution. Regulation 47 of Table A provides:

> 47. Unless a poll is duly demanded a declaration by the chairman that a resolution has been carried or carried unanimously, or by a particular majority, or lost, or not carried by a particular majority and an entry to that effect in the minutes of the meeting shall be conclusive evidence of the fact without proof of the number or proportion of the votes recorded in favour or against the resolution.

It can be seen that reg. 47 includes an additional requirement that an entry be made in the minutes. This would seem to add nothing to s. 378(4) as the regulation requires both conditions to be true. So, if the chairman had not actually made the declaration recorded in the minutes, evidence to that effect would still be admissible.

A declaration actually made by the chairman in good faith will, under s. 378(4) and articles similar to reg. 47, be conclusive and will prevent the question being reopened in legal proceedings. This is so even where there is evidence that the chairman's declaration was wrong, unless there is evidence of fraud or manifest error. At a meeting where there had been confusion as to whether a special resolution and a resolution to adjourn had been carried it was held that the declaration of the chairman (as recorded in the minutes) precluded any inquiry into the number of shareholders who voted for or against the resolutions and, in the absence of fraud, was conclusive (*Arnot* v. *United African Lands* [1901] 1 Ch. 518). Similarly on a petition for a compulsory winding up the court refused to consider the question whether an extraordinary resolution had been carried by the requisite majority (*Re Hadleigh Castle Gold Mines* [1900] 2 Ch. 419).

A special resolution to reduce a company's capital was confirmed by the court despite the fact that there was evidence that it was carried by the votes of members not qualified to vote. However, no poll was demanded and it was held that the declaration of the chairman could not be reviewed (*Graham's Morocco Co. Ltd Petitioners*, 1932 S.C. 269).

The court will, however, intervene where there has been a manifest error. Where a chairman declared the result of a vote on a show of hands to be 6 in favour and 23 against but went on to declare: 'but there are 200 voting by proxy and I declare the resolution carried as required by Act of Parliament', the court was prepared to intervene (*Re Caratal (New) Mines* [1902] 2 Ch. 498). Buckley J. said:

> I am asked to affirm a proposition that if a chairman makes a declaration and in it actually gives the numbers of votes for and against the resolution, which he is bound to recognise, and adds that there are proxies (which in law he cannot regard), and then declares the result is that the statutory majority has been obtained, although the numbers stated by him show that it has not been obtained, the declaration is conclusive. In my judgement that proposition cannot be supported.

16.8   POLL [s. 373]

A poll is a vote conducted by voting papers rather than by a show of hands. The voting rights of members on a poll will be determined by the articles and, in default, by s. 370(6). Generally speaking, members will be entitled to one vote for each share held. This means that members with larger holdings will have a greater say in the result. It is therefore more democratic than a vote on a show of hands.

Under the common law, where the method of voting used at a meeting is a show of hands, any person who is entitled to vote at a meeting may demand a poll

(*R.* v. *Wimbledon Local Board* (1882) Q.B.D. 459). This common rule applies to company meetings unless the articles provide otherwise. In practice, articles frequently modify the conditions which a person must satisfy in order to make a valid demand for a poll. In a large company with many thousands of shares, it would be ludicrous for one member holding only one share to be allowed to demand a poll without the support of other members. On the other hand, it would not be fair if the conditions imposed made it almost impossible for the members to demand a poll. To ensure that this does not happen, the Act provides that a provision in a company's articles will be void in so far as it excludes the right to demand a poll on any question other that a resolution to elect the chairman of the meeting or to adjourn the meeting [s. 373(1)(a)]. Table A allows a poll to be demanded on both the election of the chairman and a resolution to adjourn, but requires that a poll so demanded be taken immediately [reg. 51].

16.8.1   Valid demand

Under s. 373(1)(b) a demand for a poll must be capable of being made either:

(i) by not less than five members having the right to vote at the meeting; or
(ii) by a member or members representing not less than one-tenth of the total voting rights of all the members having the right to vote at that meeting; or
(iii) by a member or members holding shares in the company conferring a right to vote at the meeting, being shares on which an aggregate sum has been paid up equal to not less than one-tenth of the total sum paid up on all the shares conferring that right.

A provision contained in a company's articles will be void in so far as it would have the effect of making ineffective a demand for a poll in accordance with the above conditions. If an article is deemed to be void under s. 373(1)(b), the common law right to demand a poll will apply whereby one member may make a valid demand (*R.* v. *Wimbledon Local Board* (1882) Q.B.D. 459).

A proxy has the right to demand or join in the demand for a poll, and a demand by a person as proxy for a member is deemed to be the same as a demand by the member [s. 373(2)]. Thus two or more proxies appointed by the same member cannot defeat a requirement that more than one member must join in a demand for a poll. However a person appointed as the proxy for at least five members will always be able to demand a poll.

Articles often relax the conditions for a valid demand. For example, reg. 46 of Table A enables a valid demand to be made by two (rather than five) members having the right to vote at the meeting. It has been held that where the articles state that 'members' holding a certain percentage of shares may demand a poll, a single member holding that percentage may demand a poll (*Siemens Bros. & Co.* v. *Burns* [1918] 2 Ch. 324). In this case the company's articles stated in the definitions section (usually the first article) that words in the singular should be taken to include the plural and vice versa. Most articles track the wording of s. 373(1)(b) to avoid any problems in this regard.

In the absence of any provision to the contrary in the articles, joint holders should be counted as a single member for the purposes of demanding a poll (*Cory* v. *Reindeer Steamship Co.* (1915) 31 T.L.R. 530). Under reg. 46 of Table A only members entitled to vote may join in a demand for a poll. As only the senior of the joint holders present in person or by proxy may vote, only he may join in the demand for a poll.

The chairman has no right to direct that a poll be taken unless it is duly demanded or he is given that right by the articles (*Campbell* v. *Maund* (1836) 5 Ad. & E. 865). Reg 46 of Table A gives the chairman the right to demand a poll. The chairman may also be entitled demand a poll in his capacity as a proxy. Where the chairman has the power to call a poll, he must exercise that power if it is necessary to ascertain the true sense of the meeting. For example, where the chairman has been instructed by proxies to vote in a certain way and those votes, if cast, would produce a different result from the one on the vote on a show of hands, he has a duty to demand a poll (*Second Consolidated Trust Ltd* v. *Ceylon Amalgamated Tea & Rubber Estates Ltd* [1943] 2 All E.R. 567).

A poll may be demanded either on or before the declaration of the result of a show of hands by any person or persons entitled under the articles to do so. This will usually include the chairman and a specified number of members or proxies (as determined by reference to articles, e.g. reg. 46 of Table A).

16.8.2   Special rules

The Act provides that different rules shall apply when deciding whether a valid demand has been made in certain circumstances. For example, at a class meeting held to consider a variation in the rights of that class, any member of that class, whether present in person or by proxy, may demand a poll [s. 125(6)].

In addition, any member, whether present in person or by proxy, may demand a poll in the following circumstances:

- on a special resolution to confer, revoke or renew authority for an off-market purchase of a company's own shares [s. 164(5)];
- on a special resolution to approve a contingent purchase contract relating to the company's own shares [s. 165(2)]; and
- on a special resolution approving payment out of capital for the purchase or redemption of the company's own shares [ss. 174(3) and (5)].

16.8.3   Withdrawal of demand

Reg. 48 of Table A provides that the demand for a poll may, before the poll is taken, be withdrawn but only with the consent of the chairman. It goes on to say that a demand so withdrawn shall not be taken to have invalidated the result of a show of hands declared before the demand was made. Without such a provision it would be necessary to take another vote on a show of hands because, under the common law, the result of a show of hands ceases to have any effect once a valid demand for a poll has been made (*R. v. Cooper* (1870) L.R. 5 Q.B. 457).

If a poll demanded before a vote on a show of hands has been taken is subsequently withdrawn, it is plainly necessary to put the resolution to a vote by a show of hands.

16.8.4   Conduct of poll

Articles usually specify the manner in which the poll is to be conducted or who may determine the manner in which it is to be conducted. Reg. 49 of Table A provides that a poll shall be taken as the chairman directs and that he may appoint scrutineers (who need not be members) and fix a time and place for declaring the result of the poll and that the result of the poll shall be deemed to be the resolution of the meeting at which the poll was demanded.

A poll cannot be taken on a number of resolutions together. In other words, the members must be given an opportunity to vote for or against each resolution separately (*Patent Wood Keg Syndicate* v. *Pearse* [1909] W.N. 164). See, however, *Re R. E. Jones Ltd* (1933) 50 T.L.R. 31 where the members agreed to this procedure being used. This does not mean that separate voting papers must be used for each resolution as long as the voting papers allow members to vote for some resolutions and against others (see **Precedent 16.8A**).

Where the articles allow the chairman to determine the method of taking the poll but also require the personal attendance of the voter or the proxy appointed, the chairman has no right to direct that the poll be taken by voting papers to be returned by members through the post (*McMillan* v. *Le Roi Mining Co. Ltd* [1906] 1 Ch. 331).

Unless the articles specify the length of time for which the poll is to continue, the chairman should not close it so long as votes are still being tendered (*R. v. St Pancras Local Board* (1839) 11 Ad. & El. 356). Where the articles provide that a poll shall be taken 'in such manner as the chairman may direct' the chairman may direct that it be taken immediately (*Re Chillington Iron Co.* (1885) 29 Ch.D. 159). However, where the articles provided for a poll to be taken at a time and place to be fixed by the directors within seven days of the meeting, it was held that the chairman could not direct that a poll be taken immediately (*Re British Flax Producers Co. Ltd* (1889) 60 L.T. 215).

Reg. 51 avoids these problems by providing that a poll shall be taken either forthwith or at such time and place as the chairman directs as long as this is not more than thirty days after the poll is demanded. However, it also provides that a poll demanded on the election of a chairman or on a question of adjournment shall be taken forthwith.

Where articles require a poll to be taken forthwith (or immediately) this means as soon as practicable (*Jackson* v. *Hamlyn* [1953] Ch. 577).

Reg. 51 also provides that a demand for a poll shall not prevent the continuance of a meeting for the transaction of any business other than the question on which the poll was demanded and that, if a poll is demanded before the declaration of the result of a show of hands and the demand is duly withdrawn, the meeting shall continue as if the demand had not been made.

16.8.5   Notice of a poll

A poll taken at a later date is deemed to be a continuance of the original meeting. The original meeting is deemed to have been suspended rather than adjourned and it is not necessary to give any notice unless the articles so require (*Shaw* v. *Tati Concessions Ltd* [1913] 1 Ch. 292). Articles usually contain provisions which specify when notice of a poll must be given. Under Table A, no notice need be given of a poll not taken forthwith if the time and place at which it is to be taken is announced at the meeting at which it is demanded. In any other case at least seven clear days' notice specifying the time and place at which the poll is to be taken must be given to all the members (including those who did not attend the meeting) [reg. 52]. If the chairman does not announce the date and time of the poll at the meeting, it follows that it cannot be held for about eight or nine days and then only if proper notice has been given.

16.8.6   Votes on a poll

Under Table A, every member shall have one vote for every share held on a poll [reg. 54]. Votes may be given either personally or by proxy [reg. 59]. In the case of an equality of votes, whether on a show of hands or on a poll, the chairman shall be entitled to a casting vote in addition to any other vote he may have [reg. 50].

On a poll taken at a meeting of the company or a meeting of any class of members, a member entitled to more than one vote need not, if he votes, use all his votes or cast all the votes he uses in the same way [s. 374].

A member not present at the meeting at which a poll is demanded may vote on a poll taken at a later time or date (*R.* v. *Wimbledon Local Board* (1882) Q.B.D. 459).

16.8.7   Procedure on a poll

The articles will contain regulations governing voting by shareholders on a poll. The regulations governing holders of other securities should be contained in the trust deed constituting the stock. References to articles below should be read accordingly.

Action before the meeting

- Where proxies have given voting instructions, summarise proxy votes in favour of the chairman for each resolution indicating the number of votes for, against and giving the chairman discretion.

- Analyse proxy votes in favour of other persons.
- Appoint scrutineers (usually employees of the company or its solicitors, registrars or auditors) and arrange for their attendance.
- Prepare voting papers (see **Precedents 16.8A** and **16.8B**).
- Draft script for chairman (see **para. 21.5**).
- Ascertain the conditions under which a valid demand may be made and brief chairman accordingly.
- Brief staff and scrutineers.
- Obtain an up-to-date list of members (or if class meeting, members of that class) and annotate which, if any, are not entitled to vote owing to some restriction imposed by the articles.

When a poll is demanded

- If appropriate, chairman may suggest the demand be withdrawn in view of proxy position.
- If not withdrawn, take the names of those making the demand and check against the register of members whether they satisfy the conditions for a valid demand.
- If the demand is not valid or it is withdrawn, the chairman should rule accordingly and proceed with the business:
  (a) if the demand was made before a vote was taken on a show of hands, the chairman should invite members to vote on the resolution in that manner and declare the result accordingly;
  (b) if the demand was made after the chairman had declared the result of the vote on a show of hands, the chairman may proceed to the next item of business although it is preferable to restate the result as previously declared before doing so.

If demand valid

- The chairman should advise the meeting of the validity of the demand.
- The chairman should announce when the poll will be held. Depending on the articles and the nature of the business, this may be:
  (a) immediately;
  (b) at the conclusion of meeting; or
  (c) at a later date.
- If the poll is to be held later (i.e. not immediately), the chairman should proceed to next item of business.

Holding a poll

- The chairman should explain the procedure for the taking of the poll (see chairman's script at **para. 21.5**).
- Issue voting papers to all those entitled to vote (see **Precedents 16.8A** and **16.8B**)

- The chairman should complete voting forms in respect of proxy votes held by him (see **Precedent 16.8C**).
- Collect completed voting cards.
- Check for completeness of each voting paper.
- Where vote is given by proxy:
  (a) check that person voting has been validly appointed as a proxy;
  (b) that proxy has followed member's instruction, if any (see para. 14.11).
- Any voting paper not on the face of it valid should be referred to the scrutineers. In cases of doubt the chairman should be asked to make a ruling (see para. 16.10).
- Verify holdings with list.
- Eliminate votes given by proxy (including those given by the chairman in that capacity) where the member voted in person on the poll.
- If a member has appointed more than one proxy, ensure that the total number of votes cast does not exceed that member's holding. Refer any problems to the chairman.
- Count the votes for and against.
- Prepare a summary of the votes cast for and against in person and by proxy.
- Scrutineers to sign summary and certify the result of the poll.
- Report the result to the chairman.

Declaration of result of poll

- At the meeting:
  (a) If poll directed to be taken at a later time, the meeting to be resumed at the appointed time and the result declared.
  (b) If poll taken immediately, chairman to announce result when other business completed.
- If the resolution is passed, a copy of it may need to be filed at Companies House and, in the case of listed companies, with the Stock Exchange (see para. 7.6).

16.8.8   Result of the poll

The date of a resolution passed on a poll is the date the result of the poll is ascertained (*Holmes* v. *Keyes* [1959] Ch. 199).

Probably the least satisfactory aspect of voting on a poll rather than a show of hands is the fact that the result of the poll is rarely known until after the meeting. The only exception will be where the poll is taken immediately perhaps because the articles require it to be taken forthwith, e.g. a poll on a resolution to adjourn under Table A. This means that the members present will have no idea whether the resolution has been passed or defeated, let alone how many votes were cast for or against. There is no requirement to notify members of the results of the poll. This is the case even with regard to the members who demanded it. This is not to say that the company should refuse to reveal the results of the poll. The result must be recorded in the minutes and any member may, on payment of the prescribed fee, demand a copy of the minutes [s. 383]. In addition, if the resolution is one which must be filed at Companies House, the fact that it has been passed will become a matter of public record (see para. 7.6). Listed companies may also need to send copies of the resolution to the Stock Exchange. The results of a poll may be price-sensitive information and it may therefore be necessary to issue an announcement to the Stock Exchange.

It is good practice for the secretary to notify the members who demanded it the results of the poll and, perhaps, send them a copy of the minutes after they have been signed by the chairman. Some companies advertise the results of the poll in a newspaper.

The company may, if it so desires, inform the members how particular votes were cast. It has been held that this is not confidential information and that the company has a right to the information if the poll is conducted by independent scrutineers (*Haarhaus & Co. GmbH* v. *Law Debenture Trust Corp. plc* [1988] B.C.L.C. 640).

16.9   CHAIRMAN'S CASTING VOTE

The articles may give the chairman a casting vote. Reg. 50 states:

> 50. In the case of an equality of votes, whether on a show of hands or on a poll, the chairman shall be entitled to a casting vote in addition to any other vote he may have.

The circumstances in which it is reasonable for the chairman to use his or her casting vote on a show of hands are fairly limited. In order to ascertain the true sense of the meeting, the chairman should exercise his or her power to demand a poll rather than use the casting vote, particularly where he or she holds proxies on behalf of the members. A casting vote cannot be used to manufacture a tie.

The chairman should use his casting vote in the best interests of the company. This is, of course, a vague duty and it is unlikely that the chairman will be entirely impartial. In Parliament, the Speaker normally uses his or her casting vote to maintain the status quo. This will normally entail voting against the resolution as most resolutions seek to change the status quo.

16.10   OBJECTIONS TO QUALIFICATION OF VOTER

Articles usually provide that objections to the qualification of any voter must be raised at the meeting at which the vote objected to is tendered and that every vote not disallowed at the meeting shall be valid. Objections made in due time are normally required to be referred to the chairman whose decision shall be final and conclusive (e.g. reg. 58). Such provisions are binding and votes not disallowed cannot be challenged afterwards unless the chairman is guilty of fraud or some other misconduct (*Wall* v. *London and Northern Assets Corporation* [1898] 2 Ch. 469).

In *Re Bradford Investments plc* [1990] B.C.C. 740, such an article was held not to operate where a person who was not a member of the company had acted as the self-appointed chairman for the purposes of electing a chairman of the meeting.

16.11 FREEDOM TO EXERCISE VOTING RIGHTS

A member has a right to have any votes tendered accepted at a meeting of the company (*Pender* v. *Lushington* (1877) 6 Ch.D. 70) and a refusal to accept those votes may invalidate the resolution (see however, reg. 58 on the chairman's power to rule on the validity of votes). A member's vote is a property right which as a general rule can be exercised at that person's complete discretion. In casting their votes members are free to use their own judgment and act in their own interests even though those interests might conflict with the general interests of the company (*Carruth* v. *Imperial Chemical Industries Ltd* [1937] A.C. 707).

A director who is also a member can exercise his votes against a resolution which the court has ordered the company to effect (*Northern Counties Securities Ltd* v. *Jackson & Steeple Ltd* [1974] 1 W.L.R. 1133). Walton J. said:

> When a director votes as a director for or against any particular resolution in a directors' meeting he is voting as a person under a fiduciary duty to the company for the proposition that the company should take a certain course of action. When a shareholder is voting for or against a particular resolution he is voting as a person owing no fiduciary duty to the company and who is exercising his own right of property to vote as he thinks fit. The fact that the result of the voting at the meeting will bind the company cannot effect the position that in voting he is voting simply in exercise of his property rights.

A member may contract to vote in a certain way or at the direction of a third party, e.g. under a shareholders' agreement. The obligations under any such contract can be enforced by mandatory injunction provided that the contract is for consideration and the member continues to hold the shares (*Greenhalgh* v. *Mallard* [1943] 2 All E.R. 214). The company (unless it is a party to the contract) need only be concerned that the person tendering the vote is entitled to do so and not with the obligations of that person to vote in a certain way.

A member may vote in favour of a resolution in which he has a financial interest even if he is a director of the company (*North West Transportation Co.* v. *Beatty* (1887) 12 App. Cas. 589 and *East Pant-du United Lead Mining Co. Ltd* v. *Merryweather* (1864) 2 M. & M. 254). This rule is, of course, subject to the requirements of ss. 164 and 174 (see para. 16.2.1).

Members must, however, exercise the power to alter the articles of association in good faith for the benefit of the company as a whole (see para. 18.4).

CHAPTER SEVENTEEN

Adjournment

17.1 SUMMARY

It is not always possible or desirable to transact all the business for which a meeting has been called. In such circumstances, it may be appropriate to adjourn the meeting, i.e. to call a temporary halt to the proceedings with a view to reconvening to deal with the unfinished business at some other time and possibly at some other place.

The Companies Act 1985 has very little to say on the subject of adjournment (see paras. 17.9 and 17.5.1 below). Thus the common law rule that the power to adjourn is vested in the meeting itself will normally apply. The chairman will usually have no power to adjourn unless the articles provide otherwise. The only exceptions to this rule are that the chairman has the power to adjourn to conduct a poll, to restore order, and to facilitate the business of the meeting (see para. 17.3).

Articles usually provide that a meeting will automatically be adjourned if a quorum is not present within a specified period from the time appointed for the start of the meeting (see para. 17.4). A resolution to adjourn must specify when the adjourned meeting is to be held or who is to decide when the meeting is to be held. The articles may specify that a poll may not be demanded on a resolution to adjourn or that a poll on such a resolution must be taken immediately (see para. 17.5).

The company may need to give notice of an adjourned meeting in certain circumstances (see para. 17.6). A proxy submitted for the original meeting will also be valid at any adjournment of that meeting. The articles usually make special provision for the submission of proxies between the original meeting and the adjourned meeting (see para. 17.8).

17.2 POWER TO ADJOURN

Under the common law the right to adjourn any meeting (including a general meeting of a company) is vested in the meeting itself (*Kerr* v. *Wilkie* (1860) 1 L.T. 501). If the chairman, contrary to the wishes of the majority, purports to halt the

144

proceedings before the business of the meeting has been completed, the meeting may elect a new chairman and continue to transact the unfinished business (*Stoughton* v. *Reynolds* (1736) 2 Strange 1044). These basic common law rules are subject to a number of exceptions and are subject to modification by the articles.

17.2.1   Articles

Articles usually contain detailed provisions setting out when, how and by whom general meetings can be adjourned. Regulation 45 of Table A states: 'The chairman may, with the consent of a meeting at which a quorum is present (and shall if so directed by the meeting), adjourn the meeting from time to time and from place to place, but no business shall be transacted at an adjourned meeting other than that business which might properly have been transacted at the meeting had the adjournment not taken place.' This type of article leaves the matter of adjournment in the hands of the meeting. The chairman must adjourn the meeting if a resolution to adjourn is duly passed.

If, however, the articles provide that the chairman may adjourn with the consent of the meeting, and omit the words (and shall if so directed by the meeting), the chairman can refuse to adjourn despite the fact that a resolution to adjourn has been passed by the meeting (*Salisbury Gold Mining Co.* v. *Hathorn* [1897] A.C. 268).

Some articles give the chairman power to adjourn without the consent of the meeting (see art. 65 of Whitbread plc). These modifications are usually made in order to clarify the chairman's inherent powers under the common law (see para. 17.3 below).

17.3   CHAIRMAN'S INHERENT POWER TO ADJOURN

The chairman has inherent power to adjourn to facilitate the conduct of the meeting. The leading authority on this matter is *R.* v. *D'Oyly* (1840) 12 Ad. & El. 139, and the following extract from this case sets out the position:

> Setting aside the inconvenience that might arise if a majority of the parishioners could determine the point of adjournment, we think that the person who presides at the meeting is the proper individual to decide this. It is on him that it devolves, both to preserve order in the meeting, and to regulate the proceedings so as to give all persons entitled a reasonable opportunity of voting. He is to do the acts necessary for those purposes on his own responsibility, and subject to being called upon to answer for his conduct if he has done anything improperly.

17.3.1   To conduct a poll

In *Jackson* v. *Hamlyn* [1953] Ch. 577, it was held that the chairman's inherent power to adjourn to enable a poll to be conducted survived even though the company's articles stated that the chairman could only adjourn with consent of the meeting. In this case the chairman adjourned the meeting in order to take a poll on a resolution to adjourn the meeting. Quite naturally, those seeking to oppose the resolution to adjourn objected. However, it was held that the chairman had power to stand over the proceedings to another time, since some such power had to exist in order to give effect to the provisions as to polls in the articles. Upjohn J. stated that although this standing over was not an adjournment within the meaning of the articles, the chairman had a residual power to take such steps as would in the ordinary usage of the word amount to an adjournment.

Most articles which allow a poll on a resolution to adjourn now state that the poll must be taken immediately (see para. 17.5.1 below).

17.3.2   Room too small

The concept of the chairman's inherent or residual power to adjourn in order to facilitate the conduct of the meeting was taken a step further in *Byng* v. *London Life Association Ltd* [1989] 1 All E.R. 560. The articles of London Life provided that the chairman may, with the consent of any meeting at which a quorum is present (and shall if so directed by the meeting), adjourn the meeting from time to time and from place to place. The venue for an extraordinary general meeting of the company was not large enough to accommodate the members wishing to attend and communications between the main meeting room and overflow facilities proved to be inadequate. As it was impossible to take a proper vote, the chairman purported to adjourn the meeting himself to an alternative venue later on the same day. The Court of Appeal held that the company's articles did not exclude the chairman's inherent power to adjourn the meeting where it proved to be impossible to ascertain the wishes of the meeting. However, the chairman's inherent power was only exercisable for the purpose of giving members a proper opportunity to debate and vote on the resolutions before the meeting. On the facts of this case the chairman's decision to adjourn the meeting to the Café Royal later in the day was held to be unreasonable and declared invalid because it did not achieve this purpose. The chairman did not properly take into account the fact that a significant proportion of the members who had attended the original meeting would not be able to attend the adjourned meeting and would therefore be unable to vote because the company's articles required proxies to be delivered 48 hours before the meeting. Browne-Wilkinson V-C suggested that the correct course of action in this case would have been either to abandon the meeting or to adjourn it *sine die* and to give 21 days' notice of a fresh meeting to be held, say, a month later. He added:

> The chairman's decision will not be declared invalid unless on the facts which he knew or ought to have known he failed to take into account all the relevant factors, took into account irrelevant factors or reached a conclusion which no reasonable chairman, properly directing himself as to his duties, could have reached, i.e. the test is the same as that applicable on judicial review in accordance with the principles of *Associated Provincial Picture Houses Ltd* v. *Wednesbury Corp.* [1947] 2 All E.R. 680.

As a result of this case, some companies have modified their articles to give the chairman complete discretion to adjourn to another time or place without the consent of the meeting where it appears to him that it is likely to be impracticable to hold or continue to hold the meeting because of the number of members or their proxies present or wishing to attend (see art. 65 of Whitbread plc).

17.3.3   Adjournment to restore order

The chairman has a right to adjourn if there is persistent and violent disorder, but for no longer than is necessary to restore order (*John* v. *Rees* [1969] 2 W.L.R. 1294) (see para. 10.4.1).

17.4   AUTOMATIC ADJOURNMENT WHERE NO QUORUM

Articles usually provide that a meeting will be automatically adjourned if a quorum is not present shortly after the time appointed for the commencement of the meeting. Table A provides:

> **41.** If such a quorum is not present within half an hour from the time appointed for the meeting, or if during a meeting such a quorum ceases to be present, the meeting shall stand adjourned to the same day in the next week at the same time and place or to such time and place as the directors may determine.

This type of provision is necessary in order to avoid having to call a new meeting. Strictly speaking there is no meeting unless a quorum is present and therefore nothing to adjourn.

17.5   RESOLUTION TO ADJOURN

A formal resolution to adjourn the meeting must be proposed and passed by the meeting. The resolution can be proposed by the chairman or a member from the floor. For example scripts, see Chairman's scripts, para. 21.6.

A meeting may be adjourned for as short or long a period as is necessary. If the purpose of the adjournment is to restore order, 15 minutes may suffice. On the other hand, an indefinite adjournment may be appropriate where it is not known when the unfinished business can be dealt with, in which case the meeting is said to have been adjourned *sine die*. If an adjournment is not planned or expected, the company is not likely to have made arrangements to reserve a venue for the adjourned meeting. In these circumstances the original meeting may have to be adjourned to a time and place to be determined by the directors.

17.5.1   Poll on a resolution to adjourn

Section 371 provides members with a statutory right to demand a poll. However, s. 373(1) specifically allows a company's articles to exclude that right on a resolution to adjourn. Most articles (including Table A) do not do so but provide that a poll called on a resolution to adjourn shall be taken forthwith (e.g. reg. 51). If the right to demand a poll on a resolution to adjourn is excluded, a dissident minority may be able to obstruct the will of the majority by packing the meeting and proposing a long adjournment to prevent a poll being conducted on a resolution to which they are opposed. Under reg. 46 of Table A, the chairman would be entitled under reg. 46 to demand a poll on the question of adjournment which would be taken forthwith (reg. 51). The chairman would normally cast those proxies which he holds in favour of the substantive resolution against the resolution to adjourn (see paras. 14.14.2 and 21.6).

17.6   NOTICE OF ADJOURNED MEETING

Under the common law, there is no need to give notice of an adjourned meeting if the resolution to adjourn specifies the time and place at which the meeting is to be held. This rule obviously does not apply where the meeting is adjourned indefinitely (*sine die*) or to a time and place to be specified by the chairman or the directors.

Articles usually modify this rule by requiring notice to be given of any meeting which is adjourned for longer than a specified period. Regulation 45 of Table A states:

45. . . . When a meeting is adjourned for fourteen days or more, at least seven days' notice shall be given specifying the time and place of the adjourned meeting and the general nature of the business to be transacted. Otherwise it shall not be necessary to give any such notice.

17.7   POSTPONEMENT

Once a meeting has been duly called, it is not possible to postpone it unless the articles so provide. Thus the meeting should be held at the appointed time and place. If the chairman and the directors fail to attend, the members present can elect their own chairman and proceed to transact the business of the meeting (*Smith* v. *Paringa Mines Ltd* [1906] 2 Ch. 193). If nobody attends or there is no quorum, the meeting will normally be adjourned automatically under the articles (see para. 17.4). The correct procedure is therefore to open the meeting in the normal way and, if appropriate, to adjourn it to another time or place or, if the purpose of the meeting is redundant, to close it after passing a resolution not to put any of the business to a vote.

The immediate adjournment procedure was used by two major listed companies in the 1990s after their AGM venues were destroyed by a terrorist bomb in London. Both companies advertised the change of venue in national newspapers prior to the meeting and posted staff at access points to the original venue to direct members to the new venue. The chairman and sufficient members to form a quorum held a meeting as close as possible to the original venue at the appointed hour and immediately adjourned to the new venue. Had there been any contentious business at either meeting, the safest course of action might have been to adjourn the meeting for longer and to give notice to the members in accordance with the articles.

17.8   ATTENDANCE, VOTING AND PROXIES AT ADJOURNED MEETINGS

A member who was not present at the original meeting may attend and vote at the adjourned meeting (*R. v. D'Oyly* (1840) 12 Ad. & El. 139). An instrument of proxy deposited in time for the original meeting is also valid for any adjournment of that meeting on the basis that the adjourned meeting is merely a continuation of the original meeting (*Scadding* v. *Lorrant* (1851) 3 H.L.C. 418).

Proxies submitted after the deadline for the original meeting are not valid for the adjourned meeting unless the articles make provision to that effect (*McLaren* v. *Thomson* [1917] 2 Ch. 261). Most articles (e.g. reg. 62 of Table A) provide that a proxy lodged at least 48 hours before an adjourned meeting will be valid for that meeting. Instruments of proxy usually state that the appointment is made in respect of the original meeting 'and any adjournment thereof'. An instrument in this form submitted the appropriate number of hours before the adjourned meeting would be valid even though it was not submitted in time for the original meeting.

17.9   DATE OF RESOLUTION PASSED AT AN ADJOURNED MEETING [s. 381]

Where a resolution is passed at an adjourned meeting, it is treated for all purposes as having been passed on the date on which it is in fact passed, and not on any earlier date [s. 381].

17.10   MOTION 'THAT THE CHAIRMAN LEAVE THE CHAIR'

This is a variant of the motion to adjourn. If carried, it takes effect *sine die* (until further notice), or, in the case of a regularly recurring meeting, until the date of the next regular meeting. No amendment of such a motion is possible.

CHAPTER EIGHTEEN

Shareholder remedies

18.1 SUMMARY

Shareholders can enforce their rights as members under the articles against the company and against other members. However, the court will refuse to intervene where the breach is deemed to be a mere internal irregularity which could be cured by the majority simply by following the correct procedure (see para. 18.2).

The proper plaintiff in the case of wrongs done to the company is the company itself. The courts will only allow shareholders to bring actions on behalf of the company against the wrongdoers in very limited circumstances. As a general rule the will of the majority is allowed to prevail (see para. 18.3).

Although a company may alter its articles, the alterations must not discriminate unfairly against the minority (see para. 18.4). Shareholders may apply to the court for relief from conduct which is unfairly prejudicial. The court's remedy in most cases of unfair prejudice will be to order the majority shareholders to purchase the shares of the minority (see para. 18.5).

A member may apply to the court to have the company wound up on just and equitable grounds under s. 122(1)(g) of the Insolvency Act 1986 (see para. 18.6). The court may grant such an order even though the company has been run in accordance with the Act and the company's constitution.

The remedies outlined above tend to be used as a last resort. The Act provides various other means by which shareholders may be able to reconcile their problems (see para. 18.7).

18.2 SECTION 14 CONTRACT

The memorandum and articles, when registered, bind the company and its members to the same extent as if they had been signed and sealed by each member and contained covenants on the part of each member to observe all the provisions of the memorandum and articles [s. 14]. This provision creates a contract (known as the 'section 14 contract') between the company and its members, the terms of which are contained in the memorandum and articles. However, provisions in the memorandum or articles which conflict with the requirements of the Act will not be enforceable because s. 14 is made subject to other provisions of the Act.

The section 14 contract differs in a number of ways from normal contracts. Provision is made in the Act for its terms to be altered by a special majority [see ss. 4 and 9 on the alteration of the memorandum and articles by special resolution]. The consent of all the parties is required to vary normal contracts. And although the courts regard articles as commercial documents which should be construed so as to give them reasonable business efficacy (*Holmes* v. *Keyes* [1959] Ch. 199, 215, per Jenkins LJ), the Court of Appeal has held that terms cannot be implied into the articles in order to do so (*Bratton Seymour Service Co. Ltd* v. *Oxborough* [1992] B.C.L.C. 693).

The company can enforce the section 14 contract against its members (*Hickman's case* [1915] 1 Ch. 881) and the members can enforce it against each other (*Rayfield* v. *Hands* [1960] Ch. 1). However, the circumstances in which members can enforce the contract against the company are limited. Firstly, it has been held on a number of occasions that member may only enforce provisions in the articles which confer rights in their capacity as members. For example, it has been held that a member cannot enforce a provision in the articles that he should be the company's solicitor (*Eley* v. *Positive Government Security Life Assurance Co. Ltd* (1976) 1 Ex. D. 880) but can enforce his right to vote under the articles (*Pender* v. *Lushington* (1877) 6 Ch.D. 70). The application of this rule in cases involving shareholder directors is less certain. In *Browne* v. *La Trinidad* (1887) 37 Ch.D. 1, the Court of Appeal refused to enforce a provision in the company's articles that a member should be a director and should not be removed from office. However, in *Quinn & Axtens Ltd* v. *Salmon* [1909] A.C. 442, the court upheld a provision in the articles giving a director a right to veto certain board resolutions. This is an exceedingly difficult area of the law and one much loved by academic writers. For a more detailed analysis of the issues, see the Law Commission Consultation Paper No. 142, 'Shareholder Remedies'.

The second major exception for shareholders is that they may not be able to bring personal actions for breaches which the courts consider to be mere internal irregularities. As a general rule the courts impose this restriction where it is clear that even if the action is allowed, the majority will still get its own way by following the correct procedures. For example, in *MacDougall* v. *Gardiner* (1875)1 Ch.D. 13, the court refused to declare an adjournment passed on a show of hands invalid simply because the chairman had improperly refused to allow a minority shareholder to demand a poll. Where, however, it is clear that the breach affected the outcome of the meeting, the courts will allow an action to proceed, e.g. where the chairman improperly excluded some votes cast by a proxy in favour of a resolution which would have been passed had they been accepted (*Oliver* v. *Dalgleish* [1963] 1 W.L.R. 1274). The internal irregularities exception is founded on the same principles as the rule in *Foss* v. *Harbottle*, which is dealt with below.

18.3 THE RULE IN *FOSS* v. *HARBOTTLE*

The rule in *Foss* v. *Harbottle* limits the ability of shareholders to bring actions on behalf of the company (derivative actions) for wrongs done to the company. It is founded on two important principles. The first is that where a wrong is done to a company, only the company can take action against the wrongdoers and not individual members (the proper plaintiff principle). The second is that the will of the majority of the members should generally be allowed to prevail in the running of the company's business. Thus in *Foss* v. *Harbottle* (1843) 2 Hare 461 the court refused to intervene in a case brought by minority shareholders who alleged that the directors had misapplied the company's property, because the acts complained of were capable of being confirmed by the members and there was nothing to prevent the company from obtaining redress in its corporate capacity.

The rule in *Foss* v. *Harbottle* is subject to certain important exceptions. These were set out by the Court of Appeal in *Edwards* v. *Halliwell* [1950] 2 All E.R. 1064 and restated in *Prudential Assurance Co Ltd* v. *Newman Industries (No. 2)* [1982] Ch. 204 as follows:

(1) The proper plaintiff in an action in respect of a wrong alleged to be done to a corporation is, prima facie, the corporation.

(2) Where the alleged wrong is a transaction which might be made binding on the corporation and on all its members by a simple majority of the members, no individual member of the corporation is allowed to maintain an action in respect of that matter because, if the majority confirms the transaction, [the question is at an end]; or if the majority challenges the transaction, there is no valid reason why the company should not sue.

(3) There is no room for the operation of the rule if the alleged wrong is ultra vires the corporation, because the majority of members cannot confirm the transaction.

(4) There is also no room for the operation of the rule if the transaction complained of could be validly done or sanctioned only by a special resolution or the like, because a simple majority cannot confirm a transaction which requires the concurrence of a greater majority.

(5) There is an exception to the rule where what has been done amounts to fraud and the wrongdoers are themselves in control of the company.

In *Smith* v. *Croft (No. 2)* [1988] Ch. 114, Knox J. went even further by ruling that a shareholder could not bring a derivative action if an 'independent organ' did not want it to proceed. In this case, the wrongdoer controlled about 66 per cent of the voting rights at general meetings and the plaintiffs about 14 per cent. Another shareholder who was judged by Knox J. to be independent held about 19 per cent and opposed the action being brought. The plaintiff and this independent shareholder were deemed to constitute an independent organ and Knox J. dismissed the action on the basis that this independent organ did not want it to proceed.

Derivative actions are allowed to proceed by virtue of an equitable concession by the Court of Chancery which makes an exception to the general rule that the proper plaintiff in an action seeking redress for a wrong done to the company is the company itself. A member may be prevented from taking advantage of this concession where there is evidence of 'behaviour by the minority shareholder, which, in the eyes of equity, would render it unjust to allow a claim brought by the company at his insistence to succeed' (*Nurcumbe* v. *Nurcombe* [1985] 1 W.L.R. 370, 378, per Browne-Wilkinson LJ).

Where a derivative action is allowed, the plaintiff must bring the action against the wrongdoer for the benefit of the company rather than his own benefit. The company is enjoined as a defendant to ensure that it enforces any judgment.

18.3.1   *Ultra vires* transactions

The exception to the rule in *Foss* v. *Harbottle* that the majority cannot confirm an act which is *ultra vires* the company (i.e. beyond the capacity of the company as prescribed by the objects clause in the memorandum) is now qualified by s.35(3) (as amended by the Companies Act 1989). Section 35(3) allows a company to ratify by special resolution acts of the directors which are ultra vires the company. It follows, however, that ratification by anything less than a special resolution will still be open to challenge under the third limb of the rule in *Foss* v. *Harbottle* as restated in *Prudential Assurance Co. Ltd* v. *Newman Industries (No. 2)*.

Section 35 does not, however, allow a company to ratify transactions which are ultra vires because they are illegal (e.g. the giving of financial assistance for the purpose of acquiring shares in the company contrary to the Act) and a shareholder will be able to bring a derivative action against the wrongdoers on behalf of the company in these circumstances (*Smith* v. *Croft (No. 2)* [1988] Ch. 114).

It should also be noted that s. 35 specifically preserves a shareholder's right to bring a personal action against the company to restrain it from commiting an *ultra vires* act.

18.3.2   Special resolution procedures

Members can bring derivative actions to restrain breaches of special majority procedures (whether they are contained in the Act or the memorandum or articles) and to prevent the company from acting on resolutions passed as a result of such breaches. In *Edwards* v. *Halliwell* [1950] 2 All E.R. 1064, the Court of Appeal declared a decision by a trade union to increase its membership fees invalid because a requirement in its constitution that a two-thirds majority of the members should agree had not been observed.

18.3.3   Fraud on the minority

Shareholders may bring an action on behalf of the company where the wrongdoers have committed a fraud on the minority and control the company. This is an important exception to the rule in *Foss* v. *Harbottle*, for without it the courts would not be able to redress wrongs done by the majority for their own benefit. The word 'fraud' in this context embraces a wider equitable meaning than deceit and in reality will be a wrong done to the company rather than to the minority. Lord Davey defined fraud in *Burland* v. *Earle* [1902] A.C. 83 as embracing all cases where the wrongdoers 'are endeavouring, directly or indirectly, to appropriate to themselves money, property or advantages which belong to the company or in which the other shareholders are entitled to participate'. It should be noted that this definition does not embrace situations where the wrondoers do not benefit. Neither does it cover negligence on the part of the directors. In *Pavlides* v. *Jensen* [1956] Ch. 565, it was held that a shareholder could not sue the directors for negligently selling a mine at a gross undervalue under the fraud on the minority exception to the rule in *Foss* v. *Harbottle*. In these circumstances, the proper course would be for the company to sue the directors and, if the directors sought to prevent it from doing so for their own benefit, this would probably constitute a fraud on the minority.

In order to bring an action under the fraud on the minority exception, a plaintiff must demonstrate that the alleged wrongdoers control the company. This will be relatively simple where they own a majority of shares conferring voting rights and it is not necessary in such circumstances to demonstrate that the wrongdoers have refused to institute proceedings (*Mason* v. *Harris* (1879)11 Ch.D. 97). However, it has also been held to be sufficient to demonstrate that the wrongdoers secured with their votes the passing of a resolution that the company would not institute proceedings, even if they did not own a majority of the voting shares (*Cook* v. *Deeks* [1916] 1 A.C. 554). In *Prudential Assurance Co. Ltd* v. *Newman Industries (No. 2)* [1982] Ch. 204 it was observed as a dictum that control 'embraces a wide spectrum extending from an overall absolute majority of votes at one end to a majority of votes at the other made up of those likely to be cast by the delinquent himself plus those voting with him as a result of influence or apathy'.

It seems that a shareholder may also be prevented from bringing a derivative action under the fraud on the minority exception where an independent organ of the company does not want it to proceed (*Smith* v. *Croft (No. 2)* [1988] Ch. 114) (see para. 18.3).

18.4   ALTERATION OF ARTICLES

The Act allows a company to alter its articles by special resolution [s. 9]. However, this power must be exercised by the members in good faith for the benefit of the company as a whole (*Allen* v. *Gold Reefs of West Africa Ltd* [1900] 1 Ch. 656). In *Greenhalgh* v. *Ardene Cinemas Ltd* [1951] Ch. 286, Evershed MR said [at p. 291]:

> Certain principles, I think, can be safely stated as emerging from the authorities. In the first place, I think it is now plain that 'bona fide for the benefit of the company as a whole' means not two things but one thing. It means that the shareholder must proceed upon what, in his honest opinion, is

for the benefit of the company as a whole. The second thing is that the phrase 'the company as a whole' does not . . . mean the company as a commercial entity, distinct from the corporators: it means the corporators as a general body. That is to say, the case may be taken of an individual hypothetical member and it may be asked whether what is proposed is, in the honest opinion of those who voted in its favour, for that person's benefit. I think that the matter can, in practice, be more accurately and precisely stated by looking at the converse and saying that a special resolution of this kind would be liable to be impeached if the effect of it were to discriminate between the majority shareholders and the minority shareholders.

If the shareholders have acted honestly in what they believe to be the best interests of the company, the court is unlikely to interfere unless there are no reasonable grounds upon which such a decision could be reached (*Shuttleworth* v. *Cox Bros. & Co.* [1927] 2 K.B. 9).

Thus an alteration which gave rights of expropriation at a fair value with respect to the shares of any member who was in business as a competitor was held to be valid even though such a member existed at the time of the alteration (*Sidebottom* v. *Kershaw, Leese & Co.* [1920] 1 Ch. 154 (C.A.)). However, an alteration which enabled the majority to require any member (other than a named member) to transfer his shares was held to be invalid (*Dafen Tinplate Co. Ltd* v. *Llanelly Steel Co. Ltd* [1920] 2 Ch. 124).

An alteration giving the company a lien over fully paid shares for other debts of the holder was held to be valid because it was capable of applying to all fully paid shares, even though at the time the change only adversely affected the position of those who sought to challenge it (*Allen* v. *Gold Reefs of West Africa Ltd* [1900] 1 Ch. 656).

It should be noted that even though minority shareholders might not succeed under this heading, they could be entitled to relief under the unfair prejudice provision of s. 459.

18.5 UNFAIRLY PREJUDICIAL CONDUCT

A member may petition the court for relief from unfairly prejudicial conduct under s. 459. This statutory remedy has removed many of the obstacles which prevented minority shareholders seeking relief under the common law. Any member may petition the court and there is no need to satisfy the requirements of the rule in *Foss* v. *Harbottle*. Relief under s. 459 is not restricted to minority shareholders although the court will not grant a majority shareholder a remedy if he can easily rid himself of the prejudice by using his majority shareholding (*Re Baltic Real Estate (No. 2)* [1993] B.C.L.C. 246).

Where the court is satisfied that a petition is well founded, it may make any order it thinks fit for giving relief in respect of the matters complained of [s. 461]. The order may, for example:

- regulate the conduct of the company's affairs in the future;
- require the company to refrain from doing or continuing an act complained of or to do an act which the petitioner has complained it has omitted to do;
- authorise civil proceedings to be brought in the name of and on behalf of the company by such person or persons and on such terms as the court may direct;
- provide for the purchase of the shares of any members of the company by other members or by the company itself and in the case of a purchase by the company itself, the reduction of the company's capital accordingly; or
- alter the company's memorandum or articles of association.

The court may grant a petitioner relief under s. 459 where the company's affairs are being or have been conducted in a manner which is unfairly prejudicial to the interests of its members generally or some of the members (including at least the petitioner), or where any actual or proposed act or omission of the company (including an act or omission on its behalf) is or would be so prejudicial [s. 459(1)]. According to a study undertaken on behalf of the Law Commission for its Consultation Paper No. 142 'Shareholder Remedies', the conduct which most petitioners (over 67 per cent) complain of in cases brought under this heading is exclusion from the management of the company. It also reported that nearly 70 per cent of petitioners seek an order for the purchase of their shares.

For an example of a case on exclusion from the company's management, see *Re Saul D. Harrison & Sons plc* [1995] 1 B.C.L.C. 14, where the court held that the petitioner had a legitimate expectation of being able to participate in the management of the company and that his exclusion could therefore be unfairly prejudicial to his interests.

Relief has been given under s. 459 where a member who held 60 per cent of a company's shares voted to allot himself new shares to increase his holding to 96 per cent and reduce the holding of a minority shareholder from 40 to 4 per cent (*Re D R Chemicals* (1989) 5 B.C.C. 39). In this case the majority shareholder was ordered to purchase the minority shareholder's 40 per cent holding at a price to be fixed by independent valuation.

Cases have also been brought successfully where there has been a deliberate diversion of the company's business by those in control to another business owned by them, e.g. *Re London School of Electronics Ltd* [1986] Ch. 211.

In *Re a Company (No. 002612 of 1984)* (1986) 2 B.C.C. 99, it was held that a director's remuneration of over £350,000 over a 14 month period was plainly in excess of anything he had earned and was therefore unfairly prejudicial to the petitioner's interests. Excessive remuneration is often linked to the non-payment of dividends. However, the non-payment of dividends could in itself be unfairly prejudicial even though it affects all shareholders equally.

The courts are reluctant to grant relief for mismanagement (*Re Elingdata Ltd* [1991] B.C.L.C. 959). However, in *Re Macro (Ipswich) Ltd* [1994] 2 B.C.L.C. 354, Arden J. granted relief for specific acts of mismanagement which had been repeated over many years and which the respondent had failed to prevent or rectify. A failure to provide information about how the company is being run to a person who has a right to be consulted on major decisions could constitute unfairly prejudicial conduct (*Re R. A. Noble* [1983] B.C.L.C. 273).

The Secretary of State may also petition the court for an order if it appears to him that a company's affairs are being or have been conducted in a manner which is unfairly prejudicial to the interests of its members or some of its members [s. 460].

18.6   JUST AND EQUITABLE WINDING UP

Shareholders may in certain circumstances petition the court under s. 122(1)(g) of the Insolvency Act 1986 for an order that the company be wound up on just and equitable grounds. Indeed, this is often pleaded in the alternative to a petition under s. 459. The House of Lords has held that a member may petition for a winding up on just and equitable grounds if he can show any circumstances affecting him in his relations with the company or with the other shareholders for which winding up is a just and equitable solution (*Ebrahimi* v. *Westbourne Galleries Ltd* [1973] A.C. 360). In that case, the plaintiff and a Mr Nazar formed a private company in 1958 to carry on a business, which they had previously done as equal partners, and were appointed the company's first directors. Shortly afterwards, N's son also became a director and between them N and his son controlled the majority of votes at general meetings. All the company's profits were distributed as directors' remuneration and no dividends were ever paid. At a general meeting in 1969, Mr Ebrahimi was removed as a director by N and his son in accordance with the statutory procedures. Mr Ebrahimi petitioned the court to wind up the company on just and equitable grounds and this was allowed even though N and his son had acted in strict accordance with the Act and the company's articles. Lord Wilberforce explained the meaning of 'just and equitable' by saying:

> The words are a recognition of the fact that a limited company is more than a mere legal entity, with a personality in law of its own: that there is room in company law for recognition of the fact that behind it, or amongst it, there are individuals, with rights, expectations and obligations inter se which are not necessarily submerged in the company structure . . . The just and equitable provision does not . . . entitle one party to disregard the obligations he assumes by entering a company, nor the court to dispense him from it. It does, as equity always does, enable the court to subject the exercise of legal rights to equitable considerations; considerations, that is, of a personal character arising between one individual and another, which may make it unjust, or inequitable, to insist on legal rights, or to exercise them in a particular way.

The courts have also wound up companies under this heading where:

- it was no longer possible to achieve the purpose for which the company was formed (see *Re Eastern Telegraph Co. Ltd* [1974] 2 All E.R. 104);
- the company was promoted fraudulently (*Re Thomas Edward Brinsmead & Sons* [1897] 1 Ch. 406, C.A.); and

- the company was formed for an illegal purpose (*Re International Securities Corporation Ltd* (1908) 24 T.L.R. 837).

18.7 OTHER REMEDIES

The remedies outlined above tend to be used as a last resort. The Act provides various other means by which shareholders may be able to reconcile their problems. For example:

- The Secretary of State has wide powers to appoint inspectors to investigate matters, which may have been drawn to his attention by a member [ss. 431 and 442]. He may as a result of these investigations apply for a winding up order under the Insolvency Act 1986 or for an order under Part XVII of the Companies Act 1985.
- Shareholders representing not less than 10 per cent of the total voting rights may require the directors to convene an extraordinary general meeting [s. 368] (see para. 5.6).
- Any member may apply to the Secretary of State for an order calling a general meeting where the company is in default of its obligation to hold an annual general meeting [s. 377] (see para. 5.4).
- If for any reason it is impracticable to call a meeting of a company, or to conduct the meeting in the manner prescribed by the articles or the Act, any member may apply to the court for an order calling a meeting [s. 371] (see para. 5.5).
- Members may require the company to circulate notice of any resolution intended to be moved at the next annual general meeting and require the company to circulate a statement in connection with any business to be proposed at a general meeting [s. 376] (see para. 6.10).
- Any member of a private company which has passed an elective resolution to dispense with holding annual general meetings or to dispense with the laying of accounts or with the annual appointment of auditors may require the company to hold an annual general meeting, to lay the accounts at a general meeting or to convene a meeting to propose that the auditors' appointment be brought to an end [ss. 366A, 253 and 393] (see Chapter 24).
- Members who did not vote in favour of the change have a right to apply to the court to cancel a special resolution to alter the company's objects clause or any provision in the memorandum which could have been contained in the articles and for which no provision is made for alteration [ss. 5 and 17] (see para. 1.4.1).
- Resolutions varying the rights attached to any class of shares may be challenged by members holding not less than 15 per cent of that class who did not vote in favour of the change [s. 127].
- A special resolution passed by a private company approving the giving of financial assistance for the purchase of a company's own shares may be challenged in the court by shareholders holding at least 10 per cent by nominal value of the company's issued share capital who did not vote in favour of the resolution [s. 157].

- Shareholders may by ordinary resolution remove a director before the expiry of his term of office [s. 303] (see para. 20.11).
- Application may be made to the court for an order that the company's register of members be rectified [s. 359].
- Members have various rights of inspection of company registers and the right to copies of them on payment of a fee.
- A company must send shareholders copies of its annual accounts which must be prepared in accordance with the requirements of the Act [s. 238 and Part VII].

Organising
general meetings

CHAPTER NINETEEN

Organising annual general meetings

19.1 SUMMARY

This chapter deals with some of the more practical aspects of organising the annual general meeting, although many of the issues raised will also be relevant to other meetings. It includes a checklist for organising annual general meetings which has been cross-referenced to the relevant paragraphs and chapters in this book (see para. 19.2).

Choosing the right venue for the annual general meeting is an important task. The directors may determine where the meeting will be held, provided that the location is not chosen with the deliberate intention of excluding certain members (see para. 19.3). The venue should be large enough to accommodate all the members wishing to attend. If not, the meeting will have to be adjourned. The secretary will therefore need to estimate the attendance (see para. 19.4) and be prepared to advise the chairman on the action to take in the event that the room is too small (see para. 17.3.2).

If members are forced to sit in an uncomfortable environment, they tend to become irritable. Naturally, this is the last thing the chairman and the directors need. Attention to 'hygiene factors' is therefore important. However, shareholders may also complain if the venue is too extravagant, particularly if profits and dividends are down. The final decision will almost always be a compromise between cost, quality, size and availability (see para. 19.5).

19.2 CROSS-REFERENCED CHECKLIST FOR ANNUAL GENERAL MEETING

Preliminary questions for private limited companies (Ltd)

If an elective resolution to dispense with the AGM is in force, it is not necessary to hold an AGM unless a member has demanded that one be held. If no such elective resolution in force, consider passing one (see para. 24.3).

Date of meeting

□ Calculate last date on which AGM must be held (see para. 2.2).
□ Choose a suitable date or range of possible dates before the last date (see para. 2.4).
□ Consult chairman and other relevant personnel.
□ Fix date and inform relevant company personnel and external advisers, e.g. registrars, auditors, solicitor, broker, PR consultants, etc.
□ If a suitable opportunity arrives, inform the members.

Venue

□ Calculate likely attendance (see para. 19.4).
□ Determine other requirements, e.g. location, cost, etc. (see para. 19.5).
□ Select and visit venues.
□ Assess suitability for security purposes (see para. 10.3).
□ Provisionally book preferred venue.
□ Consult chairman.
□ If agrees, book venue and obtain confirmation of booking.
□ Agree and sign contract.
□ Obtain map of venue location.

Other arrangements

□ Make arrangements for:
   (a) catering (if required);
   (b) security and stewards (see paras. 10.2 and 10.3);
   (c) audio visual equipment (if required);
   (d) printing of signs for AGM;
   (e) stage design (if required); and
   (f) display stands (if required).

Planning the AGM mailing

□ Calculate last date notice must be sent out bearing in mind:
   (a) notice requirements (see para. 6.2);
   (b) requirement for clear days' notice (see para. 6.2.1);
   (c) date notice deemed given if sent by post (see para. 6.3).
□ Set date for posting of notice and accounts (preferably before last date).
□ If not possible within time limit, consider obtaining consent to short notice (see para. 6.8), otherwise change date of AGM.
□ Set dates for:
   (a) final draft of notice;
   (b) finalisation of accounts and audit;
   (c) board meeting to approve accounts and convene AGM (see note 1);

(d) printing of notice, proxies, circulars, accounts and other documents to go with AGM mailing (inform printers);

(e) printing of address labels (if by registrar, inform registrar stating where they are to be sent).

Drafting the notice, etc.

☐ Prepare rough outline of business to be transacted at the AGM (see para. 2.3).

☐ Check whether special notice is required for any resolution, e.g. to remove director or auditors or appoint director over age of 70, etc. (see para. 6.9).

☐ Check type of resolution required for each item of business to be proposed (see Chapter 7 and Appendix E).

☐ Calculate which (if any) of the directors must retire by rotation (see para. 20.10).

☐ Confirm that auditors are willing to be reappointed (see para. 20.3).

☐ Check whether s. 80 authority needs to be renewed (see para. 2.3).

☐ Include any valid resolutions or statements submitted by members (see para. 6.10).

☐ Draft the AGM notice and circular (see Chapter 20).

☐ Draft proxy cards (if required) (see Chapter 14).

☐ Draft attendance cards (if required) (see para. 10.2).

☐ Draft invitation to members to submit questions in advance (if required) (see para. 9.4.3).

Board meeting to convene AGM and approve results and dividends

☐ Prepare and send out notice of board meeting including resolutions:

(a) to approve report and accounts;

(b) to authorise signing of accounts and reports;

(c) to recommend a dividend;

(d) to convene the annual general meeting and approve business (see para. 5.2);

(e) to authorise secretary to sign and send out notices, etc.;

(f) to recommend the appointment of any directors (if articles require) (see para. 26.2.3 on reg. 76 of Table A);

(g) to approve the release of the preliminary announcement (plc only);

(h) nominate director to act as chairman of the general meeting in the absence of the chairman of the board (see para. 8.2).

☐ Immediately before meeting check again for any valid members' resolutions and include in papers put to the board (see para. 6.10).

☐ Hold board meeting and pass resolutions.

☐ If problems convening meeting, see para. 5.3.

Immediately after the board meeting

☐ Preliminary announcement to Stock Exchange (listed plc only).

☐ Balance sheet signed by two directors.

☐ Directors' report signed by director or secretary.
☐ Auditors' report signed by auditors.
☐ Notice signed and dated by secretary (see para. 5.2.2).
☐ Calculate required number of copies of:
    (a) annual report (including extra copies);
    (b) notice and proxy cards.
☐ Final proofs of report and accounts, notice, proxy cards, etc. sent to printers with instructions as to numbers required.
☐ Directors and relevant employees notified of close period for dealings in company's shares (listed plc only).

Sending out the notice

☐ Send report and accounts, notice, etc. to persons entitled to receive them (see para. 6.6).
☐ File annual report at Companies House.
☐ Send report and accounts to others on mailing list kept for that purpose.

Miscellaneous matters

☐ Make arrangements for the payment of the dividend (if approved).
☐ Calculate cut off day and time for valid proxies (see para. 14.7) and, if necessary, inform registrars.
☐ Monitor proxies received.
☐ If necessary, contact major shareholders to encourage submission of proxies.
☐ At appropriate time on cut off date for proxies prepare:
    (a) schedule of proxies appointed for the use of staff on the registration desk;
    (b) schedule of voting instructions for the chairman where the member has appointed chairman as proxy.
☐ Print voting cards and poll cards.

Preparations immediately before AGM

☐ Arrange for proposers and seconders of resolutions (as required).
☐ Finalise chairman's agenda/script (see Chapter 21).
☐ Prepare AGM briefing document (see Appendix G).
☐ Brief chairman.
☐ Rehearse questions and answers.
☐ Allocate following duties to staff and brief accordingly:
    (a) registration (see para. 10.2);
    (b) poll (see para. 16.8);
    (c) roving microphone;
    (d) stewards (see para. 10.2).
☐ Brief staff and rehearse AGM.

☐ Confirm final arrangements with venue, security staff, registrars, etc.
☐ Make arrangements for the release of an announcement to Stock Exchange if it is intended to reveal price-sensitive information at the meeting (listed plc only) (see para. 19.3).

Day of the annual general meeting

☐ Things to take to the meeting:
  (a) directors' service contracts (see para. 2.5);
  (b) register of directors' interests (see para. 2.5);
  (c) spare copies of report and accounts and notice;
  (d) chairman's agenda/script (plus copies for other directors who are to propose resolutions);
  (e) questions and answers script;
  (f) memorandum and articles of association (indexed);
  (g) consolidated version of Companies Act 1985 (as amended);
  (h) a textbook on the law and procedures of meetings;
  (i) summary of proxies received;
  (j) original proxy forms and summary sheets;
  (k) register of members (usually supplied by registrar);
  (l) attendance sheets for: members, proxies and corporate representatives, and guests (see para. 9.3);
  (m) notepads, pens and pencils;
  (n) name plates for top table and name badges;
  (o) reserved seats signs;
  (p) voting cards;
  (q) calculator with printed roll for counting votes on a poll;
  (r) telephone numbers of crucial participants.
☐ Final briefing of staff.
☐ Check that quorum present (see Chapter 13).
☐ Open meeting and conduct business (see Chapters 8 to 17)
☐ Record proceedings.

After the meeting

☐   Prepare minutes for signature by chairman (see Chapter 25).
☐   Take actions required as a result of resolutions passed.
☐   Authorise payment of dividend.
☐   Copy resolutions filed at Companies House (see para. 7.6).
☐   Copy resolutions sent to Stock Exchange (listed plc only) (see paras. 7.2 to 7.4).
☐   Respond to shareholder questions raised at meeting.
☐   Review the organisation of the annual general meeting.
☐   Book venue for next AGM.

Note 1:   The London Stock Exchange used to require listed companies to inform it of the date of the board meeting at which the results are finalised. This requirement was removed in June 1996. Listed companies must, however, notify the Exchange without delay after board approval of details regarding its preliminary results and any dividends to be proposed or paid [Listing Rules, para. 12.40].

19.3   LOCATION

Generally speaking, it is preferable to hold general meetings in the country of incorporation. However, the directors may determine the place at which the meeting shall be held and in the absence of fraud, their decision cannot be challenged (*Martin* v. *Walker* (1918) 145 L.T.J 377). The directors must therefore exercise their power to select the place of the meeting in the best interests of the company. If they call a meeting to be held at a time and place which clearly restricts the ability of a significant proportion of the members to attend, their decision is liable to challenge (*Cannon* v. *Trask* (1875) L.R. 20 Eq. 669).

These rules would not prevent a UK registered company holding a meeting outside the UK if, for example, the majority of its shareholders were resident in the country in which the meeting was to be held or that country was the most convenient for the members as a whole.

19.4   ESTIMATING ATTENDANCE

Ideally, the venue for the annual general meeting should be capable of accommodating all the members. For private companies with few members, this is relatively easy to arrange. However, for companies with thousands of shareholders, this is impractical. Instead, the company secretary must try to predict the number of members and guests likely to attend. The starting point for this exercise will normally be to examine attendance levels in previous years. If the number of shareholders has increased or decreased significantly, appropriate adjustments should be made.

If the company's results are not as good as expected or it has been the subject of adverse press comment, the proportion of members attending will probably be higher than normal. Numbers will also increase where food and drink or company products are offered for the first time (numbers might not fall quite so dramatically when any such perks are withdrawn – shareholders may attend to complain about the change of policy!). An interesting or unusual venue may also attract more shareholders as may a change of venue to a location which is more accessible.

Whatever figure is finally arrived at, most company secretaries tend to add a little extra for contingency purposes. Preparations for the meeting are usually made a long way in advance and it is sensible to assume that something may subsequently happen which brings shareholders out of the woodwork.

Some companies conduct surveys of a sample of their members in order to estimate the likely attendance. Others ask shareholders to return a reply-paid card if they intend to attend. Such methods usually produce a forecast which is higher than the actual attendance on the day. To this extent, they can be a useful guide to the absolute maximum attendance, particularly for a newly listed company or one which has recently undergone a major change in its shareholder base, e.g. following a takeover or merger. One company which asked all its members to return a card indicating whether they would attend, found that the responses tallied almost exactly with the actual attendance. However, on analysing the responses, it found that this was because the number of shareholders who said they would attend but did not turn up was practically the same as the number who did not respond but attended on the day. Having determined the maximum number of members for which accommodation will be provided, additional provision should be made for guests, the press and employees.

19.5   OTHER FACTORS INFLUENCING THE CHOICE OF VENUE

19.5.1   Availability

The meeting room(s) should be booked to allow for the possibility that the meeting may take longer than usual. Nothing is likely to annoy shareholders more than for discussion to be cut short because the room has to be vacated. Indeed, the chairman may find it necessary to adjourn the meeting in such circumstances which could be both costly and embarrassing.

19.5.2   Terms of licence

Are any of the terms and conditions (e.g. dress codes, security checks, etc.) inconsistent with the company's legal obligations to admit all shareholders (see para. 9.2).

19.5.3   Location

Is the venue easily accessible by road and public transport? Does it have access for the disabled? The ICSA's *Guide to best practice for Annual General Meetings* recommends that the venue for the AGM should be accessible by attendees who have disabilities, and have facilities for those with poor hearing.

19.5.4   Room size

If the estimate of the maximum attendance differs greatly from the normal attendance, the prime consideration may be flexibility. A large room capable of being partitioned off may be preferable to separate overspill rooms which need to be connected by audio visual links to the main meeting room. Such links are expensive to establish and can be unreliable. See also art. 60 of Whitbread plc on 'overflow general meetings'.

It is usual for the board of directors to be seated with the chairman, facing the shareholders. Indeed, this is one of the best practice points in ICSA's *Guide to best practice for Annual General Meetings*. The company secretary will usually be seated on the top table or platform next to the chairman. Some companies also invite the audit partner and the company's solicitor to sit on the top table. Some venues have built in stage areas and platforms. However, the seating capacity of the room may depend on the size of the platform required. It is becoming increasingly common for each director to have a VDU which is used to display either the running order or information compiled by researchers which may be helpful for the directors when answering questions from shareholders.

What seating arrangement can be provided comfortably (e.g. theatre, classroom, or boardroom styles)? Can areas be cordoned off for different classes of members or non-members? Are the chairs comfortable? Will everyone be able to see the top table?

19.5.5   Noise levels

Is the room relatively sound proof? The most common problem with hotel conference rooms is that they are situated next to the kitchen and catering staff are rarely responsive to requests to keep the noise down. Partitioned rooms should be avoided unless you can afford to reserve the whole suite as it is inevitable that the adjoining section(s) will be hired by people whose activities involve making a great deal of noise. Although the partitions themselves are normally soundproof, the connecting doors frequently are not. Also check whether the owners intend to do any building, decorating or repairs around the date of the meeting. The venue may look wonderful when you book it. Things could be very different on the day. If possible, obtain a written undertaking that no such work will be carried out on the day.

19.5.6   Lighting, heating and air conditioning

Can the lights, heating and air conditioning be adjusted easily and are they sufficient? In many hotels access to these controls is restricted. If so, will a member of staff be available to make the necessary adjustments?

19.5.7   Registration and help desks

In addition to the main meeting room, the venue will need to have a suitable area for registration. Ideally, it should not be possible for members to gain entry to the meeting room without passing through the registration area. If there is more than one entrance to the venue, the registration area might need to be located immediately outside the entrance to the meeting room. The size of the registration area will depend on the number of members and guests that are expected to attend. It may need to be large enough to accommodate several registration desks and the company's registrars may need power points if they plan to access the register of members using portable computers.

Many companies (particularly those whose private shareholders are potential or captive customers) provide shareholder help desks to deal with members' enquiries about dividends and other issues relating to their personal holdings. Retail and

Table 19.1   Venue checklist

	Main room	Overspill	Registration area	Refreshments area
Date or preferred date of meeting				
Venue required from time . . . . date				
Venue required until time . . . . date				
Maximum capacity				
Top table / platform area				
Rear/front projection				
Exhibition area				
Question points				
Help desks				
Lighting				
Power points				
Noise level				
Heat / AirCon				
Sound facilities				
Audio visual links				

Other matters

- Security
- Noticeboards / signposts
- Cloakrooms
- Telephone/fax facilities
- Boardroom
- Licence agreement
- Staff
- Catering requirements
- Cost

consumer companies often establish separate help desks to deal with enquiries which are customer related. By doing so, members are less likely to raise these issues at the meeting and the chairman is able to refer a member who asks such a question to the relevant help desk. If these facilities are to be provided, they will need to be situated in a prominent position, perhaps in the foyer.

19.5.8   Security

Space may be needed for security checks to be carried out prior to registration to prevent members bringing into the meeting any objects which could be used to disrupt the meeting, e.g. banners, missiles, whistles, klaxons, etc. (see further paras. 10.2 and 10.3).

19.5.9   Sound system and recordings

Sound equipment may be necessary for the top table and for taking questions from the floor. It should be remembered that the acoustics in an empty room are far better than when it is full of people. If the meeting room is large, it will almost certainly be necessary to provide some means of amplification for shareholders who wish to ask questions during the meeting. This can be done using roving microphones. However, the modern trend is to provide one or more fixed microphones from which shareholders must put questions. If microphones are not provided, the chairman should be briefed to repeat or summarise the questions put from the floor before answering them.

Can the proceedings (including questions from the floor) be recorded so that a transcript can be made? The company may also wish to make arrangements for the proceedings to be videotaped, possibly for transmission on a late night TV slot which shareholders who were unable to attend can record and watch at their leisure.

19.5.10   Refreshments

Where refreshments are provided, they are normally served in a separate room so that the catering staff do not disrupt the meeting. Exhibitions of company products or its history could also be placed in this area or in the main meeting room.

19.5.11   Directors' room

The availability of a meeting or preparation room for the directors and an office for the meeting organisers should also be considered.

19.5.12   Staff

Are the staff friendly and helpful? Do they have sufficient staff to cater for your needs? Will a manager be on hand throughout the meeting to handle any problems?

19.5.13   Toilets and cloakroom facilities

The standard of both the ladies and the gents toilets should be checked. Is there anywhere for members to leave their coats and baggage?

19.5.14   Other facilities

The availability of telephone, fax and photocopying facilities may be important to the organisers and to members attending.

19.6 ENHANCING THE ANNUAL GENERAL MEETING

The purpose of holding annual general meetings has been called into question on a number of occasions in recent years. This has already resulted in legislation to allow private companies (but not public companies) to dispense with holding annual general meetings, albeit with safeguards which allow any member to require one to be held (see Chapter 24). However, questions have even been raised with regard to listed companies. For example, a committee established by the DTI (under the chairmanship of Paul Myners of Gartmore plc) to examine ways of improving relationships between the City and industry reported that virtually all participants in its consultation exercise viewed the AGM as an expensive waste of time and money [Myners Report, 'Developing a Winning Partnership', 1995]. Several factors have probably caused antipathy towards the annual general meeting to increase in recent years. Probably the most important of these is the increase in the proportion of shares held by institutional investors and the fact that they do not normally attend the meeting, preferring instead to vote by proxy. One of the consequences of this is that the views of private investors who attend the meeting are not as important as they once were. In addition, single issue pressure groups tend to dominate (and often disrupt) the proceedings of an increasing number of listed companies. This can make it difficult for other shareholders to raise legitimate questions and has undoubtedly caused some shareholders to decide not to attend future meetings. Other reasons given include the constraints imposed by the Stock Exchange's rules and guidance on the release of price-sensitive information which limit the directors' ability to give meaningful answers to questions raised by shareholders at the meeting (see further para. 19.8). Companies often complain about the standard of debate and questions raised by shareholders at the meeting. Directors, in particular, complain that many shareholders only seem to attend to complain about the directors' remuneration packages.

Some commentators have called for the annual general meeting to be abolished and for companies to be allowed to conduct postal ballots (see, for example, 'The Annual General Meeting – time to go?' by David Hewit, *Chartered Secretary*, June 1996). One listed company has even included in its articles a provision which would allow it to conduct postal ballots should the law ever be changed. For the moment, however, the weight of opinion still seems to be in favour of maintaining the annual general meeting primarily as a method of holding the directors accountable for their management of the company. Company secretaries often cite as evidence of the AGM's effectiveness the fact that, when taking decisions on certain policies and strategies, directors consider whether they would feel comfortable justifying their proposed course of action at the annual general meeting. The attendance of the press at listed companies' annual general meetings also means that directors are held accountable to a wider audience.

In an attempt to stimulate new initiatives to enhance the annual general meeting, the Cadbury Committee observed that: 'If too many Annual General Meetings are at present an opportunity missed, this is because shareholders do not make the most of them and, in some cases, boards do not encourage them to do so' [Cadbury Report, para. 6.7]. Proposals to enhance the annual general meeting have subsequently been made by the DTI in its consultation document *Shareholder Communications at the Annual General Meeting,* the Myners Committee in its report 'Developing a Winning Partnership' and ICSA in its *Guide to best practice for Annual General Meetings.* The DTI consultation included proposals to make it easier for shareholders to submit resolutions for consideration at annual general meetings and for investors who hold their shares through nominee companies to attend and participate in the proceedings (see paras. 6.10.8 and 15.5.1).

The Myners Report made the following recommendations with a view to enhancing the attractiveness of annual general meetings to institutional investors:

- companies should encourage shareholders to submit questions in advance of the meeting;
- questions specific to an individual, and not of general interest, should be referred to the relevant director for response after the meeting, with the answers subsequently made available to any interested shareholder;
- companies should provide an updated trading statement at the meeting; and
- operational managers should make a presentation at the meeting and be available to answer questions from shareholders outside the formal meeting.

ICSA's *Guide to best practice for Annual General Meetings* endorsed these recommendations and made several others (see para. 19.7).

19.7   ICSA'S *GUIDE TO BEST PRACTICE FOR ANNUAL GENERAL MEETINGS*

In April 1996, the DTI issued a consultative document, *Shareholder Communications at the Annual General Meeting,* which asked whether shareholders should have a statutory right to have resolutions circulated free of charge and/or to ask questions at the AGM. It also addressed concerns raised by the NAPF that investors who hold shares through nominee companies are often unable to participate fully in the proceedings at general meetings because corporate shareholders can only appoint one corporate representative. The proposed solutions were either to allow corporate shareholders to appoint more than one representative or to give proxies a right to speak and vote on a show of hands at all company meetings.

The consultative document suggested that some of these issues could be dealt with by the development of best practice by companies and, with the encouragement of the DTI, the Institute of Chartered Secretaries and Administrators ('ICSA') established a working patty to produce a best practice guide. The working party's recommendations were published in September 1996 in a *Guide to best practice for Annual General Meetings,* and were endorsed by the National Association of Pension Funds, the Association of British Insurers and ProShare. The DTI said it 'very much welcomes the development' but stated that it was continuing to evaluate responses to the consultation document and that an announcement would be made as soon as the next steps had been decided on.

The *Guide* contains the following 24 elements of best practice which listed companies in particular are encouraged to adopt.

Shareholder communications

1. All companies should engage in an active policy of communication with all shareholders (not just institutional shareholders).
2. Companies should arrange for all correspondence from shareholders to receive a full reply from the company secretary, the chairman, another director, or another designated senior executive. If the inquiry concerns a particular product or plant, it may be appropriate for the response to come from the head of the business division or a particular factory.
3. Communications with members should be handled appropriately but sensitively in accordance with the company's shareholder communications policy.

AGM notice and venue

4. The AGM notice and accompanying documents should be circulated at least 20 working days (excluding weekends and Bank Holidays) in advance of the meeting.
5. The venue for the AGM should be accessible by attendees who have disabilities, and have facilities for those with poor hearing.
6. Companies should ensure that each item of special business included in the notice is accompanied by a full and detailed explanation.

Directors

7. Directors standing for re-election to the board should be named in the notice and form of proxy.
8. A brief description should be given of the directors standing for election or re-election, including their ages; their relevant experience (not merely a list of other directorships they hold); the dates that they were first appointed to the board; and details of any board committees to which they belong.
9. The articles of association of public companies should require all the directors to be subject to retirement by rotation.
10. Wherever possible, all directors should attend the AGM, and be seated with the chairman, facing the shareholders.
11. The chairman should not propose his own election or re-election or propose any resolution in which he has an interest.

AGM procedure

12. The resolution to receive or adopt the accounts should be separate from any resolution to approve the payment of the final dividend recommended by the directors. It is also best practice generally to deal with different items of business by way of separate resolutions.

13. Boards should provide adequate time for shareholder questions at AGMs.
14. When moving the adoption or receipt of the accounts, the chairman should allow shareholders to raise questions on any item concerning the company's past performance, its results and its intended future performance. However, the directors need not answer questions which are irrelevant to the company or its business or which could result in the release of commercially sensitive information. Nor should they disclose price-sensitive information unless it can be done in compliance with the Stock Exchange Listing Rules and guidance regarding the release of price-sensitive information.
15. Before each resolution is put to the vote, the chairman should explain again its effect and purpose. If necessary, he should elaborate on the information previously provided in the explanatory circular which accompanied the notice of the meeting. He should also invite shareholders to speak.
16. Where concerns are raised by a shareholder at the AGM and the chairman undertakes to consider them, the shareholder should subsequently be sent a full report of the action taken.

Shareholder resolutions

17. Unless the company agrees at the outset to absorb all the costs of circulation, shareholder resolutions requisitioned under section 376 of the CA 1985 should automatically be accompanied (in any notice) by another resolution giving shareholders the opportunity to decide whether the company or the requisitionists should bear the relevant costs. If the directors feel that any particular case does not justify the adoption of such a resolution, they should, however, be free to recommend a vote against it.

Polls and proxies

18. When announcing the decision on a poll, the total number of votes cast in favour of, and against, the resolution should be disclosed.
19. If the chairman informs shareholders of the number of proxy votes he holds for and against a resolution, he should clarify that those numbers refer to the proxies lodged with the company (or its registrars) before the meeting and that some of those who lodged proxies may be present and, having heard the debate, could decide to vote differently.
20. All proxy forms should be worded to allow the proxy to vote or abstain on business which may come before the meeting which was not included in the notice, e.g. amendments and formal motions.

Enhancing the AGM

21. All companies should provide an updated trading statement at their AGM unless they have recently published a scheduled financial statement.

22. At least one of the executive directors of the company should make an oral report at the AGM, on those areas of the company's operations for which he or she has responsibility.

Disorder

23. All companies should establish procedures for dealing with disturbances at their AGMs.

Proxies' right to speak

24. All chairmen should seek the consent of the meeting to proxies speaking and participating in the debate.

These 24 best practice points are supplemented by several other suggestions and recommendations intended to stimulate discussion and further development by companies. For example, the *Guide* suggests that:

- Companies could announce the date of their next AGM much earlier (possibly at the preceding AGM or with the interim report).
- Companies should avoid holding their AGM on the same day as others in the same sector in order to facilitate the attendance of shareholders with holdings across a particular sector.
- When a particular issue has been raised by a shareholder, the chairman can assist the flow of the meeting by inviting other shareholders who wish to speak on the same subject to do so at that time.
- Companies should invite shareholders to submit questions in advance, but should not use this practice as a method of manipulating the AGM by requiring written notice of questions or to replace spontaneity at the AGM.
- If a valid demand for a poll is made, shareholders should be issued with poll cards immediately and asked to deposit them as they leave the meeting. This allows the meeting to continue with the minimum of disruption and enables shareholders who have to leave the meeting early to vote on the poll.
- Although shareholders should be able to rely on the integrity of the company's registrars or auditors (properly supervised by and answerable to the company secretary, acting in that regard on behalf of the shareholders generally and not the directors) to act as scrutineers, one of the proposers of the poll could be invited to act as a joint scrutineer.

The *Guide* reports that the working party rejected proposals that shareholders should be sent a summary of the points raised at the AGM. It noted that copies of the minutes are available to shareholders and that the most important resolutions are filed at Companies House. Shareholders could also rely on the press to report anything controversial.

A guide to best practice for Annual General Meetings can be obtained from ICSA, 16 Park Crescent, London W1N 4AH (Tel: 0171 580 4741; Fax: 0171 323 1132), price £15.00.

19.8 PRICE SENSITIVE INFORMATION

The London Stock Exchange places a general obligation on listed companies to disclose certain information which is not public knowledge and which may lead to a substantial movement in the price of their securities [Listing Rules, paras. 9.1–10]. Such information must always be given to the market as a whole, by an announcement to the Company Announcements Office. Companies are free to use additional media, but selective disclosure of price-sensitive information, is not acceptable to the Exchange.

The London Stock Exchange has published additional guidance on the application of these rules, *Guidance on the dissemination of price sensitive information (1995),* which includes the following guidance on the disclosure of information at general meetings:

13.   If a meeting is to be held (e.g. with shareholders, analysts or a press conference), companies should consider in advance how to respond to questions designed to elicit price sensitive information. If it is planned to disclose price sensitive information, the information should not be given at the meeting before it is announced to the market.

17.   Companies are encouraged to make the most of existing opportunities for communicating with investors. In particular, through the annual report, or through the Chairman's address to the annual general meeting, a company may reinforce its corporate messages in non-technical terms and provide indicators of its future direction. While the annual general meeting is an opportunity for investors to discuss with directors issues affecting the company, arrangements must be made for any price sensitive information that is to be discussed at the meeting to be included in an announcement to the Company Announcements Office at or before the time of the meeting.

In order to comply with these requirements, it is usual for listed companies to release a copy of the chairman's address to the Company Announcements Office immediately prior to the meeting, particularly where this includes updated trading information. However, this will not be necessary if the chairman merely recites information already published in the annual report. It may also be necessary to release the text of any presentations to be made by operational managers. As these presentations and the chairman's address will be prepared before the meeting, it will be possible to take advice from the company's brokers on the action which should be taken where there is any doubt, although most listed companies probably err on the side of disclosure these days.

The Stock Exchange rules prohibiting the selective disclosure of price sensitive information also tend to inhibit the ability of directors to answer shareholders' questions at general meetings. Indeed, they are sometimes accused of emasculating one of the main purposes of the annual general meeting, i.e. to enable shareholders to hold the directors accountable for their stewardship of the company. This feeling may have arisen amongst shareholders because directors often cite the Stock Exchange rules as the reason for not answering certain questions even though commercial confidentiality is probably the primary reason. The acid test in this regard is whether the directors would have answered the question if there were no rules on the release of price sensitive information. In most cases, the answer would probably be no.

Nevertheless, the Stock Exchange rules do impose limitations on listed companies which are predisposed towards answering shareholders' questions. And the main problem which the directors will face is trying to decide at the meeting whether the answer which they would like to give would constitute price sensitive information. The Stock Exchange's *Guidance on the dissemination of price sensitive information* stresses that it is impossible to define any theoretical percentage movement in a share price which will make a piece of information price sensitive, and points out that no such definition is included in the insider dealing provisions of the Criminal Justice Act 1993. Favourable information could, for example, result in a static share price in a generally falling market. However, the *Guidance* goes on to say:

5.   However, price sensitive information will potentially have a significant effect on a company's share price. In particular, a company should be able to assess whether an event or information known to the company would have a significant effect on future reported earnings per share, pre-tax profits, borrowings or other potential determinants of the company's share price. The Listing Rules indicate many events which have to be announced to the market because they may be price sensitive. These include dividend announcements, board appointments or departures, profit warnings, share dealings by directors or substantial shareholders, acquisitions and disposals above a certain size, annual and interim results, preliminary results, rights issues and other offers of securities. In other areas judgement will necessarily be required . . .

6.   Companies should remember that, in general, the more specific the information, the greater the risk of it being price sensitive. For that reason, companies should not disclose significant data, least of all financial information such as sales and profit figures, to selected groups rather than to the market as a whole. *Even within these constraints, there is plenty of scope for companies to hold useful dialogue with their shareholders and other interested parties about their prospects, business environment and strategy (particularly in the medium and long term)* [our emphasis].

If in the course of a general meeting, previously unpublished price sensitive information is inadvertently disclosed, it will of course be necessary to make an announcement to the Company Announcements Office as soon as possible. It should also be noted that the decisions taken at general meetings will in themselves be price sensitive information and that the Stock Exchange therefore requires the results of meetings to be announced immediately after the meeting has closed [Listing Rules, para. 9.31].

CHAPTER TWENTY

Dealing with common items of business

20.1 SUMMARY

In this chapter we outline the procedures for dealing with some of the more common items of business at the annual general meeting as follows:

- report and accounts (see para. 20.2);
- auditors
  - (a) appointment (see para. 20.3),
  - (b) resignation (see para. 20.4),
  - (c) removal (see para. 20.5),
  - (d) remuneration (see para. 20.6);
- dividends (see para. 20.7);
- directors
  - (a) appointment (see para. 20.8),
  - (b) age limits (see para. 20.9),
  - (c) retirement by rotation (see para. 20.10),
  - (d) removal (see para. 20.11).

20.2 REPORT AND ACCOUNTS [s. 241]

The Act requires the directors of every limited company to prepare:

- a balance sheet and a profit and loss account [s. 226];
- if it is a parent company, group accounts [s. 227];
- a directors' report [s. 234].

The auditors must also make a report on the accounts to the shareholders which forms part of the statutory accounts and reports ('the accounts'), copies of which must be filed with Companies House and sent to the members. The directors must also lay the accounts before the company in general meeting [s. 241] unless the company is a private company and has passed an elective resolution to dispense with this requirement.

20.2.1   Approved by the board of directors

The annual accounts and the directors' report must be approved by the board of directors. The balance sheet must be signed on behalf of the board by one director [s. 233(1)] and the directors' report by the secretary or a director [s. 234A(1)]. The auditors' report must state the name of the auditors and be signed by them [s. 236]. The copy of the accounts and reports delivered to the registrar must be an original signed copy. The copy laid before a general meeting and any copies which are circulated, published or issued need not be signed but must state the name(s) of the person(s) who signed the balance sheet and the directors' report on behalf of the board and the name(s) of the auditors who signed the auditors' report.

The order of events for approving and signing the accounts is therefore as follows:

- Board of directors approves the accounts (including, if a parent company, its own profit and loss accounts (which is not usually published)) and the directors' report.
- Board of directors authorises a director to sign the balance sheet and the secretary or a director to sign the directors' report.
- The director authorised by the board signs the balance sheet and the secretary (or director) signs the directors' report in at least three copies of the accounts.
- The auditors then sign the auditors' report in all three copies, retaining one copy and returning the other two to the company.
- One of the returned copies is delivered to the Registrar of Companies.
- The other is kept in the company's archives.

20.2.2   Time for laying and delivering [s. 244]

The accounts must be laid before a general meeting and delivered to the Registrar within 10 months of the accounting reference date (year end) for private companies or seven months in the case of a public company [s. 244]. They do not need to be laid before they are delivered to the registrar. A company carrying on business or having interests outside the United Kingdom can claim a three month extension by giving notice in the prescribed form before the end of the period allowed for laying and delivering accounts. However, the period allowed for laying and delivering accounts is reduced for newly incorporated companies whose first accounts cover more than 12 months [s. 244(2)].

If the accounts are not laid within the appropriate period, every person who immediately before the end of that period was a director of the company is guilty of an offence and liable to a fine and, for continued contravention, to a daily default fine [s. 241(2)].

Listed companies are required by the London Stock Exchange to publish their accounts within six months of their year end [Listing Rules, para. 12.42(e)]. Publication is not the same as laying or delivering for which the usual time limits apply. Publication is the act of issuing, publishing or sending out copies of the accounts. If a listed company needs to obtain an extension to the period for laying and delivering accounts from the Registrar, it will also need to obtain an extension from the Stock Exchange of the time limit for publication.

20.2.3   Persons entitled to receive copies of the accounts and reports [s. 238]

A copy of the report and accounts must be sent at least 21 days before the date of the meeting at which they are to be laid to:

- every member of the company;
- every debenture holder; and
- every person who is entitled to receive notice of general meetings [s. 238(1)].

Copies need not be sent:

- to a member or debenture holder who is not entitled to receive notice and whose address is not known to the company, e.g. the holder of bearer shares (if the member is entitled to receive notice but the company does not know the current address, the copy should be sent to the last known address);
- to joint holders of shares or debentures who are not entitled to receive notice of general meetings unless none of the joint holders are entitled to receive notice, in which case at least one of the joint holders must be sent a copy.

Where copies of the accounts are sent out over a period of days (perhaps because of the sheer scale of the operation) they are deemed to have been sent on the last of those days [s. 238(6)]. If copies of the accounts and reports are not sent in accordance with the above requirements, the company and every officer of it in default is liable to a fine [s. 238(5)]. However, if copies of the accounts and reports are sent less than 21 days before the date of the meeting at which they are to be laid, they will be deemed to have been duly sent if it is so agreed by all the members entitled to attend and vote at the meeting [s. 238(4)] (see **Precedent 20.2A**). This is useful if the general meeting at which accounts are to be laid is held at short notice. It is arguable that accounts can be laid in accordance with s. 241 even though copies have not been sent to the members in compliance with the requirements of s. 238. There is no direct link between s. 241 and s. 238. The only consequence of a failure to comply with s. 238 would therefore seem to be that the directors may be liable to a fine.

20.2.4   Notice

The notice of the general meeting must refer to the laying of the report and accounts unless they are to be laid at an annual general meeting and the articles specify this as ordinary business (see reg. 52 of the 1948 Act Table A). There is little to commend this practice and it is only likely to confuse shareholders. In practice, most companies set out the nature of the business in the normal manner (see **Precedent 20.2B**).

In its *Guide to best practice for Annual General Meetings,* ICSA recommends that the resolution to receive or adopt the accounts should be separate from any resolution to approve the payment of the final dividend recommended by the directors.

20.2.5   Procedure at the meeting

Although s. 241 does not require a resolution to receive the report and accounts to be put to the meeting, it is normal to do so as this is the standard way of putting business before the meeting. The requirement to lay the accounts is merely a device to ensure that the shareholders are given an opportunity to question the directors about the company's performance and their own performance as managers of the company. The wording of the resolution should not give the impression that the accounts and reports can be rejected or that they will not be laid if the members vote against the resolution. If a resolution on the accounts is lost, it does not alter the fact that they are the company's report and accounts or that they have been laid in accordance with s. 241. Such a resolution would normally be interpreted as a vote of no confidence in the directors although they would not be under any obligation to resign. Thus words such as 'to approve the accounts and reports . . .' and 'to lay the accounts and reports . . .' should be avoided.

ICSA's *Guide to best practice for Annual General Meetings* recommends that when moving the adoption or receipt of the accounts, the chairman should allow shareholders to raise questions on any item concerning the company's past performance, its results and its intended future performance. However, the directors need not answer questions which are irrelevant to the company or its business or which could result in the release of commercially sensitive information. Nor should they disclose price-sensitive information unless it can be done in compliance with the Stock Exchange Listing Rules and guidance regarding the release of price-sensitive information. ICSA also recommends that where concerns are raised by a shareholder at the AGM and the chairman undertakes to consider them, the shareholder should subsequently be sent a full report of the action taken.

20.2.6   Accounts not ready for AGM

It is not uncommon (particularly for private companies with a 31 March year end and a December AGM) for the accounts not to be ready in time for the AGM. One of the most frequently asked questions in these circumstances is whether it is possible to send out notices and hold the AGM and then to adjourn it until such time as the accounts have been prepared and sent to shareholders. If the adjourned meeting is held within the period for laying of accounts, there would seem to be no objection to this procedure. The requirement is merely that the accounts be laid at a general meeting within the period. If however the adjourned meeting is held after the end of the 10 month period for laying and delivering, an offence will still be committed under s. 241. Laying the accounts in this manner would, however, prevent the accumulation of any daily default fines.

20.3   APPOINTMENT OF AUDITORS

A company must appoint auditors unless it is:
- a dormant company and has resolved not to appoint auditors [ss. 250 and 388A]; or
- is exempt as a small company from the audit requirements and not therefore obliged to appoint auditors [ss. 249A and 388A].

20.3.1   Appointment of first auditors

The directors may appoint the first auditors at any time before the first general meeting at which accounts are laid (see **Precedent 20.3A**). Auditors so appointed hold office until the conclusion of that meeting [s. 385(3)]. If the directors fail to appoint the first auditors, the company in general meeting may do so [s. 385(4)] (see **Precedent 20.3B**).

20.3.2   Periodic reappointment

Auditors must be appointed or reappointed at each general meeting at which accounts are laid [s. 385(2)]. Special procedures apply where an auditor other than the retiring auditor is being appointed (see para. 20.5). A private company which already has auditors, may elect to dispense with their annual reappointment (see further para. 24.5). A private company which has passed an elective resolution to dispense with the laying of accounts but not to dispense with the annual appointment of auditors, must appoint or reappoint auditors at a general meeting of the company held within 28 days from the date the accounts are sent to members [s. 385A].

  The resolution to appoint auditors is usually passed after the accounts have been laid. The resolution should be worded so that the auditors are appointed until the conclusion of the next general meeting at which accounts are laid rather than for a year or until the conclusion of the next annual general meeting (see **Precedent 20.3C**).

20.3.3   Appointment by Secretary of State in default

If no auditors are appointed, reappointed or deemed to be reappointed before the end of the time for appointing auditors, the company must notify the Secretary of State who may appoint a person to fill the vacancy [s. 387] and fix their remuneration [s. 390A].

20.3.4   Casual vacancies

A casual vacancy can be caused by the resignation or death of the existing auditor. The board of directors, or the company in general meeting, may fill any such vacancy in the office of auditor [s. 388(1)]. Special notice must be given of a resolution at a general meeting to fill a casual vacancy or to reappoint as auditor a person appointed by the directors to fill a casual vacancy [s. 388(3)]. On receipt of notice of the intended resolution the company must send a copy of it to the person proposed to be appointed and, if the casual vacancy was caused by the resignation of an auditor, to the auditor who resigned. See also para. 20.4 on the resignation of auditors.

20.4   RESIGNATION OF AUDITORS

Auditors may resign by notice in writing to the registered office of the company. The notice should be accompanied by a statement as to whether there are any circumstances connected with the resignation which the auditors consider should be brought to the attention of the members or creditors. Within 14 days of receipt of the notice of resignation, the company must file a copy of the notice (but not of the accompanying statement) with Companies House [s. 392].

20.4.1   Statement of circumstances

If the auditors' statement is of circumstances which they consider should be brought to the attention of the members or creditors:

- the company must within 14 days of the deposit of the statement send a copy of it to every person entitled under s. 238 to receive copies of the report and accounts or make an application to the court to restrain publication of that statement (in which case it must notify the auditors of the application);
- unless they are notified within 21 days of the deposit that an application to restrain publication has been made, the auditors must within a further 7 days (i.e. 28 days from the date of deposit) file a copy of the statement with Companies House [s. 394].

20.4.2   Rights of resigning auditors

Where the resigning auditors have deposited with their notice of resignation a statement which they consider should be brought to the attention of the members, they may deposit a requisition calling on the directors to convene an extraordinary general meeting of the company to consider their explanation of the circumstances and require the company to circulate to the members a written statement of the circumstances before that meeting [s. 392A]. They may, alternatively, require the company to circulate such a statement before any general meeting at which their term of office would have expired or at which it is proposed to fill the vacancy caused by their resignation. The company must comply with any such demands and state in the notice of meeting (possibly as a note) that representations have been made by the auditors. The resigning auditors have a right to receive notice of and to attend and speak at any such meetings. If their representations are received too late for circulation, the auditors may require them to be read out at the meeting. The court may relieve the company of these obligations if it is satisfied that the auditors are using the provisions to secure needless publicity for defamatory matter.

20.5   REMOVAL OF AUDITORS [s. 391]

Where a company wishes to change its auditors, it is normal to approach the existing auditors to see whether they would be prepared to resign voluntarily or agree not to seek reappointment. If they agree to resign, the procedures outlined above would apply and the directors could then appoint new auditors to fill the resulting casual vacancy. If the change is not urgent, it can be left until the next general meeting at which accounts are laid. If the matter is urgent, perhaps because relations have irretrievably broken down, a general meeting could be held to remove the auditors by ordinary resolution before the end of their term of office.

Special notice (see para. 6.9) must be given by a member to the company of any resolution to remove the auditors or to appoint as auditors anyone other than the retiring auditors [s. 391]. On receipt of notice of the intended resolution, the company must immediately send a copy of it to the proposed auditors and the existing auditors.

The existing auditors may make written representations to the company on the proposed resolution and demand that they be circulated to the members. The company must comply with such a demand and state in the notice of meeting that representations have been made. If the representations are not circulated to the members for any reason, the auditors may require them to be read out at the meeting. The court may relieve the company of these obligations if it is satisfied that the auditors are using the provisions to secure needless publicity for defamatory matter. As the auditors who are to be removed or not reappointed will still be the company's auditors at the start of the general meeting, they are entitled to receive notice, attend and speak at the meeting.

An auditor who is removed or not reappointed must also make a statement as to the circumstances connected with his removal or non-reappointment [s. 394].

20.6   REMUNERATION OF AUDITORS

The remuneration of auditors appointed by the directors as first auditors or to fill a casual vacancy must be fixed by the directors [s. 390A(2)].

The remuneration of auditors appointed (or re-appointed) by the company in general meeting must be fixed by the company in general meeting or in such manner as the company in general meeting may determine [s. 390A(1)]. This is usually done at the same time as the appointment by authorising the directors to fix their remuneration (see **Precedent 20.3C**). Although s. 390A(1) envisages that the members themselves may fix the auditors' remuneration, this is not normally a practicable solution. It will normally be difficult to predict the precise audit costs for the forthcoming year, not least because remuneration is deemed to include any of the auditors' expenses paid by the company [s. 390A(4)]. The members may only be able to fix the remuneration after the audit is complete. This is unlikely to be acceptable to the auditors as the members may not approve payment of the full amount.

While an elective resolution dispensing with the annual appointment of auditors is in force under s 386, the auditors are deemed to have been re-appointed each year. This can cause complications with respect to the method of fixing their remuneration (see further para. 24.5.3).

20.7   DIVIDENDS

20.7.1   Final dividends

Most articles provide that dividends must be declared by an ordinary resolution of the company in general meeting and that no dividend may exceed the amount recommended by the directors (e.g. reg. 102). Dividends can only be paid out of profits available for distribution (ss. 263 to 281). In recommending the final dividend, the directors must ensure that there are sufficient funds available for distribution. It is therefore usual for the resolution to declare a dividend to be proposed at the general meeting at which the accounts have been laid. The wording of the notice with regard to dividends is usually very simple mainly because the detailed information regarding dividends must be included in the directors' report (see **Precedents 20.7A to C**).

ICSA's *Guide to best practice for Annual General Meetings* recommends that the resolution to receive or adopt the accounts should be separate from any resolution to approve the payment of the final dividend recommended by the directors.

20.7.2   Interim dividends

Articles usually also provide that the directors may pay interim dividends without reference to the members (e.g. reg. 103) (see **Precedent 20.7D**). The directors should not pay a dividend unless it is clear that sufficient funds are available for distribution as dividends.

20.8   APPOINTMENT OF DIRECTORS

Articles usually contain detailed procedures on the appointment of directors. Any natural or legal person may be appointed as a director. A company may be appointed as a director of another company. The method of appointment and the body or person authorised to make the appointment may differ according to the type of appointment being made. Table 20.1 shows the position under the 1985 Table A. These provisions are frequently modified and it is essential to check the articles very carefully.

20.8.1   Procedure for appointment of directors

(a)   Check articles for the method of appointment (see Table 20.1 above if Table A applies).

(b)   If additional appointment, check that it will not cause the number of directors to exceed any maximum prescribed by the articles (see para. 20.8.2).

(c)   Check articles for age limits. In the case of a plc or a subsidiary of a plc, if nothing in articles, special notice required to appoint person aged 70 or over (see further para. 20.9).

(d) Check articles for share qualifications.

(e) Obtain approval for the appointment at a board meeting or, as the case may be, at a general meeting (if a private company, members' approval may be obtained by written resolution).

(f) Submit completed Form 288a to Companies House within 14 days of appointment ensuring that the new director has signed the consent to act.

(g) Enter details of the new director in the register of directors, including any former name, usual residential address, nationality, business occupation, particulars of past and present directorships and date of birth [s. 289].

(h) Remind director of any share qualification required by the articles.

(i) Remind director to disclose any interest in shares and debentures of the company.

(j) Request director to give general notice of any interest in contracts or proposed contracts with the company.

(k) Notify the company's bankers as appropriate.

(l) Obtain details of the director's PAYE coding and NI Number and instructions as to method of payment of remuneration.

(m) If appropriate, settle terms of service agreement (not to exceed five years without shareholder approval) and issue terms of reference or letter of appointment.

20.8.2 Minimum and maximum number

The Companies Act 1985 provides that every private company (whether limited by shares, limited by guarantee or unlimited) must have at least one director and that every public company formed after 1 November 1929 must have at least two [s. 282]. (Public companies formed before 1 November 1929 need only one director). Articles may require a higher number than the statutory minimum but not a lower number. Articles may also specify the maximum number of directors who may be appointed or provide a mechanism for determining such a limit. Any appointment which would cause the number of directors to exceed that maximum will be invalid.

Table 20.1 Methods of appointing directors under the 1985 Table A

Type of appointment	Appointed by	Source
First directors	Subscribers to the memorandum	CA 1985, s. 10
Additional directors	Board of directors Members	reg. 79 regs. 76 to 78
Appointments to fill a casual vacancy	Board of directors Members	reg. 79 regs. 76 to 78
Reappointment following retirement by rotation	Members	regs. 72 to 75 and 78
Reappointment following retirement at first AGM after appointment	Members	regs. 72, 78 and 79
Alternate directors	Directors	regs. 65 to 69

Reg. 64 of Table A provides that the number of directors shall not be subject to any maximum unless the members determine otherwise by ordinary resolution. This is a rather ungainly provision. It is easy to imagine circumstances where the existence of a limit imposed by ordinary resolution might be forgotten as such a resolution does not operate to amend the articles and can only be proved by reference to the minutes of the meeting at which it was passed. It is better to fix a maximum by amending the relevant article. If, however, a maximum is imposed or changed by ordinary resolution under reg. 64, it is advisable to make a note referring to that resolution on the master copy of the articles. It may also be a good idea to make a note that no such resolution has ever been passed if, indeed, that is the case. Reg. 64 can also cause problems if the members vote to impose a maximum which is less than the number of directors currently holding office. It is doubtful whether such a resolution would have the effect of removing any of the directors unless special notice was given of a resolution to remove one or more of those directors in accordance with s. 303. Such a resolution would, however, be effective in preventing any future appointments or re-appointments in breach of the maximum.

20.8.3   First directors

The first director(s) are appointed by the subscribers on Form 10 which must be filed at Companies House as part of the registration process. The people nominated on the form must indicate their willingness to act as directors by signing it. The form must also be signed by each of the subscribers or by an agent on their behalf. In effect, the first directors are appointed by the first members. On incorporation, the persons nominated are deemed to have been appointed and no further action is required. It is, however, standard practice to note in the minutes of the first board meeting the method by which they were appointed (see **Precedents 28.5B** and **C**).

If the subscribers wish to appoint a sole director of a private company, it will be necessary to appoint two initially or to modify regs. 64, 89 and 90 of Table A as they are drafted on the basis that there will be a minimum of two directors in the first instance.

20.8.4   Subsequent appointments

Subsequent appointments must be made in accordance with the procedures laid down in the company's articles of association and the requirements of the Companies Act 1985. The Act requires:

- compliance with any qualification imposed by the articles that a director must hold shares in the company [s. 291];
- special procedures to be followed to appoint as a director a person who is 70 years old or more [s. 293 and s. 294];
- resolutions to appoint directors at a general meeting of a public company to be voted on individually unless the meeting has previously resolved without dissent to take them together [s. 292].

All other questions relating to the appointment of directors can usually be resolved by reference to the articles. This is one of the areas where the Table A procedures are most likely to be modified and a careful examination of the articles will be necessary to ensure that the correct procedures are followed.

20.8.5   Appointment by the directors

Under reg. 79, the directors may appoint a director either to fill a casual vacancy or as an additional director, provided that the appointment does not cause the total number of directors to exceed any maximum fixed by or in accordance with the articles. A casual vacancy arises where an existing director has died, resigned or has been disqualified. Appointments by the board under reg. 79 are only temporary. Any directors appointed in this manner must retire at the next following annual general meeting and offer themselves for re-election. If the members resolve not to reappoint them they cease to hold office at the conclusion of the meeting. Directors retiring in this manner are not taken into account in determining the directors who are to retire by rotation at the meeting (see para. 20.10.4).

A private company may, of course, dispense with annual general meetings under the elective regime (see Chapter 24). If for any reason an annual general meeting is subsequently held, directors appointed under reg. 79 while the election was in force should retire at that meeting and offer themselves for re-election.

20.8.6   Common modifications to reg. 79

Reg. 79 applies in respect of casual vacancies and appointments of additional directors. However, articles sometimes allow the directors to make appointments to fill casual vacancies only. In these circumstances, the directors may only appoint a person to replace a director who has died, resigned or been disqualified from acting as a director. They may not fill any vacancy which arises by virtue of the procedures on rotation of directors or any vacancy which arises because an appointment made for a fixed period has ceased, e.g. an appointment for a fixed term of one year or an appointment which ceases at the conclusion of the next annual general meeting (*York Tramways Co.* v. *Willows* (1882) 8 Q.B.D. 685).

Where the articles restrict the powers of the directors to filling casual vacancies, the members retain the power to appoint additional directors.

20.8.7   Appointment by the members

If the articles give the directors power to fill casual vacancies and appoint additional directors, the members will have no power to do so unless the articles make specific provision to that effect. Under regs. 76 to 78 of Table A, the members may appoint or reappoint directors subject to certain conditions. These conditions are:

76. No person other than a director retiring by rotation shall be appointed or reappointed a director at any general meeting unless:

(a) he is recommended by the directors; or

(b) not less than fourteen nor more than thirty-five clear days before the date appointed for the meeting, notice executed by a member qualified to vote at the meeting has been given to the company of the intention to propose that person for appointment or reappointment stating the particulars which would, if he were so appointed or reappointed, be required to be included in the company's register of directors together with notice executed by that person of his willingness to be appointed or reappointed.

77. Not less than seven nor more than twenty-eight clear days before the date appointed for holding a general meeting notice shall be given to all who are entitled to receive notice of the meeting of any person (other than a director retiring by rotation at the meeting) who is recommended by the directors for appointment or reappointment as a director at the meeting or in respect of whom notice has been duly given to the company of the intention to propose him at the meeting for appointment or reappointment as a director. The notice shall give particulars of that person which would, if he were so appointed or reappointed, be required to be included in the company's register of directors.

78. Subject as aforesaid, the company may by ordinary resolution appoint a person who is willing to act to be a director either to fill a vacancy or as an additional director and may also determine the rotation in which any additional directors are to retire.

A number of points should be noted with regard to the above regulations:

- although they do not apply to the reappointment of a director retiring by rotation, they do to a director appointed by the directors to fill a casual vacancy or as an additional director who is required to retire at the annual general meeting next following his or her appointment;
- notice must be given to the members in accordance with reg. 77 in respect of any person recommended by the directors;
- a valid resolution of the board of directors will be required for a person to qualify as being recommended by the directors;
- two conditions must be satisfied for a person to be proposed who is not recommended by the directors, namely notice must be given to the company in accordance with reg. 76 (see **Precedent 20.8A**) and the company must give notice to the members in accordance with reg. 77 (see **Precedent 20.8B**).

20.8.8   1948 Act Table A

The 1948 Act Table A provisions are much simpler and are commonly adopted by public companies in preference to the 1985 Table A provisions (see for example art. 102 of Whitbread plc). Reg. 93 of the 1948 Table A provides:

93. No person other than a director retiring at the meeting shall unless recommended by the directors be eligible for election to the office of director at any general meeting unless not less than three nor more than twenty-one days before the date appointed for the meeting there shall have been left at the registered office of the company notice in writing, signed by a member duly qualified to attend and vote at the meeting for which such notice is given, of his intention to propose such person for election, and also notice in writing signed by that person of his willingness to be elected.

Regulation 93 does not apply to any director retiring at the meeting whether by rotation or otherwise. Although a member is still required to give notice to the company, there is no corresponding requirement for the company to give notice to the members.

Under reg. 97 of the 1948 Act Table A, the members may by ordinary resolution appoint another person in place of a director who has been removed from office and, without prejudice to the powers of the directors (essentially the same as under the 1985 Table A), appoint any person to be a director either to fill a casual vacancy or as an additional director. There is no corresponding requirement for the members to give notice of their intention to propose such a resolution.

20.8.9   Other methods of appointment

Although the above methods are widely used, there is no reason why some other method should not be adopted. The articles may, for example, provide that the directors may be appointed or removed from office by notice in writing signed by members holding a majority of the voting shares. This method is most likely to be used by subsidiary companies as it enables the parent company to make appointments without having to hold a meeting of the subsidiary.

A variation on this theme can be useful for joint venture companies where each of the partners in the joint venture is given the right to appoint a fixed number of directors (and replace them with others) by giving notice in writing. This can be achieved by having different classes of shares with each class having separate rights to appoint a fixed number of directors.

The articles of small owner-managed companies are frequently modified to ensure that the founders retain the right to participate in their management. Some amendment may be necessary even where all the company's shares are held equally by two people who are both appointed as directors. This is because under reg. 50 of Table A, the chairman of the general meeting has a casting vote and could therefore appoint and remove directors against the wishes of the other member to gain management control. The simplest solution in these circumstances is to amend the articles to exclude that part of reg. 50 which gives the chairman a casting vote. For a person holding less than 50 per cent of the company's shares more elaborate protection is necessary. The articles could be amended so that an extraordinary or special resolution is required (i.e. a majority of 75 per cent) to appoint new directors. The major problem for a minority shareholder however, is the fact that the members in general meeting have a statutory right to remove a director from office by ordinary resolution [s. 303]. There are a number of ways in which this problem can be overcome (see further para. 20.11 on the removal of directors) and it goes without saying that a minority shareholder should ensure that appropriate measures are taken before becoming a shareholder.

20.9 AGE LIMITS [ss. 293 and 294]

The purpose of these provisions is to enable shareholders to remove a director or to prevent the appointment of a director who has reached the age of 70. The statutory rules only apply to public companies and their subsidiaries. There is no statutory age limit in respect of private companies except where the company is a subsidiary of a public company. Table A is also silent on the matter. The following procedures can therefore be ignored by private companies unless they are a subsidiary of a public company or their articles have been amended so as to include similar age restrictions.

For directors of public companies and their subsidiaries, s. 293 sets a notional age limit of 70. It is notional because a person who has reached that age may still be appointed or reappointed as a director as long as the procedures laid down by that section are followed. In addition, the articles of a public company or any of its subsidiaries may override these statutory rules (see art. 95 of Whitbread plc).

Section 293 provides that a person who has reached the age of 70 may not be appointed as a director unless the appointment is approved by an ordinary resolution of the members in general meeting. Thus, the directors cannot appoint a person who has reached the age of 70 to fill a casual vacancy or as an additional director unless the articles make specific provision to that effect.

A director of a public company or any of its subsidiaries who reaches the age of 70 while in office must retire at the conclusion of the annual general meeting next following his or her 70th birthday, although the members may by ordinary resolution reappoint a director retiring under these rules.

Special notice must be given of the resolution (either to appoint or to reappoint the director) in accordance with s. 379 (see para. 6.9). The notice given by the member to the company (see **Precedent 20.9A**) and the notice given by the company to its members (see **Precedent 20.9B**) must state the age of the person to whom the resolution relates.

Where a director retires under these rules, any provision for the automatic reappointment of retiring directors in default of another appointment (e.g. reg. 75) does not apply and, if at the meeting at which the director retires the vacancy is not filled, it may be filled as a casual vacancy (e.g. by the directors under reg. 79) [s. 293(4)].

20.9.1 Effect on retirement by rotation

A retirement under s. 293 is ignored for the purposes of determining the order and timing of rotation of directors provided that the retiring director is reappointed or a person is appointed in place of the director so retiring [s. 293(6)]. For example, if a public company has six directors, one of whom (A) reaches the age of 70 in the third year, the following order would apply:

Year 1   A and B retire and are reappointed
Year 2   C and D retire and are reappointed
Year 3   A, E and F retire and are reappointed
Year 4   A and B retire and are reappointed

In the above example, if G was appointed in place of A in year 3, G would have to retire again in year 4 (i.e. when the person replaced would have retired if still in office).

20.9.2   Age limits in articles

If a private company which is not a subsidiary has any rules on age limits in its articles, those rules will apply irrespective of anything in s. 293 as the statutory rules apply only to public companies and their subsidiaries. The articles of a public company or its subsidiary may exclude either in whole or in part the effect of the statutory age limits [s. 293(7)].

20.10   ROTATION OF DIRECTORS

20.10.1   Is rotation necessary?

Neither the Act, the Listing Rules or the Cadbury Code of Best Practice require directors to retire by rotation. However, most articles do (including Table A). In its *Guide to best practice for Annual General Meetings,* ICSA recommends that all directors of listed companies should retire by rotation. The Association of British Insurers and the National Association of Pension Funds have also made similar recommendations, and it is likely that the Hampel Committee on Corporate Governance (the successor to the Cadbury Committee) will follow suit when it publishes its recommendations.

Retirement by rotation can cause problems for small private companies and often serves very little purpose in any case. In such circumstances, it is often preferable to modify the articles.

20.10.2   1985 Table A

The basic provisions on rotation in Table A are as follows:

73. At the first annual general meeting all the directors shall retire from office, and at every subsequent annual general meeting one-third of the directors who are subject to retirement by rotation or, if their number is not three or a multiple of three, the number nearest to one third, shall retire from office; but, if there is only one director who is subject to retirement by rotation, he shall retire.

74. Subject to the provisions of the Act, the directors to retire by rotation shall be those who have served longest in office since their last appointment or reappointment, but as between persons who became or were last reappointed directors on the same day those to retire shall (unless they otherwise agree among themselves) be determined by lot.

75. If the company, at the meeting at which a director retires by rotation, does not fill the vacancy the retiring director shall, if willing to act, be deemed to have been reappointed unless at the meeting it is resolved not to fill the vacancy or unless a resolution for the reappointment of the director is put to the meeting and lost.

20.10.3   Number to retire

In order to determine who must retire each year, it is necessary to determine which directors are subject to retirement by rotation. Under reg. 84 of Table A, the executive directors are not subject to retirement by rotation. If all the directors hold some executive office, the rotation provisions will not apply.

Most articles provide that the number nearest to one third of the directors subject to retirement by rotation shall retire. The normal rounding up and rounding down rules should be applied when calculating the number of directors who must retire unless the articles state that the number nearest to, but not exceeding, one third shall retire, in which case the figure must always be rounded down.

Under reg. 73 of the 1985 Table A, it is clear that even where only one director is subject to retirement by rotation, that person must retire at each annual general meeting. The same is true where the articles follow reg. 89 of 1948 Table A by providing that the 'number nearest one-third' shall retire (*Re New Cedos Engineering Co. Ltd* [1994] 1 B.C.L.C. 797, 810). In both cases, one person must retire at each annual general meeting if two directors are subject to retirement by rotation. However, if the articles provide that 'the number nearest to, but not exceeding, one-third' shall retire and the number of directors subject to retirement by rotation is two or less, then no directors need to retire (*Re Moseley & Sons Ltd* [1939] Ch. 719).

Table 20.2   Retirement of directors

Number of directors subject to retirement by rotation	Number to retire at each AGM	
	1948 and 1985 Table A	'Nearest to, but not exceeding one third'
One	1	0
Two	1	0
Three	1	1
Four	1	1
Five	2	1
Six	2	2

20.10.4   Who is to retire?

The directors to retire by rotation will normally be those who have served longest since their last appointment or reappointment. Articles normally provide that, where the number who must retire is less than the number who are eligible under this rule because they were appointed or last reappointed on the same day, the selection of those to retire is to be determined by lot, unless they otherwise agree among themselves (in which case their unanimous agreement is required with respect to the decision or the method of reaching that decision). A lot may be performed by the drawing of straws or some other similar method of chance. It has been held that where the articles state that the matter is to be settled by ballot, this also means by lot rather than by any method of voting (*Eyre* v. *Milton Proprietary* [1936] Ch. 244). This case is also authority for the fact that temporary directors (e.g. those appointed by the directors under reg. 79 and who must therefore automatically retire at the next following AGM) should not be included when calculating how many directors should retire under the rotation provisions.

Table 20.3   Example of retirement by rotation under 1985 Table A (all directors subject to rotation)

Event	AGM	Directors to retire
A, B, C & D appointed as first directors on formation	First AGM	A, B, C, & D (under reg. 73)
	Second AGM	C (drawn by lot between A, B, C & D)
	Third AGM	B (drawn by lot between A, B & D)
Board appoints E as additional director	Fourth AGM	A & D (under reg. 73 & 74) & E (under reg. 79)
	Fifth AGM	B & C (under reg. 73 & 74)
	Sixth AGM	A & E (by lot between A, D & E)

20.10.5   Notice and proxy forms

Unless the articles specify the re-election of directors retiring by rotation as ordinary business, it will be necessary to indicate the general nature of the business in the notice. This can be done simply by stating as an item of business 'to re-elect directors retiring by rotation'. However, it is more usual to include a separate resolution for each director who will be retiring by rotation and seeking re-election at the meeting. ICSA's *Guide to best practice for Annual General Meetings* recommends that directors standing for re-election to the board should be named in the notice and form of proxy. It also recommends that a brief description of the relevant directors should be given, including their ages; their relevant experience (not merely a list of other directorships they hold); the dates that they were first appointed to the board; and details of any board committees to which they belong. This could be done in any circular which accompanies the notice or in the directors' report if the accounts are sent to the members with the notice.

The London Stock Exchange requires proxy cards sent to members to give them the opportunity to indicate how their proxy should vote on every resolution (other than procedural resolutions) which will be put to the meeting [Listing Rules, para. 13.28]. Where the number of retiring directors standing for re-election exceeds five, the proxy form may give shareholders the opportunity to vote for or against the re-election of the retiring directors as a whole but must also allow votes to be cast for or against the re-election of the retiring directors individually [Listing Rules, para. 13.29]. The Act provides that a motion for the appointment of two or more persons as directors by a single resolution at a general meeting of a public company shall not be valid unless the meeting agrees unanimously to a proposal that the resolution be proposed in that manner [s. 292].

The Greenbury Committee's Code of Best Practice on directors' remuneration recommends that where a director of a listed company standing for re-election is a member of the company's remuneration committee, the proxy card should indicate this [see para. A5 of the Greenbury Code and para. 4 in Section A of the 'Best practice provisions: directors' remuneration in the Listing Rules].

20.10.6   Failure to hold an AGM

If a company fails to hold an annual general meeting, the directors who were due to retire at that meeting will be deemed to have retired at the end of the year in which the annual general meeting was due to be held. In *Re Consolidated Nickel Mines Ltd* [1914] 1 Ch. 883, the company's articles of association provided that a general meeting should be held once in every year and that at the ordinary meeting in 1906 all the directors should retire from office. No such meeting was held or called. It was held that the directors vacated office on 31 December 1906, i.e. the last day on which the ordinary meeting for that year could have been held . This decision was followed in *Re Zinotty Properties Ltd* [1984] 3 All E.R. 754 in a case concerning an article based on reg. 89 of the 1948 Table A. There is no reason to suppose that the result in these cases would have been any different if the article in question had been art. 73 of the 1985 Table A.

20.10.7   Position under elective regime

Re Consolidated Nickel Mines and *Re Zinotty Properties* were however both decided at a time when all companies were required by statute to hold annual general meetings. The question arises therefore as to what rules apply to a private company which has elected pursuant to ss. 366A and 381A of the Companies Act 1985 to dispense with annual general meetings if its articles also require the directors to retire by rotation at the annual general meeting. In *Re Zinotty Properties*, Mervyn Davies J. stated that the fact that the company had no directors was a consequence of the company never having held annual general meetings coupled with the operation of reg. 89 of the 1948 Act Table A and the company's article 16. Reg. 89 provides:

89. At the first annual general meeting of the company and at the annual general meeting in every subsequent year one-third of the directors for the time being, or, if their number is not three or a multiple of three, then the number nearest one-third, shall retire from office.

The company's art. 16 read:

In clause 89 of Table 'A' the words 'all the directors shall retire from office' shall be deleted.

Mervyn Davies J. seemed to indicate that the existence of an article such as reg. 89 was sufficient on its own to cause this result. This was undoubtedly correct at the time as all companies were required by law to hold annual general meetings. However, in view of the fact that private companies can now dispense with annual general meetings, this may not always be true today.

An elective resolution to dispense with holding annual general meetings is not passed as an amendment to the articles. However, it is well established that the unanimous agreement of the members can have the same effect as an amendment to the articles (*Cane* v. *Jones* [1981] 1 All E.R. 533). It could be argued that an elective resolution, being a unanimous resolution of the members, has the same effect. Thus, it might have the effect of amending any provision in the articles which is inconsistent with its purpose, e.g. a provision which requires the company to hold an annual general meeting each year, e.g. art. 47 (and, by implication, art. 89) of the 1948 Table A (the 1985 version of Table A does not include any such provision).

Even if an elective resolution does not amend any article which is inconsistent with its purpose, it must at least suspend its operation while it is in force. This distinction is irrelevant with respect to any article which requires the company to hold annual general meetings as this would be a statutory requirement if the elective resolution was revoked. However, it is a crucial point in relation to retirement by rotation as it determines whether the retirement provisions would operate if an annual general meeting is subsequently held for any reason. In the author's view, an elective resolution should be viewed as merely suspending the operation of any article which is inconsistent with its purpose, although it has to be said that art. 73 of the 1985 Table A is more conducive to this solution than, for example, art. 89 of the 1948 Act Table A which seems to imply that an annual general meeting must be held each year (art. 73 merely provides that certain directors shall retire at the first annual general meeting and at every subsequent annual general meeting).

20.10.8   Wrong directors retire

A problem which commonly arises because of a miscalculation or a lack of understanding of the articles is that the wrong directors retire at the meeting. The situation with regard to a person who should have retired depends on the articles. Such a person will cease to be a director at the conclusion of the annual general meeting unless the articles include a saving provision similar to art. 75 of Table A:

75. If the company, at the meeting at which a director retires by rotation, does not fill the vacancy the retiring director shall, if willing to act, be deemed to have been reappointed unless at the meeting it is resolved not to fill the vacancy or unless a resolution for the appointment of the director is put to the meeting and lost.

The words 'at a meeting at which a director retires by rotation' should not be interpreted as requiring any action on the part of the director. A director who is due to retire by rotation will be deemed to have retired at that meeting. Thus a vacancy will exist even though another director retired at the meeting and, provided that the other conditions of the relevant article are satisfied, the director will be deemed to have been reappointed.

The position with regard to any director who retired by mistake is complicated by the fact that the articles commonly restrict the ability of the members to appoint or reappoint directors, e.g. reg. 77 of the 1985 Table A. A director who retires earlier than is necessary does not do so by rotation under the articles. Thus any conditions in the articles on appointments by the members must be satisfied otherwise the appointment will be invalid. If the reappointment can be deemed to have been recommended by the directors, it would be valid under reg. 77 of Table A.

20.10.9   Meeting held but no resolution put

Articles such as reg. 75 of Table A also save the situation where an annual general meeting is held but no resolution is put to the meeting with respect to rotation, except where the meeting has resolved not to fill the vacancy. Thus, if the company fails by mistake or otherwise to put forward resolutions to deal with rotation at the meeting, the directors will be deemed to be reappointed. Although this type of article may be necessary to save the situation where a genuine mistake is made, it is hardly conducive to good corporate governance in so far as it allows a director to be reappointed without the approval of the members.

20.11   REMOVAL OF DIRECTORS FROM OFFICE [s. 303]

The statutory rules on removal of directors apply to public and private companies alike and cannot be excluded by the articles. The articles may, however, provide an additional method of removal, e.g. by extraordinary resolution. If so, the members may use the statutory procedures or the additional method provided by the articles to remove a director.

The statutory procedures on removal are designed primarily to ensure that a simple majority of the members have the power to remove a director. This is a crucial safeguard for the members who would otherwise have little or no control over the directors. The statutory procedures also ensure that directors are given a fair chance to defend themselves against any proposal to remove them as directors. Directors are not normally afforded similar rights where an additional procedure is provided by the articles, e.g. removal by extraordinary resolution.

Section 303 provides that the members in general meeting may by ordinary resolution remove a director provided that special notice of that resolution has been given in accordance with s. 379 (see **Precedents 20.11A** and **20.11B**). This statutory power applies notwithstanding anything in the company's articles or in any agreement between the company and the director. Special notice is also required with respect to any resolution to appoint at the same meeting another person instead of a director removed under these statutory powers.

20.11.1   Director's right to protest removal [s. 304]

On receipt of a valid notice from a member, the company must immediately send a copy of it to the director concerned (see **Precedent 20.11C**) who is entitled to speak on the resolution at the meeting whether or not he or she is a member of the company [s. 304(1)].

If the director makes written representations to the company in connection with the resolution and requests their notification to the members, the company must, unless the representations are received too late for it to do so:

(a)   state in any notice of the resolution given to members that representations have been made; and

(b)   send a copy of the director's representations to every member entitled to receive notice of the meeting [s. 304(2)].

Special notice may be served on the company up to 28 days before the meeting. The company may not have time to wait for the director to make representations if it is to meet its 21-day deadline for giving notice of the resolution to the members. If notice of the resolution has already been given or if there is not sufficient time to have the notice reprinted, the company need not comply with para. (a) above. However, even if the notice of the resolution has already been sent, the company must still send a copy of the director's representations to each member (and bear the cost of doing so) unless it is impossible to deliver them to the members before the meeting.

If, for any reason, a copy of the director's representations is not sent to the members, the director may require them to be read out at the meeting. In these circumstances, the director still has a right to speak on the resolution at the meeting [s. 304(4)].

The company or any other person who claims to be aggrieved may apply to the court for an order that the director's representations should not be sent to members or read out at the meeting on the grounds that the director is abusing the rights conferred by s. 304 to secure needless publicity for defamatory matter [s. 304(4)].

It is possible to avoid the effect of s. 303. In *Bushell* v. *Faith* [1970] A.C. 1099, the articles of a company with three equal shareholders provided that in the event of a resolution being proposed at any general meeting of the company for the removal from office of any director, any shares held by that director shall on a poll in respect of such resolution carry the right to three votes per share. When two of the shareholders tried to remove Faith as a director he was therefore able to outvote them by demanding a poll on the resolution. It was held by the House of Lords that the article was valid and did not infringe s. 303. That section simply provides that a director may be removed by ordinary resolution. It does not prevent the articles giving a member weighted voting rights.

CHAPTER TWENTY-ONE

Chairman's scripts

21.1 SUMMARY

This chapter includes specimen scripts for use by the chairman at general meetings. The examples given include scripts for:
- an annual general meeting (this is merely provided as an example and will need to be modified to reflect the resolutions to be proposed) (see para. 21.2);
- delaying the meeting to allow members to register (see para. 21.3);
- dealing with overcrowding in the meeting room (see para. 21.4);
- a poll
  (a) called by the chairman (see para. 21.5),
  (b) demanded by a member (see para. 21.5.2);
- a resolution to adjourn (see para. 21.6);
- dealing with amendments (see para. 21.7);
- dealing with disruption (see para. 21.8);
- proposing a formal motion to put the question to the vote (see para. 21.9).

21.2 CHAIRMAN'S SCRIPT FOR ANNUAL GENERAL MEETING

CHAIRMAN: Ladies and gentlemen, I am pleased to welcome you to the annual general meeting of XYZ plc and declare the meeting open. With your permission, I will take the notice of the meeting as read.

SHORT PAUSE TO SEE WHETHER ANYONE OBJECTS

CHAIRMAN: Thank you. I now call upon [name of auditor] to read the report of the auditors to the members.

AUDITOR TO READ REPORT

Resolution 1: Report and accounts

CHAIRMAN: Thank you. I propose:

> THAT the report of the directors and the audited accounts for the year ended [date], now laid before the meeting, be received.

A copy of the report and accounts was sent to members with the notice of this meeting. But before putting the resolution to the vote, I would like to draw your attention to certain matters in the report and accounts and update you on the company's performance since the end of the financial year. I will then invite questions from the floor.

CHAIRMAN TO MAKE STATEMENT

CHAIRMAN: I now invite questions from the floor on the report and accounts. I will also take questions on my statement. If you have a question or a point to make, I would be grateful if you [could make yourself known to the staff at the question point nearest to you][raise your hand and wait until a member of staff has supplied you with a microphone]. Before asking your question, you should state your name and whether you are a shareholder or a corporate representative. [I would remind you that under art. [No.] of the company's articles of association proxies are not entitled to speak at this meeting.] [Unless the meeting objects, I propose for the time being to allow proxies to speak on any resolution before the meeting but reserve the right to change my ruling in this regard should it appear necessary in order to complete the business on the agenda.]

INVITE QUESTION FROM THE FLOOR

CHAIRMAN: If nobody has any further questions or points to make on the report and accounts [pause], I would now ask you to vote on the resolution before the meeting, namely:

> THAT the report of the directors and the audited accounts for the year ended [date], now laid before the meeting, be received.

Those in favour [pause to count votes] – those against [pause to count votes] – I declare the resolution carried.

Resolution 2: Dividends

CHAIRMAN: I now propose THAT the final dividend of [5.8p] per share recommended by the directors of XYZ plc be declared payable on [date] to the holders of ordinary shares registered at the close of business on [date].

Does anyone have any questions or points to make on this resolution?

AFTER DEALING WITH QUESTIONS, IF ANY

CHAIRMAN: I now put the resolution THAT the final dividend of [5.8p] per share recommended by the directors of XYZ plc be declared payable on [date] to the holders of ordinary shares registered at the close of business on [date].

Those in favour [pause to count votes] – those against [pause to count votes] – I declare the resolution carried.

Resolutions 3 and 4: Re-election of directors

CHAIRMAN: I now turn to the re-election of directors retiring by rotation. As you may be aware, under the company's articles of association one third of your directors (including the executive directors) must retire each year and offer themselves for re-election. This year the directors to retire are [name] and me. As I am one of the directors seeking reappointment, it would not be right for me to propose that resolution. I will therefore ask my colleague [name] to do so when we come to that item. However, before doing so I have pleasure in proposing:

> THAT [name], a director retiring by rotation, be re-elected a director of the company.

INVITE QUESTIONS

CHAIRMAN: I now put the resolution to the meeting. Those in favour [pause to count votes] – those against [pause to count votes] – I declare the resolution carried.

I now call upon [name] to propose the next resolution.

[NAME]   Thank you, I propose:

> THAT [name of chairman], a director retiring by rotation, be re-elected a director of the company.

If there are no questions, I now put the resolution to the meeting. Those in favour [pause to count votes] – those against [pause to count votes] – I declare the resolution carried.

Resolution 5: Reappointment of auditors

CHAIRMAN: Thank you. The next resolution (resolution 5 in the notice) is:

> THAT [name of auditors] be reappointed auditors of the company to hold office to the conclusion of the next general meeting at which accounts are laid and that their remuneration be fixed by the directors

and I ask [name of shareholder], a shareholder, to propose this resolution.

[SHAREHOLDER]: I propose the resolution.

CHAIRMAN: Thank you. I now put the resolution to the meeting. Those in favour [pause to count votes] – those against [pause to count votes] – I declare the resolution carried.

Resolution 6: Amendment of articles

CHAIRMAN: I now turn to the last item of business on the agenda for today's meeting, namely resolution 6. I therefore propose as a special resolution:

> THAT the regulations in the document produced at the meeting, and signed by the chairman so as to identify it, be adopted as the company's articles of association in substitution for and to the exclusion of all existing articles of association of the Company.

The reasons for recommending these alterations and their effect is explained on page [No.] of the notice of this meeting. In view of the number of changes it was decided that it would be easier to adopt new articles incorporating all of the changes to the existing articles. As the adoption of new articles is proposed, a separate resolution to renew the directors' authority to allot unissued shares in the capital of the Company will not be put to the annual general meeting. Instead, new section 80 and section 89 amounts have been inserted in the new articles of association and will become effective if the resolution to adopt the new articles is passed. The relevant amounts are set out on page [No.] of the notice.

I am happy to take questions on this item of business but will ask [name] from the company's solicitors to deal with any technical or legal points which arise.

INVITE QUESTIONS

If there are no further questions, I now put the resolution to the meeting. Those in favour [pause to count votes] – those against [pause to count votes] – I declare the resolution carried as a special resolution.

Close the meeting

CHAIRMAN: That concludes the business of the meeting and I thank you for your patience. Refreshments will now be served in [place]. All the directors will be available to answer any additional questions which you may have. We will be wearing red badges so that you can identify us. Thank you.

21.3   REGISTRATION INCOMPLETE

CHAIRMAN: Despite our best efforts to speed up registration there are still people who are waiting to register. I am told that registration is likely to be completed in about [15 minutes] and I therefore propose, with your consent, to delay the start of the meeting until [time].

IF ANYONE OBJECTS

CHAIRMAN: There is room to accommodate everyone now waiting outside and I believe it would be courteous to them to wait [15 minutes] so that they can be admitted.

Note: If necessary, temporary registration cards should be used so that those affected can be admitted. If a vote is required the votes of those with temporary cards could be taken by requiring them to register.

21.4   ROOM TOO SMALL

CHAIRMAN: Despite booking a room which we expected to be easily big enough, it is clear that not everyone can be accommodated in this room.
There are approximately [   ] people waiting to get in. People other than members present in person, by corporate representative or by proxy, are reminded that they have no absolute right to be present at the meeting. In order to enable members who are outside to be accommodated in this hall, which is where the meeting is being held, it would be most helpful if about [   ] persons present who are not members or proxy holders or corporate representatives of members could volunteer to go to [another specified room]. [There is a one-way audio link so that those in the [specified room] will be able to hear the debate.]

IF ANNOUNCEMENT IS MADE AFTER TIME SET FOR THE MEETING

CHAIRMAN: I propose, with your consent, to delay the start of the meeting until [   ] to enable everyone to get settled.

IF ANYONE OBJECTS

CHAIRMAN: There is room to accommodate all members in this room and all non-members who cannot get into this room in the [   ] room. It would be courteous to those outside to wait [half an hour] to enable everyone to be accommodated.

Note: If after [15 minutes] non-members have left but registration is still not complete, temporary registration cards should be used so that those affected can be admitted. If a vote is required the votes of those with temporary cards should be taken by requiring them to register.

IF PEOPLE REFUSE TO MOVE OR THE ARRANGEMENTS FOR USING THE ROOM DO NOT WORK FOR ANY REASON

CHAIRMAN: It is clear that not everyone can be accommodated in this room. Unfortunately, if this meeting is to proceed to business it will be necessary for at least [   ] non-members to leave the meeting to enable members and proxy holders outside this room to get in. Will these people please leave [and go to the [   ] room].

IF INSUFFICIENT NON-MEMBERS LEAVE

CHAIRMAN: As non-members are unwilling to leave I propose to adjourn this meeting for [15] minutes while the stewards assist in accommodating them in the [   ] room. If insufficient non-members leave then this meeting cannot continue. If we have to reconvene this meeting further delay and additional expense will be incurred. This can be avoided if non-members (and that includes members of the press who are not themselves members) who have no entitlement to attend this meeting, now leave [and go to the [   ] room].

IF RESISTANCE IS ENCOUNTERED

CHAIRMAN: In the circumstances I have no alternative other than to propose the adjournment of this meeting to an alternative venue [which we have arranged at [   ] on [   ] at [   ]]. In order to ensure a valid vote on the question of adjournment I ask again if non-members will please leave now. They should not miss anything as they will have the opportunity to attend the adjourned meeting if the vote to adjourn the meeting is passed.

IF NON-MEMBERS DO THEN LEAVE AND MEMBERS GET IN – PUT MOTION TO ADJOURN TO A VOTE. IF NECESSARY CALL A POLL

IF EVERYBODY IS STILL NOT ACCOMMODATED

CHAIRMAN: There are still some members outside but I am going to put to the vote my proposal to adjourn to [   ] on [   ] at [   ] anyway. The stewards will attempt to count the votes of those outside.

IF THE VOTE IS LOST ON A SHOW OF HANDS, AN ATTEMPT SHOULD BE MADE TO PUT IT TO A POLL

CHAIRMAN: I also adjourn the meeting on my own authority pursuant to the inherent power vested in me as Chairman of this meeting. A further registration form will be posted to you to enable you to attend the adjourned meeting. [If you are uncertain whether you will be able to attend this meeting, proxy cards can be collected on the way out.] Proxies should be returned by [not less than 48 hours before the time of the adjourned meeting].

21.5   POLL PROCEDURES

Subject to the articles, the chairman has power to adjourn for the taking of a poll on a resolution. If the demand for a poll is valid, the poll is normally taken at the end of the meeting after any other business has been concluded unless the nature of the business requires it to be taken immediately (e.g. a poll on resolution to adjourn) or before the vote on the substantive resolution (e.g. a poll on an amendment to a resolution). See further para. 16.8 on polls, Chapter 17 on adjournments and para. 12.6 on amendments.

21.5.1   Called by chairman

CHAIRMAN: In the circumstances, I exercise my right as Chairman to call for a poll. The poll will be conducted at the end of the meeting and in the meantime I will proceed with the remaining business of the meeting.

WHEN REMAINING BUSINESS IS COMPLETE, GO TO PARA. 21.5.3

21.5.2   Demand by a member

MEMBER: [Demands a poll.]

CHAIRMAN: I should point out that I hold over [No. of proxy votes] proxies in favour of the resolution and a further [No. of proxy votes] proxies which I may vote at my discretion. There are [No. of proxy votes] votes against the resolution. In view of this [considerable] support it seems likely that the resolution will be carried. As the conduct of a poll is a lengthy process, do those calling for a poll still feel that this is a worthwhile exercise?

IF MEMBER STANDS DOWN

CHAIRMAN: Thank you. I will proceed with the business of the meeting.

IF MEMBER PERSISTS

CHAIRMAN: What is your full name and in what name is the holding registered?

ALLOW REGISTRAR TO TAKE DOWN FULL DETAILS

CHAIRMAN: Under the Company's Articles of Association, a poll can only be demanded by the Chairman or by [state relevant conditions].

Do you satisfy any of these conditions?

IF NO, RULE OUT OF ORDER.

IF YES:

CHAIRMAN: So that we can verify that the request is properly made, will you please make yourselves known to the Company's Registrar.

IF VALID DEMAND FOR POLL ON RESOLUTION TO ADJOURN, GO TO PARA. 21.5.3

OTHERWISE

CHAIRMAN: If the poll has been validly demanded, it will be conducted at the end of the meeting and I will explain the procedures when the time comes. In the meantime, I propose to proceed with the other business of the meeting.

RETURN TO MAIN SCRIPT

WHEN REMAINING BUSINESS COMPLETE, GO TO PARA. 21.5.3

21.5.3   Conduct of poll

CHAIRMAN: A poll on resolution [No.] [text of resolution] will now be conducted by our Registrars and I would ask the Secretary to describe the procedure for taking the poll.

SECRETARY: Please remain in your seats while the poll is being conducted. Polling cards will now be distributed.

On a poll each member present in person, by corporate representative or proxy has one vote for every share held. If you have already lodged a form of proxy you do not have to vote again now unless you wish to change the way you originally voted. If you do not wish to change your mind it will speed up the poll procedure if you do not vote again now.

A separate poll card should be used for each separate holding. If you are representing more than one holding, please ask for additional cards as necessary. You should indicate the number of shares to be voted in the appropriate box on the poll card. If you do not, all the shares registered in you name or in the name of the person you are representing will be included in the count. If two or more persons are jointly registered as shareholders, any one of them may vote either in person or by proxy. If more than one of the joint holders votes then only the vote of the joint holder whose name appears first on the register of members will be counted.

Corporate representatives should complete the poll card with the full details of the name of the company they represent and provide the registrars with some form of identification and their written authority to exercise the votes.

Note. Articles rarely require presentation of authority and it should only be insisted upon if a reasonable suspicion exists of wrongdoing.

Completed cards should be placed in one of the boxes at the exits from the hall. if you are unsure as to what to do our staff will be pleased to answer your queries.

IN ADDITION TO CASTING HIS OWN VOTE, CHAIRMAN SHOULD COMPLETE VOTING CARDS FOR AND AGAINST THE RESOLUTION IN ACCORDANCE WITH THE PROXIES HELD BY HIM.

AFTER A SUITABLE INTERVAL THE CHAIRMAN SHOULD GIVE NOTICE OF HIS INTENTION TO CLOSE THE POLL

CHAIRMAN: I intend to declare the poll closed in two minutes. Please ensure that your completed card has been given in.

WHEN THE CARDS HAVE ALL BEEN HANDED IN

EITHER:

CHAIRMAN: Thank you ladies and gentlemen, the poll is now closed. The poll cards will be processed by the scrutineers who will complete the poll as soon as possible. The results of the voting will be announced in this room but this will probably take about [　] hours. I therefore adjourn the meeting pending the declaration of the result of the poll.

OR:

CHAIRMAN: Thank you ladies and gentlemen. The poll is now closed. As the results of the poll will need to be checked, it will not be possible to know the result for some time. The result of the poll(s) will therefore [be published in a Stock Exchange announcement on [　] and will appear in [　] on the same day]. This concludes the business of the meeting and I now declare the meeting closed. Thank you for attending.

21.6　ADJOURNMENT

21.6.1　Proposal by chairman

The motion for adjournment should include the day, time and place of the adjourned meeting or authorise the Board to determine such matters. The Chairman should give his views on or reasons for the proposal and invite debate from the floor.

*　The Chairman has an inherent power, in limited circumstances, to adjourn the meeting if*

it is necessary to enable members to debate and vote on the business of the meeting (e.g. if the room is too small to accommodate those entitled to attend or to deal with a disturbance).

If the meeting is adjourned, further proxies may become valid as the articles may allow proxies to be lodged up to 48/24 hours before the time of the adjourned meeting.

CHAIRMAN: In accordance with Article [   ] of the Company's Articles of Association I propose that this meeting be adjourned until [date, time and place, etc.].

AFTER DEBATE ENDS

I now propose to put the proposal to adjourn to the vote. Ladies and gentlemen the proposal is that the meeting be adjourned to [date, time and place, etc.]. Will those in favour of the proposal to adjourn please raise their hands / [colour] voting cards.

Thank you.

Those against. Thank you.

IF VOTE CARRIED EITHER:

CHAIRMAN: The proposal to adjourn the meeting has been carried.

This meeting stands adjourned to [place] on [date] at [time].

OR:

This meeting is now adjourned. Notice of the adjourned meeting will be posted to shareholders as soon as possible.

IF VOTE NOT CARRIED:

CHAIRMAN: I declare the resolution not passed on a show of hands and in accordance with article [No.] of the Company's Articles of Association I therefore exercise my right to demand a poll on the proposal to adjourn the meeting.

Note: The Chairman should state how he intends to vote the proxies that he holds. When deciding how to cast the votes of proxies the Chairman should consider the intentions of the shareholders who have appointed him as their proxy and act accordingly. Therefore how the Chairman votes will depend on the circumstances. If in doubt the Chairman should seek advice on the matter.

THE POLL MAY NEED TO BE TAKEN IMMEDIATELY

GO TO PARA. 21.5.3

21.6.2 Proposal for adjournment from the floor

MEMBER: I demand that the meeting be adjourned.

CHAIRMAN: Are you a member or a representative of a corporate member?

IF NO:

CHAIRMAN: Rule out of order.

IF YES:

CHAIRMAN: I will ask the Registrars to verify your status. Will shareholders please bear with me while this exercise is completed.

Note: This must be done immediately – no other business can be carried out if a valid proposal to adjourn is outstanding.

IF STATUS IS NOT CORRECT:

CHAIRMAN: The Registrars advise me that you do not have the required status to call for an adjournment. I therefore rule the proposed adjournment out of order. (Return to main script).

IF STATUS IS CORRECT:

CHAIRMAN: What exactly is your proposal? How long is the adjournment to be for?

MEMBER: [At least [No. of days] – give reasons].

CHAIRMAN: Would your proposal then be to adjourn for a minimum of [No. of days] to a place, date and time to be fixed by the Board?

Note: The Chairman may have to assist the shareholders in formulating a suitable proposal.

MEMBER: [Yes]

Note: The Chairman should allow the Member to explain his point of view and allow debate on the motion generally.

CHAIRMAN: I now propose to put the proposal to adjourn to the vote. Ladies and gentlemen, the proposal is that the meeting be adjourned to [day, time and place]. Will those in favour of the proposal place please raise their hands/[colour] voting cards.

Thank you.

PAUSE TO ESTIMATE VOTES

Those against. Thank you.

IF PROPOSAL IS CARRIED, CHAIRMAN SHOULD CALL FOR A POLL:

Note: When deciding how to cast the votes of proxies, the Chairman must consider the intentions of the shareholders who have appointed him as their proxy and act accordingly. Therefore how the Chairman votes will depend on the circumstances. For instance, if the intention of the adjournment is to defeat the resolution, the Chairman should cast the votes of those proxies who voted against the resolution in favour of the proposal to adjourn. If in doubt the Chairman should seek advice on the matter.

CHAIRMAN: In accordance with Article [No.] of the Company's Articles of Association, I call for a poll on the proposal to adjourn the meeting. On this poll on the proposal to adjourn I am assuming that those members who have appointed me with a direction that I vote in favour of [resolution [   ]] [the resolutions proposed in the notice of meeting] approve of the conduct of the business before the meeting at this time.

Accordingly, I intend to cast those votes against the proposal to adjourn. I also propose to cast against the proposal those votes where I have been given a discretion how to vote. These amount in total to [   ] votes. [I intend to abstain] in relation to those members who have appointed me with a direction that I vote against [resolution [   ]] [the resolutions proposed in the notice of meeting].

GO TO PARA. 21.5.3

IF PROPOSAL NOT CARRIED, PROCEED WITH BUSINESS OF MEETING

IF PROPOSAL IS NOT CARRIED BUT THERE IS A CALL FOR A POLL FROM THE FLOOR:

CHAIRMAN: A proposal to adjourn the meeting has been called for. Before I explain the procedure I think the meeting should be aware that on the poll I am assuming that those members who have appointed me with a direction that I vote in favour of [resolution [   ]] [the resolutions proposed in the notice of meeting] approve of the conduct of the business before the meeting at this time. Accordingly, I intend to cast those votes against the proposal to adjourn. I also propose to cast against the proposal those votes where I have been given a discretion how to vote. These amount in total to [   ] votes. I intend to abstain in relation to those members who have appointed me with a discretion that I vote against [resolution [   ]] [the resolutions proposed in the notice of meeting]. In view of the substantial majority of votes against the proposal to adjourn and as the conducting of a poll is a lengthy process, do those calling for a poll feel that this is a worthwhile exercise?

IF PROPOSAL IS WITHDRAWN PROCEED WITH BUSINESS OF MEETING

IF MEMBER PERSISTS, GO TO PARA. 21.5.2.

21.7   DEMAND FOR AN AMENDMENT TO A RESOLUTION

An amendment to an ordinary resolution must be relevant to the resolution and with the scope of the notice convening the meeting. Otherwise, it should be ruled out of order. In addition, the amendment must not be so fundamental as to destroy the intent of the original resolution. If it does, it should be ruled out of order. A special resolution may only be passed in the form set out in the notice, so any amendment (other than typographical or grammatical corrections) should be ruled out of order.

CHAIRMAN: Can you tell me whether you are a member or a corporate representative of a member.

IF NOT, PROPOSED AMENDMENT SHOULD BE RULED OUT OF ORDER

CHAIRMAN: What is your full name and in what name is the shareholding registered?   I will ask the Registrars to verify your status.   Will shareholders please bear with me while this exercise is completed.

IF STATUS IS NOT CORRECT:

CHAIRMAN: The Registrar advises me that you do not have the required status to call for an amendment so I must rule the proposed amendment out of order.

RETURN TO THE MAIN SCRIPT.

IF STATUS IS CORRECT:

CHAIRMAN: The Registrar advises me that your status has been verified.   Would you now please state precisely what your proposed amendment is.

MEMBER: [. . . . .]

CHAIRMAN: The proposal is that we amend Resolution [   ] to read as follows [. . . . .]

Note: Chairman gives his views on the amendment (taking advice as necessary) and invites debate from the floor, taking comments/questions in turn. After debate ends, the Chairman assesses the mood of the meeting and (if appropriate) asks whether in the light of the debate the person wishes to withdraw the proposed amendment. If the member does withdraw, return to the main script. If person does not withdraw, or there appears to be support for the amendment, the Chairman should propose a vote.

CHAIRMAN: I propose to put the proposal to amend the Resolution to the vote. [Repeat proposed amendment].

Those in favour of the proposal to amend please raise your voting cards.

Thank you.

Those against?

IF AMENDMENT IS CARRIED, CHAIRMAN MAY DEMAND A POLL

CHAIRMAN: In accordance with article [No.] of the Company's Articles of Association I exercise my right to demand a poll on the proposal to amend resolution [   ].

On this poll on the proposal to amend resolution [   ], I am assuming that those members who have appointed me with a direction that I vote in favour of the resolution which it is proposed to amend approve of the resolution in its existing form. Accordingly, I intend to cast those votes against the proposal to amend the resolution. I also propose to cast against the proposal those votes where I have been given a discretion how to vote. These amount in total to [   ] votes. I intend to abstain in relation to those members who have appointed me with a discretion that I vote against the resolution which it is proposed to amend.

GO TO PARA. 21.5.3.

IF AMENDMENT NOT CARRIED, PROCEED TO A VOTE ON THE SUBSTANTIVE RESOLUTION UNLESS A POLL IS DEMANDED FROM THE FLOOR, IN WHICH CASE, PROCEED AS FOLLOWS:

CHAIRMAN: A poll on the proposed amendment to resolution [No.] has been called for. Before I explain the procedure I think that the meeting should be aware that on the poll I am assuming that those members who have appointed me with a direction that I vote in favour of the resolution which it is proposed to amend approve of the resolution in its existing form. Accordingly, I intend to cast those votes against the proposal to amend the resolution. I also propose to cast against the proposal those votes where I have been given a discretion how to vote. These amount in total to [   ] votes. I intend to abstain in relation to those members who have appointed me with a direction that I vote against the resolution which it is proposed to amend. In view of the substantial majority of votes against the proposal to amend the resolution, and as the conducting of a poll is a lengthy process, do those calling for a poll feel that this is a worthwhile exercise?

Note: As regards proxy votes against the resolution, it is difficult to decide whether the Chairman should vote them for or against the amendment. Accordingly, the safest course is to abstain. The proxy form should be drafted so as to give the Chairman the discretion to vote as he thinks fit on other business at the meeting (including adjournments and amendments validly coming before the meeting). The Chairman may wish to adopt the proposed amendment.

IF MEMBER WITHDRAWS:

CHAIRMAN: As you have now decided not to call for a poll, I will proceed with the business of the meeting. I therefore intend to propose the resolution in its original format. Are there any more questions on the resolution?

RETURN TO MAIN SCRIPT

IF MEMBER PERSISTS, GO TO PARA. 21.5.2

21.8   DISRUPTION

CHAIRMAN: Would you please be quiet so that other members can ask questions and the meeting can carry on.

MEMBER: No [or equivalent].

CHAIRMAN: If you do not stop I will have to ask you to leave the meeting.

MEMBER: No [or equivalent].

CHAIRMAN: This behaviour is intolerable. With the consent of the meeting I propose to expel you from this meeting [pause to gauge dissension]. [Mr X] would you please arrange for the stewards to escort this gentleman/lady from the meeting.

IF DISRUPTION IS SUCH AS TO REQUIRE A BRIEF ADJOURNMENT

CHAIRMAN: It is quite impossible for this meeting to continue while this disruption is going on. In order to allow tempers to cool and to enable order to be restored I adjourn this meeting for [15 minutes].

Note: In the event that disruption comes from an external source – e.g. a fire alarm is set off – consult advisers. It may be possible to have a short interruption and avoid a full adjournment.

21.9   VOTE ON CLOSURE OF THE DEBATE

CHAIRMAN: We have now debated this proposal for [time] and I believe that despite the opposition of a small minority, most members would like now to vote on the resolution.

IF NO OPPOSITION, ANNOUNCE A VOTE ON THE RESOLUTION

IF THERE IS STILL OPPOSITION TO THIS:

CHAIRMAN: In the circumstances I propose to put forward a separate motion first:

THAT the debate be closed and a vote taken on the special/ordinary resolution.

PROCEED TO VOTE ON A SHOW OF HANDS

CHAIRMAN: I declare the motion carried; we will now vote on the original resolution before the meeting.

IF CLOSURE MOTION IS NOT CARRIED, DISCUSSION ON THE RESOLUTION SHOULD BE ALLOWED TO CONTINUE

How to avoid holding general meetings

Prior to 1992, private companies were required to have at least two members. In order to comply with this requirement, many private companies were formed with one member holding 99 per cent or more of the shares and the other (usually a spouse or relative) just one. To the majority shareholder (the effective proprietor) the requirement to hold general meetings seemed to be an unnecessary administrative burden. The same was true where the vast majority of the shares were held by a small group of shareholders (usually the directors) who knew that they could pass any resolution they wanted at a general meeting.

Not surprisingly, it often used to emerge during litigation involving private companies that general meetings had not been held when they should. This could have dire consequences for the company and its directors. For example, it has been held that where the articles require a proportion of the directors to retire by rotation at the annual general meeting and no such meetings have been held, those due to retire will be deemed to have retired without being reappointed at the end of the year in which the annual general meeting at which they should have retired should have been held (*Morris* v. *Kanssen* [1946] A.C. 459). If this had gone on for a number of years, it may turn out that there were not sufficient directors to form a quorum at board meetings or, even, no directors at all.

Companies sometimes prepared minutes of meetings which had not actually taken place. This became known as holding a 'paper meeting'. Legally, no meeting had been held, and the transactions recorded in the minutes could be declared invalid if this emerged. In reality, a paper meeting is no better than no meeting at all.

Members can approve a transaction without holding a formal meeting if they all consent informally to that transaction. However, the courts apply this rule rigorously. A failure to obtain the consent of any member will be fatal, even if that member holds an insignificant number of shares (see Chapter 22).

Following pressure from the professional and business community, the government took the opportunity presented by the Companies Act 1989 to amend the 1985 Act to allow private companies to:

- pass resolutions without holding meetings by written resolution (see Chapter 23); and
- dispense with the annual general meeting (and other related formalities) under an elective regime (see Chapter 24).

CHAPTER TWENTY-TWO

Informal agreement

22.1 SUMMARY

It is now fairly well established that if all the shareholders who are entitled to vote
unanimously approve a proposal that is within the company's powers, it does not
matter whether a formal resolution was put to the vote or that the requirements as to
notice were not complied with or that the members did not give their assent at a
meeting at which they were all present (see para. 22.2).

In a recent case, the court expressed some doubt about the efficacy of passing a
special resolution for the reduction of capital in this way (see para. 22.3).

22.2 UNANIMOUS CONSENT

In *Re Express Engineering Works Ltd* [1920] 1 Ch. 466, five persons, who were the
only directors and shareholders of the company, resolved at a board meeting to
purchase some property from a syndicate in which they were interested. The
company's articles disqualified a director from voting on any contract in which he was
interested. Subsequently the liquidator sought to have the transaction set aside on the
basis that the directors were precluded from voting and that the members were only
capable of acting at a properly constituted general meeting. However, the Court of
Appeal held that although the meeting was referred to in the minutes as a board
meeting, the unanimous informal consent of the five as the members of the company
was capable of binding the company.

It has also been held that provided that all the members assent and the transaction
is within the company's powers, the members may assent at different times (*Parker &
Cooper* v. *Reading* [1926] Ch. 975). In *Cane* v. *Jones* [1981] 1 All E.R. 533, it was held
that an agreement signed by all the shareholders that the chairman should cease to be
entitled to use his casting vote, had the same effect as a special resolution altering the
articles to that effect, and it was immaterial that the statutory obligation to file such
resolutions had not been complied with.

In *Re Duomatic Ltd* [1969] 1 All E.R. 161, directors' salaries were paid without being authorised by a resolution of the shareholders as required by the articles. It was held that the agreement of the two directors who held all the voting shares amounted to an informal ratification of the payment of unauthorised salaries even though they had never constituted themselves as a shareholders' meeting. The fact that they had not informed or sought the agreement of the sole holder of the company's preference shares had no bearing because all that was required was the unanimous agreement of the members entitled to vote. A different conclusion was reached in relation to a payment made to a director for loss of office because s. 312 requires particulars of the proposed payment to be disclosed to the members and no such disclosure had taken place with regard to the preference shareholder.

The fact that the informal consent of members must be unanimous was emphasised in *EBM Co. Ltd* v. *Dominion Bank* [1937] 3 All E.R. 555. In this case, there were five shareholders, three of whom held over 99 per cent of the shares. The other two shareholders had one share each. A resolution of the three major shareholders was held not to bind the company in relation to security given to a bank for a loan despite the fact that the other two holdings were insignificant.

22.3 POSSIBLE EXCEPTIONS

Section 121 allows companies to alter their share capital in certain ways if the articles allow. Section 121(4) provides that the powers conferred by s. 121 must be exercised by the company in general meeting. It is not entirely clear whether this would exclude the operation of the principle of informal consent. However, it would be advisable to assume that this was the case.

In *Re Barry Artist plc* [1985] B.C.L.C. 283, the court confirmed a reduction in capital which had been agreed informally by all the members with 'great reluctance' and warned that this procedure would not be accepted in future reductions. Section 135 of the 1985 Act requires a reduction in capital to be passed by special resolution. It also provides that the resolution is subject to the confirmation of the court. It is not clear from the judgment of Nourse J. why this should be the case. *Cane* v. *Jones* has already established that a special resolution may be passed informally where all the members agree. The distinguishing feature in this case seems to be that to have any effect the resolution must be confirmed by the court. This is an important practical distinction because a refusal to confirm the resolution will not have any serious effect on the company. If all the members agreed to pass the resolution informally, they could just as easily do so by written resolution or at a formal meeting. In most of the other cases referred to in this chapter, if the court had not accepted that the members could bind the company by acting in his way, it would have been necessary to set aside a transaction which had been relied upon by certain parties in good faith.

It follows that it would be unwise to test the court's resolve on any resolution which must be submitted to it for confirmation. It should be added that, certainly in the case of a private limited company, it would be safer to use the statutory procedure for written resolutions (see Chapter 23). In truth, most of the cases regarding informal agreement of members have arisen because the people involved in the management of the company have not been aware of the requirement to obtain the agreement of shareholders to a particular course of action. It is rare for the members, when properly advised, to rely on this method of decision-making (see, however, para. 22.4 below).

22.4   SINGLE MEMBER COMPANIES

The sole member of a private limited company may, of course, make a decision which binds the company without holding a formal meeting at any time. The Act provides that where a sole member takes any decision which may be taken by the company in general meeting, he shall (unless the decision is taken by way of written resolution) provide the company with a written record of that decision [s. 382B(1)] (see **Precedent 22.4**). A sole member who fails to comply with this requirement will be liable to a fine [s. 382B(2)]. However, failure to comply will not invalidate the decision of the sole member [s. 382B(3)].

Whether it is advisable for the sole member to adopt this informal method for all purposes is open to question. The consultative document which preceded the regulations amending the Act in 1992 stated that s. 382B was intended to deal with the types of decision the courts have held may be taken by the members unanimously without the need for a formal meeting of the company or a written resolution. It would seem, therefore, that informal decisions should not be used for matters such as a reduction of capital where the Act specifies formalities. Informal decisions can, however, be used for passing ordinary resolutions and, it seems, changing the articles.

It will always be safer for the sole member of a private limited company to make decisions using the statutory procedures for written resolutions and there is no real advantage in using the informal arrangements in view of the recent amendments to the statutory procedures (see para. 23.2).

CHAPTER TWENTY-THREE

Written resolutions

23.1 SUMMARY

In this chapter, we examine the statutory procedures for written resolutions of private companies (see para. 23.2) and the provisions which are commonly found in the articles on written resolutions of the members (see para. 23.5).

23.2 STATUTORY PROCEDURES FOR WRITTEN RESOLUTIONS

A private company may be able to avoid holding a general meeting (or a class meeting) by using the statutory procedure for written resolutions set out in ss. 381A to 381C of the Act. The resolution must be signed by (or on behalf of) all the members who would be entitled to vote at a general meeting (or class meeting) at the date of the resolution. This is a stringent requirement. One member can prevent the resolution being passed by written resolution by refusing to sign. This does not mean that the resolution cannot be passed at all. It could still be passed at a general meeting (or class meeting) if the necessary majority can be obtained.

A resolution agreed to as a written resolution in accordance with s. 381A has effect as if it was passed by the company in general meeting (or a meeting of the relevant class of members) and any reference in any statute to a meeting at which a resolution is passed or to members voting in favour of a resolution shall be construed accordingly [s. 381A(4)].

23.2.1 Resolutions which may be passed as written resolutions

Any matter which a private company may do by a resolution at a general meeting (or at a meeting of any class of members) may be done by written resolution [s. 381A]. This includes anything required by statute or the company's articles to be done by an ordinary, extraordinary, special or elective resolution. The only exception to this rule is that a written resolution cannot be used to pass:

- a resolution under s. 303 removing a director before the expiration of his period of office;
- a resolution under s. 391 removing an auditor before the expiration of his term of office [s. 381A(7) and Part 1 of Schedule 15A].

It is not possible to hold an annual general meeting by written resolution. The Act requires a meeting to be held [s. 366]. It should also be noted that a written resolution cannot be used to lay the accounts. In order to comply with the requirements of s. 241, a general meeting must be held. Strictly speaking, it is not necessary for the members to approve or adopt the accounts to comply with s. 241 (although it is common practice to put such a resolution to the meeting). A company which lays its accounts at a general meeting will have complied with s. 241 even if the accounts are not approved by the members, either because a vote on a resolution to adopt them was lost or no such resolution was put to the meeting. It is, of course, open to a private company to dispense with holding annual general meetings and the laying of the accounts by passing an elective resolution to that effect (see Chapter 24).

23.2.2   Special rules for certain resolutions passed as written resolutions

Part II of Schedule 15A lists a number of resolutions which cannot be passed as a written resolution unless the company has furnished members with certain documents or information. If such a resolution is to be proposed as a written resolution, the relevant documents must be sent with or attached to the copy of the written resolution given to each member to sign. A copy must also be sent to the company's auditors [s. 390(2)(a)]. Matters subject to these special rules are as follows:

- a resolution under s. 95(2) regarding disapplication of pre-emption rights;
- a resolution giving approval under s. 155(4) or (5) for financial assistance for purchase of company's own shares or those of holding company;
- a resolution conferring authority to make an off-market purchase of the company's own shares under s. 164(2);
- a resolution conferring authority to vary a contract for an off-market purchase of the company's own shares under s. 164(7);
- a resolution varying, revoking or renewing any authority under s. 164(3);
- a resolution giving approval under s. 173(2) for the redemption or purchase of company's own shares out of capital;
- a resolution approving any such term as is mentioned in s. 319(1) (director's contract of employment for more than five years); and
- a resolution under s. 337(3)(a) to fund a director's expenditure in performing his duties.

23.2.3   No notice required

A written resolution may be used to pass a resolution without complying with the requirements as to notice which would apply if it was proposed at a general meeting. Effectively, no notice need be given and there is no need for the members to sign any form of consent to short notice. This is logical because, by signing the written resolution, the members effectively indicate their consent to the use of a procedure which does not require prior notice to be given.

23.2.4   Form of written resolution

To pass a written resolution, a copy of the full text of the resolution must be signed by or on behalf of all the members who at the date of the resolution would be entitled to attend and vote at a general meeting (or meeting of the relevant class of members). It is not necessary for the members' signatures to be on a single document. The members may sign separate documents provided that each document accurately states the terms of the resolution [s. 381A(2)]. In practice, this means that the wording of the resolution on each document should be identical. The form of words which precede the substantive resolution should make it clear that the resolution is being proposed as a written resolution under the statutory procedures (see **Precedent 23.2A** for a members resolution, **Precedent 23.2B** for a written resolution of a class of members).

23.2.5   Copy to auditors

If a director or secretary of a company knows that it is proposed to seek agreement to a resolution in accordance with section 381A and knows the terms of the resolution, he shall, if the company has auditors, secure that a copy of the resolution is sent to them (see **Precedent 23.2C**) or that they are otherwise notified of its contents, at or before the time the resolution is supplied to a member for signature [s. 381B(1)]. Failure to do so does not affect the validity of any resolution [s. 381B(4)]. However, the directors and the secretary will be liable to a fine unless they can prove that the circumstances were such that it was not practicable to comply with this requirement or that they believed on reasonable grounds that a copy of the resolution had been sent to the company's auditors or that the auditors had otherwise been informed of its contents. Section 381B used to require a copy of any intended written resolution to be sent to the company's auditors. It also provided that the resolution would not be effective unless and until:

- the auditors notify the company that the resolution does not concern them as auditors or that although it does concern them as auditors it need not be considered by the company in general meeting (or by a meeting of the relevant class of members); or
- a period of seven days has elapsed since the auditors received the copy of the resolution and they have not given notice that in their opinion the resolution should be considered at a general or class meeting [s. 381B].

These requirements were repealed by the Deregulation (Resolutions of Private Companies) Order 1996 which substituted a new s. 381B in the Act. The provisions of the Act relating to meetings at Appendix A have been amended to reflect this Order.

23.2.6   Company with no auditors

The new s. 381B only imposes a duty on the directors and secretary to send a copy of a proposed written resolution to the auditors where the company has auditors. A company may not have auditors because it is a new company which has not yet appointed auditors or it is a dormant company which has dispensed with the appointment of auditors under s. 250. This has clarified a failing of the old s. 381B which made no provision for companies without auditors.

23.2.7   Date written resolution passed

A written resolution will be regarded as passed on the date on which the resolution is signed by (or on behalf of) the last member to sign [s. 381A(3) and (5) as amended by the Deregulation (Resolutions of Private Companies) Order 1996]. Previously, a written resolution was not effective unless and until the auditors had notified the company that the resolution need not be considered at a general meeting (or class meeting) or had failed to respond within seven days of receipt of a copy of the resolution.

23.2.8   Filing requirements

The requirement to file copies of certain resolutions at Companies House applies even though they have been passed as written resolutions (see para. 7.6).

23.3   RECORD OF WRITTEN RESOLUTION

A record of any written resolution (and of the signatures) must be entered in the company's minute book for general meetings. Any such record signed by a director or the secretary is evidence of the passing of the resolution. [s. 382A] (see **Precedent 23.3**).

23.4   SINGLE MEMBER COMPANIES

The new statutory procedures for written resolutions will be particularly useful for the sole member of a private limited company. Before the procedures were amended, it was often quicker to pass a resolution at a general meeting called at short notice than to use the written resolution procedures because of the need to wait up to seven days after the auditors received their copy of the resolution before it took effect. However, there is now nothing to be gained from holding a formal meeting of the sole member and written resolutions will almost certainly become the standard method of decision-making. The directors and the secretary should, of course, send a copy of the proposed resolution to the auditors before the sole member signs it or ensure that they are notified in some other way of its contents.

23.5 WRITTEN RESOLUTION UNDER POWERS IN ARTICLES OF ASSOCIATION

Many companies' articles contain a clause which provides a procedure for written resolutions of the members. For example reg. 53 of Table A states:

> **53.** A resolution in writing executed by or on behalf of each member who would have been entitled to vote upon it if it had been proposed at a general meeting at which he was present shall be as effectual as if it had been passed at a general meeting duly convened and held and may consist of several instruments in the like form executed by or on behalf of one or more members.

Section 381C (as amended by the Deregulation (Resolutions of Private Companies Order) 1996) states that the statutory procedures for written resolutions have effect notwithstanding any provision of the company's memorandum or articles, but do not prejudice any power conferred by any such provision. This means that a private company may pass a written resolution in accordance with ss. 381A to 381B even if its articles require a meeting to be held. It also means that a private company can pass a written resolution in accordance with the statutory procedures or in accordance with any valid provision in its memorandum or articles of association.

As the statutory procedures have now been relaxed, there will usually be little to be gained from using the procedures specified by the articles. Indeed, it is probably safer to use the statutory procedures. There has always been a question mark over the validity of written resolutions passed in accordance with the articles where the Act requires notice of the resolution to be accompanied by other documents (see para. 23.2.2) or special notice of the resolution is required. These matters are dealt with under the statutory procedures, although it is not possible to pass a resolution to remove a director or the auditors before the conclusion of the period of office. It should also be noted that articles such as reg. 53 of Table A merely restate the position under their common law as to informal agreement. The only difference is that the agreement of the members to the resolution under provisions contained in the articles must be evidenced in writing. It probably follows that, any provision in the Act which defeats the common law rule will also defeat a provision in the articles (see para. 22.3).

Public companies cannot pass written resolutions under ss. 381A to 381C. However, many have a provision in their articles similar to reg. 53 of Table A, in which case the same caveats will apply to the use of those procedures. In practice, it is virtually impossible for most public companies to secure the agreement of all their members to a proposal and this question will only be of interest to those that are closely held.

23.5.1   Signature by a smaller proportion of members

The Act requires special, extraordinary and elective resolutions and resolutions requiring special notice to be passed at general meetings. Even where it requires something to be done by ordinary resolution, it often specifies that this must be done at a general meeting (e.g. s. 80 (authority to allot shares) and s. 385 (annual appointment of auditors)). The common law rule on informal consent is that the members must comply with the requirements of the Act unless all those who are entitled to vote at a general meeting have assented to the proposal (see *EBM Co. Ltd* v. *Dominion Bank* [1937] 3 All E.R. 555). Articles on written resolutions can be viewed as a slightly more formal codification of this rule. The articles cannot exclude the operation of the Act unless the Act allows. The articles could not therefore provide a procedure for written resolutions which does not require the agreement of all the members entitled to vote at a general meeting (e.g. require the signature of members holding only 90 per cent of the voting shares). The fact that s. 381C now states that the statutory procedures for written resolutions do not prejudice any power conferred by the articles in that regard, does not mean that any provision in the articles will be valid. All it means is that any provision which was valid before the statutory procedures were introduced will still be valid. The only possible exception to this principle would be on a resolution to approve something which was not required to be done in a particular way by the Act but by the articles, e.g. the appointment of directors or the issue of instructions by the members to the directors. In fact, articles of joint venture companies often provide for a type of written resolution procedure for the appointment of directors by each of the members. In such cases, a member holding less than 50 per cent of the shares may be able to appoint a specified number of directors by giving notice in writing to the company.

CHAPTER TWENTY-FOUR

Elective regime

24.1 SUMMARY

A private company may elect to dispense with the annual general meeting and other related formalities. This must be done by passing an elective resolution in accordance with the requirements of s. 379A (see para. 24.2). A private company can pass an elective resolution under this elective regime to:

(a) dispense with holding annual general meetings [s. 366A] (see para. 24.3);
(b) dispense with the laying of accounts and reports before general meetings [s. 252] (see para. 24.4);
(c) dispense with the annual appointment of auditors [s. 386] (see para. 24.5);
(d) extend the period for which the general meeting may authorise the directors to allot shares under s. 80 of CA 1985 [s. 80A] (see para. 24.6); or
(e) reduce the majority required to authorise short notice of meetings [s. 369(4) & s. 378(3)] (see para. 24.7).

It is possible to pass an elective resolution relating to some or all of the above dispensations. However, there is very little to be gained from dispensing with annual general meetings without electing to dispense with the requirement to lay the accounts or the annual appointment of auditors. In these circumstances, a general meeting would need to be held each year to comply with these requirements. On the other hand, it may not be necessary to extend the period for which the general meeting may authorise the directors to allot shares in order to avoid holding general meetings. Authority (if it is required) can already be granted for up to five years. Similarly, reducing from 95 to 90 per cent the majority required to authorise short notice of meetings may be pointless if each member of the company holds more than 10 per cent of the shares.

24.2 ELECTIVE RESOLUTIONS

The procedural requirements for passing an elective resolution to dispense with any of the above requirements are set out in s. 379A of the Companies Act 1985. The resolution will not be effective unless it is agreed to at a general meeting, in person or by proxy, by all the members entitled to attend and vote at the meeting. It should be stressed that this means all the members and not just those who attend the meeting. If one member fails to vote, the resolution will not be valid. This is clearly an onerous requirement. The majority required to pass other types of resolution is based on a percentage of those actually voting.

At least 21 days' notice must be given in writing of the intention to propose such a resolution as an elective resolution at a general meeting of the company and the terms of the resolution must be given in full in the notice of the meeting. Formerly, it was not possible to pass an elective resolution at short notice. This has now been changed by the Deregulation (Resolutions of Private Companies) Order 1996 which inserted a new subsection 2A in s. 379A which provides that an elective resolution shall be effective notwithstanding the fact that less than 21 days' notice in writing of the meeting has been given if all the members entitled to attend and vote at the meeting so agree.

24.2.1 Passing an elective resolution by written resolution

Even if all the members support a proposal to pass an elective resolution, it may be difficult to bring them all together at a meeting to approve the resolution. Fortunately, it is possible to pass an elective resolution without holding a meeting using the statutory procedures for written resolutions set out in ss. 381A to 381C (see para. 23.2 above and **Precedent 24.2A**). No notice need be given when passing a resolution in this manner. Therefore it is not necessary for the members to consent to short notice.

24.2.2 Revocation of elective resolution

Circumstances may change after the company passes an elective resolution which may cause a member to wish to reverse the decision permanently or to suspend its operation. These safeguards can be invoked by any member and have the effect of temporarily suspending the operation of the elective resolution.

In addition, the members may at any time revoke an elective resolution by passing an ordinary resolution to that effect at a general meeting of the company [s. 379(3)] (see **Precedent 24.2B**).

24.2.3 Filing requirement

A copy of any elective resolution (and any subsequent ordinary resolution to revoke it) must be sent to the registrar of companies within 15 days of it being passed. If an elective resolution is in force to dispense with annual general meetings or to dispense with the laying of accounts before the company in general meeting, this must be shown on the company's annual return. A resolution will be in force until it is revoked and will stay in force even though a member has demanded that a meeting be held or that accounts be laid at a general meeting called for that purpose.

24.3 DISPENSING WITH THE AGM [s. 366A]

An elective resolution to dispense with annual general meetings (see **Precedent 24.3A**) has effect for the year in which it was made and subsequent years. However, it will have no effect on any liability already incurred for failing to hold an annual general meeting in the time allowed. In other words, the elective resolution must be passed before the annual general meeting becomes due or an offence will have been committed.

24.3.1 Notice requiring AGM

If an elective resolution to dispense with annual general meetings is in force (and an annual general meeting has not been held in that year), any member may require a meeting to be held by giving notice to the company not later than three months before the end of the year (see **Precedent 24.3B**). A company which receives such a notice on any date between 1 January and 30 September must hold an annual general meeting before the end of the year. If it fails to do so, the default provisions of s. 366(4) will apply. It should be noted that in such circumstances the elective resolution continues to be in force. Thus, the company would not need to hold an annual general meeting in the following year unless required to do so again under these procedures or the elective resolution has subsequently been revoked in accordance with s. 379A(3) by an ordinary resolution of the company in general meeting.

If an elective resolution dispensing with annual general meetings is revoked by passing an ordinary resolution to that effect, the company must hold an annual general meeting before the end of the calendar year in which the ordinary resolution was passed unless it was passed after 30 September, in which case it must start holding annual general meetings the following year [s. 366A(5)].

24.4 DISPENSING WITH THE LAYING OF ACCOUNTS [s. 252]

If a resolution to dispense with annual general meetings is to serve any practical purpose, it should be accompanied by a resolution to dispense with the laying of accounts before the members in general meeting, otherwise a general meeting will need to be called each year to lay the accounts (see **Precedent 24.4A**). An election under s. 252 to dispense with the laying of accounts and reports has effect in relation to the accounts and reports of the financial year in which the resolution was passed and subsequent financial years. Thus, if the company has not already done so, it must still lay the accounts of the previous financial year before the company in general meeting. To avoid confusion amongst the members, it is probably best to propose this and any other elective resolutions at the meeting (preferably the AGM) at which accounts for the previous financial year are laid.

A company which has elected to dispense with the laying of accounts and reports must still prepare accounts and send copies to anyone entitled to receive them under s. 238. Copies must be sent not less than 28 days before the end of the period allowed for laying and delivering accounts and reports, i.e. for a private company, 10 months less 28 days after the end of the company's accounting reference period. They must be accompanied, in the case of accounts sent to a member of the company, by a notice informing him of his right to require the laying of the accounts and reports before a general meeting [s. 253(1)] (see **Precedent 24.4B**).

24.4.1 Member may require accounts to be laid

While an elective resolution dispensing with the laying of accounts is in force any member may require the company to hold a general meeting for the purpose of laying the accounts and reports [s. 253(2)]. A member must deposit at the company's registered office notice in writing to that effect (see **Precedent 24.4C**) 'before the end of the period of 28 days beginning with the day on which the accounts are sent out', e.g. if the accounts were sent out on 1 July, not later than 29 July. If within 21 days of the date of deposit of the notice, the directors do not proceed to convene a general meeting to be held within three months of the date of deposit, the person who deposited the notice may convene a meeting. In such circumstances, the member who convenes the meeting is entitled to recover from the company any reasonable expenses incurred and the company can recoup these from any outstanding or future fees or other remuneration due to the directors.

Copies of the accounts sent to members must be accompanied by a notice informing them of their rights under s. 253(2).

24.5 DISPENSING WITH THE REQUIREMENT TO APPOINT AUDITORS ANNUALLY [s. 386]

Under section 385, auditors must be appointed at the general meeting at which accounts are laid (normally the annual general meeting). Clearly, it is impossible to comply with this requirement if the company has passed an elective resolution dispensing with the requirement to lay the report and accounts. In those circumstances, s. 385A applies and the company must appoint auditors at a general meeting held within 28 days of the date on which copies of the company's annual accounts for the previous year are sent to members. Thus a company which has elected to dispense with annual general meetings and the laying of the accounts and reports, but not the requirement to appoint auditors annually, must hold a meeting to appoint auditors shortly after sending its accounts to the members. This requirement would, to say the least, be unduly burdensome and it would be unusual for a company not to take advantage of s. 386 which allows a private company to elect to dispense with the requirement to appoint auditors annually (see **Precedent 24.5A**).

When a resolution is passed to dispense with the annual appointment of auditors, the company's auditors are deemed to have been re-appointed for each succeeding financial year on the expiry of the time for appointing auditors. If the election is revoked in accordance with s. 379A, the auditors holding office at that time continue to hold office until either the conclusion of the next general meeting of the company at which accounts are laid or, if an elective resolution is still in force dispensing with the requirement to lay accounts, the expiry of the period for appointing auditors.

24.5.1   Termination of appointment of auditors not appointed annually

Usually, members have an opportunity to vote against the reappointment of the auditors at the general meeting at which accounts are laid. If the majority are opposed to their reappointment, the auditors will be removed. It should be noted that this gives the members an opportunity each year to remove the auditors without having to comply with the requirements as to special notice. Special notice is required where the auditors being proposed for appointment are not the same as those appointed previously by the members.

Where an elective resolution not to appoint auditors annually is in force, the Act provides a special procedure which allows members to vote not to reappoint auditors who would otherwise be reappointed automatically. In such circumstances, any member of the company may deposit notice in writing at the company's registered office proposing that the appointment of the company's auditors be 'brought to an end'. No member may deposit more than one such notice in any financial year of the company [s. 393(1)]. On receipt of such a notice, the directors have a duty to convene a general meeting of the company for a date not more than 28 days after the date on which the notice was given, and to propose at that meeting a resolution in a form enabling the company to decide whether the appointment of the company's auditors should be 'brought to an end'.

If the decision of the company at the meeting is that the appointment of the auditors should be 'brought to an end', the auditors shall not be deemed to be reappointed when next they would be and, if the notice was deposited within the period immediately following the distribution of the accounts (i.e. the period beginning with the day on which copies of the company's annual accounts are sent to the members under s. 238 and ending 14 days after that day), any deemed reappointment for the financial year following that to which those accounts relate which has already occurred shall cease to have effect [s. 393(2)].

If the directors fail to convene a meeting in accordance with these requirements within 14 days of the date of the deposit, the member (or members) who deposited the notice may convene the meeting themselves for a date which must be no later than three months after the date of deposit [s. 393(4)]. They must convene the meeting in the same manner as that in which meetings are to be convened by directors [s. 393(5)] and are entitled to be paid any reasonable expenses they incur in doing so [s. 393(6)].

This section does not prevent a member requisitioning a meeting to propose a resolution to remove the auditors in accordance with s. 391. Special notice of such a resolution must be given. The resolution proposed at a meeting requisitioned under s. 393 need only be framed so that the auditors appointment shall be brought to an end when they would next be deemed reappointed, etc. (e.g. to propose that the appointment of the company's auditors be brought to an end in accordance with the provisions of s. 393).

The directors could propose a resolution to remove the auditors immediately. However, to do so, they would have to comply with the requirements of s. 390. The notice given by the member under s. 393 does not constitute the first limb of the special notice requirements of s. 379.

24.5.2   Resignation of auditors while elective resolution in force

If an auditor resigns while the elective regime is in force, the directors may fill the vacancy under s. 388(1). The new auditor will, it seems, be automatically re-appointed from year to year by virtue of s. 386(2). Alternatively the appointment could be effected by a resolution of the members under s. 388(1). This would, however, require special notice of the resolution under s. 388(3). An extraordinary general meeting could be called to deal with the matter or the resolution could be passed as a written resolution under s. 381A.

24.5.3   Auditors' remuneration

Under s. 390A, the remuneration of auditors appointed by the directors as first auditors or to fill a casual vacancy must be fixed by the directors. When auditors are appointed (or re-appointed) by the company in general meeting, their remuneration must be fixed by the company in general meeting or in such manner as the company in general meeting may determine. However, while an elective resolution dispensing with the annual appointment of auditors is in force under s. 386, the auditors are deemed to have been re-appointed each year. Section 386 does not say who, if anyone, should be assumed to have reappointed them and s. 390A does not state how the auditors' remuneration should be fixed while the resolution is in force.

It is recommended that immediately after passing a resolution to dispense with the annual appointment of auditors, a resolution be passed authorising the directors to fix the remuneration of the auditors until such time as a resolution to appoint auditors is proposed at a general meeting of the company (see **Precedent 24.4B**). This may be necessary where the company in general meeting has been in the habit of fixing the auditors' remuneration itself or placing a cap on the amount which can be paid to the auditors or the previous resolution regarding auditors' remuneration was expressed in such a manner that it relates only to the financial year in which it was passed.

24.6   EXTENDING THE PERIOD OF THE DIRECTORS' AUTHORITY TO ALLOT SHARES [s.80A]

The directors cannot allot new shares unless they have been given authority to do so in accordance with the requirements of s. 80. Under s. 80(4), the maximum period for which authority can be given is five years. If required, this authority is usually renewed at the annual general meeting. In normal circumstances, it follows that a private company which has dispensed with annual general meetings and wishes to renew the directors' authority would need to call a general meeting. It can, however, avoid doing so by passing an elective resolution in accordance with s. 379A stating that the provisions of s. 80A shall apply, instead of the provisions of s. 80(4) and (5), in relation to the giving or renewal of authority to allot shares (see **Precedent 24.6A**). The provisions of s. 80A allow authority to be given to the directors by ordinary resolution for an indefinite period or for a fixed period longer than the five year maximum allowed under s. 80 (see **Precedent 24.6B**).

In order to extend the period in this manner, it is therefore necessary to pass two resolutions in the following order:

- an elective resolution stating that the provisions of s. 80A shall apply, instead of the provisions of s. 80(4) and (5), in relation to the giving or renewal of authority to allot shares; and
- an ordinary resolution authorising the directors to allot shares or other securities, specifying the maximum amount of shares of shares or other securities that may be allotted under it and the period to which the authority relates.

Any authority given in this manner (including an authority contained in the articles) may be revoked or varied by an ordinary resolution of the company in general meeting [s. 80A(3)].

24.7   ELECTION AS TO THE MAJORITY REQUIRED TO AUTHORISE SHORT NOTICE OF A MEETING [s. 369(4) and s. 378(3)]

This is perhaps the least useful of the dispensations available to private companies. It allows the majority required to authorise the holding of an extraordinary general meeting at short notice to be reduced from 95 per cent to as low as 90 per cent [s. 369(4)] and allows the majority required to authorise a special resolution to be proposed at short notice to be similarly reduced (see **Precedent 24.7**).

No advantage will be gained from passing an elective resolution along these lines if each shareholder owns more than 10 per cent of the voting shares. In these circumstances, the agreement of all the members would still be required to hold a meeting at short notice because a majority of 90 per cent could not be achieved if any member withheld consent. It must also be doubtful whether a member or members, holding between 5 and 10 per cent of the shares would vote in favour of a resolution which clearly undermines their rights. Nevertheless, there may be occasions when these relaxations may be helpful, e.g. where the company's shares are held in different names but are beneficially owned by the same person.

The elective resolution must specify the percentage which is to be substituted for the percentage in the two relevant sections. This percentage may be any figure which is less than 95 per cent but not lower than 90 per cent.

Minutes

CHAPTER TWENTY-FIVE

Minutes

25.1 SUMMARY

This chapter deals with minutes of general meetings and meetings of directors. Directors have a statutory duty to ensure that minutes are kept of general meetings and meetings of directors (see para. 25.2). It is not necessary for them to take or prepare the minutes themselves. This job normally falls to the company secretary (see para. 25.3).

Minutes should be kept securely in a minute book (see para. 25.4). They are part of the statutory books of the company and must be retained permanently (see para. 25.5). Minutes signed by the chairman will be *prima facie* evidence of the proceedings at that meeting (see paras. 25.6 and 25.7). Once they have been signed they should not be amended (see para. 25.8).

Minutes of general meetings must be made available for inspection by the members and the auditors. Members do not have a right to inspect the minutes of board meetings (see para. 25.10).

Minutes should contain certain basic information and provide an accurate record of the proceedings. There are many ways of doing this and the style adopted will depend on the use to which they are put and the preferences of the directors and secretary (see para. 25.11).

Special rules apply to members' written resolutions (see para. 25.12) and decisions taken by the sole member of a single member company (see para. 25.13).

25.2 GENERAL DUTY TO PREPARE AND KEEP

Every company is required to produce and keep minutes of all proceedings of general meetings and meetings of directors and managers [s. 382(1)]. The expression general meetings includes annual general meetings, extraordinary general meetings and class meetings. See s. 259 of the Insolvency Act and rule 5.22 of the Insolvency Rules for meetings in insolvency.

It is logical to assume that the phrase 'meetings of directors' in s. 382(1) includes committees of the board. However, in *Guinness plc* v. *Saunders* [1988] 2 All E.R. 940, the Court of Appeal held in relation to disclosure by directors of interests in contracts in accordance with s. 317 that 'a meeting of directors' does not include a committee of the board. It should be noted that for the purposes of s. 382 the phrase used is 'meetings of directors' and not 'a meeting of directors' as in s. 317. This, it is suggested, is sufficient to enable any court to distinguish the interpretation of the Court of Appeal, quite apart from the different context in which the words appear. In any case, most articles (including reg. 100 of Table A) state explicitly that the directors should keep minutes of committees of directors. In practice, where power to bind the company has been delegated to a committee, it will be necessary to keep minutes as evidence that transactions have been duly authorised. The requirement to keep minutes of committees of directors will apply even where a committee of only one director has been appointed. In this case, the minutes may take the form of a written record of decisions taken, signed by the director concerned.

25.3 WHO SHOULD TAKE THE MINUTES?

Preparing minutes of company meetings is one of the company secretary's core duties. If the company secretary is not available, it normally falls to the deputy or assistant secretary to undertake the task. Although not good practice, there is nothing to prevent someone else performing these functions. The report of the Cadbury Committee states at para. 4.25: 'It should be standard practice for the company secretary to administer, attend and prepare minutes of board proceedings.' ICSA's *Code on Good Boardroom Practice* also states:

> 9. The company secretary should be responsible to the chairman for the proper administration of meetings of the company, the board and any committees thereof. To carry out this responsibility the company secretary should be entitled to be present at (or represented at) and prepare (or arrange for the preparation of) minutes of the proceedings of all such meetings.

The company secretary and the directors can be fined for any default by the company of the provisions of the Act relating to the maintenance of minutes [s. 382(5), s. 383(4) and s. 722(3)]. Although the directors are responsible for ensuring that minutes are kept, it is difficult for them to contribute to the business of the meeting if they are also required to record the proceedings. It could also be argued that they lack the impartiality which the secretary can provide when drafting the minutes.

It is quite common for company secretaries to use an assistant to help take notes of the proceedings. This allows them to concentrate more on their advisory role during the meeting. It is also increasingly common for a recording of the meeting to be made to assist in the preparation of the minutes. This can be particularly helpful at AGMs where it is often difficult for the secretary to record all the names of speakers from the floor and, sometimes, difficult to understand the meaning of their questions or statements.

It should also be noted that transcripts and recordings of meetings can be called in evidence during legal proceedings to rebut the evidence of the minutes, and would have to be disclosed during the discovery process prior to those proceedings.

25.4 MINUTE BOOKS

Section 382 requires minutes to be entered in books kept for that purpose. However, s. 722 provides that any minute book required by the Act to be kept by the company may be kept either by making entries in bound books or 'by recording the entries in any other manner', provided in the latter case that adequate precautions are taken for guarding against falsification and for facilitating their discovery. Thus minutes may be typed or processed using a computer and included in a loose-leaf folder or pasted into a bound book. However, it is not entirely clear whether they can be kept on a computer.

25.4.1 Computerised records

According to s. 723, the words 'in any other manner' in s. 722(1) can include computer records provided that they are capable of being reproduced in a legible form. However, s. 382(2) states that minutes are evidence of the proceedings if they have been signed by the chairman of the meeting in question or the chairman of the next succeeding meeting. Until the courts recognise the validity of electronic signatures, it would seem that minutes prepared using a computer must still be produced in hard copy so that they can be signed by the chairman (for a case on electronic signatures, see *Re a Debtor (No.2021 of 1995)* [1996] 1 B.C.L.C. 538). It is less clear whether it is necessary to retain hard copies of minutes which have been signed by the chairman if, for example, they have been microfilmed or scanned into some sort of document imaging system. If either of these procedures are adopted, stringent measures to guard against falsification and for facilitating their discovery would be needed. The minutes would, of course, also have to be capable of being reproduced in legible form for the life of the company and beyond. This would mean retaining any necessary equipment or computer hardware and software. Assuming that all this can be done, the only remaining question would seem to be whether the courts will accept copies of minutes kept in this manner as evidence. In the authors' view, they would have no difficulty in doing so.

25.4.2 Guarding against falsification

Minutes may not be acceptable as evidence if inadequate precautions have been taken to guard against falsification. In a judgment prior to the current legislation, a loose-leaf minute book was rejected on the basis that: 'anyone wishing to do so . . . can take a number of leaves out and substitute any number of other leaves. It is a thing with which anyone disposed to be dishonest can easily tamper' (*Heart of Oaks Assurance Co. Ltd* v. *James Flower & Sons* [1936] 1 Ch. 76). Although the law now allows loose-leaf minute books, their content could easily be challenged if it could be proved that the security measures taken to guard against falsification were inadequate. In a more recent case, purported minutes of a directors' meeting were rejected as *prima facie* evidence of the proceedings because it was impossible to tell from the document who had chaired the meeting or who had signed them (no other evidence was submitted on the matter), and because the document had never been kept in a minute book *(POW Services* v. *Clare* [1995] 2 B.C.L.C. 435).

Some or all of the following safeguards should be adopted where minutes are kept in minute books:

- sequential numbering of the minutes of each type of meeting, e.g. if the last minute of the first meeting of directors is numbered minute 20, the first minute of the second meeting of directors should be numbered minute 21 and so on;
- the chairman should initial every page;
- pages should be numbered sequentially on specially printed paper;
- when pasted into bound books, the chairman's signature and initials should start on the printed sheet and run on to the bound page;
- the minute book should be kept in a safe (preferably fireproof) with restricted access;
- a lockable binder should be used, particularly for minutes kept in a loose-leaf folder; and
- minutes of general meetings and board meetings should be kept in separate books or folders to prevent members (who are entitled to inspect the minutes of general meetings) from gaining access to the minutes of meetings of directors and managers.

If copies of signed minutes are kept on microfiche or on a computerised document imaging system, the company should, at the very least, comply with the recommendations of the British Standards Institute for retaining documents in that form. However, it may be advisable to take additional precautions, e.g. to obtain board approval for the procedures and safeguards adopted.

25.5   RETENTION OF MINUTES

Minutes should be retained permanently, i.e. for at least the life of the company and possibly beyond in view of the provisions of s. 653(2) and reg. 32 of the Insolvency Regulations 1986. It is arguable whether it is necessary to keep the original signed copies if they have been microfilmed or recorded using a document imaging system (see para. 25.4.1 above). However, most companies still do so and this may be sensible until the matter is clarified.

25.6   SIGNATURE BY THE CHAIRMAN

Companies are given considerable leeway in the methods which they can adopt for approving the minutes and the ICSA's *Code on Good Boardroom Practice* recommends that boards should establish written procedures with regard to minutes of board meetings. Although minutes which have not been signed by the chairman may be admissible as evidence of the proceedings, they will certainly not be accorded the same weight.

25.6.1   General meetings

It is standard practice for the minutes of general meetings to be signed shortly after they have been prepared by the person who acted as the chairman of the meeting. This is often done at the first available board meeting so as to allow the other directors to make any comments but also so that an entry may be made in the board minutes to the effect that they were duly signed. If this procedure is followed, it is not necessary to seek the approval of the members at the next general meeting nor, indeed, to refer to the minutes of the previous meetings at all.

If the person who acted as the chairman of the meeting is unable or unwilling to sign the minutes, they should be signed by the chairman of the next general meeting.

If it is not possible to adopt this procedure, then the minutes should be read at the next general meeting (they cannot be taken as read unless all the members have received a copy) and a resolution put to the meeting that they be approved.

25.6.2   Meetings of directors

Board minutes are usually distributed in draft form to the directors for comment and signed by the chairman of the next succeeding board meeting. They are often included in the agenda papers for the meeting at which they are to be approved, particularly if any changes have been made to the first draft as a consequence of comments by directors. At the meeting, the minutes are usually taken as read and a motion is put recommending their adoption as a true and accurate record of the proceedings of the meeting to which they refer. If approved, they should be signed immediately by the chairman who need not have been present at the original meeting.

The chairman may, however, sign the minutes before the next succeeding meeting of the board and need not necessarily give the other directors an opportunity to comment on them. This will rarely be necessary and any chairman who follows this procedure should be prepared to explain to his fellow directors why he departed from the usual practice and expect to have the minutes scrutinised more closely than might normally be the case. If this procedure is followed and the directors disagree with the chairman's interpretation of the proceedings, they could pass a resolution to that effect which would be recorded in the minutes of that meeting. The minutes which were the subject of the disagreement should not be altered although it might be sensible for the secretary to make a marginal note in the original minutes cross-referring to the subsequent decision.

In the unlikely event that the chairman refuses to sign the minutes, it should be recorded in the minutes of the next meeting that they were approved as a true record by the other directors who were present at the original meeting, if that was the case.

25.7 EVIDENCE

Minutes are evidence of the proceedings of the relevant meeting once they have been signed by the chairman of that meeting or by the chairman of the next succeeding meeting [s. 382(2)]. However, they are only *prima facie* (on their face) evidence of the proceedings (*Re Indian Zoedone Co.* (1884) 26 Ch.D. 70). Other evidence is admissible to show that they are not an accurate record (*Re Llanharry Hematite Iron Ore Co., Roney's Case* (1864) 4 De G.J. & Sm. 426.) even if the articles state that they are to be taken as conclusive evidence without further proof (*Kerr* v. *Mottram* [1940] Ch. 657 and *Re Caratal (New) Mines Ltd* [1902] 2 Ch. 498).

25.8 AMENDMENT

Alterations can be made to the minutes before they have been signed as an accurate record by the chairman. The directors may request the chairman to amend the company secretary's original draft and may wish to amend the draft that is put before them at the next board meeting. Once the minutes have been included in the papers for a board meeting, they should be amended by longhand or typed entries on the original copy and each amendment should be initialled by the chairman before signing the minutes themselves.

Alterations should not be made after the minutes have been signed by the chairman. If the directors present at a subsequent meeting disagree with a decision taken at a previous meeting that is properly recorded in signed minutes, they should pass a further resolution rescinding or amending their previous decision which should be recorded in the minutes of that meeting. Similarly, if it is discovered after the minutes have been signed that they are inaccurate, a further resolution should be passed and recorded in the minutes of the meeting at which the inaccuracy was raised.

Details which were not available at the meeting should not be inserted in the minutes, e.g. the date of a call (*Re Cawley & Co.* (1889) 42 Ch.D. 209). However, resolutions can be framed so that they allow a director or the secretary to action a matter which is contingent upon further details being available.

25.9 RECORD OF ATTENDANCE

There is no need to keep a separate record of attendance at either general or board meetings unless the articles so provide (see, for example, reg. 86 of the 1948 Act Table A). However, it is important to include sufficient details in the minutes to show that a quorum was present or, in the case of meetings of directors, that a disinterested quorum was present. It should also be clear from the minutes who chaired the meeting. This is normally done by adding the words 'chairman' or 'in the chair' next to the name of the relevant director. If someone other than a director chairs a general meeting, this should also be apparent from the minute referring to the election of the chairman.

Reg. 100 of Table A requires the names of the directors present at meetings (including general meetings) to be included in the minutes of that meeting. If a director attends for only part of a meeting, this should be recorded in the minutes, normally by annotating the list of directors present with the words such as 'for minutes 23 to 34 only'. By doing so, it should be clear whether or not a disinterested quorum was present throughout the meeting.

Although it is not necessary to record in the minutes of general meetings the names of the members present at the meeting, it is essential to record the numbers present. As reg. 100 of Table A requires the names of the directors present at general meetings to be recorded in the minutes (whether or not they are also members), care should be taken not to include the directors who are also members in the number of other members present.

25.10   INSPECTION OF MINUTES

25.10.1   General meetings

The minutes of general meetings [s. 383(1)] and written resolutions agreed by the members [s. 382A(3)] must be kept at the company's registered office and be open to inspection by members of the company without charge. Inspection should be allowed for a minimum of two hours between 9am and 5pm on each business day (Companies (Inspection and Copying of Register, Indices and Documents) Regulations 1991 (S.I. 1991/1998)). Creditors and members of the public have no rights of inspection.

Members are entitled to be provided with copies of minutes of general meetings within 7 days of making a request. The company may make a small charge to cover administrative expenses subject to a maximum established by statutory instrument (currently 10p per 100 words). In practice, companies rarely levy the charge unless a member requests a large number of copies.

If the company wrongly refuses to allow an inspection or fails to provide copies of the minutes within the proper time, it and any responsible officer can be fined. In such circumstances, the court may order an immediate inspection or direct that the desired copies be sent.

Members are entitled to be accompanied by an advisor when they inspect the minutes of general meetings (*McCrusker* v. *McRae*, 1966 S.C. 253).

25.10.2   Meetings of directors

It is standard practice to distribute copies of the minutes to the directors before the next meeting or with the papers for the next succeeding meeting. In addition, however, directors have a common law right to inspect the minutes and to be accompanied by an advisor when they do so (*McCrusker* v. *McRae*, 1966 S.C. 253).

Members, creditors and members of the public are not entitled to inspect nor to take copies of the minutes of meetings of directors or managers.

25.10.3   By auditors

The auditors have a right of access to all books and such information and explanations necessary for the performance of their duties as auditors. This includes the minutes of general meetings, board meetings and any committees of the board. The auditors' letter of engagement will normally make some reference to the obligation of the company to make these records available for inspection.

25.11   CONTENT AND STYLE

Different people often have different views about what took place at a meeting. These views tend to become even more polarised as those present become blessed with the benefit of hindsight. There is little point holding formal meetings if no-one can remember what was decided at the meeting. The decisions taken must be recorded and those present should confirm that the record properly reflects what was decided. Preparing minutes is therefore an essential part of the decision-making process. It is also something of an art.

The secretary is expected to be psychic. Matters are decided without being expressed verbally. Individuals signal their agreement by gestures that would tax the most experienced auctioneer. Issues are discussed which no-one expects to be included in the minutes. The chairman does not follow the order of the agenda. The meeting will spend hours on trivial matters which are expected to be minuted in great detail and then gallop through the most important items. Despite all this, the secretary is expected to make sense of the meeting and produce in a timely manner (i.e. by tomorrow morning) an accurate and clear set of minutes. To cap it all, although everyone expects the minutes to record what they said in great detail, they also expect them to be concise.

The art of preparing minutes is not simply doing so concisely, accurately and clearly in the shortest possible time, although achieving these objectives requires a degree of aptitude. It is knowing when to sacrifice or adapt these principles. Egos must be smoothed. Detailed explanations may sometimes be required. On other occasions, brevity will be the only way to avoid opening old wounds.

Thus, although certain conventions are normally followed, the presentational style can be tailored. The preferences of the chairman will usually be the most influential. What can never be compromised, however, is the principle that the minutes should contain an accurate record of the decisions taken.

Although the minutes should represent a true and accurate record of the proceedings of the meeting, it is neither necessary, nor is it desirable, to include a transcript of the proceedings. According to *ICSA's Code of Good Boardroom Practice (1991)* they should 'record the decisions taken and provide sufficient background to those decisions'. Many different styles of presentation may be adopted provided that the minutes include the following basic elements:

- name of the company;
- type of meeting, e.g. annual general meeting or audit committee;
- place where the meeting was held;

- day and date of the meeting (it is not necessary to include the time);
- names and/or numbers present (see Record of attendance above);
- record of the proceedings; and
- chairman's signature.

The record of the proceedings should include the text of any resolutions put to the meeting and the result of any vote. It should also include a record of any amendments and procedural resolutions proposed at the meeting and the results of any vote on them. Any rulings made by the chairman should be recorded, e.g. on a demand for a poll. If a resolution is passed on a show of hands it is only necessary to state that the chairman declared the resolution carried. If a poll is called and taken, the number of votes for and against should be included in the minutes together with a statement as to whether the resolution was or was not carried (see **Precedent 25.11A**).

All papers presented at the meeting should be clearly identified in the minutes (see minute 77 of **Precedent 25.11C**) and retained for reference. In the interests of brevity, it is possible to refer in the minutes to papers presented at the meeting which contain the detailed proposals, rather than reproduce the proposals in full. Any such document should be initialled by the chairman for the purpose of identification and the minutes should record that fact. However, it should be noted that minutes are not user-friendly at the best of times and it will not help matters if readers have to make continuous reference to other documents in order to discern what decisions were taken. In addition, documents which are essential in order to understand the record of decisions taken in the minutes should be retained in the same way and for as long as the minutes themselves.

25.12   WRITTEN RESOLUTIONS

Where a written resolution is agreed to in accordance with s. 381A, a record of the resolution (and of the signatures) should be entered in the minute book in the same way as minutes of proceedings at general meetings [s. 382A(1)] (see **Precedent 23.3**). Any such record, if purporting to be signed by a director of the company or the company secretary, is evidence of the proceedings in agreeing to the resolution. Where a record is made in accordance with s. 382A, until the contrary is proved, the requirements of the Act with respect to those proceedings are deemed to be complied with [s. 382A(2)].

25.13   INFORMAL DECISIONS BY A SOLE MEMBER

Where a private company has only one member and that member takes any decision which may be taken by the company in general meeting and which has effect as if agreed by the company in general meeting, he shall (unless that decision is taken by way of a written resolution) provide the company with a written record of that decision [s. 382B] (see **Precedent 22.4**). Failure to do so renders the sole member liable to a fine but does not invalidate the decision [s. 382B(2) and (3)].

Meetings of directors

CHAPTER TWENTY-SIX

The board of
directors

26.1 SUMMARY

The Companies Act 1985 requires every public company formed after 1929 to have at least two directors and every other company to have at least one [s. 282]. The role of the directors is to manage the business on behalf of the shareholders. The directors and the shareholders may, of course, be the same people, particularly in small private companies. However, in larger companies the directors are more likely to be professional managers, appointed for their business acumen rather than their stake in the company.

As directors are appointed to manage the business on behalf of the shareholders, it would seem logical for the shareholders to appoint them. This is certainly the case with the first directors who must be nominated by the first members prior to incorporation in accordance with the Act (see para. 26.2.1). However, thereafter the method of appointment depends on the company's articles. The Act has very little to say on the matter. Most articles allow the members to appoint additional directors. However, they also allow the board of directors to make new appointments. In practice, this is how most directors are subsequently appointed. The articles usually preserve the primacy of the members by requiring any appointments made by the board each year to be approved by the members at the annual general meeting. In other words, the members are given an opportunity to reject people appointed by the board. Whether or not a company's articles follow this standard procedure, the Act gives the members a statutory right to remove a director by ordinary resolution at a general meeting [s. 303].

The practical procedures for the appointment of directors by the members in general meeting are dealt with in Chapter 20 at para. 20.8. Removal is dealt with at para. 20.11. This chapter includes a summary of the Table A provisions on appointment (see para. 26.2) and an analysis of the different types of director.

In the UK, all directors are members of the same board and usually have one vote each. Under this unitary system, each director has an equal say in matters put to the board. Articles usually allow the board to appoint one or more of the directors to some sort of executive office within the company (e.g. managing director) and to delegate any of its powers to them. These executive directors are usually salaried and manage the business of the company on a full-time basis (see para. 26.3.1).

Directors who are not executives are known as non-executive directors (see para. 26.3.2). The function of the board, and particularly the non-executives (if any), will be to take decisions which are outside the authority of the executive directors, to set the company's strategic objectives, and to monitor the performance of the executives.

On the continent, two-tier board systems are more common. The company is managed on a day-to-day basis by an executive board which is appointed by and is accountable to a supervisory board. The supervisory board fulfils the monitoring role performed by non-executive directors in the United Kingdom and may include shareholder and employee representatives. The system is appealing to purists as it places the non-executives above the executives in the structural hierarchy. However, it is doubtful whether these structural differences make it any easier for the part-time directors to supervise the executives.

The advantage of the unitary system is said to be that it enables the non-executive directors to contribute more effectively to the formulation of the company's strategic policies and to monitor the performance of the executives. Its major disadvantage is supposed to be that it is more difficult for the non-executive directors to be impartial and independent. This, and the fact that non-executive directors are often hand-picked by the executive directors, has caused questions to be raised about the effectiveness of the UK system of corporate governance. These criticisms were addressed in respect of listed companies in the report of the Cadbury Committee on the Financial Aspects of Corporate Governance in 1992. The report contains a code of best practice for listed companies which is intended to rectify some of these weaknesses (see further para. 32.2).

26.2   APPOINTMENT AND REMOVAL OF DIRECTORS

26.2.1   First directors

Before a company can be registered, the subscribers to the memorandum (i.e. the people who will become the company's first members) must submit a form (form 10) to the Registrar of Companies which gives the names and details of the first director(s). The form must be signed by the people nominated as proof that they are willing to act as directors. On incorporation, the people named as directors in form 10 are deemed to have been appointed the first directors of the company [s. 13(5)]. Thus the first director(s) will always be appointed by the first member(s). There is nothing to prevent the subscribers nominating themselves as the first directors.

If the articles require the directors to hold shares in the company, the Act provides that they will cease to be directors if they do not satisfy that requirement within two months or such shorter time as the articles may specify [s. 291]. The articles may also require the directors to satisfy other qualifications or provide for their removal from office on the happening of certain events.

26.2.2 Companies Act 1985

Thereafter the method of appointing replacement or additional directors will depend almost entirely on the company's articles. The Act only interferes by providing:

- that a director must comply within a certain period with any article requiring him to hold shares in the company [s. 291];
- that a motion for the appointment of two or more persons as directors by a single resolution at a general meeting of a public company shall not be valid unless the meeting agrees unanimously to a proposal that the resolution be proposed in that manner [s. 292];
- special procedures for the appointment by a public company or one of its subsidiaries of a director aged 70 or more [s. 293] (see para. 20.9); and
- that details of appointments of directors must be entered in a register by the company and notified to Companies House, although failure to do so does not invalidate the appointment [ss. 288 to 290].

Subject to these provisions, the Act does not concern itself with who may appoint directors or whether they should retire and offer themselves up for election at the annual general meeting following their appointment or retire by rotation thereafter. All these matters are left to the articles.

The Act does, however, give members a statutory right to remove any director by ordinary resolution (see para. 20.11). This right cannot be excluded by the articles, although the articles can provide an additional method of removal. If the members remove all the directors, the power to appoint directors will revert to the general meeting in default, regardless of anything the articles say.

26.2.3 Appointment provisions of Table A

Appointments by the board
Under Table A the board may appoint new directors either to fill vacancies or as additional directors (subject to any maximum fixed in accordance with the articles) [reg. 79]. Such appointments must be made by the directors at a properly constituted meeting of the board or, if the articles allow, by written resolution. See **Precedents 26.2A** and **26.2B** for examples of board resolutions appointing directors.

Directors appointed by the board must retire at the annual general meeting following their appointment and offer themselves for election by the members [reg. 79]. Not less than seven nor more than twenty eight days before the meeting the company must give notice of any person retiring in this manner who is recommended by the directors for appointment or reappointment. The notice must include the details which would be required to be included in the register of directors if that person was appointed or reappointed [reg. 77]. The purpose of this provision is to ensure that the directors cannot propose a person for appointment or reappointment without giving the members prior notice of his details, e.g. by including in the notice of the meeting an item of business to elect directors without naming them. If the company fails to give notice in accordance with reg. 77, the appointment will be invalid.

Appointment by the members
The members can also appoint directors to fill casual vacancies or as additional directors by ordinary resolution at a general meeting (subject to any maximum) [reg. 78]. However, they must give the company prior notice of their intention to propose a person as a director who is not recommended by the board not less than 14 days nor more than 35 days before the date of the meeting. The notice given to the company must include the details which would be required to be included in the register of directors if that person was appointed and notice signed by the person nominated of his willingness to act as a director [reg. 76]. The purpose of reg. 76 is to prevent the members from relying on the inclusion in the notice of the meeting of an item of business to elect or re-elect directors in order to propose a person not recommended by the directors. It should be noted, however, that the fact that a member has given notice in accordance with reg. 76 does not guarantee that the proposal will be within the scope of the notice of the meeting (see para. 12.5).

Not less than seven nor more than 28 days before the meeting, the company must give notice to every person who is entitled to receive notice of the meeting of any person in respect of whom notice has been given to the company of the intention to propose him at the meeting for appointment or reappointment as a director in accordance with reg. 76. The notice given by the company must include the details which would be required to be included in the register of directors [reg. 77].

Most companies' articles include a provision similar to reg. 76 requiring members to notify the company of their intention to propose as a director someone not recommended by the directors. The London Stock Exchange requires listed companies to adopt a similar article [Listing Rules, para. 22 of Appendix 1 to Chapter 13]. However, listed companies are not required to adopt an article similar to reg. 77 and very few do because of the potential cost of notifying the members. Under reg. 76, the members may notify the company of their intention to propose a person as a director as little as 14 days before the meeting, i.e. after the notice calling the meeting has been sent. In order to comply with the requirements of reg. 77 in these circumstances, the company would have to do a second mailing to its members.

The purpose of reg. 77 is to ensure that the members have advance warning that a person not recommended by the board is to be proposed as a director at the meeting and act accordingly, e.g. by attending the meeting or by appointing proxies to vote for or against the resolution. Giving notice in this manner enables the board to mobilise opposition to the appointment. In practice, listed companies tend to rely on the fact that the chairman controls sufficient proxy votes to defeat any such resolution.

Although it is clear that a resolution of the members in general meeting to appoint a person as a director not recommended by the board will be invalid if the members have not complied with the requirement to give the company prior notice in accordance with reg. 76, it is not clear whether such an appointment would be invalid if the company fails to give notice to the members in accordance with reg. 77. It is also not clear whether the company by giving notice in accordance with reg. 77 automatically brings the resolution to be proposed by the members within the scope of the notice of the meeting, e.g. where the reg. 77 notice was not sent within the normal period of notice for AGMs (21 clear days) or EGMs (14 clear days) and the resolution is not within the scope of the notice of the meeting already sent to members. With these difficulties in mind, it is hardly surprising that reg. 77 is rarely adopted by listed companies.

Retirement by rotation

Table A reinforces the primacy of the members in the appointment and removal process by requiring one-third of the directors to retire each year and offer themselves for re-election at the annual general meeting. This is known as retirement by rotation (see further para. 20.10). Its purpose is to ensure that the members are given a periodic opportunity to remove a director without having to propose such a resolution themselves. However, it should be noted that under Table A and many other articles, the executive directors are exempt from retirement by rotation [reg. 84]. Until recently, most listed companies adopted similar procedures. However, the trend now is for all directors to be subject to retirement by rotation.

26.3   DIRECTORS

26.3.1   Executive directors

An executive director is a director who holds some executive or management position within the company. Under Table A, the directors may appoint one or more of their number as managing director or to any other executive office (e.g. finance director) and determine the terms and remuneration of any such appointment [reg. 84]. These powers are special powers which cannot be delegated by the board under reg. 72 (see para. 29.2). The appointment of executive directors and the terms of such appointments must therefore be approved by a resolution of the board (see **Precedent 26.3A**).

Regulation 72 allows the board to delegate its powers to individual executive directors. In delegating its powers, it may limit the executive's authority by imposing certain conditions. For example, the managing director may be given power to authorise capital expenditure up to a certain value with any expenditure above that amount requiring board approval. The terms of any delegation should be approved by a resolution of the board.

Salaried executive directors should be appointed under a formal service agreement which should state the title of the job to be performed, the duties to be performed, the remuneration and other benefits associated with the appointment (including whether the remuneration payable is inclusive or exclusive of any director's fee which may be payable) and any restraints in the form of confidentiality undertakings and restrictive covenants in the event of leaving the service of the company. With regard to the duties to be performed it is normal for the service contract to include a more general provision stating that the director shall have such powers and duties as the board may determine from time to time (see **Precedent 26.3B**). This allows the board to modify authorisations generally without having to modify each executive director's contract. Limits on individual directors' authorities may also be reinforced by the adoption of a schedule of matters reserved to the board (see further para. 29.3).

The executive directors will be subject to any provisions in the articles on retirement by rotation, unless the articles specify otherwise. Under Table A, executive directors are exempt from retirement by rotation but not from the requirement to retire at the first annual general meeting following their appointment [reg. 84].

26.3.2 Non-executive directors

Non-executive directors are directors who have not been appointed to any executive office within the company. The Cadbury Committee recommended that listed companies should have a minimum of three non-executive directors and that the majority should be independent of the company [Cadbury Report, para. 4.11]. According to the report, non-executive directors will be independent if they are independent of management and free from any business or other relationship which could materially interfere with the exercise of their judgment, apart from their directors' fees and shareholdings [Cadbury Report, para. 4.12]. The London Stock Exchange requires listed companies to identify which of the non-executive directors are independent in the annual report and accounts [Listing Rules, para. 12.43(i)].

Whether or not they are independent, non-executive directors participate in the management of the company by attending board meetings and any committees of the board of which they are a member. Regulation 72 of Table A does not allow the board to delegate any of its powers to an individual non-executive director. However, the same result can be achieved by delegating to a board committee consisting of only one non-executive director.

Under Table A, all directors are entitled to be repaid any expenses they reasonably incur in connection with their duties [reg. 83]. However, the fees paid to directors in their capacity as board members must be approved by an ordinary resolution of the members in general meeting [reg. 82]. This applies to fees paid to executive and non-executive directors, although executive directors usually receive a salary instead of directors' fees which may be determined by the board without reference to the members [reg. 84]. Regulation 82 is frequently modified to enable the board to fix the fees of non-executive directors without reference to the members or subject to a maximum amount approved by the members (see art. 91 of Whitbread plc).

26.3.3 Alternate directors

An alternate director is someone appointed by a director to attend and vote at board meetings in his or her stead. The Act does not authorise a director to appoint an alternate or a proxy. Accordingly, an alternate director may only be appointed if the articles make specific provision, e.g. regs. 65 to 69 of Table A (see further para. 28.10 and **Precedents 28.10A** to **D**).

26.3.4   *De facto* **and shadow directors**

De facto directors are people who act as directors and are held out to be directors by the company even though they have never actually been appointed as directors or have ceased to be directors. A shadow director is a person in accordance with whose instructions the directors of the company are accustomed to act. A person is not deemed to be a shadow director by reason only that the directors act on advice by him in a professional capacity [s. 741]. It is probably not possible for a person to be both a shadow director and a *de facto* director. The first lurks in the shadows, sheltering behind others who, he claims, are the only directors of the company to the exclusion of himself. The second is a person who claims to act and purports to act as a director, although not validly appointed as such.

  De facto directors and shadow directors can both be disqualified under the Company Directors Disqualification Act 1986 and may be liable for wrongful and fraudulent trading under the Insolvency Act 1986. Shadow directors are subject to some of the duties and penalties prescribed by the Companies Act 1985 (e.g. ss. 330 to 346 regarding restrictions on the making of loans to directors).

CHAPTER TWENTY-SEVEN

Directors' powers

27.1 SUMMARY

The Companies Act 1985 does not confer any powers of management on the directors, either individually or as a body. This is left to the company's own constitutional documents and is normally dealt with in the articles of association.

The common law rule is that a company's powers must be exercised by its members in general meeting unless its memorandum or articles of association provide otherwise (*Mayor, Constables and Company of Merchants of the Staple of England* v. *Governor and Company of the Bank of England* (1887) 21 Q.B.D. 160). In other words, the directors will have no powers at all unless the memorandum or articles say so.

It is not normally practicable for the members to manage the business on a day-to-day basis. Every matter requiring a decision would have to be put to a general meeting called in accordance with the formal requirements of the Act. This would be impossible for a company with hundreds of shareholders. Even where there are relatively few members, it is easier for them to manage the company as directors rather than as members. This is mainly because the formalities associated with board meetings are less onerous, but also because that is the way most companies are run and doing it in any other way would complicate matters unnecessarily and would probably involve significant legal expenses.

In practice, therefore, articles include a provision known as the general management clause which gives the directors all the powers necessary to manage the company on a day-to-day basis (see para. 27.4). Other articles may give the directors special powers which they would not otherwise have, e.g. the power to delegate and the power to fix the remuneration of directors (see para. 27.5). The powers given under the general management clause are subject to other provisions in the memorandum and articles of association. Thus the directors' powers will be limited by the objects clause in the memorandum (see para. 27.3) and any other provisions in the articles which limit their scope (see para. 27.4.2). In addition, the Act gives the members certain rights and powers which cannot be excluded by the articles (see para. 27.4.1).

The articles are deemed to be a contract between the members and the company which governs the way the company is run. It follows that the only way the shareholders can interfere in matters delegated to the directors is to change that contract (i.e. to amend the articles by special resolution so as to restrict the directors' discretion) or to issue directions in accordance with procedures contained in the articles (see para. 27.4.3). Even then, such resolutions or directions will have no effect on the validity of any transaction previously entered into by the directors on behalf of the company (see para. 27.9).

Articles usually allow the directors to delegate their powers to committees of the board and to individual directors (see Chapter 29). If no such delegation has taken place or the articles make no provision for delegation by the directors, the directors must exercise their powers collectively as a board (see para. 27.7). Generally speaking this means at a properly convened and constituted meeting of the board of directors. However, where the directors all agree they may act informally, i.e. outside a formal board meeting (see para. 27.8). In addition, the articles may provide a specific mechanism to allow the directors to act without holding formal meetings, e.g. by written resolution (see para. 27.9).

If the directors are unable to act for any reason, their powers may revert in default to the members in general meeting (see para. 27.6).

27.2   EXTENT OF THE DIRECTORS' POWERS

In order to decide whether the directors are acting within their powers, the following should be considered:

- Is the proposed transaction within the powers of the company (see para. 27.3 on *ultra vires* and the objects clause)?
- If so, is there anything in the articles or the Act which specifically requires the transaction to be authorised by the members in general meeting (see, for example, Appendix E)?
- If not, is the proposed transaction concerned with the management of the company?
- If so, the directors may act under the powers given by the general management clause unless:
  - (a) some other provision in the articles restricts their powers under the general management clause in relation to the proposed transaction (see para. 27.4.2);
  - (b) the members have given the directors a valid instruction which restricts their freedom to enter into the transaction (see para. 27.4.3).
- If not, is there a special power in the memorandum or articles which authorises the directors to act in this way (see para. 27.5)?

27.3   *ULTRA VIRES* AND THE COMPANY'S OBJECTS CLAUSE

The objects clause in the memorandum of association sets out the purpose for which the company was formed and may specify the powers of the company in that regard.

By limiting the objects of the company, the clause limits its powers. For example, the objects clause may state that the company is to build and operate a railway. Such a company could not provide banking services and any transaction by the railway company with a third party in connection with banking would therefore be *ultra vires* (i.e. beyond the company's powers) and invalid.

Historically, a third party was deemed to have notice of any limitations on the company's powers by virtue of the fact that the memorandum containing the objects clause was filed at Companies House and available for public inspection. However, the *ultra vires* rule was modified in 1989 in order to comply with a European Directive and s. 35(1) of the Companies Act 1985 now provides that the validity of an act done by a company shall not be called into question on the ground of lack of capacity by reason of anything in the company's memorandum. Thus, if the directors enter into a contract with a third party for a purpose which is beyond the powers of the company, the third party can now rely on s. 35(1) to enforce it against the company (previously the contract would have been void and therefore unenforceable).

Nevertheless, s. 35(2) states that a member of the company may still bring proceedings to restrain an act which is beyond a company's capacity. In addition, s. 35(3) states that it remains the duty of the directors to observe any limitations on their powers flowing from the company's memorandum. Accordingly, the directors will be liable to compensate the company if it suffers a loss as a result of an *ultra vires* transaction approved by them. By participating in ultra vires acts, the directors are in breach of their fiduciary duty to the company, as preserved by s. 35(3).

The directors effectively bear most of the risks of an *ultra vires* transaction. However, the court can relieve the directors of their liability if it is satisfied that they have acted honestly and reasonably and ought fairly to be excused (s. 727). In addition, under s. 35(3) the members may by special resolution ratify the acts of the directors which were beyond the capaicity of the company and by a separate special resolution relieve them of any liability incurred as a result of their actions.

It can be seen from the above summary, that the *ultra vires* rule will not be a matter of great importance where the members are all directors and they all agree to a particular transaction. However, in other circumstances, the directors would be well advised to act within the powers of the company as defined by the objects clause or risk heavy personal liabilities.

27.4   GENERAL MANAGEMENT CLAUSE

Articles invariably contain a provision (known as the general management clause) which reverses the common law rule that the company's powers must be exercised by the members in general meeting. Regulation 70 of Table A is typical of this type of provision. It provides:

> **70.** Subject to the provisions of the Act, the memorandum and the articles and to any directions given by special resolution, the business of the company shall be managed by the directors who may exercise all the powers of the company.

No alteration of the memorandum or articles and no such direction shall invalidate any prior act of the directors which would have been valid if that alteration had not been made or that direction had not been given. The powers given by this regulation shall not be limited by any special power given to the directors by the articles and a meeting of directors at which a quorum is present may exercise all powers exercisable by the directors.

It can be seen that reg. 70 gives the directors authority to exercise all the powers of the company which are not specifically excluded or reserved to the members by:

- other provisions in the memorandum or articles (see para. 27.4.2); or
- the Act (see para. 27.4.1).

It also provides a special procedure under which the members in general meeting can give valid instructions to the directors (see para. 27.4.3).

It has been held that a general management clause giving the directors all powers 'necessary in the management of the company' does not authorise them to present a winding up petition without the approval of the members because winding up is not connected with the management of the company (*Re Emmadart Ltd* [1979] Ch. 540). Although directors now have a statutory power to apply for a compulsory winding up under the Insolvency Act 1986, their powers may be subject to other limitations where this wording is adopted. Modern articles seek to avoid this problem by conferring powers on the directors without the condition that they be exercised in the management of the company. Regulation 70 of Table A uses the words '. . . the business of the company shall be managed by the directors who may exercise all the powers of the company'.

Under a general management clause it is usually safe to assume that the directors can do anything the company can do as long as they are not prevented from doing that thing by the Act or another provision in the memorandum or articles. Thus in *Re Patent File Co.* (1870) L.R. 6 Ch. 83, Mellish L.J. said: 'The articles give to the directors the whole powers of the company, subject to the provisions [of the articles and] of the Companies Act . . . and I cannot find anything either in the Act or in the articles to prohibit their making a mortgage by deposit.' There are, of course, exceptions to this rule. The directors may not do anything which would be a breach of their fiduciary duty to the company unless the articles give them specific powers in that regard (e.g. pay themselves a salary). In addition, they may not delegate their powers unless the articles so provide (see para. 27.5).

This might not appear very helpful to directors, who would no doubt prefer the articles to contain a list of things which they can do. However, such an approach would be unwieldy. The relevant article would need to be similar in nature, but perhaps longer, than the objects clause in the memorandum. As such, it is doubtful whether directors would actually find it any easier. Indeed, the objects clause is the closest the directors will get to a list of their powers, although this will not be of much assistance if the company adopts the short form object authorised by s. 3A of the 1985 Act (i.e. to be a general commercial company). In this case, s. 3A states that the company has power to do anything which is incidental or conducive to the carrying on of any trade or business by it.

27.4.1   Subject to the provisions of the Act

All powers conferred on the directors by the articles are subject to the provisions of the Companies Act 1985 (as amended), whether or not this is stated in the articles. Thus, the directors cannot exercise any of the company's powers which are reserved to the shareholders by the Act and must comply with the requirements of the Act when exercising their powers. For example, directors cannot allot new shares unless they have been authorised to do so in accordance with the requirements of s. 80. For further examples of transactions which require shareholder approval, see **Appendix E** which shows the type of resolution required for various types of business at general meetings.

The Act also requires the directors to have regard to the interests of employees [s. 309], imposes restrictions on the making of loans to themselves [Part X of the Act] and generally imposes duties on the directors to comply with certain procedural requirements when exercising their powers, e.g. to keep minutes of their meetings.

27.4.2   Subject to the memorandum and articles

The general management clause is always expressed as being subject to other provisions in the memorandum and articles of association. These may include provisions which:

- limit the capacity of the company and, therefore, the directors (i.e. the objects clause in the memorandum – see para. 27.3);
- limit the powers of the directors (but not the members), e.g. a limit on directors' borrowing powers;
- reserve certain powers to the members, e.g. to approve the payment of dividend (although the articles may allow the directors to pay an interim dividend without reference to the members);
- determine the procedures which the directors must follow when exercising their powers, e.g. regulation of proceedings at meetings of directors;
- allow the directors to delegate their powers;
- relax the conditions members must satisfy in order to exercise certain statutory rights, e.g. the articles could allow members holding less than one-tenth of the voting shares to demand a general meeting (the company cannot exclude the members' minimum statutory rights);
- provide additional procedures for removal of directors, e.g. by extraordinary resolution.

27.4.3   Subject to any directions given by the members

Unless the articles contain some special provision allowing the members to give directions, the only way they can interfere in the exercise by the directors of their powers is to alter the articles in such a way that those powers revert back to the company in general meeting. In *Automatic Self-Cleansing Filter Syndicate Co. Ltd* v. *Cunninghame* [1906] 2 Ch. 34, C.A., the members in general meeting passed an ordinary resolution (i.e. by a simple majority of those voting) instructing the directors to sell part of the business to another company on certain terms. The directors refused to carry out the sale and the Court of Appeal held that they were not bound to do so because the power to sell any of the company's property had been vested in them by the articles.

Most articles provide an alternative method for the members to give instructions to the directors. In *Automatic Self-Cleansing Filter* the directors' powers were 'subject to such regulations as may from time to time be made by extraordinary resolution' (i.e. 75 per cent majority of those voting). If the resolution to sell the business had been proposed and passed as an extraordinary resolution, the result would have been different. Whether or not such provision is made, the members may achieve the same result by proposing and passing a special resolution (which also requires a 75 per cent majority but longer notice than an extraordinary resolution) to amend the articles so that, for example, the powers revert back to the company in general meeting. Having done that, they need only pass an ordinary resolution (50 per cent majority of those voting) to approve the proposed course of action.

1985 Table A

In the case of reg. 70 of the 1985 Table A, the members may give the directors binding instructions by passing a special resolution. As the articles can be amended by special resolution, this does not place them in a significantly stronger position than if no such provision was made. The only real advantage is that it is not necessary for the resolution giving directions to be framed as an amendment of the articles. This allows the members to give directions in a specific instance without limiting the directors' powers generally. Although such a resolution would not, if passed, constitute an amendment to the articles, a copy of it would have to be filed at Companies House and attached to any copy of the articles issued after it had been passed.

1948 Table A

The wording of reg. 80 of the 1948 Table A is more obscure and has caused a number of difficulties. It provides:

> **80.** The business of the company shall be managed by the directors, who . . . may exercise all such powers of the company . . . subject, nevertheless, to any of these regulations, to the provisions of the Act and to such regulations being not inconsistent with the aforesaid regulations or provisions, as may be prescribed by the company in general meeting . . .

The difficulty with this type of article is in deciding what the word 'regulations' means. In *Quin & Axtens* v. *Salmon* [1909] A.C. 442, it was held that it meant 'articles' throughout. If this interpretation is correct, the members may only interfere by changing the articles and the condition that such regulations must not be inconsistent with the articles becomes superfluous. In *Scott* v. *Scott* [1943] 1 All E.R. 582, it was held that the members in general meeting could not give the directors instructions to pay an interim dividend by ordinary resolution under an article similar to reg. 80 of the 1948 Table A. Lord Clauson pointed out (at page 444) that if an ordinary resolution could be considered to be a regulation within the meaning of those words it would still be ineffective because it would be inconsistent with the existing articles.

Other versions

Many companies still have articles modelled on the 1948 Act Table A. For example, art. 106 of Whitbread plc provides:

> 106. The business of the Company shall be managed by the Board which may exercise all such powers of the Company as are not, by the Companies Acts or by these Articles required to be exercised by the Company in General Meeting, subject nevertheless to these Articles, to the provisions of the Companies Acts and to such regulations, being not inconsistent with the aforesaid regulations or provisions, as may be prescribed by extraordinary or special resolution . . .

Under this article it is clearly anticipated that regulations which govern the behaviour of the directors shall be capable of being made by extraordinary resolution which would not have the effect of altering the articles. However, the condition that such regulations must not be 'inconsistent with the aforesaid regulations or provisions' limits the usefulness of this provision if the word regulations is taken to refer to the articles. It could be argued that any extraordinary resolution of the members which purports to fetter the discretion of the directors will be inconsistent with the articles. If so, the provision is almost superfluous because the only way the shareholders can avoid this is by amending the article which creates that inconsistency in the first place. This would seem to be a dangerous interpretation particularly for companies whose lawyers have developed a slightly modified version of the 1948 Table A provision. In the following example taken from the articles of a large UK listed company, an adverse ruling on this point could result in the members being able to give directions by ordinary resolution.

> 23.01   The business of the Company shall be managed by the Board which, in addition to all the powers and authorities by these Articles or otherwise expressly conferred on it, may exercise all such powers and do all acts and things as may be exercised or done by the Company as are not, by the Statutes or by these Articles, required to be exercised or done by the Company in general meeting, subject nevertheless to these Articles, to the provisions of the Statutes and to such directions (not inconsistent with these Articles and such provisions) as may be prescribed by the Company in general meeting.

27.4.4   Prior acts of directors not invalidated

Most articles follow reg. 70 of Table A in providing that no alteration of the memorandum or articles and no direction given in accordance with the articles shall invalidate any prior act of the directors which would have been valid if that alteration had not been made or that direction had not been given. This qualification ensures that the members cannot reverse a decision of the directors which has already been acted upon. Without it, third parties could never be sure that the company would be bound by the acts of its directors.

27.4.5 Practical points on general management clauses

If it is intended to restrict the ability of shareholders to give directions, reg. 70 of Table A should be followed. It is impossible to entrench the position of the directors any more than this as the members would be able to amend any such provision by passing a special resolution to that effect. Where the members want to retain the ability to give instructions to the directors on matters of management by ordinary resolution or extraordinary resolution, this should be stated explicitly in the articles. It is also best in such circumstances to avoid the condition that such directions must not be inconsistent with the articles or regulations. A simple modification of reg. 70 of the 1985 Table A would probably suffice for these purposes. Before making such changes, however, it is worth bearing in mind that the members may remove any of the directors by ordinary resolution [s. 303]. Often the threat of removal will be sufficient to ensure that the directors act in accordance with the wishes of the majority. It is probably for this reason that the difficulties which have previously arisen with general management clauses have all but disappeared.

27.5 SPECIAL POWERS

Other articles may give the directors special powers which they would not otherwise have under the general management clause because:

- they are not connected with the management of the company but with the relationship between the company and its members, e.g. the power to make calls (regs. 12 to 22 of Table A); or
- the exercise of such a power would otherwise be a breach of their fiduciary duties, e.g. the power to fix the remuneration of executive directors (e.g. reg. 84 of Table A).

The articles may also include special provisions dealing with powers of management which the directors would ordinarily be assumed to have under the general management clause. It is normally presumed that the existence of a special power excludes the application of any power the directors may have under a general management clause in that regard. For example, the articles may include a provision giving the directors specific power to borrow money up to a stated limit for certain defined purposes. The directors would normally be deemed to have the power to borrow under the general management clause. However, as the powers under the general management clause are expressed as being subject to other articles, it is clear that their power to borrow will be restricted, at least for the purposes stated. What may not be clear, however, is whether the directors are still authorised under the general management clause to borrow for other purposes. This will depend on the exact wording of the articles, but where there is any doubt, it should be assumed that the article containing the special power on borrowing represents the final word in this regard and excludes any powers which might normally exist under the general management clause.

Modern articles often reverse this presumption by stating in the general management clause that the powers given shall not be limited by any special power given to the directors by any other article (see, for example, reg. 70 of Table A). The purpose of these words is not to negate any restrictions contained in other articles but to preserve any powers the directors have under the general management clause which are not specifically excluded by other articles.

27.6   DEFAULT POWERS OF THE GENERAL MEETING

Where the board of directors is unable or unwilling to conduct the company's business, the members in general meeting may be entitled by default to exercise certain powers given to the directors. For example, in *Barron* v. *Potter* [1914] 1 Ch. 895, the company's articles provided that the power to appoint directors was vested in the board and fixed the quorum for board meetings as two. One of the two directors appointed refused to attend meetings so that no business could be done. It was held that the power to appoint additional directors in these circumstances reverted to the company in general meeting as this was the only way to break the deadlock.

In *Foster* v. *Foster* [1916] 1 Ch. 532, the company's articles provided that the directors could not vote on any contract in which they were interested and that the quorum for board meetings was two. Two of the three directors of the company each wanted to be appointed as its salaried managing director. Although unable to vote on their own appointment, both were able to block the appointment of the other. It was held that the power to appoint a managing director reverted by default to the general meeting.

In *Barron* v. *Potter* and to a lesser extent in *Foster* v. *Foster*, the board's failure to act paralysed the company and the general meeting merely acted in order to break the deadlock. The courts will not, however, allow the members to usurp the board's powers where the directors are unable to agree on a business decision but are otherwise capable of managing the business. Thus in *Quin & Axtens Ltd* v. *Salmon* [1909] A.C. 442, the company's articles provided that no decision regarding the acquisition or letting of certain properties would be valid if either of two named directors dissented. One of the named directors (Salmon) dissented on such a proposal. An extraordinary general meeting was then held at which the shareholders by a simple majority passed similar resolutions. The House of Lords ruled that the shareholders' resolutions were inconsistent with the articles which conferred general powers of management on the directors to the exclusion of the members.

27.7   COLLECTIVE EXERCISE OF POWERS

The directors must exercise their powers collectively, i.e. at a properly convened and constituted meeting of the board of directors, unless:

- the articles allow them to delegate their powers and they have delegated them;
- they all agree, in which case they may act informally (see para. 27.8);
- the articles allow them to make decisions in some other way, e.g. by written resolution (see para. 27.9).

Where the directors are required to act collectively as a board, unanimity is not required. Under the common law, decisions may validly be made by a majority of the directors present at board meetings, provided that there are sufficient directors to form a quorum. Under the common law, a quorum exists where a majority of the directors are present at the meeting. Thus, if there are nine directors, five must be present to form a quorum. If five attend a meeting only three of them (i.e. one third of the directors in total) need vote in favour of a proposal to bind the company. If seven attend, four must vote in favour, and so on. The common law principle that a majority of the directors present may bind the company is usually adopted in the articles (e.g. reg. 88). However, articles usually specify a fixed quorum for meetings of directors and frequently allow the directors to alter that quorum (see para. 28.7).

27.8   INFORMAL CONSENT

If the directors unanimously agree on a particular course of action, there is no need for that decision to be taken at a formal meeting of directors. It is unwise to rely on this common law rule, particularly where the articles provide an alternative method of acting without holding a meeting, e.g. written resolutions. In each of the following cases, none of the directors disputed the fact that they had concurred in the decision which was challenged in the courts. If they had, it is possible that the court's rulings would have been different. It is advisable therefore to have written evidence of the fact that all the directors agreed to act in a certain way.

In *Re Bonneli's Telegraph Co.* (1871) L.R. 12 Eq. 246, the quorum for board meetings was three. Two out of the four directors signed a letter to C stating that they would secure the agreement of the other directors to C's appointment as agent in the sale of company's business on terms set out in the letter. The remaining two directors subsequently signed and sent a copy of that letter to C signifying their agreement to the appointment. Bacon V-C held that the directors had acted in a manner which was capable of binding the company. Unfortunately, in stating his reasons, he seemed to suggest that it was only necessary for three out of the four (i.e. a quorum) to agree, even though all the directors had agreed in the case before him. This reasoning runs counter to the generally accepted principle with regard to informal decisions of the members (see *Re Express Engineering Works Ltd* [1920] 1 Ch. 466; *Re Duomatic Ltd* [1969] 1 All E.R. 161). Indeed, for many years this flaw caused some commentators to question the application of the principle of unanimous informal consent to meetings of directors.

The issue has now been clarified by two recent cases. In *Charterhouse Investments Trust Ltd* v. *Tempest Diesels Ltd* [1986] B.C.L.C. 1, the board of TD Ltd had not formally considered the disputed term in a contract for the sale of its business signed on behalf of the board by one of the directors. Hoffman J. held that the term was binding as the other directors, by their actions and subsequent testimony, were clearly content to acquiesce in whatever lawful terms were agreed by that director.

In *Runciman* v. *Walter Runciman plc* [1992] B.C.L.C. 1084, variations in a director's service contract were not put to the board for formal approval. Following a takeover, the new owners of the company challenged the validity of those variations and, in particular, an increase in the period of notice from three to five years. In holding that they were valid, Simon Brown J. said: 'The articles say nothing as to how or when the directors are to arrive at their determination. In my judgment, therefore, provided only and always that by the time the term relied upon is sought to be enforced all the other directors can be shown to have concurred in the agreement of that term, it can fairly and properly be said that they have indeed determined it as the article requires.'

The *Runciman* case also highlighted one of the factors which could easily defeat this type of informal decision-making, namely the requirement to be found in most articles for directors to disclose their interest in any contract approved by the board. Failure to do so will normally make the contract voidable at the instance of the company (in other words the company can decide whether to avoid the contract or to enforce it) (*Hely-Hutchinson* v. *Brayhead Ltd* [1967] 3 All E.R. 98). In *Runciman*, Simon Brown J. refused to apply this principle to the detriment of the director on the basis that it was a mere technical breach. In other cases, however, the courts might take a more stringent view (see para. 28.11).

Although it is not clear from the reports of the two recent cases, it is highly likely that the articles of both companies allowed the directors to act by written resolution. If so, it appears that the board may act by the unanimous consent of its directors without holding a formal meeting, irrespective of the existence of specific provisions in the articles on written resolutions.

27.9   WRITTEN RESOLUTIONS

There is no equivalent for directors to the statutory procedure for written resolutions of the members (see para. 23.2). The ability of the directors to act without holding formal meetings is therefore entirely dependent on the common law and the articles.

Most articles (including Table A) make specific provision for written resolutions of the directors even though it is now firmly established that the directors may act outside formal board meetings if they all agree. This is partly because of the uncertainties in the common law but also because articles usually provide a slightly more relaxed regime. For example, reg. 93 of Table A provides:

93. A resolution signed in writing by all the directors entitled to receive notice of a meeting of directors or of a committee of directors shall be as valid and effectual as if it had been passed at a meeting of directors or (as the case may be)

a committee of directors duly convened and held and may consist of several documents in the like form each signed by one or more directors; but a resolution signed by an alternate director need not also be signed by his appointor and, if it is signed by a director who has appointed an alternate director, it need not be signed by the alternate in that capacity.

Under the common law, the unanimous agreement of the directors is required. Under reg. 93 the resolution need only be signed by the directors entitled to receive notice of a meeting of directors or of a committee of directors as the case may be.

27.9.1 Director not entitled to receive notice

Under Table A, the only occasion on which a director is not entitled to receive notice is when he or she is absent from the United Kingdom (reg. 88). Thus, in normal circumstances, the resolution must be signed by all the directors. If, however, one or more are outside the United Kingdom, then the requirement for unanimity no longer applies.

This could give rise to some peculiar results. Say, for example, four out of seven directors travel abroad on a business trip, it would appear that the three directors who remain in the UK could pass a written resolution even though they are in the minority in terms of numbers. This is not particularly unusual because the same directors could convene a board meeting and pass the resolution in the usual manner. However, a more difficult question is whether the written resolution would still be valid where the quorum for board meetings was four.

The High Court was recently called upon to rule on a similar question under reg. 106 of the 1948 Table A, which is broadly the same as reg. 93 of the 1985 Table A. Carnwath J. held that a directors' written resolution, passed in accordance with reg. 106 of the 1948 Table A, signed by only one director where the quorum for the transaction of business by the directors was two, was invalid, notwithstanding that the only other director was outside the United Kingdom and thus not entitled to notice of a meeting of directors (*Hood Sailmakers Ltd* v. *Axford* [1996] 4 All E.R. 830). In reaching this decision, he relied on the fact that reg. 99 of the 1948 Table A refers to 'the quorum necessary for the transaction of the business' (as does reg. 88 of the 1985 Table A), and said that even though reg. 106 of the 1948 Table A indicates that a written resolution of the directors will be as valid and effectual as if it had been passed at a meeting of directors, the requirement for a quorum must be treated as a separate matter.

The absence of a director from the UK can also cause difficulties because neither version of Table A specifies the point at which the test of whether a director is entitled to receive notice should be applied.

There would be no problem if the director was away on the day that all the directors in the United Kingdom signed the resolution. However, if the directors sign on different days, it is not clear whether a person who was absent for only part of the period between the first and last signatures should also sign. Say, for example, a company has four directors (A, B, C & D) who are each given a copy of a written resolution. A and B do not agree with the proposal and do not sign it. They leave the United Kingdom on business before C & D sign the resolution. If the critical point for the test is when the last director signs, then the resolution would be valid because A & B are absent from the United Kingdom and not therefore entitled to receive notice when C & D sign it.

Alternatively it could be argued that there is no single critical point, i.e. that a director who is present in the United Kingdom at some stage during the process must sign the resolution. The process could be deemed to start from the point the first director signed and finish at the point the last director signed. This would not make any difference in the above example but would if either C or D had signed a copy of the resolution before A and B left the United Kingdom. Finally, as the test is whether a director is entitled to receive notice, it could be argued that if a director actually receives a copy of a written resolution while in the United Kingdom and does not sign it, the resolution will not be valid without his or her signature.

27.9.2   Alternate directors

Where the articles make provision for the appointment of alternate directors and one or more of the directors have appointed an alternate, it would seem that their signature will also be necessary unless some sort of saving provision is included in the articles. This is because the word 'director' will be deemed to include alternates and because alternate directors are usually entitled to receive notice of all meetings of directors and committees of which their appointor is a member. Reg. 93 provides that a written resolution signed by an alternate director need not also be signed by his appointor and, if it is signed by a director who has appointed an alternate director, it need not be signed by the alternate in that capacity.

A director who is signing in his or her own capacity and as an alternate for another director should make this clear. If a director has appointed an alternate, the alternate's signature will be required where his or her appointor is not entitled to receive notice. However, reg. 93 would seem to suggest that the signature of the alternate might also be acceptable in other circumstances.

27.9.3   Director interested in contract

It is questionable whether a written resolution will be valid where one or more of the directors has an interest in the contract which would prevent them from voting on the resolution if it were proposed at a board meeting. In *Re Charles Arkins and Co. Ltd* [1929] S.A.S.R. 129, an Australian case based on an article which allowed decision by way of written resolution signed by all the directors currently in office, a written resolution was challenged on the basis that it had been signed by a director who was interested in the contract. Napier J. rejected this argument and said: 'The signature to the resolution is not a vote . . . I can see no reason why I should qualify that article by implying something which is not expressed, namely, that the subject of the resolution must be one upon which all the directors are able to vote.' However, the decision in *Hood Sailmakers Ltd* v. *Axford* (see para. 27.9.1) would seem to suggest that a written resolution will not be valid unless amongst the directors signing it there are sufficient to form a disinterested quorum.

27.9.4   Practical points on written resolutions

Most company secretaries prefer to obtain the signatures of all the directors on the same day. If that is not possible, it is normally preferable to send out copies and obtain all the relevant signatures as quickly as possible. It is quite common for copies of the written resolution to be faxed to the directors and for the directors to be asked to sign it and fax a copy of it back to the company the same day.

It should be noted that the signature of all the directors will be required if the articles require directors who are absent from the United Kingdom to be given notice of meetings. Although this is not the case under Table A, the articles may provide for other circumstances in which a director is not entitled to receive notice. It should also be noted that there may still be some residual common law exceptions to the requirement to give notice which can be summarised as applying where the notice would not have any effect, e.g. where a director is so seriously ill that he would be unable to attend a meeting.

There is nothing to prevent the inclusion in articles of procedures to enable the directors to pass resolutions in writing if, for example, only three out of four directors or a certain percentage of them sign it.

27.9.5   Effective date and minutes

It must be presumed that a written resolution will not be effective until the last director signs. Original signed copies of the resolution should be included in the minute book [s. 382].

CHAPTER TWENTY-EIGHT

Procedures at meetings of directors

28.1 SUMMARY

Most matters concerning proceedings at meetings of directors are determined by the articles and, in default, by reference to the common law. Although companies have considerable freedom to establish their own internal board procedures, most adopt articles based on Table A. This is largely because its provisions have been tried and tested over many years and provide a solid foundation upon which new regulations and procedures can be added. The following paragraphs focus on the provisions of Table A and highlight areas where modifications to Table A are commonly made.

28.2 WHO MAY CALL A MEETING OF DIRECTORS?

Articles usually provide that any director may call a meeting of directors and that the secretary at the request of a director shall do so (e.g. reg. 88 of Table A). It is usual for the board to fix the dates of its meetings in advance so that the directors can plan their diaries. However, there may be occasions when an additional meeting is needed to deal with urgent business.

In practice, meetings are usually called by the chairman and any director wishing to call a meeting would normally consult the chairman first. This ensures that the chairman is fully informed of the circumstances and may enable an alternative solution to be found. If approached by a director, the secretary should seek to persuade the director to follow this course. Although the secretary cannot refuse to call a meeting if instructed to do so by a director, it is advisable to inform the chairman at the earliest opportunity of the situation if the director refuses to follow this advice.

28.3 DATE, TIME AND PLACE

Generally, the directors can hold their meetings wherever they wish, including overseas. However, if the court is satisfied that the reason a particular venue has been chosen is to ensure that certain directors are unable to attend, it may prevent the meeting from taking place or declare the proceedings invalid (*Martin* v. *Walker* (1918) 145 L.T.J. 377).

The person calling the meeting should specify the date, time and place at which it is to be held as this information must be given in the notice of the meeting. If a director instructs the company secretary to call a meeting, he or she may specify these matters or leave them to be settled by the secretary, perhaps after contacting the other directors to find the most suitable time and place.

The articles may specify the time and place where regular meetings are to be held, e.g. on the second Thursday of each month at the company's registered office. Obviously, no such provision is made in Table A although the directors could specify a time and place in their internal procedures or standing orders.

28.4 NOTICE

28.4.1 Introduction

The Act makes no provision with regard to notice of directors' meetings. Under the common law reasonable notice must be given to all the directors. If proper notice is not given, the meeting and any business transacted at it will be invalid. Most articles modify this basic principle, e.g. Table A provides that notice need not be given to a director who is absent from the United Kingdom. Most articles also specify the manner in which notice can be served, e.g. in writing, orally, by telephone, etc.

Where a dispute does arise as to the adequacy of the notice given, those complaining must initiate proceedings to have the meeting or its proceedings declared invalid as soon as possible, otherwise they will be deemed to have acquiesced (assented to the notice given).

28.4.2 To whom notice must be given

As a general rule, notice must be given to all the directors. However, notice need not be given where:

- all the directors agree to waive it (see para. 28.4.3);
- it can have no effect;
- the articles specifically provide.

With regard to the second heading, Lord Sterndale MR suggested in *Young* v. *Imperial Ladies Club Ltd* [1920] 2 K.B. 523 (at p. 528) that notice may not be necessary if, for example, a director is so seriously ill that he would be unable to attend. It was held in that case that notice must be given to any director who would be able to travel back in time for the meeting. In the days before air travel, this would have excluded any director in the United States. However, the rule is unlikely to be of assistance today except in the most extreme circumstances.

Articles normally contain a provision similar to reg. 88 of Table A which provides that a director who is absent from the United Kingdom is not entitled to receive notice of directors' meetings. The United Kingdom means England, Wales, Scotland or Northern Ireland. Regulation 88 is often modified so as not to exclude places outside the United Kingdom where the company's directors live.

Alternate directors are entitled under reg. 66 of Table A to receive notice of board meetings and of any meetings of board committees of which the director who appointed them is a member. Even if the articles make no provision in this regard, alternate directors are probably entitled to receive notice of such meetings under the common law principles.

Notice need not be given where the directors have agreed among themselves (or the articles prescribe) that meetings shall be held on a regular basis at a fixed time and place, e.g. on the first Thursday each month at 4.00pm at the company's registered office. In such circumstances, notice would, however, need to be given for any meeting held at a different time or place.

28.4.3   Waiver of notice

Unless the articles provide otherwise (e.g. art. 117B of Whitbread plc), directors cannot waive in advance their right to receive notice of a meeting (*Re Portuguese Consolidated Copper Mines Ltd* (1889) 42 Ch.D. 160). Table A makes no such provision and, subject to any other qualifications, notice must be given to all the directors even though some may have indicated that they are unable or unwilling to attend a future meeting.

However, notice can be waived if all the directors are present and agree to hold a board meeting without notice. In *Smith* v. *Paringa Mines Ltd* [1906] 2 Ch. 193, the two directors of a company met in the offices of one of them. The director who was the chairman proposed the appointment of a third director. Despite the objection of the other director to this appointment, the chairman declared the resolution carried by his casting vote. The appointment was held to be valid as they were both deemed to have agreed to treat their meeting as a board meeting. In *Barron* v. *Potter* [1914] 1 Ch. 895, a similar chance meeting between the directors of a company was held to be invalid as a board meeting as the director who proposed and purported to pass (by virtue of his casting vote) resolutions appointing new directors knew that the other director did not wish to attend any board meeting with him.

28.4.4   Length of notice

There is no strict rule as to the length of notice required for meetings of directors, although there is an underlying assumption that it must be reasonable in the circumstances (*Browne* v. *La Trinidad* (1887) 37 Ch.D. 1).

It is impossible to state conclusively the circumstances in which the notice given might be deemed to be unreasonable. It is fairly safe to assume that the notice given was reasonable if none of the directors object or they all attend the meeting. On the other hand, it does not necessarily follow that the notice given was unreasonable merely because a director objects. If a director does object to the notice given, the other directors should consider their position very carefully, taking into account all the other relevant factors. These might include:

(a) the length of notice usually given for similar meetings in that company;
(b) the nature and urgency of the business to be transacted.

It goes without saying that the courts are more likely to intervene if it can be inferred that the purpose of calling the meeting at short notice was to exclude a particular director from the decision-making process.

A director should register his or her objection to the length of notice given immediately and should commence legal proceedings as soon as possible, otherwise the courts may refuse to intervene. In *Browne* v. *La Trinidad*, the court accepted that the notice given to Mr Browne was unreasonable (less than ten minutes before the start of a board meeting at which it was decided to call an EGM to propose a resolution to remove him as a director). However, it refused to intervene, partly because he did not object at the time and only commenced proceedings shortly before the EGM was due to be held.

28.4.5   Form of notice

Articles usually specify the form in which notice must be given. In the absence of any provision in the articles, notice may be given in writing or orally (*Browne* v. *La Trinidad* (1887) 37 Ch.D. 1). Some articles require all notices to be given in writing.

Regulation 111 of Table A states that notice of board meetings 'need not be given in writing'. The effect of this article is not altogether clear. It certainly allows notice to be given in writing or orally. However, it would be unwise to rely on it as authorisation for giving notice by advertisement or by some other means such as electronic mail. If such methods are to be used, it is suggested that specific provision to that effect be made in the articles.

If notice is given in writing, the provisions of the articles with regard to proof of posting and the deemed date of service will apply, e.g. reg. 115 of Table A. It may be served either personally or by delivering it to the address recorded as the director's usual address in the register of directors or to an alternative address supplied by the director for these purposes. Even though it is known that a director is not at his or her usual address, notice should still be sent to that address, unless the director has given an alternative as he or she may have made arrangements to have mail forwarded.

28.4.6   Content of notice

The notice must include the date, time and place of the meeting (see **Precedent 28.4**). It need not state the nature of the business to be transacted (*La Compagnie de Mayville* v. *Whitley* [1896] 1 Ch. 788). However, where notice of the business to be transacted is given, it must not be deliberately misleading. In *Re Homer District Consolidated Gold Mines, ex parte Smith* (1888) 39 Ch.D. 546, a board meeting was called at very short notice and a resolution was passed to rescind a decision made at a meeting held only two weeks previously. The notice of the meeting was held to be invalid for a number of reasons, one of which was that it was misleading in so far as it did not mention this item of business.

28.4.7   Practical issues

It is normal practice, at least in large companies, to schedule regular board and board committee meetings for the forthcoming year. It is not uncommon for this process to be completed as early as October or November in the preceding year. This allows the directors to organise their diaries so that they are able to attend meetings. The schedule is normally appended to or included in the minutes of a board meeting. This satisfies the legal requirements as to notice provided that a copy is sent to each director and it shows the date, time and place of each meeting. It is also normal for a copy of the agenda for the meeting to be given to each director prior to the meeting. As this normally includes the date, time and place of the meeting, it may also be valid as notice of the meeting provided that it is sent out early enough to comply with the requirement that the notice given must be reasonable in the circumstances.

For small companies with relatively few directors, it may not be necessary or possible to plan so far ahead. Meetings may simply be called on an ad hoc basis at relatively short notice. Even in large public companies it is sometimes necessary to hold emergency meetings to deal with matters which cannot wait until the next scheduled meeting. In such circumstances, it is a good practice for the chairman or the secretary to contact each director in order to explain the circumstances and to offer a range of possible dates for the meeting, making it clear that the one on which the most are able to attend will be chosen. Once this has been done, each director should be notified in the usual manner.

28.5   AGENDA

The agenda is a list of the business to be transacted at a meeting. Although it is not strictly necessary to give notice of the business to be transacted at meetings of directors, it is normal for an agenda to be prepared and sent to each director prior to the meeting, together with any supporting papers that may be necessary to facilitate discussion of that business. If an agenda is sent to the directors prior to the meeting, it will constitute notice of the business and, as such, the rule that it must not be deliberately misleading will apply.

If the notice of meeting includes notice of the business to be transacted, that part of the notice can be referred to as the agenda (see **Precedent 28.5**).

Items of business on the agenda are usually placed in the order that the business is to be taken at the meeting, although the board is not bound to take them in that order (*Re Cawley & Co.* (1889) 42 Ch.D. 209).

28.5.1   Practical issues with respect to the agenda

It is normal for the agenda to refer only briefly to the nature of the business to be transacted and most items will contain some reference to supporting papers which contain the detailed proposals. If the business can be described accurately and briefly, the substance of the resolutions to be put at the meeting may be included in the agenda. Even then, however, there may be some supporting papers and, if so, the agenda should include some reference to them. The overall objective when preparing the agenda should be to keep it as short as possible. This enables the directors to assess the business of the meeting at a glance.

Where supporting papers are required, they should be clearly identified and numbered and placed in the order in which they appear on the agenda. This task normally falls to the secretary, who should ensure that all reports and papers have been submitted and are listed in the proper form on the agenda.

The agenda and supporting papers should be sent so that they are in the hands of the directors about a week before the meeting. This gives them adequate opportunity to read the papers carefully. Many directors will not do so until the very last minute no matter when they receive the board papers. Nevertheless, they tend to forget this when they receive the board papers late and normally will not hesitate to complain. As any secretary would tell you, the reason why the agenda is late is normally because one of the directors was late in submitting a paper for inclusion. Of course, it can be argued that one of the secretary's jobs is to chase these recalcitrant directors.

Any Other Business
In view of the fact that it is not necessary to give notice of the business to be transacted at board meetings, it would seem to be perfectly in order for business not included in the notice or the agenda to be raised under the heading 'Any Other Business'. Two qualifications must be made to this principle. The first is that, in accordance with the ruling in *Homer*, the notice may be deemed to be invalid if the item is omitted so as to mislead members of the board that it will not be raised. The second is that it is unreasonable to expect the directors to make reasoned decisions if they are not given sufficient time to consider the merits of a proposal or the opportunity to consider any alternative proposals. Many chairmen refuse as a matter of principle to put matters raised under Any Other Business to a vote until the following meeting. In practice, however, it may sometimes be necessary to do so, e.g. where there is likely to be a considerable delay before the next meeting.

28.6   CHAIRMAN

In theory, the duties of the chairman at meetings of directors are largely the same as those of the chairman of general meetings. However, meetings of directors are usually less formal than general meetings. Decisions are often reached on a consensual basis and the chairman is less likely to be called upon to exercise formal control over the proceedings. At general meetings the chairman does not usually owe his position to the members but to his office as chairman of the board. In contrast, the chairman of the board is invariably elected by the board and can be removed by the board. Unless also the majority shareholder, the chairman's position will therefore be more tenuous. As a result, the chairman of the board tends to acts more as facilitator or arbiter as opposed to an autocrat or judge.

28.6.1   Role and duties

The common law duties of the chairman, as expressed by Chitty J. in *National Dwelling Society Ltd* v. *Sykes* [1894] 3 Ch. 159, are also applicable to meetings of directors. It is therefore the duty of the chairman to ensure that:

(a)   the meeting is properly conducted;
(b)   all directors are given a fair opportunity to contribute to the deliberations;
(c)   the sense of the meeting is properly ascertained and recorded; and
(d)   order is preserved.

The chairman's authority is derived from the body which made the appointment. In other words, by electing a chairman, the directors are deemed to have conferred upon him all the powers necessary to fulfil the role. At general meetings, the chairman is deemed to have authority to rule on points of order and on other incidental questions which arise during the meeting (*Re Indian Zoedone Co.* (1884) 26 Ch. D 70). This is probably the case at meetings of directors, although if challenged at the meeting, the chairman should bend to the will of the majority unless he is given specific authority by the articles to determine the matter himself. For example, reg. 98 of Table A provides that any question at a meeting of directors or of a committee of directors as to the right of a director to vote may, before the conclusion of the meeting, be referred to the chairman of the meeting and his ruling in relation to any director other than himself shall be final and conclusive.

In the unlikely event that a meeting is disorderly, the chairman will probably have inherent power to adjourn it in order to restore order (*John* v. *Rees* [1969] 2 W.L.R. 1294). Otherwise the power to adjourn will rest with the meeting and the chairman should not adjourn or close the meeting without the consent of the meeting until all the business is transacted.

28.6.2   Governance role

Most articles allow any director to call a meeting [e.g. reg. 88]. In practice, it will be the chairman who usually decides whether meetings are necessary and who settles the agenda. In doing so, he will take account of the views of other directors (particularly the chief executive) and the advice of the company secretary (particularly on formal items of business, but also on matters of governance). The Cadbury Committee suggested that the chairman should be primarily responsible for:

• the working of the board;
• its balance of membership (subject to board and shareholders' approval);

- ensuring that all relevant issues are on the agenda; and
- ensuring that all directors, executive and non-executive alike, are enabled and encouraged to play their full part in its activities [Cadbury Report, para. 4.7].

It goes on to say that chairmen should be able to stand sufficiently back from the day-to-day running of the business to ensure that their boards are in full control of the company's affairs and alert to their obligations to their shareholders. It is for them to make certain that non-executive directors receive timely, relevant information tailored to their needs, that they are properly briefed on the issues arising at board meetings, and that they make an effective contribution as board members in practice. It is equally for the chairman to ensure that executive directors look beyond their executive duties and accept their full share of the responsibilities of governance [Cadbury Report, paras. 4.7 and 4.8].

The Cadbury Committee recommended that the role of chairman should in principle be separate from that of the chief executive. There should therefore be a clearly accepted division of responsibilities at the head of the company, which will ensure a balance of power and authority, such that no individual has unfettered powers of decision. Where the chairman is also the chief executive, it is essential that there should be a strong and independent element on the board [Cadbury Report, para. 4.9 and Cadbury Code, para. 1.2].

28.6.3   Appointment

Articles usually specify the method by which the chairman of the board of directors is to be appointed. For example, Table A provides:

> **91.** The directors may appoint one of their number to be chairman of the board of directors and may at any time remove him from that office. Unless he is unwilling to do so, the director so appointed shall preside at every meeting of directors at which he is present. But if there is no director holding that office, or if the director holding it is unwilling to preside or is not present within five minutes after the time appointed for the meeting, the directors present may appoint one of their number to be chairman of the meeting.

The main objective of this provision is to avoid the need to elect a chairman at each meeting of directors. A director appointed to the office of 'chairman of the board of directors' has a right to chair subsequent meetings until removed from office.

If, unusually, the articles make no provision with regard to the appointment of the chairman, the directors present at each meeting may elect one of their number to be the chairman of it.

If the office of chairman is unsalaried, a director is not deemed to have an interest in his or her appointment to that office and may therefore vote on a resolution to that effect (*Foster* v. *Foster* [1916] 1 Ch. 532). Where the office is salaried, a director will have a personal interest and may be prevented by the articles from voting on his or her own appointment. The same principles apply to any resolution to remove the chairman.

A salaried chairman can therefore be removed more easily than an unsalaried chairman. Some articles specifically allow directors to be counted in the quorum at the meeting at which they are appointed to an office but not to vote, e.g. reg. 84(4) of the 1948 Act Table A.

28.6.4   Problems appointing a chairman

Under Table A, the person appointed as 'chairman of the board of directors' is automatically entitled (until removed from office) to:

- chair subsequent meetings of directors [reg. 91];
- a casting vote at any meeting of directors which he chairs [reg. 88];
- chair meetings of the company [reg. 42]; and
- a casting vote at general meetings [reg. 50].

The ability to exercise a casting vote at board and general meetings could easily tip the balance of power and it is not unusual for the directors to be unable to reach agreement on the appointment of someone as 'chairman of the board of directors'. In these circumstances, the directors may prefer at each board meeting to elect one of their number as 'chairman of the meeting', leaving the office of 'chairman of the board of directors' vacant and the issue of who is to chair general meetings to be determined by the default provisions of reg. 42 (see further para. 8.2). The person elected as chairman at each meeting would, however, still have a casting vote because reg. 88 confers that right on the 'chairman of the meeting' rather than on the 'chairman of the board of directors'.

Where reg. 88 or a similar article applies, it is not uncommon for the directors to be unable to agree on the appointment of a chairman at all, particularly where there are only two or some other even number of directors. To avoid this problem, it may be advisable at the outset to remove the chairman's right to a casting vote at meetings of directors and/or general meetings by amending the articles. This could be done by a written resolution of the members or the unanimous agreement of all the members (*Cane* v. *Jones* [1981] 1 All E.R. 533).

In the event of complete deadlock, the power to appoint the chairman may revert to the company in general meeting (*Foster* v. *Foster* [1916] 1 Ch. 532). However, if the two sides each control half the shares, this is unlikely to provide a solution. It may be possible for the directors to appoint someone as chairman of the meeting on the condition that they refrain from exercising the right to a casting vote, the assumption being that the person will automatically be removed if he attempts to exercise that right. It might however be safer to appoint no chairman at all.

28.6.5   No chairman

The board may act without a chairman. The chairman is said to derive authority from the meeting. If no chairman is appointed, the meeting retains those powers itself. Matters which the chairman would normally be called upon to decide could be resolved by the meeting. In addition, Table A merely provides that the directors 'may' appoint one of their number to be chairman of the board or chairman of the meeting. This would seem to imply that they need not do so. The directors could even invite someone who is not a director to chair or act as the facilitator at board meetings.

The board may also act without a chairman by way of written resolution in accordance with the provisions of the articles (if any) or by unanimous resolution of the directors (preferably evidenced in writing) if the articles do not specifically provide for written resolutions.

28.6.6   Chairman not present

Articles commonly provide that if the chairman of the board is not present within five minutes of the start of the meeting, the directors may elect one of their number to chair the meeting. If the chairman of the board arrives after the directors have elected a person to chair the meeting, the person elected is under no obligation to vacate the chair, although it is normal practice to do so.

28.7   QUORUM

The quorum is the minimum number of directors who must be present and entitled to vote at a meeting of directors in order for it to transact business. A quorum must be present for each item of business considered and a director who is not entitled to vote (e.g. because he is interested in the transaction) cannot be counted in calculating whether a quorum exists for that item (see para. 28.7.3).

The quorum is normally fixed by the articles. If the articles are silent on the matter, the basic common law rule is that the quorum is a majority of the directors (see para. 28.7.1).

Articles normally give the directors limited powers to act where their number (i.e. the total number of directors in office and not merely the number present at the meeting) falls below the number fixed as the quorum (see para. 28.7.7).

A third party dealing with the company in good faith may by virtue of s. 35A be able to enforce a contract entered into by the directors in breach of the requirements of the articles. In such circumstances, the company could sue the directors for damages for breach of duty. It is therefore in the directors' interests to act in accordance with the articles and to ensure that a quorum is present when they make decisions.

28.7.1   Quorum fixed by or in accordance with the articles

Articles invariably specify the quorum for meetings of directors or a method of fixing one. For example, reg. 89 states:

> **89.** The quorum for the transaction of business of the directors may be fixed by the directors and unless so fixed at any other number shall be two. A person who holds office only as an alternate director shall, if his appointor is not present, be counted in the quorum.

The articles may fix a quorum of one, and there is nothing to prevent the directors from doing so under articles such as reg. 89 (*Re Fireproof Doors Ltd* [1916] 2 Ch. 142).

If the articles do not fix or provide for a method of fixing a quorum, the quorum for meetings of directors will be a majority of the directors currently holding office (*York Tramways Co.* v. *Willows* (1882) 8 Q.B.D. 685) or, where it can be shown that a standard practice has evolved over time, the number of directors who usually act in conducting the business of the company (*Re Tavistock Ironworks Co.* (1867) L.R. 4 Eq. 233). It goes without saying that where the articles make no provision as to the quorum, it is safer to assume that it is a majority of the directors. It is interesting to note that, whilst it is preferable for the articles to specify a quorum or a method of fixing one, the advantage of not doing so is that under the common law the number required to form a quorum (being a majority of the directors) automatically falls as the number of directors falls.

Where the articles do not specify a quorum but provide a method for fixing one, e.g. by a resolution of the directors, the quorum will be a majority of the directors until such time as alternative provision is made by that method (*York Tramways Co.* v. *Willows* (1882) 8 Q.B.D. 685). However, where the articles allow the directors to fix their own quorum and no resolution to that effect has ever been passed, the majority rule may be dispensed with if the court is satisfied that there was an understanding between all the directors which was followed (*Re Regent's Canal Iron Co.* [1867] W.N. 79). Again, it is safer to assume that the quorum is a majority of the directors unless the alternative quorum has been applied for a number of years.

28.7.2   Changing the quorum

Where the articles give the directors power to fix or alter the quorum, they may only exercise that power if they act in accordance with the existing rules and procedures governing their meetings, including the existing quorum requirements (*Re Portuguese Consolidated Copper Mines Ltd* (1889) 42 Ch.D. 160). In other words, they cannot change the quorum unless there are sufficient directors present at the meeting to form a quorum under the existing rules.

If the articles allow the directors to fix or alter the quorum, they may do so by a written resolution of all the directors as long as the articles allow them to act in this manner. It is doubtful whether such a resolution would be valid, however, if there were insufficient directors to form a quorum under the existing rules (*Hood Sailmakers Ltd* v. *Axford* [1996] 4 All E.R. 830).

If the quorum is fixed by the articles and they make no separate provision for alteration, the quorum can only be changed by passing a special resolution at a general meeting to amend the relevant article.

28.7.3   Disinterested quorum

Under the common law a quorum must be present for each item of business at a meeting and only those entitled to vote may be counted in calculating whether a quorum exists (*Re Greymouth Point Elizabeth Railway and Coal Co. Ltd* [1904] 1 Ch. 32). These principles apply to meetings of directors unless they are specifically excluded by the articles. Table A specifically provides that a director shall not be counted in the quorum present at a meeting in relation to a resolution on which he is not entitled to vote [reg. 95].

This rule can be of crucial importance because articles frequently restrict the right to vote at meetings of directors where a director has a personal interest in the matter under consideration, e.g. reg. 94 of Table A. Where such restrictions operate, a quorum may in fact be present for some but not all items of business. Care should be taken to check that a competent or disinterested quorum exists for each item of business.

The courts do not look favourably on techniques used by directors to avoid the operation of rules restricting their right to vote on matters in which they have an interest. Two such techniques were rejected in a case where a company's articles allowed directors to contract with the company but not to vote on any such contract. The quorum for board meetings had been fixed at three by the directors under powers given to them by the articles. At a meeting attended by four directors a contract in which two of them were interested was passed by two separate resolutions. Each interested director voted only on the resolution concerning the other director. These resolutions were held to be invalid because there was in reality only one item of business. Treating it as two separate resolutions was merely a device to avoid the operation of the articles (this rule would prevent directors from voting on a number of separate resolutions to take out directors' and officers' insurance cover for each director where only one policy to cover them all is to be taken out). At a subsequent meeting attended by three directors, those present voted to reduce the quorum to two so as to allow a resolution to be passed issuing a debenture to one of the directors present. The resolution to alter the quorum was also held to be invalid because its sole purpose was to enable something to be done indirectly which could not be done directly (*Re North Eastern Insurance Co. Ltd* [1919] 1 Ch. 198). In this case, the reason for altering the quorum was blatantly obvious. If it could be shown that the quorum was altered for other legitimate reasons, the resolutions at this second meeting would have been valid.

If the number of directors in office and the number required to form a quorum are equal and the articles include restrictions on the right to vote, the directors may be unable to deal with any item of business in which any of them has an interest. This sort of blanket prohibition may not be desirable as it could prevent the directors from acting in the best interests of the company merely because one of them has an interest in a particular transaction. It is usual therefore for the articles to specify a number of exceptions to the general prohibition on voting, e.g. reg. 94 of Table A. Modifications and additions can be made from time to time to these exceptions by amending the articles. In addition, articles often provide that the members in general meeting may by ordinary resolution suspend or relax the operation of any restrictions on directors' voting, e.g. reg. 96 of Table A. If so, it would normally be simpler to call a meeting to propose such a relaxation.

For small owner-managed companies, it is usually sensible to exclude or modify the relevant provisions of Table A (regs. 94 to 96) so as to allow the directors to vote on any matter irrespective of any interest they may have in it (see **Precedent 28.7A**).

From a practical point of view, there is no need for a director to withdraw from the meeting when a matter in which he or she is interested is being considered, although it is usual to do so if the board so requests.

28.7.4   Alternate directors

Under the common law, directors must be present in person at the venue specified in the notice to be counted in the quorum. The articles may, however, provide otherwise, and commonly do so where provision is made for the appointment of alternate directors. They may also provide that directors who are in contact with the meeting by telephone or audio visual links can be counted in the quorum (e.g. art. 119 of Whitbread plc) (see also para. 28.9).

Where the articles provide for the appointment of alternate directors (a type of proxy), special provision will usually be made regarding the quorum. For example, reg. 89 of Table A provides that 'a person who holds office only as an alternate director shall, if his appointor is not present, be counted in the quorum'. It should be noted that this provision does not apply where the person appointed is already a director and it is highly questionable whether such a person can be counted in the quorum more than once. There is no other provision in Table A which specifically excludes the common law rule in these circumstances, even though the director appointed as the alternate would be entitled to more than one vote if a quorum was actually present by some other means (see reg. 88).

Table A also provides that an alternate director is deemed to be interested in any contract in which his or her appointee is interested [reg. 94]. If a director is by virtue of his interest in a contract disqualified from voting and from being counted in the quorum, his alternate will be similarly disqualified. This may be the case even where the articles are silent on the matter as any other conclusion would enable the directors to circumvent restrictions on voting when they are interested in a contract. It should also be noted that an alternate director will also be disqualified from voting under reg. 94 where he is interested in the transaction.

28.7.5   Sole director

The default figure of two for the quorum at meetings of directors in reg. 89 is wholly inappropriate for a private company to be formed with only one director and suitably modified articles should be submitted with the application for registration (see **Precedent 28.7B**). If this is not done, the sole director will be incapable of acting and will need to apply to the court order under s. 371 calling a general meeting to appoint an additional director or to amend the article specifying the quorum. In practice, it would probably be cheaper and less time-consuming to form a new company.

28.7.6   Practical issues when fixing a quorum

Generally speaking, it is preferable to fix a low quorum. Doing so facilitates the conduct of the board's business. If the quorum is too high, one or more of the directors may be able to obstruct the board by deliberately absenting themselves from meetings. A director cannot be forced to attend board meetings against his will. In *Barron* v. *Potter* [1914] 1 Ch. 895, the quorum was two and Barron, one of only two directors, refused to attend board meetings. Had he done so, Potter, the other director who was entitled to a casting vote as chairman, would have been able to appoint his own nominee as an additional director. Potter tried to hold a board meeting at a railway station and again at the company's offices at which he purported to propose and carry with his casting vote a resolution to appoint his nominee as an additional director. Barron made it clear that he refused to attend board meetings and it was held that he could not be forced to do so against his will. The appointment by Potter was therefore invalid.

In *Re Opera Photographic Ltd* (1989) 5 B.C.C. 601, a director tried to prevent the board convening a general meeting to remove him as a director by absenting himself from board meetings, thereby making it impossible to obtain a quorum at board meetings. The court ordered that a general meeting be called. In *Barron* v. *Potter*, it would have served no purpose for Potter to apply to the court for an order calling a general meeting. Barron had already requisitioned a general meeting to appoint new directors at which he would have been in the majority. Potter's only chance of success was therefore to entice Barron to attend a board meeting at which he had the casting vote.

Thus, although a director may be able to obstruct the business of the company by absenting himself from board meetings, the will of the majority will nearly always prevail as they will be in a position to remove him or to appoint additional directors unless the director has special class rights which enable him to veto appointments and removals (see para. 28.8.3).

It is, of course, sometimes desirable to establish a deadlocked company, e.g. where two members hold the same number of voting shares and are the only directors. In this case, it will be necessary to remove the chairman's casting vote at board and general meetings and fix a quorum of two at board meetings. If the directors fail to agree, it would serve no purpose applying to the court to call a general meeting as the balance of power would be the same.

The advantages of setting a relatively low figure as the quorum are plain. The other directors cannot call a meeting without giving reasonable notice. If the meeting is called to deal with routine or uncontroversial business, only sufficient directors to form a quorum need attend. However, whether all the directors attend or not, when an important or controversial item of business is considered, the will of the majority and not the minority will hold sway.

The final point that is worthy of consideration is that the quorum for board meetings may also affect the quorum for committees of the board where the articles provide that the regulations governing proceedings at board meetings shall also apply to committees of the board (see para. 30.6).

28.7.7 Number below quorum

Articles which allow the directors to act notwithstanding any vacancy in their number do not allow them to act where their number falls below that required to constitute a quorum. This issue is, however, normally addressed in modern articles. For example, Table A, which specifies that the minimum number of directors shall be two unless otherwise determined by ordinary resolution (reg. 64) and that the quorum for meetings of directors shall be two unless otherwise fixed by the directors (reg. 88), provides:

> **90.** The continuing directors or a sole continuing director may act notwithstanding any vacancies in their number, but, if the number of directors is less than the number fixed as the quorum, the continuing directors or director may act only for the purpose of filling vacancies or of calling a general meeting.

Under this type of article the directors may act in the normal way where their number falls below the minimum prescribed by the articles but is still sufficient to form a quorum. However, if the number remaining is not sufficient to form a quorum the directors may only act to appoint new directors and to call a general meeting.

It should be noted that under s. 35A, a company will be bound by the acts of its board of directors in favour of a third party dealing with the company in good faith even though the board acted in breach of the company's memorandum or articles of association. Thus, whether the number of directors is less than the minimum prescribed by the articles or there are not sufficient directors to form a quorum, the directors may bind the company in a transaction with an innocent third party. By doing so, however, the directors will have acted in breach of duty and may therefore be liable to compensate the company.

28.8 VOTING

The rules on voting at directors' meetings are based on the common law but are subject to modification by the articles. Board meetings and board committees are usually conducted with a great deal less formality than company meetings. Decisions are normally reached by concensus and matters are rarely put to a formal vote because it will normally be apparent without doing so which side would win.

When a resolution is put to a vote, each director will have one vote unless the articles provide otherwise. Questions are usually decided on a majority of votes cast for or against the resolution, although the articles may require a special majority for certain types of business. Most articles restrict the right to vote where a director has a personal interest in the matter under consideration. The chairman is commonly given a second or casting vote to be used in the event of a deadlock.

Table A provides:

> **88.** ... Questions arising at a meeting shall be decided by a majority of votes. In the case of an equality of votes, the chairman shall have a second or casting vote.

A director who is also an alternate director shall be entitled in the absence of his appointor to a separate vote on behalf of his appointor in addition to his own vote.

28.8.1 Method of voting

Articles rarely specify the method of voting, e.g. reg. 88 of Table A simply states that questions shall be decided on a majority of votes. Voting is normally conducted by a show of hands with each director having one vote. This method may not be satisfactory if any of the directors is entitled to more than one vote, e.g. a personal vote and one as an alternate for another director. A director who is present at the meeting and who has more than one vote has a right to have each of those votes counted and may have a right to demand a poll if they are not counted (see *R. v. Wimbledon Local Board* (1882) 8 Q.B.D. 459). The method of voting used should take account of the fact that some directors may have more votes than others. It is not necessary to follow the formal procedures used at company meetings. Voting papers could be used where it is difficult for the chairman to calculate the true number of votes for and against the resolution on a show of hands.

28.8.2 Casting vote

Unless the articles so provide, the chairman has no right to a casting vote (*Nell v. Longbottom* [1894] 1 Q.B. 767). Under reg. 88 of Table A the person who acts as the chairman of a meeting of directors is given a casting vote. A casting vote may only be used where there has already been a vote and the number of votes for and against the resolution are exactly equal. It cannot be used where there is a majority in favour or against in order to manufacture a tie.

There is no legal necessity for the chairman to use the casting vote in the event of a tie. Although failure to use the casting vote has the same effect as voting against the resolution, this may be preferable if the chairman wishes to remain impartial. The chairman need not use the casting vote in the same way as his or her original vote on the resolution.

In exercising a casting vote the chairman can follow one of two guiding principles (which are quite capable of producing the opposite result). The first, which is adopted by the Speaker of the House of Commons, is that the casting vote should be used to preserve the status quo. This may mean voting for or against the resolution depending on which way the resolution is worded. The second, which is perhaps more commonly applied, is that the chairman should use the casting vote in the best interests of the company. Clearly this second principle is more subjective than the first and depends on the chairman's view of what is in the interest of the company.

A casting vote may be exercised contingently. In *Bland v. Buchanan* [1901] 2 K.B. 75, the validity of a town councillor's vote was challenged during a meeting. The chairman realised that if the challenge proved to be well-founded, there would be a tied vote on a particular resolution. As he was not certain of the true position, he stated that if there was an equality of votes, he would use his casting vote in a particular way. The court commended the chairman's actions, stating that he had taken 'a very practical and business like view'.

28.8.3   Weighted voting

Under the common law each director has only one vote unless the articles provide otherwise. It is unusual for any director to have more than one vote except where the chairman is given a casting vote or a director is also an alternate for another director. However, weighted voting is sometimes used in owner-managed companies to ensure that the founder or major shareholder can outvote the other directors at board meetings. It is not strictly necessary for a director who is the majority shareholder because he or she would be able to remove any other director by passing an ordinary resolution at a general meeting. Neither will it offer a director who is a minority shareholder protection against removal as a director, unless he or she is also entitled to additional votes on a resolution to remove him or her at a general meeting.

28.8.4   Record of votes

Directors have a right to have their opposition to a resolution recorded in the minutes whether or not a formal vote was put to the meeting. This is mainly because a director who was not present when a decision was taken or who voted against it at the meeting will not be liable for the consequences of that transaction, unless it can be proved that he subsequently acquiesced in the decision.

28.8.5   Restrictions on voting

Articles frequently impose restrictions on the right to vote where a director has a personal interest in the subject of the resolution. As has already been seen, these restrictions can cause the board to become inquorate, as a director who is unable to vote on a resolution cannot normally be included in calculating whether a quorum exists for that item of business (see reg. 95 of Table A). However, provided that a quorum exists there is nothing to prevent the other directors from entering into a contract in which a director is interested.

In practice the restrictions on voting are themselves normally subject to a number of qualifications and articles usually provide a mechanism which allows the members to suspend or relax the restrictions contained in the articles (e.g. reg. 96 of Table A).

Regulation 94 of Table A provides that a director shall not vote at a meeting of directors or a committee of directors on any resolution concerning a matter in which he has, directly or indirectly, an interest or duty which is material and which conflicts or may conflict with the interests of the company. However, it goes on to list a number of exceptions to this general rule. These exceptions cover the giving of guarantees, security or indemnities, subscribing for shares or other securities, underwriting an issue of securities, and pension scheme arrangements.

Regulation 94 also states that an interest of a person who is, for any purpose of the Companies Act 1985 (as amended at the time the company was formed), connected with a director shall be treated as an interest of the director. It also provides in relation to an alternate director that an interest of his appointor shall be treated as an interest of the alternate director without prejudice to any interest which the alternate director has otherwise. Thus an alternate director may not vote if either he or his appointor has a relevant interest.

The London Stock Exchange requires the articles of listed companies to prohibit directors from voting on matters in which they have an interest, subject to certain limited exceptions [Listing Rules, para. 20 of Appendix 1 to Chapter 13].

28.8.6   Practical issues on voting

It is difficult to frame many of the issues discussed at board meetings as formal resolutions and it can sometimes be counter-productive to do so. When the chairman feels that a consensus has been reached, he or she should attempt to summarise it. This gives the other directors an opportunity to object to that interpretation and is obviously helpful for the secretary in preparing the minutes. What often happens, however, is that the chairman will often end the discussion by saying: 'I think we are all agreed on that subject and suggest we move on to the next item of business.' In such circumstances, if one were to go round the table asking each director what they thought had been agreed, each one would probably give a different answer. The other directors should not allow the chairman to get away with this, although it is often left to the secretary to ask the chairman to summarise what has been decided so that it can be properly recorded in the minutes.

28.9   MEETINGS BY TELEPHONE

Recent cases have confirmed that the board may act without holding a formal meeting if all the directors give their consent informally (see para. 27.8). There is no reason why that informal consent should not be given over the telephone. A more difficult question is whether directors can participate in board meetings over the telephone (or by audio-visual link). In other words, can they be counted in the quorum and can they vote even though they are not personally present so that the board can act without unanimity in the usual manner.

To avoid the need for argument as to the common law position, some companies have amended their articles to expressly provide for the holding of board meetings by telephone. In the case of meetings conducted using a conference type telephone system this can be done fairly simply. For example, the articles of Whitbread plc state:

119.   The quorum necessary for the transaction of business of the Board may be fixed from time to time by the Board and unless so fixed at any other number shall be two. For the purposes of these Articles any Director who is able (directly or by telephonic communication) to speak and be heard by each of the other

Directors present or deemed to be present at any meeting of the Board, shall be deemed to be present in person at such meeting and shall be entitled to vote or be counted in the quorum accordingly. Such meeting shall be deemed to take place where the largest group of those participating is assembled, or, if there is no such group, where the chairman of the meeting then is, and the word 'meeting' shall be construed accordingly.

Such an article deals with the potential conceptual problems which could arise under the common law. It clarifies that directors who are in contact with the meeting by conference telephone connection may be counted in the quorum. Without such an article the board could be deemed by the courts to be incapable of transacting any business where the number of directors physically present at the meeting is not sufficient to meet the quorum fixed by or established in accordance with the articles. Where the quorum has been fixed at a relatively low number, this might not be a problem.

If sufficient directors are physically present at the meeting to form a quorum (proper notice having been given to all directors entitled to receive notice), there is no doubt that those directors are able to transact business in the usual manner. This will also be the case even if some directors vote by telephone, provided that the votes of those directors would not have altered the outcome of any vote on a resolution. The matter is only open to argument when the result of a vote would have been different if those participating by telephone had not voted.

Regulation 88 of Table A provides:

Questions arising at a meeting shall be decided by a majority of votes. In the case of an equality of votes, the chairman shall have a second or casting vote. A director who is also an alternate director shall be entitled in the absence of his appointor to a separate vote on behalf of his appointor in addition to his own vote.

It also provides that, subject to the provisions of the articles, the directors may regulate their proceedings as they think fit. As Table A makes no specific provision as to the method by which directors must vote at meetings of directors, it can be argued that the directors may make their own regulations which allow them to vote by telephone.

The courts have already demonstrated a willingness to accept the fact that the participants in a general meeting need not all be in the same room (in other words, that a meeting may take place at several different locations at once). In *Byng* v. *London Life Association Ltd* [1989] 1 All E.R. 560, the company provided overflow facilities at an extraordinary general meeting to accommodate members who were unable to find a place at the venue given in the notice of that meeting (Cinema 1, Barbican). The overflow facilities were also in the Barbican complex and were intended to be connected to the main body of the meeting by audio-visual links. During the meeting those audio-visual links did not work as intended and the chairman purported to adjourn it to another place on the same day. The plaintiff sought to have the extraordinary resolution passed at the adjourned meeting declared invalid on a number of grounds. The first of these was that the original meeting was not a valid meeting because it was held in more than one place and as such could not be adjourned. The Court of Appeal dismissed this argument. In the leading judgment, Browne-Wilkinson V-C stated (at 565):

> The rationale behind the requirement for meetings in the 1985 Act is that the members shall be able to attend in person so as to debate and vote on matters affecting the company. Until recently this could only be achieved by everyone being physically present in the same room face to face. Given modern technological advances, the same result can now be achieved without all the members coming face to face; without being physically in the same room they can be electronically in each other's presence so as to hear and be heard and to see and be seen. The fact that such a meeting could not have been foreseen at the time the first statutory requirements for meetings were laid down, does not require us to hold that such a meeting is not within the meaning of the word 'meeting' in the 1985 Act.

Although in this case the Court of Appeal accepted that a general meeting need not be held in one room, it indicated that, for general meetings at least, the participants must be in visual as well as audio contact. In addition, it should be noted that whilst the overflow facilities were obviously in different rooms they were both in the place given in the notice of the meeting (i.e. the Barbican). In his judgment in the *Byng* case, Mustill LJ said (at 572):

> I also accept that it possible to have a meeting, not all of whose members are present in the same room. It is unnecessary to consider the extreme case where none of the participants are face to face, but are linked by simultaneous audio-visual transmissions. This would require consideration of whether it is possible to convene a meeting which does not take place in any single location, and which consists only of the exchange of electronic impulses. No such problem arises here. If the arrangements had gone according to plan, and if the participants had first occupied Cinema 1 until it was full, and had then all found a place in the adjacent rooms by the time the business had commenced, and if they had been able to see hear and communicate with the other participants I would have seen no intellectual or practical objection to regarding this as a 'meeting'. Moreover, it would have been a meeting held at the place of which notice had been given, namely Cinema 1, since this was where the centre of gravity of the meeting was to be found.

In this respect Byng does not seem to advance the cause for telephone board meetings much further. However, it at least demonstrates the courts' willingness to adapt long-established legal principles in order to allow technology to be used to facilitate meetings. It should also be borne in mind that the courts normally impose less stringent rules for meetings of directors.

Thus it is likely that a meeting of directors at which each of the directors was able to hear and be heard but not see and be seen and at which some of the directors participating were at a different location would be held to be a valid meeting, provided that there was a quorum at the place nominated in the notice as the place where the meeting was to be held.

28.9.1   Series of telephone calls

Except where the directors approve a proposal unanimously, it seems unlikely that the courts would accept as valid a resolution of the board reached as a result of a series of one-to-one telephone calls conducted by the chairman, unless the articles made specific provision to this effect. This would stretch the common law concept of a meeting too far. It would not allow the simultaneous transfer of views. It is not a meeting of minds at a particular point in time. Those who were contacted first may have changed their minds by the time the chairman has spoken to the last director. They might also have reached a different conclusion if they had heard the views of other directors. The same might be true of those who are contacted later in the series of calls if the chairman fails to explain adequately the views of the minority.

Some companies have articles which specifically allow decisions of the board to be reached in this manner. On the whole such a method of decision-making is only suitable for issues which are simple or mere formalities.

28.10   ALTERNATE DIRECTORS

At common law there is no automatic right to vote by proxy. The Act confers a statutory right on the members to vote by proxy but does not make similar provision with regard to the directors. Thus a director who is unable to attend a meeting of directors will be unable to vote at that meeting unless the articles provide otherwise.

Table A provides a mechanism which allows directors to appoint another person to attend and vote in their stead at board and committee meetings (see also arts. 118 and 133 of Whitbread plc). A person so appointed is known as an alternate director.

Regulation 68 provides that alternate directors may be appointed or removed by notice to the company signed by the director making or revoking the appointment or in any other manner approved by the directors (see **Precedents 28.10A–D**). However, reg. 65 states that the approval of the board is required regarding the appointment as an alternate of a person who is not a director. Such approval is not required where another director is appointed and reg. 88 provides that a director who is also an alternate director shall be entitled in the absence of his appointor to a separate vote on behalf of his appointor in addition to his own vote.

Regulation 89 provides that a person who holds office only as an alternate director shall, if his appointor is not present, be counted in the quorum. This provision does not deal with the position of a director who is also appointed as an alternate for one or more of the other directors (see para. 28.7.4).

Regulation 69 provides that an alternate director shall be deemed to be a director and shall alone be responsible for his own acts and defaults and shall not be deemed to be the agent of the director appointing him. Thus the chairman need not be concerned as to whether the alternate is voting in accordance with the instructions of his appointor. If the appointee is not already a director of the company, his appointment as alternate director will cause him to be regarded as a director and the usual formalities (such as notification of appointment on form 288a) should be followed.

Regulation 94 provides in relation to alternate directors that an interest of his appointor shall be treated as an interest of the alternate director without prejudice to any interest which the alternate director has otherwise. Thus an alternate director may not vote if either he or his appointor is interested in a transaction put to the vote at either a board or committee meeting.

An alternate director may sign a written resolution instead of his appointor under reg. 93.

28.11   INTERESTS IN CONTRACTS

Under s. 317, directors have a duty to declare at a meeting of directors the nature of any direct or indirect interest they may have in any contract or proposed contract with the company. This provision is intended to assist in avoiding conflicts of interest on the part of directors and to ensure that the requirements of the articles (e.g. reg. 94 of Table A) restricting a director's right to vote on such matters are observed. The type of interest which is relevant for these purposes is extremely wide and would include being a director of another company which is to be a party to a proposed transaction.

Section 317(3) allows general notice of a director's interests as a shareholder of other companies to be given to the company. This notice has no effect unless it is given at a meeting of directors or the director takes reasonable steps to secure that it is brought up and read at the next meeting of directors after it is given. This procedure cannot be used where a director's interest is only as a director of another company and in such circumstances separate disclosure is required in relation to each relevant transaction.

In the case of a proposed contract, the declaration must be made at the meeting of the directors at which the question of entering into the contract was first considered or, if the director was not at the date of that meeting interested in the proposed contract, at the next meeting of directors held after he became so interested. If a director becomes interested in an existing contract, the declaration must be made at the first meeting of directors after he becomes so interested.

The requirements of s. 317 are not satisfied by giving notice of an interest at a meeting of a committee of the board and it makes no difference that all the board members knew of the interest in question (*Guinness plc* v. *Saunders* [1988] 2 All E.R. 940). It has also been held that a sole director must comply with the formalities of s. 317 by holding a meeting and making a declaration at that meeting (*Re Neptune (Vehicle Washing Equipment) Ltd* [1995] 1 B.C.L.C. 352).

Articles frequently provide that directors may be a party to or otherwise interested in certain transactions or arrangements with the company provided that they have disclosed the nature and extent of that interest in accordance with s. 317. Any failure on the part of a director to comply with such an article renders any contract between the company and the director concerned voidable at the instance of the company (*Hely-Hutchinson* v. *Brayhead Ltd* [1967] 3 All E.R. 98).

28.12   ADJOURNMENT

Articles rarely make specific provision with respect to adjournment of directors' meetings other than to state that the directors may adjourn (see art. 117 of Whitbread plc). As a result, the common law rules on adjournment will normally apply and the power to adjourn will rest with the meeting (*National Dwelling Society Ltd* v. *Sykes* [1894] 3 Ch. 159). It follows that, in order to exercise that power, a quorum must be present. Thus, it is impossible to adjourn a board meeting at which a quorum is not present, unless the articles make specific provision to that effect, and a further meeting will need to be called.

If a quorum is present, the directors may adjourn. In practice, it is unusual for directors' meetings to be adjourned for any longer than a few hours, perhaps to allow lunch to be taken or further negotiations to take place before a final decision is made. Although there is strictly no need to give notice of an adjourned meeting (*Scadding* v. *Lorrant* (1851) 3 H.L.C. 418), it is normal practice to notify directors who were unable to attend the original meeting, if only to ensure that there is a quorum at the adjourned meeting. The quorum required at an adjourned meeting will be the same as for the original meeting.

28.13   STANDING ORDERS AND INTERNAL REGULATIONS

Articles frequently provide that, subject to the articles, the directors may regulate their proceedings as they think fit (e.g. reg. 88 of Table A). As a result, boards may adopt standing orders or internal regulations which govern their own conduct and procedures. The areas in which the board may establish such regulations might include:

- length of notice of board meetings;
- location and frequency of meetings;
- requirements to give notice of business to be transacted in the agenda;
- procedures for the approval and circulation of the minutes of meetings;
- schedule of matters reserved to the board.

Assuming that such regulations are consistent with the articles, the question arises as to their status and enforceability. Much will depend on the way they are drafted. If they are framed as a code of best practice (in other words they are aspirational rather than mandatory), they are unlikely to be enforceable. If, however, they are drafted as regulations and are intended to be mandatory, it is arguable that they should be complied with as if they were contained in the articles.

Articles often confer a similar power on the directors to fix the quorum at board meetings. It has been held that they may only exercise that power if they act in accordance with the existing rules and procedures governing their meetings, including the existing quorum requirements (*Re Portuguese Consolidated Copper Mines Ltd* (1889) 42 Ch.D. 160). In other words, they cannot change the quorum unless there are sufficient directors present at the meeting to form a quorum under the existing rules.

It could be argued that the same principle applies to internal regulations made by the board under reg. 88 or a similar article. For example, an internal regulation requiring at least seven days' notice of board meetings, could not be amended at a meeting held with notice of less than seven days. In theory, the board meeting would not have been validly called and any business transacted at it would therefore be invalid. In practice, the validity of the meeting would only be liable to challenge by a director or, in the event of insolvency, an administrator. No one else would be likely to have notice of the breach. Third parties would be protected from any breach by the indoor management rule (see para. 31.6). A director wishing to challenge the validity of the proceedings would need to act quickly otherwise he may be deemed by the courts to have acquiesced in the breach. The board could of course subsequently ratify the decisions taken at the meeting and the court could refuse to declare the proceedings invalid where it is satisfied that the irregularities could be cured by the board going through the proper process (*Bentley-Stevens* v. *Jones* [1974] 1 W.L.R. 638).

CHAPTER TWENTY-NINE

Delegation of directors' powers

29.1 SUMMARY

The directors must exercise their powers collectively as a board unless the articles authorise them to delegate those powers. This is because the directors are deemed to be agents of the company and because of the operation of the universal rule that agents may not sub-delegate without the authority of their principal (*delegatus non potest delegare*). The power to delegate is not one of the powers given to the directors by the general management clause and will therefore depend on the existence of a specific power in the articles.

Most articles follow reg. 72 of Table A and allow the board of directors to delegate to board committees and to individual executive directors. In addition, articles usually give the board specific power to appoint agents by power of attorney or otherwise (see para. 29.4).

Committees, executive directors and agents appointed by the board may not sub-delegate unless given specific authority to do so by the board. In effect the power to delegate must itself be delegated (see para. 29.2.4).

Although reg. 72 states that the directors may delegate 'any of their powers', the courts have held that this does not necessarily include special powers given to them by the articles, e.g. the power to pay the directors special remuneration (see para. 29.2.5).

The Cadbury Code requires directors of listed companies to produce a schedule of matters reserved for the decision of the board (see para. 29.3).

29.2 DELEGATION TO COMMITTEES AND EXECUTIVE DIRECTORS

Articles usually allow boards to delegate their powers to board committees and to individual executive directors. If no such provision is made in the articles, no committee or executive director may validly exercise the powers given to the directors.

The power to delegate to a committee cannot be used for an improper purpose, e.g.

to exclude one or more of the directors from the forum where the board's decisions are taken (*Pullbrook* v. *Richmond Consolidated Mining Co.* (1878) 9 Ch.D. 610).

29.2.1 Table A

Regulation 72 of Table A is typical of the sort of provision one would expect to find on delegation in the articles. It provides:

> **72.** The directors may delegate any of their powers to any committee consisting of one or more directors. They may also delegate to any managing director or any director holding any other executive office such of their powers as they consider desirable to be exercised by him. Any such delegation may be made subject to any conditions the directors may impose, and either collaterally with or to the exclusion of their own powers and may be revoked or altered. Subject to any such conditions, the proceedings of a committee with two or more members shall be governed by the articles regulating the proceedings of directors so far as they are capable of applying.

29.2.2 Revocation and amendment of delegated authority

The board may at any time revoke a previous decision to delegate its powers (*Huth* v. *Clarke* (1890) 25 Q.B.D. 391). It follows that it must also be able to amend the extent of any delegation as it could achieve the same result by revoking the original powers and then delegating new powers. It is, of course, unnecessary to go through this convoluted procedure and a board resolution amending the delegated authority will suffice. Regulation 72 specifically states that any delegation by the board may be revoked or altered. However, this will be the case unless the articles specify otherwise.

29.2.3 Exclusive authority

In *Huth* v. *Clarke* it was also held that the body which delegates the powers retains the authority to exercise them itself. Thus, unless the articles provide otherwise, the board retains collateral power to act even though it has delegated those powers to a committee or executive director. Regulation 72 of Table A states that the directors may delegate their powers either collaterally or to the exclusion of their own powers. However, it also provides that the directors may revoke any delegated powers. Accordingly, even if it has delegated to a committee to the exclusion of its own powers, it could revoke that authority and act itself. It is doubtful whether the courts would intervene even if the board failed to revoke the delegated authority before acting itself if it was clear that the board would have done so if it had known that this was necessary. In practice therefore in order to grant exclusive authority the articles must allow the directors to delegate their powers irrevocably.

29.2.4   Sub-delegation

Committees and executive directors cannot sub-delegate their powers unless author-ised to do so by the board (*Cook* v. *Ward* (1877) 2 C.P.D. 255). This does not mean that a committee may not ask one or more of its members to make recommendations to a future meeting of the committee as long as the committee takes the final decision.

It is doubtful whether the articles need to make specific provision authorising sub-delegation. However, some listed companies have recently amended their articles to do so, presumably to clarify the position and to avoid any possibility of an adverse ruling following the *Guinness* case (see para. 29.2.5 below). Companies have survived without making specific provision in this regard for hundreds of years. Although it is rare for board committees to sub-delegate, it is obvious that the managing director or chief executive of a large company must sub-delegate to other managers and employees of the company.

29.2.5   Restrictions on power to delegate

Although articles usually state that the directors may delegate 'any of their powers', this may not include special powers given to the directors by the articles (e.g. the power to fix the remuneration of directors). This is a difficult area and the answer will depend on the construction of the articles in each case. What is beyond doubt is that the general power to delegate will, unless otherwise stated, cover the powers given to the directors under the general management clause (e.g. reg. 70 of Table A).

In *Guinness plc* v. *Saunders* [1990] 1 All E.R. 652, the House of Lords held that an article giving 'the Board' of Guinness general power to delegate to committees did not authorise them to delegate a special power conferred by another article authorising 'the Board' to fix the special remuneration of a director serving on a committee. It reached this decision despite the fact 'the Board' was defined elsewhere in the articles as being: 'The Directors for the time being (or a quorum of such Directors assembled at a meeting of Directors duly convened) or any Committee authorised by the Board to act on its behalf.' Lord Templeman, who gave the main judgment, said: 'It cannot have been intended that any committee should be able to grant special remuneration to *any* director who serves on *any* committee.'

This decision arose from a dispute between Guinness plc and one of its former non-executive directors, Mr Ward, who had been paid £5.2m for services rendered to Guinness during its bid for Distillers. The payment had not been authorised by the board but by two out of the three members of the committee established by the board (of which Mr Ward was a member) with full power and authority to settle the terms of the offer, to approve any revisions of the offer and to authorise and approve, execute and do all such documents, deeds, acts and things as they may consider necessary or desirable in connection with the making or implementation of the offer.

There can be no doubt that the House of Lords bent over backwards to ensure that Mr Ward accounted to Guinness for the money he had received and it may be that the effect of the judgment is only relevant to directors' remuneration. Directors are treated as fiduciaries under the common law and cannot claim remuneration unless the articles expressly provide for payment. The ability of the board to fix directors' remuneration is therefore dependent upon the existence of a special power contained in the articles. It seems from the *Guinness* case that this power cannot be delegated unless the articles make it absolutely clear that this is in fact intended. This is particularly important in view of the recommendations of the Greenbury Committee that executive directors' remuneration should be determined by a committee of non-executive directors (see para. 30.12). Previously, remuneration committees were established to make recommendations to the board in this regard.

However, it is possible that the *Guinness* case will have wider ramifications. Most articles include provisions giving the directors special powers in addition to the powers conferred by the general management clause, and these special powers are expressed as being given to the directors collectively. This is certainly the case under Table A which contains special powers authorising the directors:

- to declare a share to be wholly or in part free from a lien (reg. 8);
- to authorise a person to give effect to the sale of shares subject to a lien (reg. 9);
- to make calls (regs. 12 to 22);
- to reject share transfers (regs. 24 and 25);
- to call general meetings (reg. 37);
- to appoint and fix the remuneration of any managing or other executive director (reg. 84);
- to appoint the chairman of the board (reg. 91);
- to appoint and fix the remuneration of the secretary (reg. 99);
- to pay interim dividends (reg. 103).

It may well be that the board cannot delegate these powers under reg. 72 to a committee or an individual executive director. It is therefore advisable for the board to exercise these powers itself.

Following the decision in the *Guinness* case, most listed companies amended their articles to state that the general power to delegate is not intended to be limited by anything in the articles which requires powers to be exercised by the board. For example, Whitbread plc's article on delegation to committees concludes by saying:

124(C) The power to delegate contained in this Article shall be effective in relation to the powers, duties and discretions of the Board generally whether or not express reference is made in these Articles to powers, duties or discretions being exercised by the Board or by a committee authorised by the Board.

This will be particularly important if, for example, authority to fix the remuneration of executive directors is to be delegated to the remuneration committee (see also art. 92 of Whitbread plc).

29.3 SCHEDULE OF MATTERS RESERVED FOR THE BOARD

If the board has not delegated any of its powers, it must exercise those powers itself on behalf of the company. When it delegates various powers to committees and to individual executive directors, it may no longer be entirely clear what matters must still be referred to the board for decision. In order to decide, it may be necessary to trawl through the terms of reference of every committee and executive director. This can cause problems in large companies as the powers delegated to executive directors may in certain circumstances allow them to act where the board would have expected to have the final say.

To address this problem, the Cadbury Committee recommended that boards of listed companies should have a formal schedule of matters specifically reserved to them for their collective decision [Cadbury Code, para. 1.4]. This, it suggested, was to ensure that the direction and control of the company remains firmly in the hands of the board and to provide 'a safeguard against misjudgments and possible illegal practices'. A copy of the schedule should be given to each director on appointment and kept up to date [Cadbury Report, para. 4.23]. The schedule should include at the minimum:

- acquisition and disposal of assets of the company or its subsidiaries that are material to the company;
- investments;
- capital projects;
- authority levels;
- treasury policies; and
- risk management policies [Cadbury Report, para. 4.24].

The existence of such a schedule is one of the recommendations of the Code which is subject to review by the auditors of listed companies.

The ICSA's Company Secretaries Panel has published a model schedule of matters reserved for the board (see **Precedent 29.3**). The model schedule is not a definitive list or even an indication of best practice but may be useful as a starting point for boards of directors. Some of the matters in the draft schedule may not be material to the affairs of the company and there may well be matters which are material to the company's particular business which are not included in it. Some of the matters included will, of course, be relevant to all companies, e.g. those that derive from company law. The schedule is subdivided into matters governed by company law, stock exchange requirements, Cadbury recommendations and other matters.

When adopting a schedule of reserved matters, procedures should be laid down for dealing with urgent matters between board meetings. The schedule should also make clear which transactions require multiple board signatures on the relative documentation [Cadbury Report, para. 4.24].

29.4   APPOINTMENT OF OTHER AGENTS

Articles usually give the directors specific power to appoint other agents. For example, reg. 71 of Table A provides:

> **71.** The directors may, by power of attorney or otherwise, appoint any person

to be the agent of the company for such purposes and on such conditions as they determine, including authority for the agent to delegate all or any of his powers.

It is noteworthy that reg. 71 specifically states that the board may authorise an agent to delegate all or any of his powers. The power to appoint an agent would normally be deemed to include this power.

CHAPTER THIRTY

Board committees

30.1 SUMMARY

Committees of directors may only be appointed by a resolution of the board which should specify its membership and duties (see para. 30.2). Only directors may be appointed as members unless the articles provide otherwise (see para. 30.2.3). Articles usually provide that the proceedings at committees of directors shall be governed by the regulations governing board meetings (see paras. 30.4 to 30.9) except where a committee of one director is appointed (see para. 30.10). The Cadbury Committee recommended that all listed companies should establish an audit committee (see para. 30.11) and a remuneration committee. The Greenbury Committee made further detailed recommendations concerning the operation of remuneration committees (see para. 30.12).

30.2 APPOINTMENT OF COMMITTEES

The power to delegate to committees of directors is a special power which must be exercised by the board at a properly convened and constituted meeting of the board. In other words, the establishment of a committee with delegated powers must be the subject of a valid board resolution.

The resolution establishing a committee must deal with its:

- membership;
- duties and powers; and
- any conditions imposed by the board on the exercise of those powers.

This can sometimes be done in one simple resolution (see **Precedent 30.2A**). However, it is normal to pass a resolution establishing the committee's terms of reference (including its delegated powers) and to deal with appointments separately when establishing a standing committee.

30.2.1   Membership

Most articles state that the directors may appoint a committee of one or more directors. However, the power to delegate to a committee is deemed to include the power to delegate to a committee consisting of only one director, unless the articles specifically provide otherwise (*Re Fireproof Doors Ltd* [1916] 2 Ch. 142).

In most cases, it will be preferable to appoint named individuals to a committee. This will be so for standing committees such as the audit and remuneration committees which are usually comprised wholly or mainly of non-executive directors. It is, however, perfectly acceptable to appoint post-holders rather than named individuals. This might be a more suitable method for an executive committee where the membership is drawn from particular office-holders.

30.2.2   Committees of 'any two directors'

It is also quite common for boards of directors to establish a committee of 'any two directors' or 'any three directors', etc. (see **Precedent 30.2B**). This method is most commonly used to allow one or more directors to complete a transaction which the board has already authorised or to sign a document on behalf of the board. In such cases, it arguable whether it is necessary to establish a committee. It would be sufficient for the board to resolve, for example, that any two directors be authorised to sign the balance sheet on behalf of the board.

The 'any two director' method is slightly less satisfactory where the committee is to be given discretionary powers. The technique was used by board of Guinness during its takeover of Distillers in the 1980s to appoint a committee of any three directors:

> with full power and authority to settle the terms of the offer, to approve any revision of the offer which the committee might consider it desirable to make and [amongst other things] (vi) to authorise and approve, execute and do, or procure to be executed and done all documents, deeds, acts and things as they may consider necessary or desirable in connection with the making or implementation of the offer and/or the proposals referred to above and any revision thereof . . . (see *Guinness* v. *Saunders* [1990] 1 All E.R. 654).

Appointing such a committee could be viewed as appointing the whole board as a committee and fixing the quorum at the number of directors specified. In theory, all the directors are potential members of such a committee and are therefore entitled to receive notice of its meetings. It is, however, debatable whether this method could be used to avoid any restrictions in the articles as to the quorum at committee meetings. If it is possible to appoint a committee of any two directors, it must also be acceptable to appoint a committee of 'any two' of a number of named directors. The end result is, of course, the same as if the board had appointed a committee of, say, four named directors and specified the quorum as two. If the articles prevent the board doing this by the normal method, it must be doubtful whether it can achieve the same result by using the 'any two director' method of appointment. It is worthy of note on this score that the articles of Guinness gave the board specific power to fix the quorum of committees of the board.

It is also questionable what the position would be if, say, four directors attended a meeting of a committee of 'any two directors'. Could they all vote? And what would happen if two were in favour and two opposed to a proposal? Which (if any) of the directors would constitute the committee? In *Guinness* v. *Saunders*, Lord Templeman said, somewhat pointedly perhaps, that the three directors in that case 'constituted themselves as a committee'. Could three other directors have constituted themselves as a committee with the same powers?

In order to avoid these problems, there ought, perhaps, to be some sort of control exercised on the calling of meetings of such a committee. Usually this will be the task of the person who prepares the documentation for the meeting. Indeed, it may be preferable to specify in the board resolution establishing the committee that it may not meet unless the company secretary or some other specified person is present. These sort of safeguards may not be necessary where the committee is established to execute a document or perform some other mechanical process.

30.2.3 Co-opted members

Only directors may be appointed as members of board committees unless the articles provide otherwise. Regulation 72 of Table A makes no such provision. Non-directors cannot therefore be appointed as voting members, although they can be given rights of attendance.

Until recently, the London Stock Exchange required directors to form the majority on board committees of listed companies whose articles allow co-opted members, and insisted that such committees act only where the majority of members present were directors. Although this rule was abolished in 1995, the articles of many listed companies still include such restrictions (see art. 124 of Whitbread plc).

30.3 POWERS AND DUTIES

The extent of the powers delegated to a committee should be specified in the board resolution or the terms of reference approved by the board. Generally speaking, this will be apparent from the committee's duties or functions. However, it is safer to set out these powers explicitly. For example, if a committee is to be established to negotiate, agree and execute a contract for the purchase of a specified freehold property, it might be preferable to state explicitly that the committee has the power to appoint surveyors and solicitors and incur other costs which are necessary in the performance of its duties.

It is not necessary to delegate any powers to a committee established solely to make recommendations to the board. Any director may make recommendations to the board. However, committees established for this purpose may also benefit from having certain incidental powers (e.g. to retain external professional advisers) and it is preferable to specify these powers at the outset.

It is normal to draft more formal rules for standing committees. A standing committee is one which is established permanently to perform certain duties on a regular basis. Terms of reference for such committees are usually adopted by a specific board resolution. Named individuals are then appointed as members of such committees by a seprate resolution(s). See **Precedent 30.11** for specimen terms of reference of an audit committee and **Precedent 30.13** for a nomination committee.

30.4   PROCEEDINGS AT COMMITTEE MEETINGS

The proceedings at committees of the board will be governed by the articles and in default by the common law of meetings. Articles usually provide that the proceedings at committee meetings shall be governed by the articles regulating the proceedings at board meetings so far as they are capable of applying. Regulation 72 of Table A adopts this style but only with respect to committees of two or more directors. The issues raised in connection with meetings of only one director are covered at para. 30.10.

30.4.1   Conditions imposed by the board

Regulation 72 provides that the board may impose conditions on the exercise by a committee of its delegated powers. The application to committees of the articles governing the proceedings at board meetings is made subject to any such conditions imposed by the directors. The word 'conditions' would seem to imply that the board may impose additional restrictions but may not relax the application of the articles. For example, the board could appoint the chairman of the committee and thereby limit the application of reg. 91 which would otherwise allow the committee to choose its own chairman. However, the board could not relax the application of reg. 95 which states that a director shall not be counted in the quorum present at a meeting in relation to a resolution on which he is not entitled to vote. To do so would be to remove an obstacle rather than impose an additional obstacle. It is acknowledged, however, that this theory can cause problems with regard to the quorum at committee meetings (see para. 30.6).

Some articles use the word 'regulations' instead of 'conditions' (see art. 124 of Whitbread plc). This would appear to give the directors more latitude in disapplying the articles. It should be noted, however, that even this form of wording would not allow the directors to disapply an article which specifically states that it shall apply to committees of directors as well as the board, e.g. reg. 94 of Table A which sets out the circumstances in which a director cannot vote on a resolution.

30.5   APPOINTMENT OF THE COMMITTEE CHAIRMAN

Under Table A, the committee members may appoint (and remove) one of their number as chairman of the committee (applying reg. 91 and reg. 72), unless the board appoints a chairman itself. The board may nominate the chairman as a condition on the exercise of the committee's powers. A chairman appointed in this manner cannot be removed by the committee and will have a casting vote if the articles confer a casting vote on the chairman of the board of directors, unless, of course, the board removes the casting vote as a condition on the exercise of the committee's powers.

The board may also appoint one or more deputy or vice chairmen to act in the chairman's absence. If it fails to do so and the committee's quorum is such that meetings can be held without the nominated chairman, the committee members present will have the power (in accordance with reg. 91) to appoint one of their number to chair meetings in the absence of the chairman.

30.6 QUORUM

The common law rule is that a committee can only act if all its members are present. This rule can, of course, be modified by the articles. For example, the articles may give the board specific power to fix the quorum for board committees. Where this is the case, the common law rule will apply in default if the board fails to specify a quorum (*Re Liverpool Household Stores Association Limited* (1890) 59 L.J. Ch. 616). Even though this may be what the board intended, it is preferable to state the quorum in the resolution appointing the committee or the terms of reference approved by the board.

Unfortunately, most articles do not give the board specific power to fix the quorum for committees but rely on provisions like reg. 72 of Table A, which state that the proceedings of committees shall be governed by the articles regulating the proceedings of the board so far as they are capable of applying. In these circumstances, the article which deals with the quorum at board meetings will also govern the quorum at board committees so far as it is capable of applying. The Table A provision dealing with the quorum at board meetings (reg. 89) is capable of applying (see below). However, if the number of members appointed to a committee (say, three) is less than than the number specified by the articles as the quorum at board meetings (say, four), that article will not be capable of applying and the common law rule will apply in default. In other words the quorum will be all three members of the committee.

Under Table A, the quorum for the transaction of the business of the directors may be fixed by the directors and unless so fixed at any other number shall be two [reg. 89]. This article also governs the quorum at committee meetings by virtue of reg. 72. However, it is capable of more than one interpretation when applied to a committee. It could mean that the quorum for the transaction of the business of a committee of directors may be fixed by the *board of directors* and unless so fixed at any other number shall be two. Or it could mean that the quorum for the transaction of the business of a committee of directors may be fixed by the *committee* and unless so fixed at any other number shall be two. Both interpretations cannot be correct, otherwise the committee would be able to change the quorum fixed by the board. It is suggested that the first of these interpretations is correct and that if the board fails to fix the quorum at some other number, it will be two.

30.6.1   Quorum of one

The basic common law rule established in *Sharp* v. *Dawes* is that in order to hold a valid meeting there must be a meeting of minds, in other words, that there must be at least two people present who are entitled to attend and vote. However, even the common law recognises that a valid meeting can be held with only one person present where he or she is the only person entitled to attend and vote at meetings of that body, e.g. the sole holder of a class of shares (*East* v. *Bennett Bro. Ltd* [1911] 1 Ch. 163).

In any case, the principle laid down in *Sharp* v. *Dawes* is a common law rule and, as such, is liable to modification by the articles. If the articles allow the directors to fix a quorum of one at board meetings and provide that the regulations governing board meetings shall also apply to committee meetings, it would seem that they may also fix a quorum of one for a committee of more than one director (*Re Fireproof Doors Ltd* [1916] 2 Ch. 142). Regulation 89 of Table A allows the directors to fix a quorum of one for board meetings and therefore to do likewise for any committee.

30.6.2   Disinterested quorum

Regulation 95 of Table A provides that a director shall not be counted in the quorum present at a meeting in relation to a resolution on which he is not entitled to vote. This is merely a restatement of the common law rule and will always be the case unless the articles make specific provision to the contrary. Any article on this matter will also apply to meetings of a committee of directors by virtue of reg. 72 and it is doubtful whether the directors can exclude the application of any such article by imposing a condition in accordance with reg. 72. It is also arguable that reg. 95 should be read in conjunction with reg. 94 which specifically states that it is applicable to committees of directors.

30.6.3   Minimum number

Articles specifying the minimum number of directors are clearly not intended to apply to committees of the board and can be considered to be excluded by the words 'so far as they are capable of applying' in reg. 72 and similarly worded articles. The board may, however, specify as a condition in the board resolution establishing the committee the minimum number of members of that committee. If so, the committee will not be authorised to act if the number of members falls below that figure, say as a result of the death or resignation of committee members (*Re Liverpool Household Stores Association Ltd* (1890) 59 L.J. Ch. 616). If the board resolution states that the committee shall consist of three members and then proceeds to name them, that would be equivalent to fixing a minimum number.

Regulation 90 of Table A provides that the continuing directors or sole continuing director may act notwithstanding any vacancies in their number. If reg. 90 applies to committees by virtue of reg. 72, it would appear that a committee may act notwithstanding any vacancies provided that there are sufficient members present to form a quorum. This would seem to defeat the object of setting a minimum in the first place. However, one might also say the same about the situation with regard to the board of directors.

30.7   VOTING

At common law, directors are excluded from voting where they are interested in the contract under discussion. This rule can be modified wholly or partially by the articles and any such provisions will apply to board committee meetings. Regulation 94 of Table A allows the directors to vote in certain limited circumstances where they are interested but otherwise imposes a general prohibition. It specifically states that it applies to committees of directors as well as the board.

Where non-directors are appointed as members of a board committee, it is a good idea to clarify in the terms of reference their duties with regard to disclosure of interests and their right to vote on contracts in which they have an interest. Non-directors do not have a statutory duty to disclose such interests and articles on voting usually refer only to directors.

Articles sometimes provide that the majority of members present at a meeting must be directors where they allow non-directors to be appointed. This could also be included as a condition in the committee's terms of reference.

Under the common law, each member of the committee will have one vote. The articles may, however, make alternative provision with regard to board meetings and any such provisions may be adopted by default for committees by virtue of clauses like reg. 72. The most obvious example is where the articles provide for the appointment of alternate directors. If a director appoints another director as his or her alternate, the director so appointed will have two votes. Great care should, however, be taken where one or more directors have weighted voting rights in respect of the exercise by the board of certain powers and it is proposed to delegate those powers to a committee.

30.7.1   Disclosure of interests

In order to comply with s. 317, it is not sufficient for a director to declare an interest in a contract at a committee meeting. This must be done at a board meeting (*Guinness plc* v. *Saunders* [1988] 2 All E.R. 940). The same will be true with regard to any article which requires disclosure in accordance with the requirements of the Act, e.g. regs. 85 and 86.

30.7.2   Alternate directors

There is no automatic right to appoint a proxy or an alternate at meetings of committees. The right to appoint an alternate depends entirely on the articles. Table A deals explicitly with the position of alternates with regard to committees (see regs. 65 to 71). To summarise, it provides that an alternate is entitled to receive notice of all meetings of committees of which his or her appointor is a member and to attend and vote at any such meeting in the absence of his or her appointor. It is doubtful whether a non-director who is a member of a committee can appoint an alternate unless the articles specifically provide.

30.8   DEFECTS IN APPOINTMENT

Section 285 and articles based on it (e.g. reg. 92 of Table A) serve to validate the acts of committees where it is subsequently discovered that there is a defect in the appointment or qualification of directors who were members of it (see para. 31.2).

30.9   WRITTEN RESOLUTIONS

Most articles on directors' written resolutions specifically extend this form of decision-making to committees of the board. This is certainly the case with regard to reg. 93 of Table A, although not reg. 106 of the 1948 Table A.

30.10   COMMITTEE OF ONE DIRECTOR

As a general rule, there must be at least two people present in order to hold a meeting (*Sharp* v. *Dawes* (1876) 2 Q.B.D. 26). The power to delegate to a committee is, however, deemed to include the power to delegate to a committee of only one director unless the articles provide otherwise (*Re Fireproof Doors Ltd* [1916] 2 Ch. 142). Although it is not necessary, most articles specify that the board may delegate its powers to a committee of one or more directors.

   Most articles follow reg. 72 of Table A by providing that the articles governing proceedings at board meetings shall apply to committees consisting of two or more directors. In other words, they make no provision for proceedings at meetings of committees of one director. Even if the articles do not follow this precise form, the words 'so far as they are capable of applying' will exclude the application of many of the articles. However, any article which specifically states that it is applicable to committees of directors will still be relevant, e.g. reg. 93 (written resolutions) and reg. 94 (restrictions on voting). In theory, it is still necessary for a director who is the sole member of a committee to hold meetings. In practice, it will not be necessary for him to give himself any notice and whenever he exercises his delegated powers he can be said to be holding a meeting. What is important is that the director maintains a formal record of his decisions. Regulation 100 requires the directors to keep minutes of all proceedings at meetings of committees of directors. Probably the best way of doing this is for the director to act by written resolution (see **Precedent 30.10**) and for each resolution to be entered into a minute book kept for that purpose.

30.11   AUDIT COMMITTEE

The Cadbury Committee recommended that listed companies establish a committee of non-executive directors to review and make recommendations to the board on all aspects of the audit and financial reporting process (for specimen terms of reference see **Precedent 30.11**). The Cadbury Code states that the committee should consist of at least three non-executives and that it should have written terms of reference which deal clearly with its authority and duties [Cadbury Code, para. 4.3]. The London Stock Exchange requires listed companies to report on their compliance with the Cadbury Code and give reasons for any non-compliance [Listing Rules, para. 12.43(j)]. Accordingly, the vast majority of listed companies have established audit committees.

The establishment of an audit committee as envisaged by the Cadbury Committee is not intended to undermine the ultimate responsibility of the board for reviewing and approving the annual report and accounts and the half-year report. Rather, it is intended to ensure that the non-executive directors become actively involved in that process and have access to the resources necessary to enable them to make independent judgments. It also offers the auditors a direct link with the non-executive directors. To summarise, it provides an important assurance that a key area of the board's duties will be rigorously discharged.

30.11.1   Duties of the audit committee

The duties of an audit committee established to comply with the Cadbury Code and Report should include reviewing and making recommendations to the board on:

- the appointment of the external auditor, the audit fee, and any question of resignation or dismissal;
- the nature and scope of the audit and co-ordination where more than one audit firm is involved;
- the half-year and annual financial statements before submission to the Board;
- problems and reservations arising from the interim and final audits, and any matters the auditor may wish to discuss (in the absence of management where necessary);
- the auditor's management letter and management's response;
- the company's statement on internal control prior to endorsement by the Board;
- the internal audit programme;
- the major findings of internal investigations and management's response.

30.11.2   Membership

As the purpose of the audit committee is to review financial statements and controls initiated by the executive directors, there would seem to be little point in having members drawn from the executive directors. The Cadbury Committee recommended that the committee consist of at least three non-executives and that a majority of the non-executives serving on the committee should be independent. It also recommended that the committee's membership should be disclosed in the annual report.

Although not members of the committee, it is usual for the finance director, the external auditor and the head of internal audit to be invited to attend meetings. The Cadbury Committee recommended, however, that the committee should have a discussion with the external auditors, at least once a year, without executive board members present, to ensure that there are no unresolved issues of concern.

30.11.3   Powers

The primary purpose of the audit committee is not to exercise powers delegated by the board but to monitor and review matters connected with the financial statements and to make recommendations to the board arising from these activities. Strictly speaking, there is no need to delegate any powers to the committee for these purposes. However, the audit committee may need to be given certain incidental powers to enable it to function effectively. It could, for example, be given explicit powers of internal investigation and rights of access to any company information it requires. In theory, this would enable the audit committee to cut through the usual chain of authority when conducting investigations, although it is questionable whether the committee could enforce such powers without recourse to the board in the face of concerted opposition by the executive directors. The committee will almost certainly need to be given power to retain independent professional advisers. This is a far more concrete power and undoubtedly involves the delegation of powers by the board.

30.11.4   Secretary

The specimen terms of reference for an audit committee contained in the Cadbury Report (see **Precedent 30.11**) envisage that the company secretary will act as the secretary to the audit committee. This is consistent with the Cadbury Committee's Code of Best Practice which states that all directors should have access to the advice and services of the company secretary. However, this may not be desirable where the company secretary is also a director.

30.12   REMUNERATION COMMITTEE

Although articles often require directors' fees to be approved by the members in general meeting (e.g. reg. 82 of Table A), they usually give the board of directors power to fix the salaries of the executive directors (e.g. reg. 84 of Table A). Executive directors may be paid directors' fees in addition to any salary they receive. If so, those fees will be subject to the approval of the members if the articles so provide. However, their executive salaries will be fixed by the board and the members will have no direct say in the amount they are paid. This distinction is necessary because executive directors are usually employed under a service contract, the terms of which need to be settled before the executive joins the board. It is usually suggested that they would not be prepared to join a company if their remuneration was conditional on the approval of the members in general meeting.

The usual procedure is therefore for the board to enter into a contract with the executive director on behalf of the company when it appoints him. If the director is subsequently dismissed (e.g. by the members at the next annual general meeting), he will be entitled to damages for breach of contract (see, for example reg. 84 of Table A). The amount of damages will depend on the director's remuneration but also on the period of notice the company is required to give under the contract.

The members are therefore reliant on the board to exercise restraint in the matter of executive salaries. Not surprisingly, shareholders often feel that the salaries of executive directors approved by the board are too generous. Where the majority of directors are executive directors, it is generally believed that the board cannot be sufficiently impartial. Although each director is unable to vote on his or her own salary, the suspicion is that they tend to approve larger increases for their colleagues than perhaps they ought on the basis that their colleagues will approve a similar increase for them.

In an attempt to combat spiralling pay increases, shareholders began to call on boards of directors to establish remuneration committees consisting of a majority of non-executive directors to be responsible for making recommendations to the board on executive directors' salaries. These proposals were adopted by the Cadbury Committee in 1992 [Cadbury Code, para. 3.3] and the London Stock Exchange introduced a requirement that listed companies report on their compliance with the Committee's recommendations [Listing Rules, para. 12.43(j)].

30.12.1   Greenbury Code of Best Practice

Despite the recommendations of the Cadbury Committee, there continued to be considerable public disquiet over the salaries paid to executive directors, particularly in the privatised utility companies, and, in February 1995, the CBI formed a study group chaired by Sir Richard Greenbury 'to identify good practice in determining directors' remuneration and to prepare a code of such practice for use by UK plcs'. The study group (the 'Greenbury Committee') published its final report and code of practice on 17 July 1995 (Directors' Remuneration: Report of a Study Group chaired by Sir Richard Greenbury, Gee Publishing, South Quay Plaza, 183 Marsh Wall, London E14 9FS, price £10.00). The London Stock Exchange agreed to adopt the new Code with certain minor modifications and with effect from 31 December 1995 withdrew the requirement for listed companies to report on their compliance with section 3 of the Cadbury Code (regarding executive directors' service contracts, disclosure of emoluments and remuneration committees).

In its place, the Exchange introduced a requirement that listed companies incorporated in the United Kingdom report on their compliance with section A of the Greenbury Code on remuneration committees (see para. 30.12.2 below) and include in their annual reports a report by the remuneration committee (or by the Board itself if there is no remuneration committee) which must contain:

- a statement of the company's policy on executive directors' remuneration;
- a statement that, in framing its remuneration policy, the committee (or the Board itself if there is no such committee) has given full consideration to Section B of the best practice provisions annexed to the listing rules (see para. 30.12.3 below);

- the amount of each element in the remuneration package for the period under review of each director by name;
- information on share options, including SAYE options, for each director by name;
- details of any other long-term incentive schemes;
- explanation and justification of any element of remuneration, other than basic salary, which is pensionable;
- details of any directors' service contract with a notice period in excess of one year or with provisions for pre-determined compensation on termination which exceeds one year's salary and benefits in kind, giving the reasons for such notice period; and
- the unexpired term of any directors' service contract of a director proposed for election or re-election at the forthcoming annual general meeting and, if any director proposed for election or re-election does not have a directors' service contract, a statement to that effect.

The scope of the auditors' report on the financial statements must cover the disclosures made pursuant to paragraph (iii), (iv) and (v) above. The auditors must state in their report if in their opinion the company has not complied with any of the requirements of paragraph 1 2.43(x)(iii), (iv) and (v) of the Listing Rules and, in such a case, must include in their report, so far as they are reasonably able to do so, a statement giving the required particulars.

30.12.2 Greenbury on remuneration committees

Section A of the Greenbury Code deals with remuneration committees and their operation. The London Stock Exchange requires listed companies to include a statement in their annual report indicating whether the provisions of section A (as annexed to the Listing Rules in a slightly modified form) have been complied with and, if not, giving the reasons for any areas of non-compliance. Compliance with Section A of the Greenbury Code is not therefore mandatory for listed companies. However, pressure from institutional investors will probably ensure that the vast majority follow the recommendations.

The provisions of Section A as adopted in modified form by the London Stock Exchange are as follows:

1. Boards of directors should set up remuneration committees to determine, within agreed terms of reference, the company's policy on executive remuneration and specific remuneration packages for executive directors, including pension rights and any compensation payments.
2. Remuneration committees should consist exclusively of non-executive directors with no personal financial interest other than as shareholders in the matters to be decided, no potential conflicts of interest arising from cross-directorships and no day-to-day involvement in running the business.
3. Remuneration committee chairmen should report to directors through means specified in the listing rules.
4. The members of the remuneration committee should be listed each year in the

committee's report to shareholders. When they stand for election or re-election, the proxy cards should indicate their membership of the committee.

5. The Board itself, or where required by the Articles of Association, the shareholders, should determine the remuneration of all non-executive directors, within the limits set out in the Articles of Association.
6. Remuneration committees should consult the company chairman and/or chief executive about their proposals relating to the remuneration of other executive directors and have access to professional advice inside and outside the company.
7. The remuneration committee chairman, or other member of the remuneration committee, should attend the company's annual general meeting to answer shareholders' questions about directors' remuneration.
8. The committee's annual report to shareholders need not be a standard item of agenda for annual general meetings, but the committee should consider each year whether the circumstances are such that the annual general meeting should be invited to approve the policy set out in its report and should minute its conclusions.

30.12.3   Section B

The Listing Rules require the remuneration committee's report to include a statement that, in framing its remuneration policy, the committee has given full consideration to the best practice provisions set out in section B of the best practice provisions annexed to the listing rules. Section B as it appears in the Listing Rules is in fact a modified version of sections C and D of the Greenbury Code. It covers general remuneration policies and service contracts and includes some of the Greenbury Committee's more controversial recommendations, e.g. that notice or contract periods should be reduced to one year or less.

In theory, section B is purely advisory. All remuneration committees have to do is to consider these recommendations. They are not obliged to comply with them or to explain or justify any areas of non-compliance.

30.13   NOMINATION COMMITTEE

Paragraph 2.4 of the Cadbury Code recommends that non-executive directors should be selected through a formal process. This recommendation is expanded further in the Report which advocates the establishment of a nomination committee responsible for the recommendation of persons for appointment to the board, as executive or non-executive directors. It suggests that the committee should include a majority of non-executive directors and be chaired either by the chairman of the board or by a non-executive director. [Cadbury Report, paras. 4.15 and 4.30]. See **Precedent 30.13** for specimen terms of reference for a nomination committee drawn up by the ICSA's Company Secretaries Panel.

A practical issue which will arise in operating a nomination committee is that the minutes/reports to the board of the committee will, for reasons of discretion, usually not include details of internal candidates considered in principle but rejected. The names of outside candidates under serious consideration by the committee (e.g. for non-executive directorship) would, again for reasons of discretion, no doubt be 'sounded out' with the full board prior to the committee commencing discussions with the person concerned with a view to possibly making a recommendation for his or her appointment.

CHAPTER THIRTY-ONE

Failure to comply with proper procedures

31.1 SUMMARY

Although the directors have a duty to act in accordance with the provisions of the company's memorandum and articles of association in order to avoid personal liability, their failure to do so will not always invalidate the transaction, at least as far as innocent third parties are concerned. Protection against defects in the decision-making process is provided by statute, articles and the common law where, for example:

- there is a defect in the appointment or qualification of a director (see para. 31.2);
- the number of directors is less than the minimum prescribed by or in accordance with the articles (see para. 31.3);
- the directors act beyond their powers (see para. 31.4);
- the directors act beyond the company's powers (see para. 31.5); or
- the directors fail to follow proper procedures (see para. 31.6).

31.2 DEFECTS IN APPOINTMENT OR QUALIFICATION OF DIRECTORS

31.2.1 CA 1985, section 285

Section 285 serves to validate the acts of a director or manager notwithstanding any defect that may afterwards be discovered in his or her appointment or qualification. This allows third parties to deal with the company through its directors without having to investigate whether they have been properly appointed. Articles usually contain similarly worded provisions, e.g. reg. 92 of Table A (see para. 31.2.2). Section 285 and such articles operate between the company and outsiders and between the company and its members (*Dawson* v. *African Consolidated Land & Trading Co.* [1898] 1 Ch. 6).

Anyone seeking to rely on such provisions must have acted in good faith. A person who merely has notice of the facts which give rise to the defect will not be prevented from relying on s. 285 unless they are also aware of the consequences of those facts

(*Channel Collieries Trust Ltd* v. *Dover, St Margaret's and Martin Hill Light Railway Co.* [1914] 2 Ch. 506). The requirements of good faith will normally prevent a director from benefiting under s. 285. However, it has also been held that a director who allotted himself shares in the knowledge that his appointment was invalid (i.e. in bad faith) could not subsequently avoid the allotment on the ground that it could not therefore be validated by a clause similar in terms to reg. 92 of Table A (*York Tramways* v. *Willows* (1882) 8 Q.B.D. 685).

Section 285 applies only where there has been an appointment and not where there has been no appointment or reappointment at all. Thus, a provision similar to s. 285 in a company's articles did not validate the acts of a director who had vacated office at the end of the year in which he was due to retire by rotation owing to the fact that no annual general meeting had been held in that year at which he could be reappointed (*Morris* v. *Kanssen* [1946] A.C. 459). See, however, para. 31.2.2 below.

Section 285 operates to validate the acts of a director appointed without the necessary share qualification required by the articles (*Channel Collieries Trust Ltd* v. *Dover*, etc.). It also operates where a director becomes disqualified because 'he ceases to hold the requisite number of shares or does some act or suffers something to happen which causes him to vacate his office' (Farwell J. in *British Asbestos Co.* v. *Boyd* [1903] 2 Ch. 439). In *British Asbestos*, the director was appointed secretary and became disqualified by virtue of the articles which prohibited the person appointed as secretary from being a director.

31.2.2   Reg. 92 of Table A

Reg. 92 of Table A goes further than s. 285 and the relevant article in the *Morris* v. *Kanssen* case by validating acts of a director who has vacated office. It provides:

> **92.** All acts done by a meeting of directors, or of a committee of directors, or by a person acting as a director shall, notwithstanding that it be afterwards discovered that there was a defect in the appointment of any director or that any of them were disqualified from holding office, or had vacated office, or were not entitled to vote, be as valid as if every such person had been duly appointed and was qualified and had continued to be a director and had been entitled to vote.

It should also be noted that reg. 92 also seeks to validate the acts of a director who is not entitled to vote at any meeting of directors or any committee thereof.

31.3   NUMBER OF DIRECTORS LESS THAN THE PRESCRIBED MINIMUM AND QUORUM

Under the common law, where articles prescribe a minimum number of directors and the actual number of directors falls below that minimum, the continuing directors cannot exercise any of their powers even though there are sufficient of them to form a quorum (*Re Alma Spinning Co.* (1880) 16 Ch.D. 681). This rule can give rise to serious problems because the continuing directors will be unable to exercise either their power to appoint new directors or their power to call a general meeting to allow the members to do so. Indeed, the only way to resolve the problem may be for a member or a director to make an application to the court under s. 371 for an order calling a general meeting to allow the members to appoint new directors.

In order to avoid such difficulties, it is normal for the articles to include a clause allowing the continuing directors to act notwithstanding any such vacancy in their number, e.g. reg. 90 of Table A. This type of article allows the directors to continue to act if their number falls below the minimum specified in the articles. For example, where a company's articles provided that the number of directors shall be not less than four, that two directors shall constitute a quorum and that the continuing directors may act notwithstanding any vacancy in the board, an allotment of shares by only two directors following the resignation of two out of the original four was held to be valid (*Re Scottish Petroleum Co.* (1883) 23 Ch.D. 413).

However, a similar article giving the continuing directors power to act notwithstanding any vacancy in their body was held not to operate where the minimum number of directors prescribed by the articles had never been reached (*Re Sly, Spink and Co.* [1911] 2 Ch. 430).

A question that begs to be asked is whether there is any point prescribing a minimum number of directors if the articles say that such a minimum can be ignored? The best answer that can be given is that the remaining directors may have a general duty to take steps to fill the vacancies so as to bring their number back to the prescribed minimum. In other words, they could not continue indefinitely to opertate below the prescribed minimum. It may also be that if they fail to fill the vacancies, the members in general meeting may do so in default regardless of anything in the articles to the contrary (see para. 27.6).

The articles of a company with four equal shareholders might require a minimum of four directors, the implication being that each of the members will be appointed as a director. The promoters or incorporators of a company may set a high figure to give the impression that the company is more respectable and that the executive directors will be monitored by an independent element on the board.

In reality, prescribing a minimum number of directors in the articles that is higher than the statutory minimum is likely to cause more problems than it is worth and company formation agents frequently modify Table A accordingly, not least to allow private companies to be established with only one director.

31.3.1   Number of directors falls below quorum

Articles which allow the directors to act notwithstanding any vacancy in their number do not operate where the number of directors is less than that required to constitute a quorum unless specific provision is made. Modern articles usually give the continuing directors limited powers to act in these circumstances. For example, reg. 90 of Table A provides:

90.   The   continuing   directors   or   sole   continuing   director   may   act notwithstanding any vacancy in their number, but, if the number of directors is less than the number fixed as the quorum, the continuing directors or director may act only for the purpose of filling vacancies or of calling a general meeting.

Under this type of article the continuing directors may only act for the purposes stated where their number is less than the number fixed as the quorum if the minimum number of directors prescribed by the articles has at some time been reached. Some articles go further than reg. 90 by giving the continuing directors power to act where there is a matter which must be dealt with urgently.

31.4   ACTS BEYOND THE POWERS OF THE DIRECTORS

In favour of a person dealing with a company in good faith, the power of the board of directors to bind the company, or authorise others to do so, is deemed by virtue of s. 35A to be free of any limitation under the company's constitution. Limitations under the company's constitution are deemed to include limitations deriving from a resolution of the company in general meeting or a meeting of any class of shareholders or from any shareholders' agreement [s. 35A(3)].

A person will not be regarded as acting in bad faith by reason only of his knowing that an act is beyond the powers of the directors under the company's constitution and will be presumed to have acted in good faith unless the contrary is proved [s. 35A(2)].

A member may still bring proceedings to restrain the doing of an act which is beyond the powers of the directors provided that the act is not required to be done in fulfilment of a legal obligation arising from a previous act of the company [s. 35A(4)].

The liability incurred by the directors, or any other person, by reason of the directors exceeding their powers is also not affected [s. 35A(5)]. The company could therefore sue the directors itself. A shareholder would not normally be allowed to sue the directors on behalf of the company where the act complained of was outside the authority of the directors but within the powers of the company, unless it could be shown that the directors control the company and have profited from their actions (see para. 18.3).

Section 35B provides that a third party is not bound to make any enquiries as to the limitations on the powers of the board, whether these limitations derive from the objects of the company as stated in its memorandum or some other source.

31.5   ACTS BEYOND THE COMPANY'S CAPACITY

The validity of an act done by a company cannot be called into question on the ground of lack of capacity by reason of anything contained in the company's memorandum (e.g. the objects clause). A member may still bring proceedings to restrain the doing of an act which is beyond the company's capacity; but no such proceedings shall lie in respect of an act to be done in fulfilment of a legal obligation arising from a previous act of the company [s. 35(2)].

It remains the duty of the directors to observe any limitations on their powers flowing from the memorandum and action by the directors which, but for s. 35(1), would be beyond the company's capacity may only be ratified by the company by special resolution. A resolution ratifying such action shall not however affect any liability incurred by the directors, or any other person. Relief from such liability must be agreed to separately by special resolution [s. 35(3)].

31.5.1 · Where a director is party to a transaction

Both s. 35 and s. 35A are qualified with respect to transactions to which directors or their associates are a party by s. 322A. It provides that where the board of directors exceeds its powers under the company's constitution and one of the parties to the transaction with the company is a director of the company or its holding company or an associate of such a director, the transaction will be voidable at the instance of the company. This means that the company may decide whether to treat the contract as void or to enforce its contractual rights. Whether or not the transaction is avoided, the director or his associate will be liable to account to the company for any gain which he has made directly or indirectly by the transaction and to indemnify the company for any loss or damage resulting from the transaction [s. 322A(3)].

The transaction ceases to be voidable if:

- restitution of any money or other asset which was the subject of the transaction is no longer possible; or
- the company is indemnified for any loss or damage resulting from the transaction; or
- rights acquired in good faith for value and without actual notice of the directors' exceeding their powers by a person who is not a party to the transaction would be affected by the avoidance; or
- the transaction is ratified by the company in general meeting, by ordinary or special resolution or otherwise as the case may require [s. 322A(5)].

31.6   THE INDOOR MANAGEMENT RULE

This rule protects third parties dealing with the company from irregularities in the decision-making process, including acts of the board, board committees and individual directors. It can be applied in three different situations:

- where a director has no authority to act (*Re County Life Assurance Co. Ltd* (1870) L.R. 5 Ch. App. 288);
- where the director would have had authority had certain conditions been satisfied (*Royal British Bank* v. *Turquand* (1856) 119 E.R. 886);
- where the director has authority to act but fails to follow the correct procedure (*Duck* v. *Tower Galvanising Co. Ltd* [1901] 2 K.B. 314).

CHAPTER THIRTY-TWO

Corporate governance

32.1 SUMMARY

Corporate governance is concerned amongst other things with the balance of power between the directors and shareholders. As such, the law of meetings is one of the central elements of the governance process. The other important element is the financial reporting process and the role of the auditors within that process.

32.2 COMMITTEE ON THE FINANCIAL ASPECTS OF CORPORATE GOVERNANCE (THE CADBURY COMMITTEE)

The Committee on the Financial Aspects of Corporate Governance chaired by Sir Adrian Cadbury ('the Cadbury Committee') was established following a series of high-profile corporate failures in the 1980s which had not been signalled in the audited accounts of the respective companies. Following each collapse, shareholders and the media looked for scapegoats and the auditors were one of the first ports of call. Auditors claimed that each company's audited accounts complied with existing accounting standards and that the failures had arisen because of factors over which they had no control or which they could not be expected to uncover during an audit. The Accounting Standards Board, headed by Sir David Tweedie, began a fundamental review of accounting standards in an attempt to ensure better and more uniform disclosure. However, the accountancy profession was still concerned about the public's expectations gap in relation to the role of the auditors and it was the prime mover behind the formation of the Cadbury Committee.

The Committee's terms of reference were to consider and make recommendations on:

- the responsibilities of directors for reviewing and reporting on performance to shareholders;
- the case for audit committees of the board;
- the principal responsibilities of auditors and the extent and value of the audit;

- the links between shareholders, boards, and the auditors;
- any other relevant matters.

On its formation, the Committee had almost universal support and was urged to broaden its investigation into areas such as directors' remuneration, the structure of the board and the role of the company secretary.

The Report of the Committee on the Financial Aspects of Corporate Governance (Gee, South Quay Plaza, 183 Marsh Wall, London E14 9FS) was published in 1992 and included a Code of Best Practice (see para. 32.2.2). The London Stock Exchange amended its Listing Rules to require listed companies to report on their compliance with the Code in their report and accounts and give reasons for any area of non-compliance [Listing Rules para. 12.43(j)]. Parts of companies' statements of compliance must be reviewed by the auditors before publication.

Many of the Committee's recommendations fall outside the scope of this book. However, the following are covered elsewhere:

- schedule of matters reserved to the board (see para. 29.3);
- audit committees (see para. 30.11);
- remuneration committees (see para. 30.12);
- nomination committees (see para. 30.13);
- role of the chairman (see para. 28.6); and
- role of the company secretary (see para. 32.4).

The Committee also recommended that institutional investors should disclose their voting policies. Many are now doing so by issuing their own codes on governance related issues.

32.2.1   Issues for the future

The Cadbury Committee identified several issues which it felt ought to be addressed by its successor body:
- the disclosure of directors' remuneration (subsequently considered by the Greenbury Committee – see para. 30.12);
- auditors' liability (the subject of a Law Commission study and a DTI consultation paper in 1996); and
- procedures for putting forward resolutions at general meetings (the subject of a DTI consultation paper in 1996 – see para. 6.10).

32.2.2   Cadbury Committee's Code of Best Practice

1   The board of directors

1.1 The board should meet regularly, retain full and effective control over the company and monitor the executive management.

1.2 There should be a clearly accepted division of responsibilities at the head of a company, which will ensure a balance of power and authority, such that no one individual has unfettered powers of decision. Where the chairman is also the chief executive, it is essential that there should be a strong and independent element on the board, with a recognised senior member.

1.3 The board should include non-executive directors of sufficient calibre and number for their views to carry significant weight in the board's decisions.

1.4 *The board should have a formal schedule of matters specifically reserved to it for decision to ensure that the direction and control of the company is firmly in its hands.*

1.5 *There should be an agreed procedure for directors in the furtherance of their duties to take independent professional advice if necessary at the company's expense.*

1.6 All directors should have access to the advice and services of the company secretary, who is responsible to the board for ensuring that board procedures are followed and that applicable rules and regulations are complied with. Any question of the removal of the company secretary should be a matter for the board as a whole.

2   Non-executive directors

2.1 Non-executive directors should bring an independent judgement to bear on issues of strategy, performance, resources, including key appointments, and standards of conduct.

2.2 The majority should be independent of management and free from any business or other relationship which could materially interfere with the exercise of their independent judgement, apart from their fees and shareholding. Their fees should reflect the time which they commit to the company.

2.3 *Non-executive directors should be appointed for specified terms and reappointment should not be automatic.*

2.4 *Non-executive directors should be selected through a formal process and both this process and their appointment should be a matter for the board as a whole.*

[3   ~~Executive directors~~ (Note 1)

3.1 ~~Directors' service contracts should not exceed three years without shareholders' approval.~~

3.2 ~~There should be full and clear disclosure of directors' total emoluments and those of the chairman and highest-paid UK director, including pension contributions and stock options. Separate figures should be given for salary and performance-related elements and the basis on which performance is measured should be explained.~~

3.3 ~~Executive directors' pay should be subject to the recommendations of a remuneration committee made up wholly or mainly of non-executive directors.~~]

4   Reporting and controls

4.1 It is the board's duty to present a balanced and understandable assessment of the company's position.

4.2 The board should ensure that an objective and professional relationship is maintained with the auditors.

4.3 *The board should establish an audit committee of at least three non-executive directors with written terms of reference which deal clearly with its authority and duties.*

4.4 *The directors should explain their responsibility for preparing the accounts next to a statement by the auditors about their reporting responsibilities.*

4.5 *The directors should report on the effectiveness of the company's system of internal control.*

4.6 *The directors should report that the business is a going concern, with supporting assumptions or qualifications as necessary.*

Notes:

1. Section 3 has been superseded by the Code of Best Practice issued by the Greenbury Committee (see further para. 30.12).

2. The company's statement of compliance should be reviewed by the auditors in so far as it relates to the paragraphs in italics.

32.3 ICSA CODE ON GOOD BOARDROOM PRACTICE

Prior to the formation of the Cadbury Committee, the Institute of Chartered Secretaries and Administrators (ICSA) issued a code on good boardroom practice (see **Precedent 32.3**). ICSA recommended that boardroom procedures should be periodically reviewed to ensure both the satisfactory operation of its code and the identification of matters which individual companies could advantageously bring within its scope. Some of the recommendations in the ICSA code were subsequently adopted by the Cadbury Code. However, it is still a useful guide on board procedures.

32.4 COMPANY SECRETARY

The Cadbury Code states (at para. 1.6) that 'All directors should have access to the advice and services of the company secretary, who is responsible to the board for ensuring that board procedures are followed and that applicable rules and regulations are complied with. Any question of the removal of the company secretary should be a matter for the board as a whole.'

The Cadbury Committee said in its report:

The company secretary has a key role to play in ensuring that board procedures are both followed and regularly reviewed. The chairman and the board will look to the company secretary for guidance on what their responsibilities are under the rules and regulations to which they are subject and on how those responsibilities should be discharged. All directors should have access to the advice and services of the company secretary and should recognise that the chairman is entitled to the strong and positive support of the company secretary in ensuring the effective functioning of the board. It should be standard practice for the company secretary to administer, attend and prepare minutes of board meetings. [Cadbury Report, para. 4.25]

See also ICSA's Code on good boardroom practice at **Precedent 32.3** for ICSA's recommendations regarding the company secretary's right to attend meetings of the board and its committees.

Under the Companies Act the directors have a duty to appoint as secretary someone who is capable of carrying out the duties which the post entails [s. 283]. The Cadbury Committee said 'the responsibility for ensuring that the secretary remains capable, and any question of the secretary's removal, should be a matter for the board as a whole' [Cadbury Report, para. 4.26].

The Cadbury Committee also said it 'expects that the company secretary will be a source of advice to the chairman and to the board on the implementation of the Code of Best Practice' [Cadbury Report, para. 4.27].

CHAPTER THIRTY-THREE

Precedents

CHAPTER 4: CLASS MEETINGS

P. 4.4 Notice of class meeting

XYZ Limited

Notice is hereby given that a separate meeting of the holders of the six per cent £1 preference shares in the capital of the company will be held on [date] at [place] at [time] to propose the following resolution as an extraordinary resolution:

> THAT this separate class meeting of the holders of the six per cent £1 preference shares in the capital of the company hereby sanctions [resolution being sanctioned] and hereby sanctions any variation, modification or abrogation of the rights and privileges attached or belonging to the six per cent £1 preference shares effected thereby or necessary to give effect thereto.

By order of the Board
[Signature]
Secretary
[registered office address]
[date]

Notes:

Holders of six per cent preference shares in the company are entitled to attend and vote at this meeting or to appoint a proxy to attend and vote in their stead. A proxy need not be a member of the company.

CHAPTER 5: CALLING GENERAL MEETINGS

P. 5.2A   Minute of board resolution convening annual general meeting

It was resolved:

THAT the Annual General Meeting of the Company be convened and held at [place] on [date] at [time] for the following purposes:

1. To receive the accounts and the reports of the directors and auditors for the financial year ending [date].
2. To re-appoint ABC as auditors until the conclusion of the next meeting at which accounts are laid and to authorise the directors to fix their remuneration.
3. To authorise the Directors to allot shares pursuant to section 80 of the Companies Act 1985.

THAT the secretary be authorised to sign the notice on behalf of the Board and to issue notices accordingly, together with a form of proxy in accordance with the proof print submitted to and approved by this meeting.

P. 5.2B   Minute of board resolution convening extraordinary general meeting

It was resolved:

THAT an Extraordinary General Meeting of the Company be convened and held at [place] on [date] at [time] for the following purpose:

1. to increase the share capital of the Company.

THAT the Secretary be authorised to sign the notice on behalf of the Board and to issue notices accordingly, together with a form of proxy in accordance with the proof print submitted to and approved by this meeting.

P. 5.6A   Members' requisition for extraordinary general meeting

The Directors
XYZ plc

We the undersigned, being members of XYZ plc holding in the aggregate [number] ordinary shares of £1 each out of the issued and paid-up capital of [number] ordinary shares of £1 each, require you, pursuant to section 368 of the Companies Act 1985, to convene an extraordinary general meeting of the company for the purpose of considering the following resolutions, which will be proposed as ordinary resolutions:

1. THAT [name] be appointed a director of the company.

2. THAT the share capital of the company be increased to £[amount] by the creation of [number] additional ordinary shares of £1 each.

[Signatures]   [Addresses]
[Date]
[Note: If (unusually) the company's articles provide a more relaxed regime for a members requisition and the members are unable to meet the statutory requirements, the wording of the requisition should refer to the relevant article.]

P. 5.6B Notice of requisitioned meeting given by requisitionists

XYZ plc

NOTICE IS HEREBY GIVEN that, pursuant to a requisition dated [date] made in accordance with the provisions of section 368 of the Companies Act 1985, and deposited at the registered office of the company on [date of deposit], an Extraordinary General Meeting of the company will be held at [place] on [date], at [time] for the purpose of considering the following resolutions, which will be proposed as ordinary resolutions:

RESOLUTIONS

1. THAT [name] be appointed a director of the company.
2. THAT the share capital of the company be increased to £[amount] by the creation of [number] additional ordinary shares of £1 each.

A member entitled to attend and vote at the meeting is entitled to appoint one or more proxies to attend and vote instead of him. A proxy need not also be a member.

[Signatures and names]   [Addresses]
[Date]

CHAPTER 6: NOTICE OF GENERAL MEETINGS

P. 6.5A Notice of Annual General Meeting of Public Limited Company

XYZ plc
Notice is hereby given that the annual general meeting of XYZ plc (the Company) will be held at [place] on [date] at [time] for the following purposes:

Resolutions – ordinary business

1. To receive the report of the Directors and the audited accounts for the year ended [year end].
2. To re-elect the following Directors:
   [Name]
   [Name]
3. To reappoint [name of auditors] as auditors and authorise the Directors to determine their remuneration.

Resolutions – special business

4. To consider and, if thought fit, to pass the following resolution as a Special Resolution:

   THAT the authority and power conferred on the Directors by Article [No.] (Authority to allot securities) of the Articles of Association of the Company be and they are hereby renewed for the period expiring on the date of the annual general meeting of the Company to be held in [year + 1] and that:

   (a) for the purposes of Article [No.], the prescribed amount for the above period shall be £[amount 1] and

   (b) for the purposes of the proviso to Article [No.], the aggregate nominal amount of equity securities allotted wholly for cash during such period, otherwise than as mentioned in such proviso, shall not exceed £[amount 2].

By order of the Board
ABC Delta, Secretary
[Registered office address]
[date]

Notes

1. A member entitled to attend and vote at the meeting is entitled to appoint a proxy or more than one proxy to attend and vote instead of him. A proxy need not be a member.

2. To be entitled to attend and vote at the meeting (and for the purpose of the determination by the company of the number of votes they may cast), members must be entered on the company's register of members by [time and date not more than 48 hours before the time fixed for the meeting] ('the specified time'). If the meeting is adjourned to a time not more than 48 hours after the specified time for the original meeting, that time will also apply for the purpose of determining the entitlement of members to attend and vote (and for the purpose of the determining the number of votes they may cast) at the adjourned meeting. If the meeting is adjourned for a longer period, to be entitled to attend and vote at the adjourned meeting (and for the purpose of the determination by the company of the number of votes they may cast), members must be entered on the company's register of members [number of hours] before the time fixed for the adjourned meeting or, if the company gives notice of the adjourned meeting, the time specified in that notice.

See **Precedent 25.11A** for the minutes of the above meeting.

P. 6.5B   Notice of extraordinary general meeting

XYZ Limited
Notice is hereby given that an extraordinary general meeting of XYZ Limited will be held at [place] on [date] at [time] for the purpose of considering and, if thought fit, passing the following resolution as a special resolution:

SPECIAL RESOLUTION

THAT the name of the company be changed to '[name] Limited'.

By order of the Board
[Name]
Secretary
[Registered office address]
[Date]

Note

A member entitled to attend and vote at the meeting is entitled to appoint a proxy to attend and vote instead of him. A proxy need not be a member.

P. 6.8A   Consent to short notice of an annual general meeting

We, the undersigned, all the members for the time being of XYZ Limited, and having a right to attend and vote at the annual general meeting of the company to be held on [date], hereby agree:

(a) to accept shorter notice of the said meeting than the period of notice prescribed by section 369(2)(a) of the Companies Act 1985; and
(b) to accept copies of the company's accounts less than 21 days before the date of the said meeting as required by section 238(1) of the Companies Act 1985.

Dated this . . . . day of . . . . 19. . . .
[Signatures]

P. 6.8B   Consent to short notice of an extraordinary general meeting

We, the undersigned, being a majority in number of the members together holding not less than 95 per cent of the share capital of XYZ Limited having a right to attend and vote at the meeting referred to below, hereby agree to an extraordinary general meeting of the company being held on [date], notwithstanding that shorter notice has been given of the said meeting than the period of notice prescribed by section 369(2) of the Companies Act 1985.

Dated this . . . . day of . . . . 19. . . .
[Signatures]

P. 6.8C   Consent to short notice of an extraordinary general meeting to pass a special resolution

We, the undersigned, being a majority in number of the members together holding not less than 95 per cent of the share capital of XYZ Limited having a right to attend and vote at the meeting referred to below, hereby agree to an extraordinary general meeting of the company being held on [date], for the purpose of considering the special resolution set out in the notice of the said meeting notwithstanding that less than twenty-one days' notice of the meeting has been given.

Dated this . . . . day of . . . . 19. . . .
[Signatures]

P. 6.9A   Special notice from member to company

To: The directors,
XYZ plc
[Registered Office]
I hereby give notice, pursuant to section 379 and section [293 / 303 / 388 / 391A] of the Companies Act 1985, of my intention to propose the following resolution as an ordinary resolution at the next [annual/extraordinary] general meeting of the company:

ORDINARY RESOLUTION
[Text of resolution]

[Signed]   [Address]
[Date]

P. 6.9B   Notice of resolution requiring special notice

To consider and, if thought fit, to pass as an ordinary resolution the following resolution for which special notice has been given in accordance with section 379 of the Companies Act 1985:

THAT . . . .

P. 6.10A   Requisition of resolution [and supporting statement] under section 376 of the Companies Act 1985

The Directors
XYZ plc
[Registered office address]
We the undersigned being members of XYZ plc representing not less than one-twentieth of the total voting rights of all the members having at the date hereof a right to vote at the next annual general meeting of the company, hereby require you to give to the members entitled to receive notice of the next annual general meeting notice of the following resolution, which it is intended to move thereat as an ordinary resolution [, and to circulate to the members entitled to have notice of the meeting sent to them the annexed statement with respect to the matter referred to in the proposed resolution]:

ORDINARY RESOLUTION
[Text of resolution]

[STATEMENT IN SUPPORT]
[Text of statement of not more than 1,000 words]

[Signed]   [Address]
[Date]

P. 6.10B   Requisition for circulation of statement under section 376 of the Companies Act 1985

The Directors
XYZ plc
[Registered office address]
We the undersigned being members of XYZ plc representing not less than one-twentieth of the total voting rights of all the members having at the date hereof a right to vote at the annual general meeting/extraordinary general meeting of the company convened for [insert date of meeting], hereby require you to circulate to the members entitled to have notice of the meeting sent to them the following statement with respect of the resolution set out in the notice of the said meeting:

STATEMENT
[Text of statement of not more than 1,000 words]

[Signed]   [Address]
[Date]

P. 6.10C   Requisitioned resolution in notice of annual general meeting

To consider the following resolution intended to be moved at the meeting as a special resolution, notice of which is given by the company pursuant to section 376 of the Companies Act 1985 on the requisition of certain members:

SPECIAL RESOLUTION
[Text of resolution]

P. 6.10D   Notice of requisitioned resolution

XYZ plc
NOTICE OF RESOLUTION

Notice is hereby given, upon the requisition of certain members pursuant to section 376 of the Companies Act, that the company has been advised of an intention to move the following resolution as an extraordinary resolution at the annual general meeting of the company to be held on [date] at [place] at [time]:

EXTRAORDINARY RESOLUTION
[Text of resolution]

By order of the board upon a requisition pursuant to section 376 of the Companies Act 1985

By Order of the Board
[Signed]
Secretary

CHAPTER 7: RESOLUTIONS

P. 7.6   Copy resolution for filing with Registrar of Companies

[Company Number]

THE COMPANIES ACT 1985

AND

THE COMPANIES ACT 1989

COMPANY LIMITED BY SHARES

[NAME OF COMPANY]

At an [annual/extraordinary] general meeting of the members of the above-named company held at [place] on [date] the following resolutions were duly passed:

AS SPECIAL RESOLUTIONS
[Resolutions]

AS ORDINARY RESOLUTION
[Resolutions]

AS EXTRAORDINARY RESOLUTIONS
[Resolutions]

Chairman/Secretary

CHAPTER 9: RIGHT TO ATTEND AND SPEAK

P. 9.3   Attendance sheet (members)

XYZ plc

Members present at the annual general meeting held on [date]

NAME (IN BLOCK CAPITALS)	SIGNATURE
[Names]	[Signatures]

CHAPTER 10: SECURITY AND DISORDER

P. 10.2   Article of NatWest allowing security checks at general meetings

74   The chairman of a meeting, or the company secretary, can take any action they consider appropriate for:

● the safety of people attending a general meeting;
● proper and orderly conduct at a general meeting; or

- the meeting to reflect the wishes of the majority.

For example, they can require any people to prove who they are, they can carry out security searches, and stop certain things being taken into the meeting. They can refuse to allow any person into a meeting, or can arrange for any person who refuses to comply with any requirements imposed under this Article to be removed from a meeting.

[*Note:* NatWest's articles are written in plain English]

CHAPTER 14: PROXIES

P. 14.6 Two-way proxy which complies with The Listing Rules of The London Stock Exchange

XYZ plc

Form of appointment of proxy

I/We, [name of member/names of joint holders], of [address/addresses], being a member/members of the above-named company, hereby appoint the chairman of the meeting* or [name of proxy] of [address of proxy] as my/our proxy to vote in my/our name[s] and on my/our behalf at the annual/extraordinary general meeting of the company to be held on [date], and at any adjournment thereof.

[* Delete if it is desired to appoint any other person and insert his or her name and address in the space provided.]

I/We hereby authorise and instruct the proxy to vote on the resolutions to be proposed at such meeting as indicated in the boxes below. Unless otherwise directed, the proxy will vote or abstain from voting as he or she thinks fit. Should any resolutions, other than those specified, be proposed at the meeting, the proxy may vote thereon as he or she thinks fit.

Resolutions	For	Against
1. Ordinary resolution to receive the report and accounts		
2. Ordinary resolution to declare a dividend		
3. Ordinary resolution to reappoint AC&B as auditors and to authorise the directors to fix their remuneration		
4. Ordinary resolution to re-elect [name] as a director		
5. Ordinary resolution to authorise directors to allot shares		
6. Special resolution to alter articles of association		

Date
Signature

Notes:

1. To be effective this form must be lodged at the offices of the Company's Registrars, [address], not later than [48] hours before the time of the meeting together, if

appropriate, with the power of attorney or other authority under which it is signed or a notarially certified copy of such power or authority.

2. In the case of a corporation this proxy should be given under its common seal or should be signed on its behalf by an attorney or officer so authorised and the words 'authorised signatory' added under the signature.

3. In the case of joint holders the vote of the senior who tenders a vote, whether in person or by proxy, will be accepted to the exclusion of the votes of the other holders. For this purpose seniority is determined by the order in which the names stand in the register of members in respect of the joint holding.

4. A proxy need not be a member of the company.

CHAPTER 15: CORPORATE REPRESENTATIVES

P. 15.4 Board minute appointing corporate representative

It was resolved:

THAT [name] or, failing him, [name] or, failing her, [name] be appointed, pursuant to section 375 of the Companies Act 1985, to act as the company's representative at any meeting of the members or creditors of other companies in which the company is or may become interested as a member or creditor.

CHAPTER 16: VOTING

P. 16.5 Specimen article giving enhanced voting rights

(a) Subject to sub-paragraphs 2 and 3 below, on a show of hands every member who (being an individual) is present in person or (being a corporation) is present by a duly authorised representative, not being himself a member, shall have one vote and on a poll every member shall have one vote for every share of which he is the holder.

(b) If at any general meeting a poll is duly demanded on a resolution to remove a director from office, the director named in the resolution shall be entitled to [number] votes for each share of which he is the holder.

(c) If at any general meeting a poll is duly demanded on a resolution to delete or amend the provisions of this article, every director shall have shall have [number] votes for each share of which he is the holder if voting against such a resolution.

P. 16.8A Voting card for use by members and corporate representatives on a poll

VOTING CARD
For the [Annual/Extraordinary] General Meeting of
XYZ plc
held on [date]

(To be used as instructed by the chairman)

Name of shareholder . . . .
   (In Block Capitals)

Signature . . . .

Number of shares held . . . .

	Number of votes	
	For	Against
Resolution 1		
Resolution 2		
Resolution 3		

Notes

1. Please record your votes by placing an X in the appropriate column above.
2. It is not necessary to complete the number of shares held, provided the vote is being given in respect of the entire holding.
3. If you wish to cast some of your votes for and some against a resolution, you may do so by indicating the number of votes cast for and against in the appropriate columns.

P. 16.8B   Voting card for use by proxies on a poll

VOTING CARD
For the [Annual/Extraordinary] General Meeting of
XYZ plc
held on [date]
(To be used as instructed by the chairman)

Name of proxy . . . .
   (In Block Capitals)
Signature of proxy . . . .
Name of shareholder represented . . . .
   (In Block Capitals)
Number of shares represented by proxy . . . .

	Number of votes	
	For	Against
Resolution 1		
Resolution 2		
Resolution 3		

Notes

1. Please record your votes by placing an X in the appropriate column above.
2. It is not necessary to complete the number of shares held, provided the vote is being given in respect of the entire holding.
3. If you wish to cast some of your votes for and some against a resolution, you may do so by indicating the number of votes cast for and against in the appropriate columns.
4. If you represent more than one member (other than members who hold shares jointly), you should complete a separate voting card in respect of each holding.

P. 16.8C   Voting card for use by chairman on a poll

CHAIRMAN'S VOTING CARD
For the [Annual/Extraordinary] General Meeting of
XYZ plc
held on [date]

Signature of chairman of meeting . . . .

See attached sheet for names and holdings of shareholders represented.

	Number of votes	
	For	Against
Resolution 1		
Resolution 2		
Resolution 3		

CHAPTER 20: DEALING WITH COMMON ITEMS OF BUSINESS

P. 20.2A   Agreement to accept accounts less than 21 days before general meeting

We, the undersigned, being all the members of XYZ Limited entitled to attend and vote at the [annual/extraordinary] general meeting, convened for [date of meeting], hereby agree that copies of the documents required to be sent to us in accordance with section 238 of the Companies Act 1985 not later than twenty-one days before the date of the said meeting shall be deemed to have been duly sent notwithstanding that they are sent less than twenty-one days before the date of the meeting.

[Date]
[Signatures]

P. 20.2B   Notice of AGM re laying of accounts

To receive the accounts and reports of the directors and the auditors for the year ended [date].

P. 20.3A   Board resolution to appoint first auditors

THAT [name of auditors] be appointed auditors of the company to hold office until the conclusion of the first general meeting at which accounts are laid before the company.

P. 20.3B   Resolution of company to appoint first auditors

THAT [name of auditors] be appointed auditors of the company to hold office until the conclusion of the first general meeting at which accounts are laid before the company [and that their remuneration be fixed by the directors*].
* See further para. 20.6.

P. 20.3C   Resolution to reappoint auditors at general meeting

THAT [name of auditors] be reappointed auditors of the company until the conclusion of the next general meeting at which accounts are laid before the company [and that their remuneration be fixed by the directors*].
* See further para. 20.6

P. 20.5A   Resolution of general meeting for removal of auditors

THAT [name of auditors] be removed from office as auditors of the company with immediate effect [and that [name of new auditors] be appointed auditors of the company in their place to hold office until the conclusion of the next general meeting a which accounts are laid and that their remuneration be fixed by the directors].

P. 20.5B   Resolution of general meeting for appointment of auditors other than retiring auditors

THAT [name of auditors] be appointed auditors of the company in place of the retiring auditors to hold office until the conclusion of the next general meeting at which accounts are laid before the company and that their remuneration be fixed by the directors.

P. 20.7A   Directors' report re dividends

An interim dividend of 5p per share has been paid and the directors recommend a final dividend of 9p per share in respect of the year ended [date], making a total for the year of 14p per share. The proposed dividend will, if approved at the annual general meeting, be paid on [date] to shareholders on the register at the close of business on [date].

P. 20.7B   Notice of resolution to declare a dividend

To declare a dividend.

P. 20.7C   Minute of resolution to declare a dividend

It was resolved:

> THAT a final dividend of 9p per 25p ordinary share in respect of the year ended [date] be declared payable on [date] to shareholders registered at the close of business on [date].

P. 20.7D   Directors' resolution to pay an interim dividend

It was resolved:

> THAT an interim dividend for the year ended [date] of 7p per share on the ordinary shares of 25p each be paid on [date] to shareholders registered at the close of business on [date].

P. 20.8A   Notice given by member to the company of intention to propose person (not recommended by the directors) for appointment or reappointment as a director

To the Directors
XYZ Ltd
Pursuant to reg. 76 of Table A, I hereby give notice of my intention to propose [name] for election as a director at the annual general meeting of the company to be held on [date]. The particulars regarding [name] which would, if he were so appointed or reappointed, be required to be included in the company's register of directors are set out below.

[Particulars]
[Signature]
[Date]

I, [name], hereby give notice that I am willing, if elected, to act as a director of XYZ Ltd.

[Signature]
[Date]

P. 20.8B   Notice given by company to members in accordance with reg. 77 of resolution to appoint director not retiring by rotation

To elect [name] as a director (see Note 1).

Note 1: [Particulars which would be required to be included in the register of directors.]

P. 20.9A   Special notice to company to comply with s. 293

The Directors
XYZ Limited
I hereby give notice pursuant to sections 293 and 379 of the Companies Act 1985 of my intention to propose the following resolution as an ordinary resolution at the next annual general meeting of the company:

> THAT Mrs S. Brown, who has attained the age of 70 years, be re-elected a director of the company.

[Signature]
[Address]   [Date]

P. 20.9B   Notice given by company to its members to comply with s. 293

To re-elect Mrs S. Brown a director of the company, special notice having been given to the company pursuant to sections 293 and 379 of the Companies Act 1985 of the intention to propose the following resolution as an ordinary resolution:

> THAT Mrs S. Brown, who has attained the age of 70 years, be re-elected a director of the company.

P. 20.11A   Special notice to company to remove director

The Directors
XYZ Limited
I hereby give notice pursuant to sections 303 and 379 of the Companies Act 1985 of my intention to propose the following resolution as an ordinary resolution at the next annual general meeting of the company:

> THAT Mrs S. Brown be removed from office as a director of the company.

[Signature]
[Address]   Date]

P. 20.11B Notice given by the company to its members

Special notice has been given to the company in accordance with sections 303 and 379 of the Companies Act 1985 of the intention to propose the following resolution as an ordinary resolution:

THAT Mrs S. Brown be removed from office as a director of the company.

P. 20.11C Letter from company accompanying copy of notice sent to the director concerned

Dear Mrs Brown,
Please find enclosed a copy of a notice received by the company from Mr Brown (a member of the company) stating that he intends at the next general meeting of the company to propose a resolution to remove you as a director of the company.
Yours sincerely,

[Secretary]
[Copy of notice enclosed]

CHAPTER 22: INFORMAL AGREEMENT

P. 22.4 Written record of decision by sole member of a company

XYZ Limited
Written record under s. 382B of the Companies Act 1985 (as amended) of a decision (which may be taken by the company in general meeting) taken by the sole member on [date].

The following resolution, having effect as an [ordinary] resolution, was approved on the above date by the undersigned sole member of the company:

THAT . . . .

[Signature]
[Date]

CHAPTER 23: WRITTEN RESOLUTIONS

P. 23.2A Written resolution (members)

XYZ Limited
Pursuant to Section 381A of the Companies Act 1989, we the undersigned being all the members of the company who at the date of this resolution are entitled to vote at a general meeting of the company, hereby resolve:

THAT . . . .

[Signatures and dates]*
* The date of the resolution is the date when it was signed by the last member to sign.

P. 23.2B   Written resolution (class of members)

XYZ Limited

Pursuant to Section 381A of the Companies Act 1989, we the undersigned being all the members of the company who at the date of this resolution are entitled to vote at a meeting of the holders of the [description of class] of the company, hereby resolve:

THAT . . . .

[Signatures and dates]*
* The date of the resolution is the date when it was signed by the last member to sign.

P. 23.2C   Letter to auditors to accompany copy of statutory written resolution

To: the Auditors

We enclose a copy of a resolution which it is proposed to be agreed as a written resolution of the company pursuant to Section 381A of the Companies Act 1985 ('the Act'). This copy is being sent to you in accordance with the requirements of Section 381B of the Act.

Yours faithfully,

Secretary
On behalf of XYZ Limited

P. 23.3   Record of a written resolution

Record of a written resolution of XYZ Limited
The following resolution(s) was/were passed as a written resolution on [date] being the date of the last signature.

A copy of the resolution was delivered to the auditors on [date].

The signatories to the resolution were:
[Names of directors]

Signature
[Director/Secretary]
[Date]

CHAPTER 24: ELECTIVE REGIME

P. 24.2A   Written resolution to dispense with the AGM.

XYZ Limited

Pursuant to Section 381A of the Companies Act 1985 we the undersigned, being all the members of the company who at the date of this resolution are entitled to attend and vote at general meetings of the company, hereby unanimously resolve as an elective resolution in accordance with Section 379A of the Companies Act 1985 (the Act):

THAT the company hereby elects:

(1) pursuant to Section 252 of the Act, to dispense with the laying of accounts and reports before the company in general meeting;

(2) pursuant to Section 366A of the Act, to dispense with the holding of annual general meetings; and

(3) pursuant to Section 386 of the Act, to dispense with the obligation to appoint auditors annually.

[Members' signatures and date signed]

P. 24.2B   Ordinary resolution to revoke an elective resolution

THAT pursuant to Section 379A of the Companies Act 1985, the company hereby revokes the elective resolution passed on [date] [purpose of resolution].

P. 24.3A   Elective resolution to dispense with AGM

To resolve as an elective resolution in accordance with Section 379A of the Companies Act 1985:

THAT pursuant to Section 366A of the Companies Act 1985, the company elects to dispense with the holding of annual general meetings.

P. 24.3B   Notice by member to company requiring annual general meeting while elective resolution is in force

To: The Directors   [Date]
XYZ Ltd
[Registered Office]
As a member of the company I hereby give notice, pursuant to section 366A(3) of the Companies Act 1985, that I require the company to hold an annual general meeting for the year ending 19 . . notwithstanding that an elective resolution to dispense with the holding of annual general meetings is in force.

[Signature]
[Name and address]

P. 24.2A   Elective resolution to dispense with laying of accounts & report

To resolve as an elective resolution in accordance with Section 379A of the Companies Act 1985:

THAT pursuant to Section 252 of the Companies Act 1985, the company elects to dispense with the laying of accounts and reports before the company in general meeting.

P. 24.4B Notice to members in annual report & accounts informing them of their rights under s. 253(2)

An elective resolution dispensing with the requirement to lay the accounts and reports at a general meeting of the company is currently in force. This means that the accounts and reports for the year ended . . . . . 19 . . (enclosed with this notice) will not be laid at a general meeting, unless a member of the company requires a general meeting to be held for this purpose.

Under s. 253 of the Companies Act 1985 any member may require the company to hold a general meeting for the purpose of laying the accounts and reports by giving notice in writing to that effect to the company at its registered office (addressed to the secretary) within 28 days of the date of this notice.

[Dated]

P. 24.4C Notice to company from member requiring general meeting to be held for the purpose of laying accounts and reports

To: The Directors   [Date]
XYZ Ltd
[Registered Office]

As a member of the company I hereby give notice, pursuant to section 253(2) of the Companies Act 1985, that I require a general meeting of the company to be held for the purpose of laying the accounts and reports of the company for the year ending 19 . . .

[Signature]
[Name and address]

P. 24.5A Elective resolution to dispense with appointment of auditors annually

To resolve as an elective resolution in accordance with Section 379A of the Companies Act 1985:

THAT pursuant to Section 386 of the Companies Act 1985, the company elects to dispense with the obligation to appoint auditors annually.

P. 24.5B Ordinary resolution authorising the directors to fix the remuneration of auditors while an elective resolution dispensing with their annual appointment is in force

THAT the directors be authorised to fix the remuneration of the auditors until such time as a resolution to appoint auditors is passed at a general meeting of the company.

P. 24.6A Elective resolution electing that the provisions of s. 80A apply in relation to the giving or renewal of authority to allot shares

To resolve as an elective resolution in accordance with Section 379A of the Companies Act 1985 ('the Act'):

THAT in relation to the giving or renewal of authority under Section 80 of the Act, the provisions of Section 80A of the Act shall apply, instead of the provisions of Section 80(4) and 80(5) of the Act, after the passing of this resolution.

P. 24.6B Ordinary resolution authorising the directors to allot shares for an indefinite period

THAT the directors be generally and unconditionally authorised, pursuant to Section 80 of the Companies Act 1985, to exercise for an indefinite period any power of the company to allot and grant rights to subscribe for or to convert securities into shares of the company up to a maximum nominal amount equal to the nominal amount of the authorised but unissued share capital at the date of the passing of this resolution.

P. 24.7 Elective resolution to reduce the majority required to authorise short notice of meetings

To resolve as an elective resolution in accordance with Section 379A of the Companies Act 1985 ('the Act'):

THAT pursuant to Sections 369(4) and 378(3) of the Act, the provisions of those Sections shall have effect in relation to the company as if for the references to 95 per cent in those provisions there was substituted references to 90 per cent.

CHAPTER 25: MINUTES
See also **Precedent 28.5C: Minutes of first board meeting**

P. 25.11A Minutes of annual general meeting of public limited company

Minutes of the annual general meeting of XYZ plc held on [date] at [place]
Present: [Name of director], Chairman
               [Names of other directors]
               [Number] members
               [Number] proxies representing [number] members
In attendance Secretary

34. The chairman opened the meeting at 11.00 am.
35. The chairman proposed and the meeting agreed to take the notice of the meeting as read.
36. [Name] representing [name of auditors] read the report of the auditors to the members.

Resolution 1

37. The chairman proposed THAT the report of the Directors and the audited accounts for the year ended [date], now laid before the meeting, be received.

    After dealing with questions, the chairman put the resolution to the meeting and declared it carried.

Resolution 2

38. The chairman proposed THAT [name 1], a director retiring by rotation, be re-elected a director of the company.

    The resolution was put to the meeting and the chairman declared it carried.

Resolution 3

39. The chairman proposed THAT [name 2], a director retiring by rotation, be re-elected a director of the company.

    During the discussion of this proposal, [name], a proxy for a member of the company opposed to the reappointment of [Name 2], attempted to make a speech in breach of article [No.] of the company's articles of association. Despite repeated warnings from the chairman, the proxy refused to be quiet. To general acclamation, the chairman warned him that if he did not comply he would be asked to leave the meeting. The proxy continued speak in a highly aggressive manner. Accordingly, the chairman ordered him to leave the meeting. The proxy ignored the chairman's order and advanced towards the stage in a threatening manner. The chairman ordered the stewards to remove him from the meeting and he was removed following a brief struggle.

    After dealing with further questions, the chairman put the resolution to the meeting and declared it carried.

Resolution 4

40. The chairman proposed THAT [name of auditors] be reappointed as auditors to hold office until the conclusion of the next general meeting at which accounts are laid before the company and that their remuneration be determined by the directors.

    The resolution was put to the meeting and the chairman declared it carried.
    [Name], a member of the company holding [number] shares, demanded a poll.

The chairman ruled that the member was not able satisfy the requirements of article [No.] of the company's articles of association and that the demand was therefore invalid, and confirmed that the resolution had been carried.

Resolution 5

41. The chairman proposed as a special resolution:

> THAT the authority and power conferred on the Directors by Article [No.] (Authority to allot securities) of the Articles of Association of the Company be renewed for the period expiring on the date of the annual general meeting of the Company to be held in [year + 1] and that:
>
> (a) for the purposes of Article [No.], the prescribed amount for the above period shall be £[amount 1] and
> (b) for the purposes of the proviso to Article [No.], the aggregate nominal amount of equity securities allotted wholly for cash during such period, otherwise than as mentioned in such proviso, shall not exceed £[amount 2].

[Name], a member of the company, proposed an amendment the effect of which would have been to substitute £[amount 3] as the prescribed amount for the purposes of Article [No.]. The chairman ruled the amendment out of order and explained that it was not possible to amend the substance of a special resolution.

After further discussion, the chairman put the resolution to the meeting and declared it carried.

[Name], a member of the company, and [name], a proxy representing a member of the company, demanded a poll on the resolution. The chairman informed the meeting that the demand was valid and that a poll would be held immediately at which representatives of the company's auditors would act as scrutineers. After the chairman informed the meeting of the poll procedures, voting papers were issued and collected by the company's registrars.

The results of the poll were as follows:

For: [   ]
Against: [   ]

42. The chairman closed the meeting.

[Signature]
Chairman

P. 25.11B   Minutes of general meeting of a single member company

XYZ Limited

Minutes of an extraordinary general meeting held at [place] on [date]

Present: Mr XYZ (Chairman)
In attendance: C. Sec (Company Secretary)

The chairman proposed as a [special] resolution:

THAT . . . .

After declaring an interest in the resolution to the extent that [nature of interest] this was passed by the sole member of the company as a [special] resolution of the company.

[Signature]
Chairman

P. 25.11C Minutes of board meeting of a public company

EXAMPLE plc

Minutes of a meeting of the BOARD OF DIRECTORS held on [date] at 27 Fitzwilliam Place, London W1.

Present:	Julian Gold	Director (in the chair)
	Susan Silver	Director
	Richard Wood	Director
	Samuel Johnson	Director (for minutes 74 to 79 only)
	George Hawkins	Director

In attendance: Alan Scribe   Secretary

72. The chairman signed the minutes of the board meeting held on [date], copies having been circulated to the directors.

73. Subsequent to a recommendation by the Nomination Committee it was resolved:

THAT Mr Andrew de Chancery be and is hereby appointed a director of the company and shall hold office until the next annual general meeting.

74. Mr George Hawkins joined the meeting.

75. It was resolved:

THAT pursuant to article [No.] of the company's articles of association, any two directors be appointed a committee to take any actions and to complete all documents necessary to purchase the freehold on 27 Fitzwilliam Place, London W1.

76. There were produced and considered:

(a) group management accounts made up to 30th September 1994 (Board paper 94/10);

(b) predicted cash flow statement for the six months to 30th April 1995 (Board paper 94/11).

It was resolved:

THAT the company's bankers be approached by Richard Wood to negotiate an increase in the company's overdraft facilities to £2,000,000 to cover the cash shortfall predicted to arise between [date] and [date].

77. There was produced and discussed a paper a document prepared by Susan Silver entitled 'Going greener' (Board paper 94/12), on the company's environmental policy. It was resolved:

> THAT no decision could be made to implement the proposals in the paper without detailed costings. The chairman requested Susan Silver to resubmit the proposals at the next board meeting together with a schedule of the projected costs of implementing each of the recommendations for each of the company's subsidiaries.

78. The chairman stated that the next meeting of the board of directors would be held on [date] at Fitzwilliam Place.
79. There being no further business the meeting was closed.

[Signature]
Chairman

CHAPTER 26: THE BOARD OF DIRECTORS

P. 26.2A Board resolution to fill a casual vacancy

THAT [name of new director] be appointed a director of the company in the place of [name of former director] with effect from [date] and shall hold office until the next annual general meeting.

P. 26.2B Board resolution to appoint an additional director

THAT [name of new director] be appointed a director of the company with effect from [date] and shall hold office until the next annual general meeting.

P. 26.2C Appointment of additional director by sole continuing director

XYZ Limited

Pursuant to the authority given by regulation 90 of Table A in the Companies (Tables A to F) Regulations 1985 (which regulation is incorporated in the company's articles of association), I, [name], the sole continuing director of the company, hereby appoint [name of person to be appointed] to be a director of the company to fill the vacancy caused by [circumstances, e.g. death or resignation] of [name].

[Date]
[Signature]

P. 26.3A Extract from directors' service agreement

The director shall exercise such powers and functions and perform such duties in relation to the company or any of its subsidiaries and associates as may from time to time be vested in or assigned to him by the board and shall comply with all directions from time to time given to him by the Board (or anyone authorised by the board) and with all rules and regulations from time to time laid down by the company concerning employees.

P. 26.3B   Board minute of resolution to appoint managing director

There was produced a draft of a service contract between the company and [name] appointing [name] as managing director of the company with effect from [date], on the terms and conditions set out in the service contract.

It was resolved:

THAT [name] be appointed managing director of the company with effect from [date] on the terms set out in the service contract produced at the meeting and that the chairman be authorised to sign the service agreement on behalf of the company.

CHAPTER 27: DIRECTORS' POWERS

P. 27.9   Written resolution of the directors

XYZ Limited

Pursuant to the authority given by article [no.] of the company's articles of association, we, the undersigned, being all the directors of XYZ Limited [entitled to receive notice of a meeting of directors], hereby resolve:

THAT . . . . .

[Date]
[Signatures]

CHAPTER 28: PROCEDURES AT MEETINGS OF DIRECTORS

P. 28.4   Notice of board meeting

XYZ Limited
[Address]
[Date]

To the directors of XYZ Limited

Notice of board meeting
A meeting of the directors of the company will be held at [place] on [date] at [time].

[Signature]
Secretary
By order of the chairman

P. 28.5A Example of notice of board meeting including the agenda

XYZ Limited
A board meeting will be held at [place] on [date] at [time]

AGENDA
1. *Minutes*
   To approve the minutes of the board meeting held on 24 August 1996 (board paper no. 09/96/01).
2. *Management accounts*
   To consider the management accounts for August 1996 (board paper no. 09/96/02).
3. *Appointment of directors*
   To consider the recommendations of the nomination committee on the appointment of non-executive directors (board paper no. 09/96/03).
4. *Charitable donation*
   To consider and, if thought fit, to approve the following charitable donations:
5. *Date of next meeting*
   To note that the next meeting will be held on 26 October 1996 at 299 Kingsdown Place at 10.30am.

. . . .

Secretary

P. 28.5B Agenda for first board meeting (private company)

XYZ Limited
Agenda for board meeting to be held at [place] on [date] at [time]

1. To produce the certificate of incorporation and a copy of the memorandum and articles of association as registered.
2. To note that the first directors of the company named by the subscribers in the documents delivered to the Registrar of Companies with the memorandum of association are: [names].
3. To consider and, if thought fit, resolve that [name of director] be appointed chairman of the board.
4. To note that [name] was named by the subscribers as secretary in the documents delivered to the Registrar of Companies and to consider and, if thought fit, resolve:

   THAT the appointment of [name] as secretary be confirmed at a salary payable from [date] at the rate of [amount] per annum, such appointment being terminable by [period] notice in writing given by either party to the other at any time.

5. To consider and, if thought fit, resolve:

   THAT the situation of the company's registered office shown in the documents delivered with the memorandum to the Registrar of Companies (namely, [address]) be confirmed.

6. To consider and, if thought fit, resolve:

    THAT the seal, of which an impression is affixed in the margin hereof, be adopted as the common seal of the company.

7. To consider opening a bank account with [name of bank] and, if thought fit, resolve:
    [Resolutions in accordance with bank's printed form for opening an account.]

8. To consider and, if thought fit, resolve:

    THAT [name] be appointed auditors of the company to hold office until the conclusion of the first general meeting at which accounts are laid before the company.

9. To produce and read to the meeting notices given by the directors pursuant to section 317(3) of the Companies Act 1985.

10. To produce forms of application for 98 shares of £1 each in the capital of the company, together with cheques for a total of £100, being payment in full for the said shares and the two shares taken by the subscribers to the memorandum of association.
    To consider and, if thought fit, resolve:
    (a) THAT 49 shares of £1 each, fully paid and numbered 3 to 51 inclusive, be alloted to [applicant 1];
    (b) THAT 49 shares of £1 each, fully paid and numbered 52 to 100 inclusive, be alloted to [applicant 2];
    (c) THAT the undermentioned share certificates drawn in respect of subscribers' shares and the allotments made by resolutions (a) and (b) above be approved and that the common seal be affixed thereto:
    No. 1   [applicant 1]   50 shares numbered 1 to 50 inclusive
    No. 2   [applicant 2]   50 shares numbered 51 to 100 inclusive

11. To consider and, if thought fit, resolve:

    THAT all the shares of the company shall henceforth cease to bear distinguishing numbers.

12. To consider fixing dates for future board meetings.

P. 28.5C   Minutes of first board meeting (private company)

XYZ Limited
Minutes of board meeting held at [place] on [date] at [time]

1. There were produced the certificate of incorporation and a copy of the memorandum and articles of association as registered.

2. It was noted that the first directors of the company named by the subscribers in the documents delivered to the Registrar of Companies with the memorandum of association are: [names].

3. It was resolved:

> THAT [name of director] be appointed chairman of the board.

4. It was noted that [name] was named by the subscribers as secretary in the documents delivered to the Registrar of Companies and resolved:

> THAT the appointment of [name] as secretary be confirmed at a salary payable from [date] at the rate of [amount] per annum, such appointment being terminable by [period] notice in writing given by either party to the other at any time.

5. It was resolved:

> THAT the situation of the company's registered office shown in the documents delivered with the memorandum to the Registrar of Companies (namely, [address]) be confirmed.

6. It was resolved:

> THAT the seal, of which an impression is affixed in the margin hereof, be adopted as the common seal of the company.

7. It was resolved:

> THAT a bank account be opened with [name of bank] and . . . [Resolutions in accordance with bank's printed form for opening an account.]

8. It was resolved:

> THAT [name] be appointed auditors of the company to hold office until the conclusion of the first general meeting at which accounts are laid before the company.

9. There were produced and read to the meeting notices given by [names of directors] pursuant to section 317(3) of the Companies Act 1985.

10. There were produced forms of application for 98 shares of £1 each in the capital of the company, together with cheques for a total of £100, being payment in full for the said shares and the two shares taken by the subscribers to the memorandum of association.

    It was resolved:

    (a) THAT 49 shares of £1 each, fully paid and numbered 3 to 51 inclusive, be allotted to [applicant 1];

    (b) THAT 49 shares of £1 each, fully paid and numbered 52 to 100 inclusive, be allotted to [applicant 2];

    (c) THAT the undermentioned share certificates drawn in respect of subscribers' shares and the allotments made by resolutions (a) and (b) above be approved and that the common seal be affixed thereto:

    No. 1   [applicant 1]   50 shares numbered 1 to 50 inclusive
    No. 2   [applicant 2]   50 shares numbered 51 to 100 inclusive

11. It was resolved:

> THAT all the shares of the company shall henceforth cease to bear distinguishing numbers.

12. It was resolved that the next meeting of the board of directors would be held at [place] on [date] at [time].

[Signed]
[Chairman]

P. 28.5D   Agenda for board meeting of public company

XYZ plc

Agenda for board meeting to be held at [place] on [date] at [time].

1. The chairman to sign the minutes of the board meeting held on [date] and the committee meeting held on [date], copies having been circulated to the directors.
2. To produce transfer audit reports dated [date] from the company's registrars and to resolve:

   (a) THAT share transfers Nos. . . . to . . . inclusive and loan stock transfers Nos. . . . to . . . inclusive be approved.

   (b) THAT the sealing and issue of share certificates Nos. . . . to . . . inclusive and loan stock certificates Nos. . . . to . . . inclusive be confirmed.

3. To produce the seal book and resolve:

   > THAT the affixing of the common seal of the company to the documents set out against items Nos. . . . to . . . inclusive in the seal book be confirmed.

4. To produce and consider:

   (a) a list of bank balances as at [date]
   (b) cash flow statements for the period to [date]
   (c) financial statement as at [date].

5. To produce and consider a proof print of the report of the directors and the accounts for the year ended [date], and a draft of the chairman's statement and operating and financial review to be circulated with the report and accounts. To consider and, if thought fit resolve:

   (a) THAT, with reference to minute No. [   ] of the annual general meeting held on [date], the remuneration of the auditors be fixed at [amount].

   (b) THAT the report of the directors, the chairman's statement, the operating and financial review and the accounts for the year ended [date], including the final dividend of [   ]p per share recommended therein (making a total dividend of [   ]p per share for the year) be approved and that, subject to approval by the company in general meeting, such dividend be paid on [date] to shareholders registered at the close of business on [date].

(c)   THAT the signature of the balance sheet by two directors on behalf of the board be authorised.

(d)   THAT the signature of the directors' report by the secretary be authorised.

(e)   THAT the annual general meeting of the company be convened and held at [place] on [date] at [time] to transact the ordinary business of the company and that the secretary be authorised to issue notices accordingly, together with a form of proxy in accordance with the proof print submitted to and approved by this meeting.

(f)   THAT [the company's bankers] be requested to open dividend account No. [   ] in the name of the company and be authorised to honour warrants dated [date], drawn on the said account bearing the facsimile or autographic signature of the secretary without other signature thereto.

6. To consider and, if thought fit, resolve:

THAT the secretary be authorised to release forthwith to the London Stock Exchange and to the company's press agents a preliminary announcement of the results of the year ended [date].

P. 28.7A   Board resolution to fix quorum for meetings of directors

THAT the quorum necessary for the transaction of the business of the directors be fixed at three.

P. 28.7B   Article allowing interested directors to vote and be counted in quorum

A director may vote at a meeting of directors or any committee of directors on any contract or arrangement in which he is interested and on any incidental matter, and a director who is so interested shall be counted in calculating whether a quorum exists for that item of business; [and Regulation 94 of Table A shall be modified accordingly].

P. 28.7C   Article allowing sole director to act

The quorum for the transaction of business of the directors may be fixed by the directors and unless so fixed at any other number shall be two; but if and so long as there is a sole director, he may exercise all the powers and authorities vested in the directors by these Articles [and Table A; and Regulation 89 of Table A shall be modified accordingly]. A person who holds office only as an alternate director shall, if his appointor is not present, be counted in the quorum.

P. 28.10A   Form of appointment of alternate director

Pursuant to article [no.] of the articles of association of [name of company] and subject to the approval of the board of [name of company], I [name of director making appointment] being a director of [name of company] hereby appoint [name of person to be appointed as alternate] to be my alternate director.

P. 28.10B   Resolution approving appointment of alternate director

There was produced a form of appointment dated [date] by which [name of director] appoints [name of alternate] to be his alternate director.

It was resolved THAT the appointment by [name of director] of [name of alternate] to be his alternate director be approved.

P. 28.10C   Form of revocation of appointment of alternate director

Pursuant to article [no.] of the articles of association of [name of company], I hereby revoke the appointment dated [date] of [name of alternate appointed] as my alternate director.

P. 28.10D   Board minute noting revocation of appointment of alternate director

A form of revocation dated [date] by which [name of director] revokes the appointment of [name of alternate] as his alternate was produced and noted.

CHAPTER 29: DELEGATION OF DIRECTORS' POWERS

P. 29.3   ICSA's aide memoir for compiling a schedule of matters to be reserved for the approval of the board

Companies Act requirements
1. Approval of interim and final financial statements.*
2. Approval of the interim dividend and recommendation of the final dividend.*
3. Approval of any significant change in accounting policies or practices.*
4. Appointment or removal of company secretary.*
5. Remuneration of auditors (where, as is usual, shareholders have delegated this power to the board) and recommendations for appointment or removal of auditors.*

Stock Exchange
6. Approval of all circulars and listing particulars (approval of routine documents such as periodic circulars re scrip dividend procedures or exercise of conversion rights might perhaps be delegated to a committee).*

7. Approval of press releases concerning matters decided by the board.*

Management
8. Approval of the group's commercial strategy and the annual operating budget.
9. Changes relating to the group's capital structure or its status as plc.
10. Appointments to boards of subsidiaries.
11. Terms and conditions of directors [and senior executives].*
12. Changes to the group's management & control structure.

Board membership and board committees
13. Board appointments and removals.*
14. Terms of reference of chairman, vice chairman, chief executive and other executive directors.*
15. Terms of reference and membership of board committees.*

Cadbury recommendations
16. Major capital projects.
17. Material contracts of the company [or any subsidiary] in the ordinary course of business e.g. bank borrowing (above £xxx) and acquisition or disposal of fixed assets (above £xxx).
18. Contracts of the company [or any subsidiary] not in the ordinary course of business e.g. loans & repayments (above £xxx); foreign currency transactions (above £xxx); major acquisitions or disposals (above £xxx).
19. Major investments [including the acquisition or disposal of interests of more than [5] per cent in the voting shares of any company or the making of any take-over bid].
20. Risk management strategy.
21. Treasury policies (including foreign exchange exposures).

Miscellaneous
22. Major changes in the rules of the company pension scheme, or changes of trustees or (when this is subject to the approval of the company) changes in the fund management arrangements.
23. Major changes in employee share schemes and the allocation of executive share options.
24. Formulation of policy regarding charitable donations.
25. Political donations.
26. Prosecution, defence or settlement of litigation (involving above £xxx or being otherwise material to the interests of the company).
27. Internal control arrangements.
28. Health & safety policy.
29. Environmental policy.
30. Directors' & officers' liability insurance.

Note: Items marked * are not considered suitable, in any event, for delegation to a committee of the board e.g. because of Companies Act requirements or because, under the recommendations of the Cadbury Report, they are the responsibility of, e.g. an audit, nomination or remuneration committee with the final decision on the matter required to be taken by the whole board.

CHAPTER 30: BOARD COMMITTEES

P. 30.2A Board resolution to appoint committee

THAT, pursuant to article [no.] of the company's articles of association, A, B, and C (any two of whom shall be a quorum) be appointed a committee with power to . . .

P. 30.2B Board resolution to appoint committee

THAT, pursuant to article [no.] of the company's articles of association, any two directors be appointed a committee to take such action and to complete all documents necessary for [reason].

P. 30.10 Written resolution of committee of one director

XYZ Limited
Pursuant to the authority given by article [no.] of the company's articles of association, I, the undersigned, being the sole member of a committee established by the board of directors on [date] to [short prescription of purpose], hereby resolve;

THAT . . . . .

[Date]
[Signature]

P. 30.11 Specimen terms of reference of an audit committee

Constitution
1. The Board hereby resolves to establish a Committee of the Board to be known as the Audit Committee.

Membership
2. The Committee shall be appointed by the Board from amongst the non-executive directors of the Company and shall consist of not less than three members. A quorum shall be two members.
3. The chairman of the committee shall be appointed by the Board.

Attendance at meetings
4. The Finance Director, the Head of Internal Audit, and a representative of the external auditors shall normally attend meetings. Other Board members shall also

have the right of attendance. However, at least once a year the Committee shall meet with the external auditors without executive Board members present.

5. The Company secretary shall be the Secretary of the Committee.

Frequency of meetings

6. Meetings shall be held not less than twice a year. The external auditors may request a meeting if they consider that one is necessary.

Authority

7. The Committee is authorised by the Board to investigate any activity within its terms of reference. It is authorised to seek any information it requires from any employee and all employees are directed to co-operate with any request made by the Committee.

8. The Committee is authorised by the Board to obtain outside legal or other independent professional advice and to secure the attendance of outsiders with relevant experience and expertise if it considers necessary.

Duties

9. The duties of the Committee shall be:
   (a) to consider the appointment of the external auditor, the audit fee, and any question of resignation or dismissal;
   (b) to discuss with the external auditor before the audit commences the nature and scope of the audit, and ensure co-ordination where more than one audit firm is involved;
   (c) to review the half-year and annual financial statements before submission to the Board, focusing particularly on:
      (i)   any changes in accounting policies and practices
      (ii) major judgemental areas
      (iii) significant adjustments resulting from the audit
      (iv) the going concern assumption
      (v)   compliance with accounting standards
      (vi) compliance with stock exchange and legal requirements;
   (d) to discuss problems and reservations arising from the interim and final audits, and any matters the auditor may wish to discuss (in the absence of management where necessary);
   (e) to review the auditor's management letter and management's response;
   (f) to review the Company's statement on internal control systems prior to endorsement by the Board;
   (g) to review the internal audit programme, ensure co-ordination between internal and external auditors, and ensure that the internal audit function is adequately resourced and has appropriate standing within the Company;
   (h) to consider the major findings of internal investigations and management's response;
   (i) to consider other topics as defined by the Board.

Reporting procedures
10. The Secretary shall circulate minutes of meetings of the Committee to all members of the Board.

P. 30.13 Specimen terms of reference for nomination committee

Constitution
1. The Board hereby resolves to establish a Committee of the Board to be known as the Nomination Committee.

Membership
2. The Committee shall comprise three Directors appointed by the Board, the majority of whom must be non-executive directors. A quorum shall be two members.
3. The Chairman of the Committee shall be appointed by the Board.

Frequency of meetings
4. The Committee shall meet at least once a year.

Powers
5. The committee shall have the power to employ the services of such advisers as it deems necessary to fulfil its responsibilities.

Duties
6. The duties of the Committee shall be:
   (a) to nominate candidates for the approval of the board to fill vacancies on the board of directors;
   (b) to consider and make recommendations to the board at least annually on its composition and balance.

Reporting procedures
7. The company secretary shall act as secretary to the committee and shall keep an appropriate record of its proceedings.

CHAPTER 32: CORPORATE GOVERNANCE

P.32.3 ICSA code on good boardroom practice

The Institute of Chartered Secretaries and Administrators (ICSA) believes that reliance on unwritten boardroom procedures and practices is no longer acceptable in the modern business environment. Whilst it is acknowledged that company law should not attempt to prescribe any particular style of boardroom management, ICSA believes that certain basic principles of good boardroom practice can be considered to be universally applicable.

Accordingly, ICSA has formulated this Code for directors and company secretaries as a guide to matters which it believes should be addressed and, wherever applicable, accepted formally by boards of directors in recognition of a commitment to adhere to an overall concept of best practice.

ICSA also recommends that boardroom procedures should be periodically reviewed to ensure both the satisfactory operation of the Code and the identification of matters which individual companies could advantageously bring within its scope.

Good Boardroom Practice: A Code for Directors and Company Secretaries

1. The board should establish written procedures for the conduct of its business which should include matters covered by this Code. A copy of these written procedures should be given to each director. Compliance should be monitored, preferably by an audit committee, and breaches of the procedures should be reported to the board.
2. The board should ensure that each director is given on appointment sufficient information to enable him to perform his duties. In particular, guidance for non-executive directors should cover procedures:
   (i) for obtaining information concerning the company; and
   (ii) for requisitioning a meeting of the board.
3. In the conduct of board business, two fundamental concepts should be observed:
   (i) each director should receive the same information at the same time; and
   (ii) each director should be given sufficient time in which to consider any such information.
4. The board should identify matters which require the prior approval of the board and lay down procedures (note 1) to be followed when, exceptionally, a decision is required before its next meeting on any matter not required by law to be considered at board level.
5. As a basic principle, all material contracts, and especially those not in the ordinary course of business, should be referred to the board prior to commitment by the company.
6. The board should approve definitions of the terms 'material' (note 2) and 'not in the ordinary course of business' and these definitions should be brought to the attention of all relevant persons.
7. Where there is any uncertainty regarding the materiality or nature of a contract, it should normally be assumed that the contract should be brought before the board.
8. Decisions regarding the content of the agenda for individual meetings of the board and concerning the presentation of agenda items should be taken by the chairman in consultation with the company secretary.
9. The company secretary should be responsible to the chairman for the proper administration of the meetings of the company, the board and any committees thereof. To carry out this responsibility the company secretary should be entitled to be present at (or represented at) and prepare (or arrange for the preparation of) minutes of the proceedings of all such meetings.

10. The minutes of meetings should record the decisions taken and provide sufficient background to those decisions. All papers presented at the meeting should be clearly identified in the minutes and retained for reference. Procedures for the approval and circulation of minutes should be established.

11. Where the articles of association allow the board to delegate any of its powers to a committee, the board should give its prior approval to:

   (i) the membership and quorum of any such committee;

  (ii) its terms of reference; and

 (iii) the extent of any powers delegated to it.

12. The minutes of all meetings of committees of the board (or a written summary thereof) should be circulated to the board prior to its next meeting and the opportunity should be given at that meeting for any member of the board to ask questions thereon.

13. Notwithstanding the absence of a formal agenda item, the chairman should permit any director or the company secretary to raise at any board meeting any matter concerning the company's compliance with this Code of Practice, with the company's memorandum and articles of association and with any other legal or regulatory requirement.

Notes

1. If it is practicable, the approval of all the directors should be obtained by means of a written resolution. In all cases, however, the procedures should balance the need for urgency with the overriding principle that each director should be given as much information as possible and have an opportunity to requisition an emergency meeting of the board to discuss the matter prior to the commitment of the company.

2. Different definitions of the term 'material' should be established for 'contracts not in the ordinary course of business' and 'contracts in the ordinary course of business'. Financial limits should be set where appropriate.

Appendices

Companies Act 1985 provisions on meetings

The following provisions include all amendments up to the end of April 1997.

CHAPTER II

CLASS RIGHTS

125. Variation of class rights

(1)   This section is concerned with the variation of the rights attached to any class of shares in a company whose share capital is divided into shares of different classes.

(2)   Where the rights are attached to a class of shares otherwise than by the company's memorandum, and the company's articles do not contain provision with respect to the variation of the rights, those rights may be varied if, but only if –

(a)   the holders of three-quarters in nominal value of the issued shares of that class consent in writing to the variation; or

(b)   an extraordinary resolution passed at a separate general meeting of the holders of that class sanctions the variation;

and any requirement (howsoever expressed) in relation to the variation of those rights is complied with to the extent that it is not comprised in paragraphs (a) and (b) above.

(3)   Where –

(a)   the rights are attached to a class of shares by the memorandum or otherwise;

(b)   the memorandum or articles contain provision for the variation of those rights; and

(c)   the variation of those rights is connected with the giving, variation, revocation or renewal of an authority for allotment under section 80 or with a reduction of the company's share capital under section 135;

those rights shall not be varied unless –

(i)   the condition mentioned in subsection (2)(a) or (b) above is satisfied; and

(ii)   any requirement of the memorandum or articles in relation to the variation of rights of that class is complied with to the extent that it is not comprised in that condition.

(4)   If the rights are attached to a class of shares in the company by the memorandum or otherwise and –

(a) where they are so attached by the memorandum, the articles contain provision with respect to their variation which had been included in the articles at the time of the company's original incorporation; or
(b) where they are so attached otherwise, the articles contain such provision (whenever first so included),

and in either case the variation is not connected as mentioned in subsection (3)(c), those rights may only be varied in accordance with that provision of the articles.

(5)   If the rights are attached to a class of shares by the memorandum, and the memorandum and articles do not contain provision with respect to the variation of those rights, those rights may be varied if all the members of the company agree to the variation.

(6)   The provisions of section 369 (length of notice for calling company meetings), section 370 (general provisions as to meetings and votes) and sections 376 and 377 (circulation of members' resolutions) and the provisions of the articles relating to general meetings shall, so far as applicable, apply in relation to any meeting of shareholders required by this section or otherwise to take place in connection with the variation of the rights attached to a class of shares, and shall so apply with the necessary modifications and subject to the following provisions, namely –

(a) the necessary quorum at any such meeting other than an adjourned meeting shall be two persons holding or representing by proxy at least one-third in nominal value of the issued shares of the class in question and at an adjourned meeting one person holding shares of the class in question or his proxy;
(b) any holder of shares of the class in question present in person or by proxy may demand a poll.

(7)   Any alteration of a provision contained in a company's articles for the variation of the rights attached to a class of shares, or the insertion of any such provision into the articles, is itself to be treated as a variation of those rights.

(8)   In this section and (except where the context otherwise requires) in any provision for the variation of the rights attached to a class of shares contained in a company's memorandum or articles, references to the variation of those rights are to be read as including references to their abrogation.

126. Savings for court's powers under other provisions

Nothing in subsections (2) to (5) of section 125 derogates from the powers of the court under the following sections of this Act, namely –

sections 4 to 6 (company resolution to alter objects),

section 54 (litigated objection to public company becoming private by re-registration),

section 425 (court control of company compromising with members and creditors),

section 427 (company reconstruction or amalgamation),

sections 459 to 461 (protection of minorities).

127. Shareholders' right to object to variation

(1)   This section applies if, in the case of a company whose share capital is divided into different classes of shares –

(a) provision is made by the memorandum or articles for authorising the variation of the rights attached to any class of shares in the company subject to –

   (i)   the consent of any specified proportion of the holders of the issued shares of that class, or

   (ii)   the sanction of a resolution passed at a separate meeting of the holders of those shares,

and in pursuance of that provision the rights attached to any such class of shares are at any time varied; or

(b) the rights attached to any class of shares in the company are varied under section 125(2).

(2)   The holders of not less in the aggregate than 15 per cent of the issued shares of the class in question (being persons who did not consent to or vote in favour of the resolution for the variation), may apply to the court to have the variation cancelled; and if such an application is made, the variation has no effect unless and until it is confirmed by the court.

(3)   Application to the court must be made within 21 days after the date on which the consent was given or the resolution was passed (as the case may be), and may be made on behalf of the shareholders entitled to make the application by such one or more of their number as they may appoint in writing for the purpose.

(4)   The court, after hearing the applicant and any other persons who apply to the court to be heard and appear to the court to be interested in the application, may, if satisfied having regard to all the circumstances of the case, that the variation would unfairly prejudice the shareholders of the class represented by the applicant, disallow the variation and shall, if not satisfied, confirm it.

The decision of the court on any such application is final.

(5)   The company shall within 15 days after the making of an order by the court on such an application forward a copy of the order to the registrar of companies; and if default is made in complying with this provision, the company and every officer of it who is in default is liable to a fine and, for continued contravention, to a daily default fine.

(6)   'Variation', in this section, includes abrogation; and 'varied' is to be construed accordingly.

128. Registration of particulars of special rights

(1)   If a company allots shares with rights which are not stated in its memorandum or articles, or in any resolution or agreement which is required by section 380 to be sent to the registrar of companies, the company shall deliver to the registrar of companies, within one month from allotting the shares, a statement in the prescribed form containing particulars of those rights.

(2)   This does not apply if the shares are in all respects uniform with shares previously allotted; and shares are not for this purpose to be treated as different from shares previously allotted by reason only that the former do not carry the same rights to dividends as the latter during the 12 months immediately following the former's allotment.

(3)   Where the rights attached to any shares are varied otherwise than by an amendment of the company's memorandum or articles or by a resolution or agreement subject to section 380, the company shall within one month from the date on which the variation is made deliver to the registrar of companies a statement in the prescribed form containing particulars of the variation.

(4)   Where a company (otherwise than by any such amendment, resolution or agreement as is mentioned above) assigns a name or other designation, or a new name or other designation, to any class of its shares, it shall within one month from doing so deliver to the registrar of companies a notice in the prescribed form giving particulars of the name or designation so assigned.

(5)   If a company fails to comply with this section, the company and every officer of it who is in default is liable to a fine and, for continued contravention, to a daily default fine.

129. Registration of newly created class rights

(1)   If a company not having a share capital creates a class of members with rights which are not stated in its memorandum or articles or in a resolution or agreement to which section 380 applies, the company shall deliver to the registrar of companies within one month from the date on which the new class is created a statement in the prescribed form containing particulars of the rights attached to that class.

(2)   If the rights of any class of members of the company are varied otherwise than by an amendment of the memorandum or articles or by a resolution or agreement subject to section 380, the company shall within one month from the date on which the variation is made deliver to the registrar of companies a statement in the prescribed form containing particulars of the variation.

(3)   If a company (otherwise than by any such amendment, resolution or agreement as is mentioned above) assigns a name or other designation, or a new name or other designation, to any class of its members, it shall within one month from doing so deliver to the registrar of companies a notice in the prescribed form giving particulars of the name or designation so assigned.

(4)   If a company fails to comply with this section, the company and every officer

of it who is in default is liable to a fine and, for continued contravention, to a daily default fine.

CHAPTER IV
MEETINGS AND RESOLUTIONS

366. Annual General Meeting

(1)   Every company shall in each year hold a general meeting as its annual general meeting in addition to any other meetings in that year, and shall specify the meeting as such in the notices calling it.

(2)   However, so long as a company holds its first annual general meeting within 18 months of its incorporation, it need not hold it in the year of its incorporation or in the following year.

(3)   Not more than 15 months shall elapse between the date of one annual general meeting and that of the next.

(4)   If default is made in holding a meeting in accordance with this section, the company and every officer of it who is in default shall be liable to a fine.

366A. Election by private company to dispense with annual general meetings

(1)   A private company may elect (by elective resolution in accordance with section 379A) to dispense with the holding of annual general meetings.

(2)   An election has effect for the year in which it is made and subsequent years, but does not affect any liability already incurred by reason of default in holding an annual general meeting.

(3)   In any year in which an annual general meeting would be required to be held but for the election, and in which no such meeting has been held, any member of the company may, by notice to the company not later than three months before the end of the year, require the holding of an annual general meeting in that year.

(4)   If such a notice is given, the provisions of section 366(1) and (4) apply with respect to the calling of the meeting and the consequences of default.

(5)   If the election ceases to have effect, the company is not obliged under section 366 to hold an annual general meeting in that year if, when the election ceases to have effect, less than three months of the year remains. This does not affect any obligation of the company to hold an annual general meeting in that year in pursuance of a notice given under subsection (3).

367. Secretary of State's power to call meeting in default

(1)   If default is made in holding a meeting in accordance with section 366, the Secretary of State may, on the application of any member of the company, call, or direct the calling of, a general meeting of the company and give such ancillary or

consequential directions as he thinks expedient, including directions modifying or supplementing, in relation to the calling, holding and conduct of the meeting, the operation of the company's articles.

(2)   The directions that may be given under subsection (1) include a direction that one member of the company present in person or by proxy shall be deemed to constitute a meeting.

(3)   If default is made in complying with directions of the Secretary of State under subsection (1), the company and every officer of it who is in default is liable to a fine.

(4)   A general meeting held under this section shall, subject to any directions of the Secretary of State, be deemed to be an annual general meeting of the company; but, where a meeting so held is not in the year in which the default in holding the company's annual general meeting occurred, the meeting so held shall not be treated as the annual general meeting for the year in which it is held unless at that meeting the company resolves that it be so treated.

(5)   Where a company so resolves, a copy of the resolution shall within 15 days after its passing, be forwarded to the registrar of companies and recorded by him; and if default is made in complying with this subsection, the company and every officer of it who is in default is liable to a fine and, for continued contravention, to a daily default fine.

368. Extraordinary general meeting on members' request

(1)   The directors of a company shall, on a members' requisition, forthwith proceed duly to convene an extraordinary general meeting of the company.

This applies notwithstanding anything in the company's articles.

(2)   A members' requisition is a requisition of-

(a)   members of the company holding at the date of the deposit of the requisition not less than one-tenth of such of the paid-up capital of the company as at that date carries the right of voting at general meetings of the company; or

(b)   in the case of a company not having a share capital, members of it representing not less than one tenth of the total voting rights of all the members having at the date of deposit of the requisition a right to vote at general meetings.

(3)   The requisition must state the objects of the meeting, and must be signed by the requisitionists and deposited at the registered office of the company, and may consist of several documents in like form each signed by one or more requisitionists.

(4)   If the directors do not within 21 days from the date of deposit of the requisition duly convene a meeting, the requisitionists, or any of them representing more than one half of the total voting rights of all of them, may themselves convene a meeting, but any meeting so convened shall not be held after the expiration of three months from that date.

(5)   A meeting convened under this section by requisitionists shall be convened in the same manner, as nearly as possible, as that in which meetings are to be convened by directors.

(6)   Any reasonable expenses incurred by the requisitionists by reason of the failure of the directors duly to convene a meeting shall be repaid to the requisitionists by the company out of any sums due or to become due from the company by way of fees or other remuneration in respect of their services to such of the directors as were in default.

(7)   In the case of a meeting at which a resolution is to be proposed as a special resolution, the directors are deemed not to have duly convened the meeting if they do not give the notice required for special resolutions by section 378(2).

(8)   The directors are deemed not to have duly convened a meeting if they convene a meeting for a date more than 28 days after the date of the notice convening the meeting.

369. Length of notice for calling meetings

(1)   A provision of a company's articles is void in so far as it provides for the calling of a meeting of the company (other than an adjourned meeting) by a shorter notice than –

(a) in the case of the annual general meeting, 21 days' notice in writing; and
(b) in the case of a meeting other than an annual general meeting or a meeting for the passing of a special resolution –
   (i)   7 days' notice in writing in the case of an unlimited company; and
   (ii) otherwise, 14 days' notice in writing.

(2)   Save in so far as the articles of a company make other provision in that behalf (not being a provision avoided by subsection (1)), a meeting of the company (other than an adjourned meeting) may be called –

(a) in the case of the annual general meeting, 21 days' notice in writing; and
(b) in the case of a meeting other than an annual general meeting or a meeting for the passing of a special resolution –
   (i)   7 days' notice in writing in the case of an unlimited company; and
   (ii) otherwise, 14 days' notice in writing.

(3)   Notwithstanding that a meeting is called by shorter notice than that specified in subsection (2) or in the company's articles (as the case may be), it is deemed to have been duly called if it is so agreed –

(a) in the case of a meeting called as the annual general meeting, by all the members entitled to attend and vote at it; and
(b) otherwise, by the requisite majority.

(4)   The requisite majority for this purpose is a majority in number of the members having a right to attend and vote at the meeting, being a majority –

(a) together holding not less than 95 per cent in nominal value of the shares giving a right to attend and vote at the meeting; or

(b) in the case of a company not having a share capital, together representing not less than 95 per cent of the total voting rights at that meeting of all the members.

A private company may elect (by elective resolution in accordance with section 379A) that the above provisions shall have effect in relation to the company as if for the references to 95 per cent there were substituted references to such lesser percentage, but not less than 90 per cent, as may be specified in the resolution or subsequently determined by the company in general meeting.

370. General provisions as to meetings and votes

(1)   The following provisions have effect in so far as the articles of the company do not make provision in that behalf.

(2)   Notice of the meeting of the company shall be served on every member of it in the manner in which notices are required to be served by Table A (as for the time being in force).

(3)   Two or more members holding not less that one-tenth of the issued share capital or, if the company does not have a share capital, not less than 5 per cent in number of the members of the company may call a meeting.

(4)   Two members personally present are a quorum.

(5)   Any member elected by the members present at the meeting may be chairman of it.

(6)   In the case of a company originally having a share capital, every member has one vote in respect of each share or each £10 of stock held by him; and in any other case every member has one vote.

370A. Quorum at a meeting of the sole member

Notwithstanding any provision to the contrary in the articles of a private company limited by shares or by guarantee having only one member, one member present in person or by proxy shall be a quorum.

371. Power of court to order meeting

(1)   If for any reason it is impracticable to call a meeting of a company in any manner in which meetings of that company may be called, or to conduct the meeting in the manner prescribed by the articles or this Act, the court may either of its own motion or on the application –

(a) of any director of the company, or
(b) of any member of the company who would be entitled to vote at the meeting,

order a meeting to be called, held and conducted in any manner the court thinks fit.

(2)   Where such an order is made, the court may give such ancillary or consequential directions as it thinks expedient; and these may include a direction that

one member of the company present in person or by proxy be deemed to constitute a meeting.

(3)   A meeting called, held and conducted in accordance with an order under subsection (1) is deemed for all purposes a meeting of the company duly called, held and conducted.

372. Proxies

(1)   Any member of a company entitled to attend and vote at a meeting of it is entitled to appoint another person (whether a member or not) as his proxy to attend and vote instead of him; and in the case of a private company a proxy appointed to attend and vote instead of a member has also the same right as the member to speak at the meeting.

(2)   But, unless the articles otherwise provide –

(a) subsection (1) does not apply in the case of a company not having a share capital; and

(b) a member of a private company is not entitled to appoint more than one proxy to attend on the same occasion; and

(c) a proxy is not entitled to vote except on a poll.

(3)   In the case of a company having a share capital, in every notice calling a meeting of the company there shall appear with reasonable prominence a statement that a member entitled to attend and vote is entitled to appoint a proxy or, where that is allowed, one or more proxies to attend and vote instead of him, and that a proxy need not also be a member.

(4)   If default is made in complying with subsection (3) as respects any meeting, every officer of the company who is in default is liable to a fine.

(5)   A provision contained in a company's articles is void in so far as it would have the effect of requiring the instrument appointing a proxy, or any other document necessary to show the validity of, or otherwise relating to, the appointment of a proxy, to be received by the company or any other person more than 48 hours before a meeting or adjourned meeting in order that the appointment may be effective.

(6)   If for the purpose of any meeting of a company invitations to appoint as proxy a person or one of a number of persons specified in the invitations are issued at the company's expense to some only of the members entitled to be sent a notice of the meeting and to vote at it by proxy, then every officer of the company who knowingly and wilfully authorises or permits their issue in that manner is liable to a fine.

However, an officer is not so liable by reason only of the issue to a member at his request in writing of a form of appointment naming the proxy, or of a list of persons willing to act as proxy, if the form or list is available on request in writing to every member entitled to vote at the meeting by proxy.

(7)   This section applies to meetings of any class of members of a company as it applies to general meetings of the company.

373. Right to demand a poll

(1)   A provision contained in a company's articles is void in so far as it would have the effect either –

(a)   of excluding the right to demand a poll at a general meeting on any question other than the election of the chairman of the meeting or the adjournment of the meeting; or

(b)   of making ineffective the demand for a poll on any such question which is made either –

   (i)   by not less than 5 members having the right to vote at the meeting; or

   (ii)   by a member or members representing not less than one-tenth of the total voting rights of all the members having the right to vote at the meeting; or

   (iii)   by a member or members holding shares in the company conferring the right to vote at the meeting, being shares on which an aggregate sum has been paid up equal to not less than one-tenth of the total sum paid up on all the shares conferring that right.

(2)   The instrument appointing a proxy to vote at a meeting of a company is deemed also to confer authority to demand or join in demanding a poll; and for the purposes of subsection (1) a demand by a person as proxy for a member is the same as a demand by a member.

374. Voting on a poll

On a poll taken at a meeting of a company or a meeting of any class of members of a company, a member entitled to more than one vote need not, if he votes, use all his votes or cast all the votes he uses in the same way.

375. Representation of corporations at meetings

(1)   A corporation, whether or not a company within the meaning of this Act, may –

(a)   if it is a member of another corporation, being such a company, by resolution of its directors or other governing body authorise such persons as it thinks fit to act as its representative at any meeting of the company or at any meeting of any class of members of the company;

(b)   if it is a creditor (including a holder of debentures) of another corporation, being such a company, by resolution of its directors or other governing body authorise such persons as it thinks fit to act as its representative at any meeting of creditors of the company held in pursuance of this Act or of rules made under it, or in pursuance of the provisions contained in any debenture or trust deed, as the case may be.

(2)   A person so authorised is entitled to exercise the same powers on behalf of the corporation which he represents as that corporation could exercise if it were an individual shareholder, creditor or debenture-holder of the other company.

376. Circulation of members' resolutions

(1)   Subject to the section next following, it is the duty of a company, on the requisition in writing of such members as is specified below and (unless the company otherwise resolves) at the expense of the requisitionists –

(a)   to give to members of the company entitled to receive notice of the next annual general meeting notice of any resolution which may properly be moved and is entitled to be moved at the meeting;
(b)   to circulate to members entitled to have notice of any general meeting sent to them any statement of not more than 1,000 words with respect to the matter referred to in any proposed resolution or the business to be dealt with at that meeting.

(2)   The number of members necessary for a requisition under subsection (1) is –

(a)   any number of members representing not less than one-twentieth of the total voting rights of all the members having at the date of the requisition a right to vote at the meeting to which the requisition relates; or
(b)   not less than 100 members holding shares in the company on which there has been paid up an average sum, per member, of not less than £100.

(3)   Notice of any such resolution shall be given, and any such statement shall be circulated, to members of the company entitled to have notice of the meeting sent to them, by serving a copy of the resolution or statement on each such member in any manner permitted for service of notice of the meeting.

(4)   Notice of any such resolution shall be given to any other member of the company by giving notice of the general effect of the resolution in any other manner permitted for giving him notice of meetings of the company.

(5)   For compliance with subsections (3) and (4), the copy must be served, or notice to the effect of the resolution be given (as the case may be) in the same manner and (as far as practicable) at the same time as the notice of the meeting; and where it is not practicable for it to be served or given at the same time, it must be served or given as soon as practicable thereafter.

(6)   The business which may be dealt with at an annual general meeting includes any resolution of which notice is given in accordance with this section; and for the purposes of this subsection notice is deemed to have been so given notwithstanding the accidental omission, in giving it, of one or more members. This has effect notwithstanding anything in the company's articles.

(7)   In the event of default in complying with this section, every officer of the company who is in default is liable to a fine.

377. In certain cases, compliance with s. 376 not required

(1)   A company is not bound under section 376 to give notice of a resolution or to circulate a statement unless –

(a) a copy of the requisition signed by the requisitionists (or two or more copies which between them contain the signatures of all the requisitionists) is deposited at the registered office of the company –

   (i)   in the case of a requisition requiring notice of a resolution, not less than 6 weeks before the meeting, and

   (ii)   otherwise, not less than a week before the meeting; and

(b) there is deposited or tendered with the requisition a sum reasonably sufficient to meet the company's expenses in giving effect to it.

(2)   But if, after a copy of a requisition requiring notice of a resolution has been deposited at the company's registered office, an annual general meeting is called for a date 6 weeks or less after the copy has been deposited, the copy (though not deposited within the time required by subsection (1)) is deemed properly deposited for the purposes of that subsection.

(3)   The company is also not bound under section 376 to circulate a statement if, on the application either of the company or of any other person who claims to be aggrieved, the court is satisfied that the rights conferred by that section are being abused to secure needless publicity for defamatory matter; and the court may order the company's costs on such application to be paid in whole or in part by the requisitionists, notwithstanding that they are not parties to the application.

378. Extraordinary and special resolutions

(1)   A resolution is an extraordinary resolution when it has been passed by a majority of not less than three-fourths of such members as (being entitled to do so) vote in person or, where proxies are allowed, by proxy, at a general meeting of which notice specifying the intention to propose the resolution as an extraordinary resolution has been duly given.

(2)   A resolution is a special resolution when it has been passed by such a majority as is required for the passing of an extraordinary resolution and at a general meeting of which not less than 21 days' notice, specifying the intention to propose the resolution as a special resolution, has been duly given.

(3)   If it is so agreed by a majority in number of the members having the right to attend and vote at such a meeting, being a majority –

(a) together holding not less than 95 per cent in nominal value of the shares giving that right; or

(b) in the case of a company not having a share capital, together representing not less than 95 per cent of the total voting rights at that meeting of all the members,

a resolution may be proposed and passed as a special resolution at a meeting of which less than 21 days' notice has been given.

A private company may elect (by elective resolution in accordance with section 379A) that the above provisions shall have effect in relation to the company as if for the references to 95 per cent there were substituted references to such lesser percentage, but not less than 90 per cent, as may be specified in the resolution or subsequently determined by the company in general meeting

(4)   At any meeting at which an extraordinary resolution or a special resolution is submitted to be passed, a declaration by the chairman that the resolution is carried is, unless a poll is demanded, conclusive evidence of the fact without proof of the number or proportion of the votes recorded in favour of or against the resolution.

(5)   In computing the majority on a poll demanded on the question that an extraordinary resolution or a special resolution be passed, reference is to be had to the number of votes cast for and against the resolution.

(6)   For the purposes of this section, notice of a meeting is deemed duly given, and the meeting duly held, when the notice is given and the meeting held in the manner provided by this Act or the company's articles.

379. Resolution requiring special notice

(1)   Where by any provision of this Act special notice is required of a resolution, the resolution is not effective unless notice of the intention to move it has been given to the company at least 28 days before the meeting at which it is moved.

(2)   The company shall give its members notice of any such resolution at the same time and in the same manner as it gives notice of the meeting or, if that is not practicable, shall give them notice either by advertisement in a newspaper having an appropriate circulation or in any other mode allowed by the company's articles, at least 21 days before the meeting.

(3)   If after notice of the intention to move such a resolution has been given to the company, a meeting is called for a date 28 days or less after the notice has been given, the notice is deemed properly given, though not given within the time required.

379A. Elective resolution of private company

(1)   An election by a private company for the purposes of –

(a) section 80A (election as to duration of authority to allot shares),
(b) section 252 (election to dispense with laying of accounts and reports before general meeting),
(c) section 366A (election to dispense with holding annual general meeting),
(d) section 369(4) or 378(3) (election as to majority required to authorise short notice of meetings), or
(e) section 386 (election to dispense with appointment of auditors annually),

shall be made by resolution of the company in general meeting in accordance with this section.

Such a resolution is referred to in this Act as an 'elective resolution'.

(2)   An elective resolution is not effective unless –

(a) at least 21 days' notice in writing is given of the meeting, stating that an elective resolution is to be proposed and stating the terms of that resolution, and

(b) the resolution is agreed to at the meeting, in person or by proxy, by all the members entitled to attend and vote at the meeting.

(2A)   An elective resolution is effective notwithstanding the fact that less than 21 days' notice in writing of the meeting is given if all the members entitled to attend and vote at the meeting so agree.

(3)   The company may revoke an elective resolution by passing an ordinary resolution to that effect.

(4)   An elective resolution shall cease to have effect if the company is registered as a public company.

(5)   An elective resolution may be passed or revoked in accordance with this section, and the provisions referred to in subsection (1) have effect, notwithstanding any contrary provision in the company's articles of association.

380. Registration, etc. of resolutions and agreements

(1)   A copy of every resolution or agreement to which this section applies shall, within 15 days after it is passed or made, be forwarded to the registrar of companies and recorded by him; and must be either a printed copy or else a copy in some other form approved by the registrar.

(2)   Where articles have been registered, a copy of every such resolution or agreement for the time being in force shall be embodied in or annexed to every copy of the articles issued after the passing of the resolution or the making of the agreement.

(3)   Where articles have not been registered, a printed copy of every such resolution or agreement shall be forwarded to any member at his request on payment of 5 pence or such lesser sum as the company may direct.

(4)   This section applies to –

(a)   special resolutions;
(b)   extraordinary resolutions;
(bb) an elective resolution or a resolution revoking such a resolution;
(c)   resolutions or agreements which have been agreed to by all the members of a company but which, if not so agreed to, would not have been effective for their purpose unless (as the case may be) they had been passed as special resolutions or as extraordinary resolutions;
(d)   resolutions or agreements which have been agreed to by all the members of some class of shareholders but which, if not so agreed to, would not have been effective for their purpose unless (as the case may be) they had been passed by some particular majority or otherwise in some particular manner, and all resolutions or agreements which effectively bind all the members of any class of shareholders though not agreed to by all those members.
(e)   a resolution passed by the directors of a company in compliance with a direction under section 31(2) (change of name on Secretary of State's direction);
(f)   a resolution of a company to give, vary, revoke or renew an authority to the directors for the purposes of section 80 (allotment of relevant securities);

(g)   a resolution of the directors passed under section 147(2) (alteration of memorandum on company ceasing to be a public company, following acquisition of its own shares);

(h)   a resolution conferring, varying, revoking or renewing authority under section 166 (market purchase of company's own shares);

(j)   a resolution for voluntary winding up, passed under section 84(1)(a) of the Insolvency Act;

(k)   a resolution passed by the directors of an old public company, under section 2(1) of the Consequential Provisions Act, that the company should be re-registered as a public company;

(l)   a resolution of the directors passed by virtue of regulation 16(2) of the Uncertificated Securities Regulations 1995 (which allow title to a company's shares to be evidenced and transferred without written instrument); and

(m)   a resolution of a company passed by virtue of regulation 16(6) of the Uncertificated Securities Regulations 1995 (which prevents or reverses a resolution of the directors under regulation 16(2) of those Regulations).

(5)   If a company fails to comply with subsection (1), the company and every officer of it who is in default is liable to a fine and, for continued contravention, to a daily default fine.

(6)   If a company fails to comply with subsection (2) or (3), the company and every officer of it who is in default is liable to a fine.

(7)   For the purposes of subsections (5) and (6), a liquidator of a company is deemed an officer of it.

381. Resolution passed at an adjourned meeting

Where a resolution is passed at an adjourned meeting of (a) a company; (b) the holders of any class of shares in a company; (c) the directors of a company; the resolution is for all purposes to be treated as having been passed on the date on which it was in fact passed, and is not to be deemed passed on any earlier date.

381A. Written resolutions of private companies

(1)   Anything which in the case of a private company may be done (a) by resolution of the company in general meeting, or (b) by resolution of a meeting of any class of members of a company, may be done, without a meeting and without previous notice being required, by resolution in writing signed by or on behalf of all the members of the company who at the date of the resolution would be entitled to attend and vote at such a meeting.

(2)   The signatures need not be on a single document provided each is on a document which accurately states the terms of the resolution.

(3)   The date of the resolution means when the resolution is signed by or on behalf of the last member to sign.

(4)   A resolution agreed to in accordance with this section has effect as if passed –

(i) by the company in general meeting, or

(ii) by a meeting of the relevant class of members of the company,

as the case may be; and any reference in any enactment to a meeting at which a resolution is passed or to members voting in favour of a resolution shall be construed accordingly.

(5)   Any reference in any enactment to the date of passing of a resolution is, in relation to a resolution agreed in accordance with this section, a reference to the date of the resolution.

(6)   A resolution may be agreed to in accordance with this section which would otherwise be required to be passed as a special, extraordinary or elective resolution; and any reference in any enactment to a special, extraordinary or elective resolution includes such a resolution.

(7)   This section has effect subject to the exceptions specified in Part I of Schedule 15A; and in relation to certain descriptions of resolutions under this section the procedural requirements of this Act have effect with the adaptations specified in Part II of that Schedule.

381B. Duty to notify auditors of proposed written resolution

(1)   If a director or secretary of a company –

(a) knows that it is proposed to seek agreement to a resolution in accordance with section 381A, and

(b) knows the terms of the resolution,

he shall, if the company has auditors, secure that a copy of the resolution is sent to them or that they are otherwise notified of its contents, at or before the time the resolution is supplied to a member for signature.

(2)   A person who fails to comply with subsection (1) is liable to a fine.

(3)   In any proceedings for an offence under this section it is a defence for the accused to prove –

(a) that the circumstances were such that it was not practicable for him to comply with subsection (1), or

(b) that he believed on reasonable grounds that a copy of the resolution had been sent to the company's auditors or that they had otherwise been informed of its contents.

(4)   Nothing in this section affects the validity of any resolution.

381C. Written resolutions: supplementary provisions

(1)   Sections 381A and 381B have effect notwithstanding any provision of the company's memorandum or articles, but do not prejudice any power conferred by any such provision.

(2)   Nothing in those sections affects any enactment or rule of law as to –

(a) things done otherwise than by passing a resolution, or
(b) cases in which a resolution is treated as having been passed, or a person is precluded from alleging that a resolution has not been duly passed.

382. Minutes of meetings

(1)   Every company shall cause minutes of all proceedings of general meetings, all proceedings at meetings of its directors and, where there are managers, all proceedings at meetings of its managers to be entered in books kept for that purpose.

(2)   Any such minute, if purporting to be signed by the chairman of the meeting at which the proceedings were had, or by the chairman of the next succeeding meeting, is evidence of the proceedings.

(3)   Where a shadow director by means of a notice required by section 317(8) declares an interest in a contract or a proposed contract, this section applies –

(a) if it is a specific notice under paragraph (a) of that subsection, as if the declaration had been made at the meeting there referred to, and
(b) otherwise, as if it had been made at the meeting of directors next following the giving of the notice;

and the making of the declaration is in either case deemed to form part of the proceedings at the meeting.

(4)   Where minutes have been made in accordance with this section of the proceedings at any general meeting of the company or meeting of directors or managers, the, until the contrary is proved, the meeting is deemed duly held and convened, and all proceedings had at the meeting to have been duly had; and all appointments of directors, managers or liquidators are deemed valid.

(5)   If a company fails to comply with subsection (1), the company and every officer of it who is in default is liable to a fine and, for continued contravention, to a daily default fine.

383. Inspection of minute books

(1)   The books containing the minutes of proceedings of any general meeting of a company held on or after 1st November 1929 shall be kept at the company's registered office, and . . . be open to the inspection of any member without charge.

(2)   . . .

(3)   Any member shall be entitled [on payment of such fee as may be prescribed] to be furnished, within 7 days after he has made a request in that behalf to the company, with a copy of any such minutes as are referred to above . . .

(4)   If an inspection required under this section is refused or if a copy required under this section is not sent within the proper time, the company and every officer of it who is in default is liable in respect of each offence to a fine.

(5)   In the case of any such refusal or default, the court may by order compel an immediate inspection of the books in respect of all proceedings of general meetings, or direct that copies required be sent to the persons requiring them.

CHAPTER V

AUDITORS

Appointment of auditors

384. Duty to appoint auditors

(1)   Every company shall appoint an auditor or auditors in accordance with this Chapter.

This is subject to section 388A (certain companies exempt from obligation to appoint auditors).

(2)   Auditors shall be appointed in accordance with section 385 (appointment at general meeting at which accounts are laid), except in the case of a private company which has elected to dispense with the laying of accounts, in which case the appointment shall be made in accordance with section 385A.

(3)   References in this Chapter to the end of the time for appointing auditors are to the end of the time within which an appointment must be made under section 385(2) or 385A(2), according to whichever of those sections applies.

(4)   Sections 385 and 385A have effect subject to section 386 under which a private company may elect to dispense with the obligation to appoint auditors annually.

385. Appointment at general meeting at which accounts laid

(1)   This section applies to every public company and to a private company which has not elected to dispense with the laying of accounts.

(2)   The company shall, at each general meeting at which accounts are laid, appoint an auditor or auditors to hold office from the conclusion of that meeting until the conclusion of the next general meeting at which accounts are laid.

(3)   The first auditors of the company may be appointed by the directors at any time before the first general meeting of the company at which accounts are laid; and auditors so appointed shall hold office until the conclusion of that meeting.

(4)   If the directors fail to exercise their powers under subsection (3), the powers may be exercised by the company in general meeting.

385A. Appointment by private company which is not obliged to lay accounts

(1)   This section applies to a private company which has elected in accordance with section 252 to dispense with the laying of accounts before the company in general meeting.

(2)   Auditors shall be appointed by the company in general meeting before the end of the period of 28 days beginning with the day on which copies of the company's annual accounts for the previous year are sent to members under section 238 or, if notice is given under section 253(2) requiring the laying of the accounts before the company in general meeting, the conclusion of that meeting.

Auditors so appointed shall hold office from the end of that period or, as the case may be, the conclusion of that meeting until the end of the time for appointing auditors for the next financial year.

(3)   The first auditors of the company may be appointed by the directors at any time before –

(a) the end of the period of 28 days beginning with the day on which copies of the company's first annual accounts are sent to members under section 238, or

(b) if notice is given under section 253(2) requiring the laying of the accounts before the company in general meeting, the beginning of that meeting;

and auditors so appointed shall hold office until the end of that period or, as the case may be, the conclusion of that meeting.

(4)   If the directors fail to exercise their powers under subsection (3), the powers may be exercised by the company in general meeting.

(5)   Auditors holding office when the election is made shall, unless the company in general meeting determines otherwise, continue to hold office until the end of the time for appointing auditors for the next financial year; and auditors holding office when an election ceases to have effect shall continue to hold office until the conclusion of the next general meeting of the company at which accounts are laid.

386. Election by private company to dispense with annual appointment

(1)   A private company may elect (by elective resolution in accordance with section 379A) to dispense with the obligation to appoint auditors annually.

(2)   When such a resolution is in force the company's auditors shall be deemed to be re-appointed for each succeeding financial year on the expiry of the time for appointing auditors for that year, unless –

(a) a resolution has been passed under section 250 by virtue of which the company is exempt from the obligation to appoint auditors, or

(b) a resolution has been passed under section 393 to the effect that their appointment should be brought to an end.

(3)   If the election ceases to be in force, the auditors then holding office shall continue to hold office –

(a) where section 385 then applies, until the conclusion of the next general meeting of the company at which accounts are laid;

(b) where section 385A then applies, until the end of the time for appointing auditors for the next financial year under that section.

(4)   No account shall be taken of any loss of the opportunity of further deemed re-appointment under this section in ascertaining the amount of any compensation or damages payable to an auditor on his ceasing to hold office for any reason.

387. Appointment by Secretary of State in default of appointment by company

(1) If in any case no auditors are appointed, re-appointed or deemed to be re-appointed before the end of the time for appointing auditors, the Secretary of State may appoint a person to fill the vacancy.

(2)   In such a case the company shall within one week of the end of the time for appointing auditors give notice to the Secretary of State of his power having become exercisable.

If a company fails to give the notice required by this subsection, the company and every officer of it who is in default is guilty of an offence and liable to a fine and, for continued contravention, to a daily default fine.

388. Filling of casual vacancies

(1)   The directors, or the company in general meeting, may fill a casual vacancy in the office of auditor.

(2)   While such a vacancy continues, any surviving or continuing auditor or auditors may continue to act.

(3)   Special notice is required for a resolution at a general meeting of a company –
(a) filling a casual vacancy in the office of auditor, or
(b) re-appointing as auditor a retiring auditor who was appointed by the directors to fill a casual vacancy.

(4)   On receipt of notice of such an intended resolution the company shall forthwith send a copy of it –
(a) to the person proposed to be appointed, and
(b) if the casual vacancy was caused by the resignation of an auditor, to the auditor who resigned.

388A. Dormant company exempt from obligation to appoint auditors

(1)   A company which by virtue of section 249A (certain categories of small company) or section 250 (dormant companies) is exempt from the provisions of Part VII relating to the audit of accounts is also exempt from the obligation to appoint auditors.

(2)   The following provisions apply if a company which has been exempt from those provisions ceases to be exempt.

(3)   Where section 385 applies (appointment at general meeting at which accounts are laid), the directors may appoint auditors at any time before the next meeting of the company at which accounts are to be laid; and auditors so appointed shall hold office until the conclusion of that meeting.

(4)   Where section 385A applies (appointment by private company not obliged to lay accounts, the directors may appoint auditors at any time before –
(a) the end of the period of 28 days beginning on the day on which copies of the company's annual accounts are next sent to members under section 238, or
(b) if notice is given under section 253(2) requiring the laying of the accounts before the company in general meeting, the beginning of the meeting;
and auditors so appointed shall hold office until the end of that period or, as the case may be, the conclusion of that meeting.

(5)   If the directors fail to exercise their powers under subsection (3) or (4), the powers may be exercised by the company in general meeting.

390.   Right to attend company meetings, &c

(1)   A company's auditors are entitled –

(a)   to receive notices of, and all other communications relating to, any general meeting which a member of the company is entitled to receive;
(b)   to attend any general meeting of the company; and
(c)   to be heard at any general meeting which they attend on any part of the business of the meeting which concerns them as auditors.

(2)   In relation to a written resolution proposed to be agreed to by a private company in accordance with section 381A, the company's auditors are entitled –

(a)   to receive all such communications relating to the resolution as, by virtue of any provision of Schedule 15A, are required to be supplied to a member of the company.

(3)   The right to attend or be heard at a meeting is exercisable in the case of a body corporate or partnership by an individual authorised by it in writing to act as its representative at the meeting.

390A.   Remuneration of auditors

(1)   The remuneration of auditors appointed by the company in general meeting shall be fixed by the company in general meeting or in such manner as the company in general meeting may determine.

(2)   The remuneration of auditors appointed by the directors or the Secretary of State shall be fixed by the directors or the Secretary of State, as the case may be.

PART XXV

MISCELLANEOUS AND SUPPLEMENTARY PROVISIONS

722.   Form of company registers, etc.

(1)   Any register, index, minute book or accounting records required by the Companies Acts to be kept by a company may be kept either by making entries in bound books or by recording the matters in question in any other manner.

(2)   Where any such register, index, minute book or accounting record is not kept by making entries in a bound book, but by some other means, adequate precautions shall be taken for guarding against falsification and facilitating its discovery.

(3)   If default is made in complying with subsection (2), the company and every officer of it who is in default is liable to a fine and, for continued contravention, to a daily default fine.

723. Use of computers for company records

(1)   The power conferred on a company by section 722(1) to keep a register or other record by recording the matters in question otherwise than by making entries in bound books includes the power to keep the register or other record by recording those matters otherwise than in a legible form, so long as the recording is capable of being reproduced in a legible form.

(2)   Any provision of an instrument made by a company before 12th February 1979 which requires a register of holders of the company's debentures to be kept in legible form is to be read as requiring the register to be kept in a legible or non-legible form.

(3)   If any such register or other record of the company as is mentioned in section 722(1), or a register of holders of company debentures, is kept by the company by recording the matters in question otherwise than in a legible form, any duty imposed on the company by this Act to allow inspection of, or to furnish a copy of, the register or other record or any part of it is to be treated as a duty to allow inspection of, or to furnish, a reproduction of the recording or of the relevant part of it in a legible form.

(4)   The Secretary of State may by regulations in a statutory instrument make such provision in addition to subsection (3) as he considers appropriate in connection with such registers or other records as are mentioned in that subsection, and are kept as so mentioned; and the regulations may make modifications of provisions of this Act relating to such registers or other records.

(5)   A statutory instrument under subsection (4) is subject to annulment in pursuance of a resolution of either House of Parliament.

SCHEDULE 15A

Section 381A(7)

WRITTEN RESOLUTIONS OF PRIVATE COMPANIES

PART I

EXCEPTIONS

1. Section 381A does not apply to –

(a) a resolution under section 303 removing a director before the expiration of his period of office, or

(b) a resolution under section 391 removing an auditor before the expiration of his term of office.

PART II

ADAPTATION OF PROCEDURAL REQUIREMENTS

Introductory

2.–(1)   In this Part of this schedule (which adapts certain requirements of this Act in relation to proceedings under section 381A) –

(a) a 'written resolution' means a resolution agreed to, or proposed to be agreed to, in accordance with that section, and

(b) a 'relevant member' means a member by whom, or on whose behalf, the resolution is required to be signed in accordance with that section.

(2)   A written resolution is not effective if any of the requirements of this Part of this Schedule is not complied with.

Section 95 (disapplication of pre-emption rights)

3.–(1)   The following adaptations have effect in relation to a written resolution under section 95(2) (disapplication of pre-emption rights), or renewing a resolution under that provision.

(2)   So much of section 95(5) as requires the circulation of a written statement by the directors with a notice of meeting does not apply, but such a statement must be supplied to him for signature.

(3)   Section 95(6) (offences) applies in relation to the inclusion in any such statement of matter which is misleading, false or deceptive in a material particular.

Section 155 (financial assistance for purchase of company's own shares or those of holding company)

4.   In relation to a written resolution giving approval under section 155(4) or (5) (financial assistance for purchase of company's own shares or those of holding company), section 157(4)(a) (documents to be available at meeting) does not apply, but the documents referred to in that provision must be supplied to each relevant member at or before the time at which the resolution is supplied to him for signature.

Sections 164, 165 and 167 (authority for off-market purchase or contingent purchase contract of company's own shares)

5.–(1)   The following adaptations have effect in relation to a written resolution –

(a)   conferring authority to make an off-market purchase of the company's own shares under section 164(2),

(b)   conferring authority to vary a contract for an off-market purchase of the company's own shares under section 164(7), or

(c)   varying, revoking or renewing any such authority under section 164(3).

(2)   Section 164(5) (resolution ineffective if passed by exercise of voting rights by member holding shares to which the resolution relates) does not apply; but for the purposes of section 381A(1) a member holding shares to which the resolution relates shall not be regarded as a member who would be entitled to attend and vote.

(3)   Section 164(6) (documents to be available at the company's registered office and at meeting) does not apply, but the documents referred to in that provision and, where that provision applies by virtue of section 164(7), the further documents referred to in that provision must be supplied to each relevant member at or before the time at which the resolution is supplied to him for signature.

(4)   The above adaptations also have effect in relation to a written resolution in relation to which the provisions of section 164(3) to (7) apply by virtue of –

(a)   section 165(2) (authority for contingent purchase contract), or

(b)   section 167(2) (approval of release of rights under contract approved under section 164 or 165).

Section 173 (approval for payment out of capital)

6.–(1)   The following adaptations have effect in relation to a written resolution giving approval under section 173(2) (redemption or purchase of company's own shares out of capital).

(2)   Section 174(2) (resolution ineffective if passed by exercise of voting rights by member holding shares to which resolution relates) does not apply; but for the purposes of section 381A(1) a member holding shares to which the resolution relates shall not be regarded as a member who would be entitled to attend and vote.

(3)   Section 174(4) documents to be available at meeting) does not apply, but the documents referred to in that provision must be supplied to each relevant member at or before the time at which the resolution is supplied to him for signature.

Section 319 (approval of director's service contracts)

7.   In relation to a written resolution approving any such term as is mentioned in section 319(1) (director's contract of employment for more than five years), section 319(5) (documents to be made available at company's registered office and at meeting) does not apply, but the documents referred to in that provision must be supplied to each relevant member at or before the time at which the resolution is supplied to him for signature.

Section 337 (funding of director's expenditure in performing duties)

8.   In relation to a written resolution giving approval under section 337(3)(a) (funding a director's expenditure in performing his duties), the requirement of that provision that certain matters be disclosed at the meeting at which the resolution is passed does not apply, but those matters must be disclosed to each relevant member at or before the time at which the resolution is supplied to him for signature.

Companies Act 1985 Table A

TABLE A

REGULATIONS FOR MANAGEMENT OF A COMPANY LIMITED BY SHARES

INTERPRETATION

1. In these regulations –

"the Act" means the Companies Act 1985 including any statutory modification or re-enactment thereof for the time being in force.
"the articles" means the articles of the company.
"clear days" in relation to the period of notice means that period excluding the day when the notice is given or deemed to be given and the day for which it is given or on which it is to take effect.
"executed" includes any mode of execution.
"office" means the registered office of the company.
"the holder" in relation to shares means the member whose name is entered in the register of members as the holder of the shares.
"the seal" means the common seal of the company.
"secretary" means the secretary of the company or any person appointed to perform the duties of the secretary of the company, including a joint, assistant or deputy secretary.
"the United Kingdom" means Great Britain and Northern Ireland.

Unless the context otherwise requires, words or expressions contained in these regulations bear the same meaning as in the Act but excluding any statutory modification thereof not in force when these regulations become binding on the company.

SHARE CAPITAL

2. Subject to the provisions of the Act and without prejudice to the rights attached to any existing shares, any share may be issued with such rights or restrictions as the company may by ordinary resolution determine.

3. Subject to the provisions of the Act, shares may be issued which are to be redeemed or are to be held liable to be redeemed at the option of the company or the holder on such terms and in such manner as may be provided by the articles.

4. The company may exercise the powers of paying commissions conferred by the Act. Subject to the provisions of the Act, any such commissions may be satisfied by the payment of cash or by the allotment of fully or partly paid shares or partly in one way and partly in the other.

5. Except as required by law, no person shall be recognised by the company as holding a share upon any trust and (except as otherwise provided by the articles or by law) the company shall not be bound by or recognise any interest in any share except an absolute right to the entirety thereof in the holder.

SHARE CERTIFICATES

6. Every member, upon becoming the holder of any shares, shall be entitled without payment to one certificate for all the shares of each class held by him (and, upon transferring part of his holding of shares of any class, to a certificate for the balance of such holding) or several certificates each for one or more of his shares upon payment for every certificate after the first of such reasonable sum as the directors may determine. Every certificate shall be sealed with the seal and shall specify the number, class and respective amounts paid thereon. The company shall not be bound to issue more than one certificate for shares held jointly by several persons and delivery of a certificate to one joint holder shall be sufficient delivery to all of them.

7. If a share certificate is defaced, worn-out, lost or destroyed, it may be renewed on such terms (if any) as to evidence and indemnity and payment of the expenses reasonably incurred by the company in investigating evidence as the directors may determine but otherwise free of charge, and (in the case of defacement or wearing-out) on delivery up of the old certificate.

LIEN

8. The company shall have a first and paramount lien on every share (not being a fully paid share) for all moneys (whether presently payable or not) payable at a fixed time or called in respect of that share. The directors may at any time declare any share to be wholly or in part exempt from the provisions of this regulation. The company's lien on a share shall extend to any amount payable in respect of it.

9. The company may sell in such manner as the directors determine any shares on which the company has a lien if a sum in respect of which the lien exists is presently payable and is not paid within fourteen clear days after notice has been given to the holder of the share or to the person entitled to it in consequence of the death or bankruptcy of the holder, demanding payment and stating that if the notice is not complied with the shares may be sold.

10.   To give effect to a sale the directors may authorise some person to execute an instrument of transfer of the shares sold to, or in accordance with the directions of, the purchaser. The title of the transferee to the shares shall not be affected by any irregularity in or invalidity of the proceedings in reference to the sale.

11.   The net proceeds of the sale, after payment of the costs, shall be applied in payment of so much of the sum for which the lien exists as is presently payable, and any residue shall (upon surrender to the company for cancellation of the certificate for the shares sold and subject to a like lien for any moneys not presently payable as existed upon the shares before the sale) be paid to the person entitled to the shares at the date of the sale.

CALLS ON SHARES AND FORFEITURE

12.   Subject to the terms of allotment, the directors may make calls upon the members in respect of any moneys unpaid on their shares (whether in respect of nominal value or premium) and each member shall (subject to receiving at least fourteen clear days' notice specifying when and where payment is to be made) pay to the company as required by the notice the amount called on his shares. A call may be required to be paid by instalments. A call may, before receipt by the company of any sum due thereunder, be revoked in whole or part and payment of a call may be postponed in whole or part. A person upon whom a call is made shall remain liable for calls made upon him notwithstanding the subsequent transfer of the shares in respect whereof the call was made.

13.   A call shall be deemed to have been made at the time when the resolution of the directors authorising the call was passed.

14.   The joint holders of a share shall be jointly and severally liable to pay all calls in respect thereof.

15.   If a call remains unpaid after it has become due and payable the person from whom it is due and payable shall pay interest on the amount unpaid from the day it became due and payable until it is paid at the rate fixed by the terms of allotment of the share or in the notice of the call or, if no rate is fixed, at the appropriate rate (as defined by the Act) but the directors may waive payment of the interest wholly or in part.

16.   An amount payable in respect of a share on allotment or at any fixed date, whether in respect of nominal value or premium or as an instalment of a call, shall be deemed to be a call and if it is not paid the provisions of the articles shall apply as if the amount had become due and payable by virtue of a call.

17.   Subject to the terms of allotment, the directors may make arrangements on the issue of shares for a difference between the holders in the amounts and times of payment of calls on their shares.

18.   If a call remains unpaid after it has become due and payable the directors may give to the person from whom it is due not less than fourteen clear days' notice

requiring payment of the amount unpaid together with any interest which may have accrued. The notice shall name the place where payment is to be made and shall state that if the notice is not complied with the shares in respect of which the call was made will be liable to be forfeited.

19.   If the notice is not complied with any share in respect of which it was given may, before the payment required by the notice has been made, be forfeited by a resolution of the directors and the forfeiture shall include all dividends or other moneys payable in respect of the forfeited shares and not paid before the forfeiture.

20.   Subject to the provisions of the Act, a forfeited share may be sold, re-allotted or otherwise disposed of on such terms and in such manner as the directors determine either to the person who was before the forfeiture the holder or to any other person and at any time before sale, re-allotment or other disposition, the forfeiture may be cancelled on such terms as the directors think fit. Where for the purposes of its disposal a forfeited share is to be transferred to any person the directors may authorise some person to execute an instrument of transfer of the shares to that person.

21.   A person any of whose shares have been forfeited shall cease to be a member in respect of them and shall surrender to the company for cancellation the certificate for the shares forfeited but shall remain liable to the company for all moneys which at the date of forfeiture were presently payable by him to the company in respect of those shares with interest at the rate at which interest was payable on those moneys before the forfeiture or, if no interest was so payable, at the appropriate rate (as defined by the Act) from the date of forfeiture until payment but the directors may waive payment wholly or in part or enforce payment without any allowance for the value of the shares at the time of forfeiture or for any consideration received on their disposal.

22.   A statutory declaration by a director or the secretary that a share has been forfeited on a specified date shall be conclusive evidence of the facts stated in it as against all persons claiming to be entitled to the share and the declaration shall (subject to the execution of an instrument of transfer if necessary) constitute a good title to the share and the person to whom the share is disposed of shall not be bound to see to the application of the consideration, if any, nor shall his title to the share be affected by any irregularity in or invalidity of the proceedings in reference to the forfeiture or disposal of the share.

TRANSFER OF SHARES

23.   The instrument of transfer of a share may be in any usual form or in any other form which the directors may approve and shall be executed by or on behalf of the transferor and, unless the share is fully paid, by or on behalf of the transferee.

24.   The directors may refuse to register the transfer of a share which is not fully paid to a person of whom they do not approve and they may refuse to register the transfer of a share on which the company has a lien. They may also refuse to register a transfer unless –

(a)   it is lodged at the office or at such other place as the directors may appoint and is accompanied by the certificate for the shares to which it relates and such other evidence as the directors may reasonably require to show the right of the transferor to make the transfer;

(b) it is in respect of only one class of shares; and

(c) it is in favour of not more than four transferees.

25.   If the directors refuse to register a transfer of a share, they shall within two months after the date on which the transfer was lodged with the company send to the transferee notice of the refusal.

26.   The registration of transfers of shares or of transfers of any class of shares may be suspended at such times and for such periods (not exceeding thirty days in any year) as the directors may determine.

27.   No fee shall be charged for the registration of any instrument of transfer or other document relating to or affecting the title to any share.

28.   The company shall be entitled to retain any instrument of transfer which is registered, but any instrument of transfer which the directors refuse to register shall be returned to the person lodging it when notice of the refusal is given.

TRANSMISSION OF SHARES

29.   If a member dies the survivor or survivors where he was a joint holder, and his personal representatives where he was a sole holder or the only survivor of joint holders, shall be the persons recognised by the company as having any title to his interest; but nothing herein contained shall release the estate of a deceased member from any liability in respect of any share which had been jointly held by him.

30.   A person becoming entitled to a share in consequence of the death or bankruptcy of a member may, upon such evidence being produced as the directors may properly require, elect either to become the holder of the share or to have some other person nominated by him registered as the transferee. If he elects to become the holder he shall give notice to the company to that effect. If he elects to have another person registered he shall execute an instrument of transfer of the share to that person. All the articles relating o the transfer of shares shall apply to the notice or instrument of transfer as if it were an instrument of transfer executed by the member and the death or bankruptcy of the member had not occurred.

31.   A person becoming entitled to a share in consequence of the death or bankruptcy of a member shall have the rights to which he would be entitled if he were the holder of the share, except that he shall not, before being registered as the holder of the share, be entitled in respect of it to attend or vote at any meeting of the company or at any separate meeting of the holders of any class of shares in the company.

ALTERATION OF SHARE CAPITAL

32. The company may by ordinary resolution –

(a) increase its share capital by new shares of such amount as the resolution prescribes;

(b) consolidate and divide all or any of its share capital into shares of larger amount than its existing shares;

(c) subject to the provisions of the Act, sub-divide its shares, or any of them, into shares of smaller amount and the resolution may determine that, as between the shares resulting from the sub-division, any of them may have any preference or advantage as compared with the others; and

(d) cancel shares which, at the date of the passing of the resolution, have not been taken or agreed to be taken by any person and diminish the amount of its share capital by the amount of the shares so cancelled.

33. Whenever as a result of a consolidation of shares any members would become entitled to fractions of a share, the directors may, on behalf of those members, sell the shares representing the fractions for the best price reasonably obtainable to any person (including, subject to the provisions of the Act, the company) and distribute the net proceeds of sale in due proportion among those members, and the directors may authorise some person to execute an instrument of transfer of the shares to, or in accordance with the directions of, the purchaser. The transferee shall not be bound to see to the application of the purchase money nor shall his title to the shares be affected by any irregularity in or invalidity of the proceedings in reference to the sale.

34. Subject to the provisions of the Act, the company may by special resolution reduce its share capital, any capital redemption reserve and any share premium account in any way.

PURCHASE OF OWN SHARES

35. Subject to the provisions of the Act, the company may purchase its own shares (including any redeemable shares) and, if it is a private company, make a payment in respect of the redemption or purchase of its own shares otherwise than out of distributable profits of the company or the proceeds of a fresh issue of shares.

GENERAL MEETINGS

36. All general meetings other than annual general meetings shall be called extraordinary general meetings.

37. The directors may call general meetings and, on the requisition of members pursuant to the provisions of the Act, shall forthwith proceed to convene an extraordinary general meeting for a date not later than eight weeks after receipt of the requisition. If there are not within the United Kingdom sufficient directors to call a general meeting, any director or any member of the company may call a general meeting.

NOTICE OF GENERAL MEETINGS

38. An annual general meeting and an extraordinary general meeting called for the passing of a special resolution or a resolution appointing a person as a director shall be called by at least twenty-one clear days' notice. All other extraordinary general meetings shall be called by at least fourteen clear days' notice but a general meeting may be called by shorter notice if it is so agreed –

(a)   in the case of an annual general meeting, by all the members entitled to attend and vote thereat; and

(b)   in the case of any other meeting by a majority in number of the members having a right to attend and vote being a majority together holding not less than ninety-five per cent in the nominal value of the shares giving that right.

The notice shall specify the time and place of the meeting and the general nature of the business to be transacted and, in the case of an annual general meeting, shall specify the meeting as such.

Subject to the provisions of the articles and to any restriction imposed on any shares, the notice shall be given to all members, to all person entitled to a share in consequence of the death or bankruptcy of a member and to the directors and auditors.

39.   The accidental omission to give notice of a meeting to, or the non-receipt of notice of a meeting by, any person entitled to receive notice shall not invalidate the proceedings at that meeting.

PROCEEDINGS AT GENERAL MEETINGS

40.   No business shall be transacted at any meeting unless a quorum is present. Two persons entitled to vote upon the business to be transacted, each being a member or a proxy for a member or a duly authorised representative of a corporation, shall be a quorum.

41.   If such a quorum is not present within half an hour from the time appointed for the meeting, or if during a meeting such a quorum ceases to be present, the meeting shall stand adjourned to the same day in the next week at the same time and place or to such time and place as the directors may determine.

42.   The chairman, if any, of the board of directors or in his absence some other director nominated by the directors shall preside as chairman of the meeting, but if neither the chairman nor any such other director (if any) be present within fifteen minutes after the time appointed for holding the meeting and willing to act, the directors present shall elect one of their number to be chairman and, if there is only one director present and willing to act, he shall be chairman.

43.   If no director is willing to act as chairman, or if no director is present within fifteen minutes after the time appointed for holding the meeting, the members present and entitled to vote shall choose one of their number to be chairman.

44.   A director shall, notwithstanding that he is not a member, be entitled to attend and speak at any general meeting and at any separate meeting of the holders of any class of shares in the company.

45.   The chairman may, with the consent of a meeting at which a quorum is present (and shall if so directed by the meeting), adjourn the meeting from time to time and from place to place, but no business shall be transacted at an adjourned meeting other than that business which might properly have been transacted at the meeting had the adjournment not taken place. When a meeting is adjourned for fourteen days or more, at least seven days' notice shall be given specifying the time and place of the adjourned meeting and the general nature of the business to be transacted. Otherwise it shall not be necessary to give any such notice.

46.   A resolution put to the vote of a meeting shall be decided on a show of hands unless before, or on the declaration of the result of, the show of hands a poll is duly demanded. Subject to the provisions of the Act, a poll may be demanded –

(a)   by the chairman; or

(b)   by at least two members having the right to vote at the meeting; or

(c)   by a member or members representing not less than one-tenth of the total voting rights of all the members having the right to vote at the meeting; or

(d)   by a member or members holding shares conferring a right to vote at the meeting being shares on which an aggregate sum has been paid up equal to not less than one-tenth of the total sum paid up on all the shares conferring that right;

and a demand by a person as proxy for a member shall be the same as a demand by the member.

47.   Unless a poll is duly demanded a declaration by the chairman that a resolution has been carried unanimously, or by a particular majority, or lost, or not carried by a particular majority and an entry to that effect in the minutes of the meeting shall be conclusive evidence of the fact without proof of the number or proportion of the votes recorded in favour or against the resolution.

48.   The demand for a poll may, before the poll is taken, be withdrawn but only with the consent of the chairman and a demand so withdrawn shall not be taken to have invalidated the result of a show of hands declared before the demand was made.

49.   A poll shall be taken as the chairman directs and he may appoint scrutineers (who need not be members) and fix a time and place for declaring the result of the poll. The result of the poll shall be deemed to be the resolution of the meeting at which the poll was demanded.

50.   In the case of an equality of votes, whether on a show of hands or on a poll, the chairman shall be entitled to a casting vote in addition to any other vote he may have.

51.   A poll demanded on the election of a chairman or on a question of adjournment shall be taken forthwith. A poll demanded on any other question shall be taken either forthwith or at such time and place as the chairman directs not being more than thirty days after the poll is demanded. The demand for a poll shall not prevent the continuance of a meeting for the transaction of any business other than the question on which the poll was demanded. If a poll is demanded before the declaration of the result of a show of hands and the demand is duly withdrawn, the meeting shall continue as if the demand had not been made.

52.   No notice need be given of a poll not taken forthwith if the time and place at which it is to be taken are announced at the meeting at which it is demanded. In any other case at least seven clear days' notice shall be given specifying the time and place at which the poll is to be taken.

53.   A resolution in writing executed by or on behalf of each member who would have been entitled to vote upon it if it had been proposed at a general meeting at which he was present shall be as effectual as if it had been passed at a general meeting duly convened and held and may consist of several instruments in the like form executed by or on behalf of one or more members.

VOTES OF MEMBERS

54.   Subject to any rights or restrictions attached to any shares, on a show of hands every member who (being an individual) is present in person or (being a corporation) present by a duly authorised representative, not being himself a member entitled to vote, shall have one vote and on a poll every member shall have one vote for every share of which he is the holder.

55.   In the case of joint holders the vote of the senior who tenders a vote, whether in person or by proxy, shall be accepted to the exclusion of the votes of the other joint holders; and seniority shall be determined by the order in which the names of the holders stand in the register of members.

56.   A member in respect of whom an order has been made by any court having jurisdiction (whether in the UK or elsewhere) in matters concerning mental disorder may vote, whether on a show of hands or on a poll, by his receiver, curator bonis or other person authorised in that behalf appointed by that court, and any such receiver, curator bonis or other person may, on a poll, vote by proxy. Evidence to the satisfaction of the directors of the authority of the person claiming to exercise the right to vote shall be deposited at the office, or at such other place as is specified in accordance with the articles for the deposit of instruments of proxy, not less than 48 hours before the time appointed for holding the meeting or adjourned meeting at which the right to vote is to be exercised and in default the right to vote shall not be exercisable.

57.   No member shall vote at any general meeting or at any separate meeting of the holders of any class of shares in the company, either in person or by proxy, in respect of any share held by him unless all moneys presently payable by him in respect of that share have been paid.

58.   No objection shall be raised to the qualification of any voter except at the meeting or adjourned meeting at which the vote objected to is tendered, and every vote not disallowed at the meeting shall be valid. Any objection made in due time shall be referred to the chairman whose decision shall be final and conclusive.

59.   On a poll votes may be given either personally or by proxy. A member may appoint more than one proxy to attend on the same occasion.

60.   An instrument appointing a proxy shall be in writing, executed by or on behalf of the appointor and shall be in the following form (or in a form as near thereto as circumstances allow or in any other form which is usual or which the directors may approve) –

"   PLC/Limited

  I/We,   , of   , being a member/members of the above-named company, hereby appoint   of

, or failing him,   of   , as my/our proxy to
vote in my/our name[s] and on my/our behalf at the annual/extraordinary general
meeting of the company to be held on   19   , and at any adjournment
thereof.
Signed on   19   ."

61.   Where it is desired to afford members an opportunity of instructing the proxy
how he shall act the instrument appointing a proxy shall be in the following form (or
in a form as near thereto as circumstances allow or in any other form which is usual or
which the directors may approve) –

"   PLC/Limited
I/We,   , of   , being a member/members
of the above-named company, hereby appoint   of
, or failing him,   of   , as my/our proxy to
vote in my/our name[s] and on my/our behalf at the annual/extraordinary general
meeting of the company to be held on   19   , and at any adjournment
thereof.

This form is to be used in respect of the resolutions mentioned below as follows:
Resolution No. 1 *for *against
Resolution No. 2 *for *against.
*Strike out whichever is not desired.

Unless otherwise instructed, the proxy may vote as he thinks fit or abstain from voting.
Signed this   day of   19   ."

62.   The instrument appointing a proxy and any authority under which it is
executed or a copy of such authority certified notarially or in some other way approved
by the directors may –

(a) be deposited at the office or such other place within the United Kingdom as is
     specified in the notice convening the meeting or in any instrument of proxy sent
     out by the company in relation to the meeting not less than 48 hours before the
     time for holding the meeting or adjourned meeting at which the person named
     in the instrument proposes to vote; or
(b) in the case of a poll taken more than 48 hours after it is demanded, be deposited
     as aforesaid after the poll has been demanded and not less than 24 hours before
     the time appointed for the taking of the poll; or
(c) where the poll is not taken forthwith but is taken not more than 48 hours after it
     was demanded, be delivered at the meeting at which the poll was demanded to the
     chairman or to the secretary or to any director;

and an instrument of proxy which is not deposited or delivered in a manner so
permitted shall be invalid.

63.   A vote given or poll demanded by proxy or by the duly authorised
representative of a corporation shall be valid notwithstanding the previous
determination of the authority of the person voting or demanding a poll unless notice

of the determination was received by the company at the office or at such other place at which the instrument of proxy was duly deposited before the commencement of the meeting or adjourned meeting at which the vote is given or the poll demanded or (in the case of a poll taken otherwise than on the same day as the meeting or adjourned meeting) the time appointed for taking the poll.

NUMBER OF DIRECTORS

64.   Unless otherwise determined by ordinary resolution, the number of directors (other than alternate directors) shall not be subject to any maximum but shall be not less than two.

ALTERNATE DIRECTORS

65.   Any director (other than an alternate director) may appoint any other director, or any other person approved by resolution of the directors and willing to act, to be an alternate director and may remove from office an alternate director so appointed by him.

66.   An alternate director shall be entitled to receive notice of all meetings of directors and of all meetings of committees of directors of which his appointor is a member, to attend and vote at any such meeting at which the director appointing him is not personally present, and generally to perform all the functions of his appointor as a director in his absence but shall not be entitled to receive any remuneration from the company for his services as an alternate director. But it shall not be necessary to give notice of such a meeting to an alternate director who is absent from the United Kingdom.

67.   An alternate director shall cease to be an alternate director if his appointor ceases to be a director; but if a director retires by rotation or otherwise but is reappointed or deemed to have been reappointed at the meeting at which he retires, any appointment of an alternate director made by him which was in force immediately prior to his retirement shall continue after his reappointment.

68.   Any appointment or removal of an alternate director shall be by notice to the company signed by the director making or revoking the appointment or in any other manner approved by the directors.

69.   Save as otherwise provided in the articles, an alternate director shall be deemed for all purposes to be a director and shall alone be responsible for his own acts and defaults and he shall not be deemed to be the agent of the director appointing him.

POWERS OF DIRECTORS

70.   Subject to the provisions of the Act, the memorandum and the articles and to any directions given by special resolution, the business of the company shall be managed by the directors who may exercise all the powers of the company. No alteration of the memorandum or articles and no such direction shall invalidate any prior act of the directors which would have been valid if that alteration had not been made or that direction had not been given. The powers given by this regulation shall not be limited by any special power given to the directors by the articles and a meeting of directors at which a quorum is present may exercise all powers exercisable by the directors.

71.   The directors may, by power of attorney or otherwise, appoint any person to be the agent of the company for such purposes and on such conditions as they determine, including authority for the agent to delegate all or any of his powers.

DELEGATION OF DIRECTORS' POWERS

72.   The directors may delegate any of their powers to any committee consisting of one or more directors. They may also delegate to any managing director or any director holding any other executive office such of their powers as they consider desirable to be exercised by him. Any such delegation may be made subject to any conditions the directors may impose, and either collaterally with or to the exclusion of their own powers and may be revoked or altered. Subject to any such conditions, the proceedings of a committee with two or more members shall be governed by the articles regulating the proceedings of directors so far as they are capable of applying.

APPOINTMENT AND RETIREMENT
OF DIRECTORS

73.   At the first annual general meeting all the directors shall retire from office, and at every subsequent annual general meeting one-third of the directors who are subject to retirement by rotation or, if their number is not three or a multiple of three, the number nearest to one third shall retire from office; but, if there is only one director who is subject to retirement by rotation, he shall retire.

74.   Subject to the provisions of the Act, the directors to retire by rotation shall be those who have served longest in office since their last appointment or reappointment, but as between persons who became or were last reappointed directors on the same day those to retire shall (unless they otherwise agree among themselves) be determined by lot.

75.   If the company, at the meeting at which a director retires by rotation, does not fill the vacancy the retiring director shall, if willing to act, be deemed to have been reappointed unless at the meeting it is resolved not to fill the vacancy or unless a resolution for the reappointment of the director is put to the meeting and lost.

76.   No person other than a director retiring by rotation shall be appointed or reappointed a director at any general meeting unless –

(a) he is recommended by the directors; or
(b) not less than fourteen nor more than thirty-five clear days before the date appointed for the meeting, notice executed by a member qualified to vote at the meeting has been given to the company of the intention to propose that person for appointment or reappointment stating the particulars which would, if he were

so appointed or reappointed, be required to be included in the company's register of directors together with notice executed by that person of his willingness to be appointed or reappointed.

77.   Not less than seven nor more than twenty-eight clear days before the date appointed for holding a general meeting notice shall be given to all who are entitled to receive notice of the meeting of any person (other than a director retiring by rotation at the meeting) who is recommended by the directors for appointment or reappointment as a director at the meeting or in respect of whom notice has been duly given to the company of the intention to propose him at the meeting for appointment or reappointment as a director. The notice shall give particulars of that person which would, if he were so appointed or reappointed, be required to be included in the company's register of directors.

78.   Subject as aforesaid, the company may by ordinary resolution appoint a person who is willing to act to be a director either to fill a vacancy or as an additional director and may also determine the rotation in which any additional directors are to retire.

79.   The directors may appoint a person who is willing to act to be director, either to fill a vacancy or as an additional director, provided that the appointment does not cause the number of directors to exceed the number fixed by or in accordance with the articles as the maximum number of directors. A director so appointed shall hold office only until the next following annual general meeting and shall not be taken into account in determining the directors who are to retire by rotation at the meeting. If not reappointed at such annual general meeting, he shall vacate office at the conclusion thereof.

80.   Subject as aforesaid, a director who retires at an annual general meeting may, if willing to act, be reappointed. If he is not reappointed, he shall retain office until the meeting appoints someone in his place, or if it does not do so, until the end of the meeting.

DISQUALIFICATION AND REMOVAL OF DIRECTORS

81.   The office of director shall be vacated if –

(a) he ceases to be a director by virtue of any provision of the Act or becomes prohibited by law from being a director; or

(b) he becomes bankrupt or makes any arrangement or composition with his creditors generally; or

(c) he is, or may be, suffering from mental disorder and either –

    (i) he is admitted to hospital in pursuance of an application for treatment under the Mental Health Act 1983 or, in Scotland, an application for admission under the Mental Health (Scotland) Act 1960, or

    (ii) an order is made by a court having jurisdiction (whether in the United Kingdom or elsewhere) in matters concerning mental disorder for his detention or for the appointment of a receiver, curator bonis or other person to exercise powers with respect to his property or affairs; or

(d) he resigns his office by notice to the company; or

(e) he shall for more than six consecutive months have been absent without permission of the directors from meetings of the directors held during that period and the directors resolve that his office be vacated.

REMUNERATION OF DIRECTORS

82. The directors shall be entitled to such remuneration as the company may by ordinary resolution determine and, unless the resolution provides otherwise, the remuneration shall be deemed to accrue from day to day.

DIRECTORS' EXPENSES

83. The directors may be paid all travelling, hotel, and other expenses properly incurred by them in connection with their attendance at meetings of directors or committees of directors or general meetings or separate meetings of the holders of any class of shares or of debentures of the company or otherwise in connection with the discharge of their duties.

DIRECTORS' APPOINTMENTS
AND INTERESTS

84. Subject to the provisions of the Act, the directors may appoint one or more of their number to the office of managing director or to any other executive office under the company and may enter into an agreement or arrangement with any director for his employment by the company or for the provision by him of any services outside the scope of the ordinary duties of a director. Any such appointment, agreement or arrangement may be made on such terms as the directors determine and they may remunerate any such director for his services as they think fit. Any appointment of a director to an executive office shall terminate if he ceases to be a director but without prejudice to any claim for damages for breach of the contract of service between the director and the company. A managing director and a director holding any other executive office shall not be subject to retirement by rotation.

85. Subject to the provisions of the Act, and provided that he has disclosed to the directors the nature and extent of any material interest of his, a director notwithstanding his office –

(a) may be a party to, or otherwise interested in, any transaction or arrangement with the company or in which the company is otherwise interested;

(b) may be a director or other officer of, or employed by, or party to any transaction or arrangement with, or otherwise interested in, any body corporate promoted by the company or in which the company is otherwise interested; and

(c) shall not, by reason of his office, be accountable to the company for any benefit which he derives from any such office or employment or from any such transaction or arrangement or from any interest in any such body corporate and no such transaction or arrangement shall be liable to be avoided on the ground of any such interest or benefit.

86. For the purposes of regulation 85 –

(a) a general notice given to the directors that a director is to be regarded as having an interest of the nature and extent specified in the notice in any transactions or arrangement in which a specified person or class of persons is interested shall be deemed to be a disclosure that the director has an interest in any such transaction of the nature and extent so specified; and

(b) an interest of which a director has no knowledge and of which it is unreasonable to expect him to have knowledge shall not be treated as an interest of his.

DIRECTOR'S GRATUITIES AND PENSIONS

87. The directors may provide benefits, whether by payment of gratuities or pensions or by insurance or otherwise, for any director who has held but no longer holds any executive office or employment with the company or with any body corporate which is or has been a subsidiary of the company or a predecessor in business of the company or of any such subsidiary, and for any member of his family (including a spouse and a former spouse) or any person who is or was dependent upon him, and may (as well before as after he ceases to hold such office or employment) contribute to any fund and pay premiums for the purchase of any such benefit.

PROCEEDINGS OF DIRECTORS

88. Subject to the provisions of the articles, the directors may regulate their proceedings as they think fit. A director may, and the secretary at the request of a director shall, call a meeting of the directors. It shall not be necessary to give notice of a meeting to a director who is absent from the United Kingdom. Questions arising at a meeting shall be decided by a majority of votes. In the case of an equality of votes, the chairman shall have a second or casting vote. A director who is also an alternate director shall be entitled in the absence of his appointor to a separate vote on behalf of his appointor in addition to his own vote.

89. The quorum for the transaction of business of the directors may be fixed by the directors and unless so fixed at any other number shall be two. A person who holds office only as an alternate director shall, if his appointor is not present, be counted in the quorum.

90. The continuing directors or a sole continuing director may act notwithstanding any vacancies in their number, but, if the number of directors is less than the number fixed as the quorum, the continuing directors or director may act only for the purpose of filling vacancies or of calling a general meeting.

91. The directors may appoint one of their number to be the chairman of the board of directors and may at any time remove him from that office. Unless he is unwilling to do so, the director so appointed shall preside at every meeting of directors at which he is present. But if there is no director holding that office, or if the director holding it is unwilling to preside or is not present within five minutes after the time appointed for the meeting, the directors present may appoint one of their number to be chairman of the meeting.

92. All acts done by a meeting of directors, or of a committee of directors, or by a person acting as a director shall, notwithstanding that it be afterwards discovered that there was a defect in the appointment of any director or that any of them were disqualified from holding office, or had vacated office, or were not entitled to vote, be as valid as if every such person had been duly appointed and was qualified and had continued to be a director and had been entitled to vote.

93. A resolution signed in writing by all the directors entitled to receive notice of a meeting of directors or of a committee of directors shall be as valid and effectual as if it had been passed at a meeting of directors or (as the case may be) a committee of directors duly convened and held and may consist of several documents in the like form each signed by one or more directors; but a resolution signed by an alternate director need not also be signed by his appointor and, if it is signed by a director who has appointed an alternate director, it need not be signed by the alternate in that capacity.

94. Save as otherwise provided by the articles, a director shall not vote at a meeting of directors or a committee of directors on any resolution concerning a matter in which he has, directly or indirectly, an interest or duty which is material and which conflicts or may conflict with the interests of the company unless his interest or duty arises only because the case falls within one or more of the following paragraphs –

(a) the resolution relates to the giving to him of a guarantee, security, or indemnity in respect of money lent to, or an obligation incurred by him for the benefit of, the company or any of its subsidiaries;

(b) the resolution relates to the giving to a third party of a guarantee, security, or indemnity in respect of an obligation the company or any of its subsidiaries for which the director has assumed responsibility in whole or in part and whether alone or jointly with others under a guarantee or indemnity or by the giving of security;

(c) his interest arises by virtue of his subscribing or agreeing to subscribe for any shares, debentures or other securities of the company or any of its subsidiaries, or by virtue of his being, or intending to become, a participant in the underwriting or sub-underwriting of an offer of any such shares, debentures or other securities by the company or any of its subsidiaries for subscription, purchase or exchange;

(d) the resolution relates in any way to a retirement benefits scheme which has been approved, or is conditional upon approval, by the Board of Inland Revenue for taxation purposes.

For the purposes of this regulation, an interest of a person who is, for any purpose of the Act (excluding any statutory modification thereof not in force when this regulation becomes binding on the company), connected with a director shall be treated as an interest of the director and, in relation to an alternate director, an interest of his appointor shall be treated as an interest of the alternate director without prejudice to any interest which the alternate director has otherwise.

95.   A director shall not be counted in the quorum present at a meeting in relation to a resolution on which he is not entitled to vote.

96.   The company may by ordinary resolution suspend or relax to any extent, either generally or in respect of any particular matter, any provision of the articles prohibiting a director from voting at a meeting of directors or of a committee of directors.

97.   Where proposals are under consideration concerning the appointment of two or more directors to offices or employments with the company or any body corporate in which the company is interested the proposals may be divided and considered in relation to each director separately and (provided he is not for another reason precluded from voting) each of the directors concerned shall be entitled to vote and be counted in the quorum in respect of each resolution except that concerning his own appointment.

98.   If a question arises at a meeting of directors or of a committee of directors as to the right of a director to vote, the question may, before the conclusion of the meeting, be referred to the chairman of the meeting and his ruling in relation to any director other than himself shall be final and conclusive.

SECRETARY

99.   Subject to the provisions of the Act, the secretary shall be appointed by the directors for such term, at such remuneration and upon such conditions as they may think fit; and any secretary so appointed may be removed by them.

MINUTES

100.   The directors shall cause minutes to be made in books kept for the purpose –

(a)   of all appointments of officers made by the directors; and

(b)   of all proceedings at meetings of the company, of the holders of any class of shares in the company, and of the directors, and of committees of directors, including the names of the directors present at each such meeting.

THE SEAL

101.   The seal shall only be used by the authority of the directors or of a committee of directors authorised by the directors. The directors may determine who shall sign any instrument to which the seal is affixed and unless otherwise so determined it shall be signed by a director and by the secretary or by a second director.

DIVIDENDS

102. Subject to the provisions of the Act, the company may by ordinary resolution declare dividends in accordance with the respective rights of members, but no dividend shall exceed the amount recommended by the directors.

103. Subject to the provisions of the Act, the directors may pay interim dividends if it appears to them that they are justified by the profits of the company available for distribution. If the share capital is divided into different classes, the directors may pay interim dividends on shares which confer deferred or non-preferred rights with regard to dividend as well as on shares which confer preferential rights with regard to dividend, but no interim dividend shall be paid on shares carrying deferred or non-preferred rights if, at the time of payment, any preferential dividend is in arrears. The directors may also pay at intervals settled by them any dividend payable at a fixed rate if it appears to them that the profits available for distribution justify the payment. Provided the directors act in good faith they shall not incur any liability to the holders of shares conferring preferred rights for any loss they may suffer by the lawful payment of an interim dividend on any shares having deferred or non-preferred rights.

104. Except as otherwise provided by the rights attached to shares, all dividends shall be declared and paid according to the amounts paid up on the shares on which the dividend is paid. All dividends shall be apportioned and paid proportionately to the amounts paid up on the shares during any portion or portions of the period in respect of which the dividend is paid; but, if any share is issued on terms providing that it shall rank for dividend from a particular date, that share shall rank for dividend accordingly.

105. A general meeting declaring a dividend may, upon the recommendation of the directors, direct that it shall be satisfied wholly or partly by the distribution of assets and, where any difficulty arises in regard to the distribution, the directors may settle the same and in particular may issue fractional certificates and fix the value for distribution of any assets and may determine that cash shall be paid to any member upon the footing of the value so fixed in order to adjust the rights of members and may vest assets in trustees.

106. Any dividend or other moneys payable in respect of a share may be paid by cheque sent by post to the registered address of the person entitled or, if two or more persons are the holders of the share or are jointly entitled to it by reason of the death or bankruptcy of the holder, to the registered address of that one of those persons who is first named on the register of members or to such person and to such address as the person or persons entitled may in writing direct. Every cheque shall be made payable to the order of the person or persons entitled or to such other person as the person or persons entitled may in writing direct and payment of the cheque shall be a good discharge to the company. Any joint holder or other person jointly entitled to a share as aforesaid may give receipts for any dividend or other moneys payable in respect of the share.

107. No dividend or other moneys payable in respect of a share shall bear interest against the company unless otherwise provided by the rights attached to the share.

108. Any dividend which has remained unclaimed for twelve years from the date when it became due for payment shall, if the directors so resolve, be forfeited and cease to remain owing by the company.

ACCOUNTS

109. No member shall (as such) have any right of inspecting any accounting records or other book or document of the company except as conferred by statute or authorised by the directors or by ordinary resolution of the company.

CAPITALISATION OF PROFITS

110. The directors may with the authority of an ordinary resolution of the company –

(a) subject as hereinafter provided, resolve to capitalise any undivided profits of the company not required for paying any preferential dividend (whether or not they are available for distribution) or any sum standing to the credit of the company's share premium account or capital redemption reserve;

(b) appropriate the sum resolved to be capitalised to the members who would have been entitled to it if it were distributed by way of dividend and in the same proportion and apply such sum on their behalf either in or towards paying up the amounts, if any, for the time being unpaid on any shares held by them respectively, or in paying up in full unissued shares or debentures of the company of a nominal amount equal to that sum, and allot the shares or debentures credited as fully paid to those members, or as they may direct, in those proportions, or partly in one way and partly in the other: but the share premium account, the capital redemption reserve, and any profits which are not available for distribution may, for the purposes of this regulation, only be applied in paying up unissued shares to be allotted members credited as fully paid;

(c) make such provision by the issue of fractional certificates or by payment in cash or otherwise as they determine in the case of shares or debentures becoming distributable under this regulation in fractions; and

(d) authorise any person to enter on behalf of all members concerned into an agreement with the company providing for the allotment to them respectively, credited as fully paid, of any shares or debentures to which they are entitled upon such capitalisation, any agreement made under such authority being binding on all such members.

NOTICES

111. Any notice to be given to or by any person pursuant to the articles shall be in writing except that notice calling a meeting of directors need not be in writing.

112. The company may give any notice to a member either personally or by sending it by post in a prepaid envelope addressed to the member at his registered address or by leaving it at that address. In the case of joint holders of a share, all notices shall be given to the joint holder whose name stands first in the register of members in respect of the joint holding and notice so given shall be sufficient notice to all the joint holders. A member whose registered address is not within the United Kingdom and who gives to the company an address within the United Kingdom at which notices may be given to him shall be entitled to have notices given to him at that address, but otherwise no such member shall be entitled to receive any notice from the company.

113.   A member present, either in person or by proxy, at any meeting of the company or of holders of any class of shares in the company shall be deemed to have received notice of the meeting and, where requisite, of the purposes for which it was called.

114.   Every person who becomes entitled to a share shall be bound by any notice in respect of that share which, before his name is entered in the register of members, has been duly given to a person from whom he derives his title.

115.   Proof that an envelope containing a notice was properly addressed, prepaid and posted shall be conclusive evidence that the notice was given. A notice shall be deemed to be given at the expiration of 48 hours after the envelope containing it was posted.

116.   A notice may be given by the company to the persons entitled to a share in consequence of death or bankruptcy of a member by sending or delivering it, in any manner authorised by the articles for the giving of notice to a member, addressed to them by name, or by the title of representatives of the deceased, or trustee of the bankrupt or by any description at the address, if any, within the United Kingdom supplied for that purpose by the persons claiming to be so entitled. Until such an address has been supplied, a notice may be given in any manner in which it might have been given if the death or bankruptcy had not occurred.

WINDING UP

117.   If the company is wound up, the liquidator may, with the sanction of an extraordinary resolution of the company and any other sanction required by the Act, divide among the members in specie the whole or any part of the assets of the company and may, for that purpose, value any assets and determine how the division shall be carried out as between members or different classes of members. The liquidator may, with the like sanction, vest the whole or any part of the assets in trustees upon such trusts for the benefit of the members as he with the like sanction determines, but no member shall be compelled to accept any assets upon which there is a liability.

INDEMNITY

118.   Subject to the provisions of the Act, but without prejudice to any indemnity to which a director may otherwise be entitled, every director or other officer or auditor of the company shall be indemnified out of the assets of the company against any

liability incurred by him in defending any proceedings, whether civil or criminal, in which judgment is given in his favour or in which he is acquitted or in connection with any application in which relief is granted to him by the court from liability for negligence, default, breach of duty or breach of trust in relation to the affairs of the company.

Index to 1985 Table A

Articles of Association of Whitbread plc

REGULATIONS FOR MANAGEMENT

OF A COMPANY LIMITED BY SHARES

INTERPRETATION

1.   No regulations set out in any statute, or in any statutory instrument or other subordinate legislation made under any statute, concerning companies shall apply as regulations or articles of the Company.

2.   In these Articles, if not inconsistent with the subject or context, the words standing in the first column of the following table shall bear the meanings set opposite them respectively.

Ordinary Shares	Ordinary Shares of 25 pence each.
Auditors	The auditors for the time being of the Company or, in the case of joint auditors, any one of them.
The Board	The Directors or any of them acting as the Board of the Company.
Companies Act	Every statute (including orders, regulations or other subordinate legislation made under it) from time to time in force concerning companies insofar as it applies to the Company.
The Directors	The Directors for the time being of the Company.
In writing	Written or produced by any visible substitute for writing, or partly one and partly another.
The London Stock Exchange	The International Stock Exchange of the United Kingdom and the Republic of Ireland.
Month	Calendar month.
Office	The Registered Office of the Company.
Paid	Paid or credited as paid.

Preference Capital	The First Cumulative Preference Stock, the Second Cumulative Preference Stock and the Third Cumulative Preference Stock.
Register	The register of members required to be kept pursuant to the Companies Acts.
Seal	The Common Seal of the Company or any seal of the Company permitted under the Companies Acts.
Secretary	Any person appointed by the Board to perform the duties of the secretary of the Company and includes any assistant or deputy secretary.
These Articles	These Articles of Association as from time to time altered and the expression 'this Article' shall be construed accordingly.
The United Kingdom	Great Britain and Northern Ireland.
Year	Calendar year.

Words denoting the singular number only shall include the plural number also and vice versa.

Words denoting the masculine gender only shall include the feminine gender.

Words denoting person only shall include corporations.

The expressions "Debenture" and "Debenture holder" shall include "Debenture Stock" and "Debenture Stockholder".

The provisions of these Articles applicable to paid up shares shall apply to stock, and the words "share" and "shareholder" shall be construed accordingly.

References to any statute or statutory provision shall be construed as relating to any statutory modification or re-enactment thereof for the time being in force.

Any words or expressions defined in the Companies Acts in force when these Articles or any part of these Articles are adopted shall (if not inconsistent with the subject or context) bear the same meanings in these Articles or that part (as the case may be) save that the word "company" shall include any body corporate.

Headings are included for convenience only and shall not affect the construction of these Articles.

GENERAL MEETINGS

Annual General Meetings

55.   The Company shall in each year hold a General Meeting as its Annual General Meeting in addition to any other meetings in the year, and shall specify the meeting as such in the notices calling it. The Annual General Meeting shall be held at such time (within a period of not more than fifteen months after the holding of the last preceding Annual General Meeting) and place as may be determined by the Board. All General Meetings other than Annual General Meetings shall be called Extraordinary General Meetings.

Extraordinary General Meetings

56.   The Board may call an Extraordinary General Meeting whenever it shall think

fit, and shall, on requisition in accordance with the Companies Acts proceed to convene an Extraordinary General Meeting as required by the Companies Acts and shall do so upon receipt of a requisition of members pursuant to the provisions of the Companies Acts. If at any time there are not within the United Kingdom sufficient Directors capable of acting to form a quorum, any Director or any two members of the Company may convene an Extraordinary General Meeting in the same manner as nearly as possible as that in which meetings may be convened by the Board.

NOTICE OF GENERAL MEETINGS

Notice of General Meetings
57.   An Annual General Meeting and any General Meeting at which it is proposed to pass a Special Resolution or (save as provided by the Companies Acts) a resolution of which special notice has been given to the Company shall be called by twenty-one clear days' notice in writing at the least, and any other General Meeting by fourteen days' clear notice in writing at the least given in such manner hereinafter mentioned to the Auditors and to all members other than such as are not under the provisions of these Articles entitled to receive such notices from the Company, provided that a General Meeting notwithstanding that it has been called by a shorter notice than that specified above shall be deemed to have been duly called if it is so agreed:

(A) in the case of an Annual General Meeting, by all the members entitled to attend and vote thereat; and

(B) in the case of an Extraordinary General Meeting, by a majority in number of the members having a right to attend and vote thereat, being a majority together holding not less than 95 per cent in nominal value of the shares giving that right.

Contents of notice
58.   (A)   Every notice calling a General Meeting shall specify the place and the day and hour of the meeting, and there shall appear with reasonable prominence in every such notice a statement that a member entitled to attend and vote is entitled to appoint a proxy to attend and vote instead of him and that a proxy need not be a member of the Company.
(B)   In the case of an Annual General Meeting, the notice shall also specify the meeting as such.
(C)   In the case of any General Meeting the notice shall specify the general nature of the business and if any resolution is to be proposed as an Extraordinary Resolution or as a Special Resolution, the notice shall contain a statement to that effect.

Omission or non-receipt of notice or form of proxy
59.   The accidental omission to give notice of any meeting or (in cases where forms of proxy are sent out with the notice) the omission to send such form of proxy with the notice to, or the non-receipt of the notice of the meeting or such form of proxy by, any member shall not invalidate the proceedings at the meeting.

OVERFLOW GENERAL MEETINGS

Simultaneous attendance at several places

60.   (A)   The Board may make arrangements for simultaneous attendance and participation in General Meetings by members and proxies entitled to attend such meetings at places other than the place specified in the Notice convening the meeting ('the specified place').

Meeting treated as held at place specified in notice

(B)   Any arrangements for simultaneous attendance at other places shall operate so that any members and proxies excluded from attendance at the specified place are able to attend at one or more of the other places. For the purposes of all other provisions of these Articles any such meeting shall be treated as being held and taking place at the specified place.

Right of Board to facilitate organisation and administration of meeting

(C)   The right of any member or proxy otherwise entitled to attend a General Meeting at the specified place shall be subject to any arrangements that the Board may at its discretion make from time to time (whether before or after the date of the Notice convening the meeting) for facilitating the organisation and administration of any General Meeting by requiring any such person (selected on such basis as the Board may at its discretion decide) to attend the meeting at one or more of the other places.

PROCEEDINGS AT GENERAL MEETINGS

Business of Ordinary Meeting

61.   All business shall be deemed special that is transacted at an Extraordinary General Meeting and also all business that is transacted at an Annual General Meeting with the exception of the following:

(A)   declaring dividends,
(B)   receiving the accounts and reports of the Directors and Auditors and other documents required to be annexed to the accounts,
(C)   electing the Directors in place of those or re-electing as Directors those retiring by rotation or otherwise,
(D)   appointing Auditors where special notice of the resolution for such appointment is not required by the Companies Acts, and
(E)   fixing or determining the method of fixing the remuneration of the Auditors.

Quorum

62.   No business shall be transacted at any General Meeting unless a quorum is present when the meeting proceeds to business. Save as herein otherwise provided three members present in person or by proxy and entitled to vote shall be a quorum for all purposes.

Adjournment if quorum not present

63.   If within thirty minutes from the time appointed for the meeting a quorum is not present, the meeting, if convened on the requisition of members, shall be dissolved. In any other case it shall stand adjourned to such other day (not being less than seven nor more than twenty-eight days thereafter) and at such other time or place as the Chairman may determine, and if at such adjourned meeting a quorum is not present within thirty minutes from the time appointed for holding the meeting, the members present shall be a quorum.

Chairman

64.   The Chairman, Deputy Chairman or Vice Chairman of the Board shall preside as Chairman at every General Meeting of the Company. If there be no such Chairman, Deputy Chairman or Vice Chairman, or at any meeting neither of them be present within fifteen minutes after the time appointed for holding the meeting, or if neither of them be willing to act as Chairman, the Directors present shall choose some Director, or if no Director be present, or if all the Directors present decline to take the chair, the members present shall choose some member present to be Chairman. Each Director shall be entitled to attend and speak at any General Meeting of the Company and at any separate General Meeting of the holders of any class of shares in the Company.

Adjournment

65.   The Chairman of a General Meeting may, with the consent of any meeting at which a quorum is present (and shall if so directed by the meeting) adjourn the meeting from time to time (or sine die) and from place to place, but no business shall be transacted at any adjourned meeting except business left unfinished at the meeting from which the adjournment took place. If it appears to the Chairman of the meeting that it is likely to be impracticable to hold or continue the meeting because of the number of members or their proxies present or wishing to attend or that an adjournment is otherwise necessary so that the business of the meeting may be properly conducted, he may without the need for such consent adjourn the meeting to such other time and place as he may determine (or sine die). When a meeting is adjourned sine die the time and place of the adjourned meeting shall be fixed by the Board. When a meeting is adjourned for thirty days or more or sine die, notice of the adjourned meeting shall be given as in the case of the original meeting. Save as expressly provided by these Articles it shall not be necessary to give any notice of an adjournment or of the business to be transacted at an adjourned meeting.

Voting

66.   At any General Meeting a resolution put to the vote of the meeting shall be decided on a show of hands unless a poll is (before or on the declaration of the result of the show of hands) demanded:

(A) by the Chairman of the Meeting; or
(B) by at least three members present in person or by proxy and entitled to vote; or

(C)   by a member or members entitled either by reason of their own holding or as representatives or as proxies, to cast one-tenth or more of the votes which could be cast in respect of that resolution if all persons entitled to vote thereon were present at the meeting; or

(D)   by a member or members holding shares in the Company conferring a right to vote at the meeting being shares on which an aggregate sum has been paid up equal to not less than one-tenth of the total sum paid up on all the shares conferring that right.

Demand of poll

67.   Unless a poll is so demanded and the demand is not withdrawn, a declaration that a resolution has been carried, or carried unanimously, or by a particular majority, or lost, and an entry to that effect in the minute book shall be conclusive evidence of the fact without proof of the number or proportion of the votes recorded in favour or against such resolution.

Amendment of resolution

68.   If an amendment shall be proposed to any resolution under consideration but shall in good faith be ruled out by the Chairman of the meeting the proceedings on the substantive resolution shall not be invalidated by any error in such ruling. In the case of a resolution duly proposed as a Special or Extraordinary resolution no amendment thereto (other than a mere clerical amendment to correct a manifest error) may in any event be considered or voted upon.

Votes counted in error

69.   If any votes shall be counted which ought not to have been counted or might have been rejected, the error shall not vitiate the resolution unless it be pointed out at the same meeting, or at any adjournment thereof, and not in that case unless it shall in the opinion of the Chairman of the meeting be of sufficient magnitude to vitiate the resolution.

Procedure for poll

70.   Except as provided in Article 72, if a poll is duly demanded, it shall be taken at such time and in such a manner (including the use of ballot or voting papers or tickets) as the Chairman of the meeting may direct, and the result of a poll shall be deemed to be the resolution of the meeting at which the poll was demanded. The Chairman of the meeting may in the event of a poll, appoint scrutineers and may adjourn the meeting to some time and place fixed by him for the purpose of declaring the result of the poll. The demand for a poll may be withdrawn but only with the consent of the Chairman.

Chairman's casting vote

71.   In the case of an equality of votes, whether on a show of hands or on a poll, the chairman of the meeting at which the show of hands takes place or at which the poll is demanded shall be entitled to a further or casting vote in addition to any vote to which he may be entitled as a member.

Time for taking a poll

72.   A poll demanded on the election of a chairman or on a question of adjournment shall be taken forthwith. A poll demanded on any other question shall be taken at such time and place as the Chairman of the meeting may direct. No notice need be given of a poll not taken immediately.

Continuance of business after demand for poll

73.   The demand for a poll shall not prevent the continuance of a meeting for the transaction of any business other than the question on which the poll has been demanded.

VOTES OF MEMBERS

74.   Subject to any special rights or restrictions as to voting attached by or in accordance with these Articles to the Preference Capital or to any new class of shares issued, on a show of hands every member who is present in person shall have one vote, and on a poll every member who is present in person or by proxy shall have one vote for every 25 pence of paid-up Preference Capital held by him and one vote for each £1 of paid-up Ordinary Shares held by him.

75.   In the case of joint holders of a share the vote of the senior who tenders a vote, whether in person or by proxy, shall be accepted to the exclusion of the votes of the other joint holders and for this purpose seniority shall be determined by the order in which the names of the holders stand in the Register.

Voting rights of members of unsound mind

76.   A member in respect of whom an Order has been made by any competent court or official on the ground that he is or may be suffering from mental disorder or is otherwise incapable of managing his affairs may vote by any person authorised in such circumstances to do so on his behalf and that person may vote on a poll by proxy, provided that evidence to the satisfaction of the Board of the authority of the person claiming to exercise the right to vote has been delivered at the Office (or at such other place as is specified in accordance with these Articles for the delivery of instruments appointing a proxy) not later than the last time at which an instrument of proxy should have been delivered in order to be valid for use at that meeting or on the holding of a poll.

No right to vote where call is unpaid

77.   No member shall, unless the Board otherwise determines be entitled to vote at a General Meeting either personally or by proxy, or to exercise any privilege as a member unless all calls or other sums presently payable by him in respect of shares in the Company have been paid.

Removal of voting, dividend and transfer rights

78.   (A) If any member, or any other person appearing to be interested in shares

held by such member, has been duly served with a notice under Section 212 of the Companies Act 1985 (a "Section 212 Notice") and is in default in supplying to the Company the information thereby required within the prescribed period, the Board may in its absolute discretion at any time thereafter serve a notice (a "default notice") upon such member as follows:

(i)   a default notice may provide that, in respect of shares in relation to which the default occurred and any shares issued after the date of the Section 212 Notice in right of those shares ('default shares'), the member shall not be entitled to exercise either personally or by proxy the votes attaching thereto or to exercise any right conferred thereby in relation to meetings of the Company or of the holders of any class of shares of the Company; and

(ii)   where the default shares represent at least the prescribed percentage, then the default notice may additionally provide that:

(a)   in respect of the default shares, any dividend or other distribution which would otherwise be payable or made on such shares may (if so determined by the Board in relation to such dividend or other distribution) be withheld in whole or in part (as the Board determines) by the Company without any liability to pay interest thereon when such money is finally paid to the member (in which case any election made pursuant to Article 148 by the holder of default shares in respect of a dividend thereon which is so withheld shall be ineffective);

(b)   no transfer other than an approved arm's length transfer of any shares held (by such member shall be registered unless the member is not himself in default as regards supplying the information requested and the transfer when presented for registration is accompanied by a certificate by the member in a form satisfactory to the Board to the effect that after due and careful enquiry (the member is satisfied that no person in default as regards supplying (information is interested in any of the shares the subject of the transfer.

The Company shall send to each other person appearing to the Board to be interested in the shares the subject of any default notice a copy of the notice, but a failure or omission by the Company to do so or the non-receipt of such notice by any such person shall not invalidate such notice.

(B)   Any default notice shall have effect in accordance with its terms for as long as the default (in respect of which the default notice was issued) continues but shall cease to have effect in relation to any shares which are transferred by means of an approved arm's length transfer as defined in paragraph (C) (iv) below. Written notice of such determination shall be given to the member.

(C)   For the purpose of this Article:

(i)   a person shall be treated as appearing to be interested in any shares if the member holding such shares has given to the Company a notification under the said Section 212 or otherwise which either (a) names such person as being so interested or (b) fails to establish the identities of those interested in the shares and (after taking into account the said notification and any other relevant information) the Company knows or has reasonable cause to believe that the person in question is or may be interested in shares;

(ii)   the prescribed period shall be 14 days from the date of service of the said notice under the said Section 212;

(iii)   the prescribed percentage shall be 0.25 per cent in nominal value of the issued shares of their class;

(iv)   a transfer of shares is an approved arm's length transfer if but only if:

(a)   it is a transfer of shares to an offeror by way or in pursuance of acceptance of a take-over offer for the Company (as defined in Section 14 of the Company Securities (Insider Dealing) Act 1985); or

(b)   the Board is satisfied that the transfer is made pursuant to a sale at arm's length of the whole of the beneficial ownership of the shares to a party unconnected with the transferor and with other persons appearing to be interested in such shares immediately prior to such sale (including any such sale made through a recognised investment exchange (as defined in the Financial Services Act 1986) or any stock exchange outside the United Kingdom on which the Company's shares of the class are normally traded). For the purposes of this paragraph any associate (as that term is defined in Section 435 of the Insolvency Act 1986) shall be included amongst the persons who are connected with the member or any person appearing to be interested in such shares.

(D)   Any notice referred to in this Article may be served by the Company upon the addressee either personally or by sending it through the post in a pre-paid letter addressed to the addressee at his usual or last known address.

(E)   Nothing contained in this Article shall limit the powers of the Board under Section 216 of the Companies Act 1985 and, in particular, the Company shall be entitled to apply to the Court under Section 216(1) whether or not these provisions apply or have been applied.

Objections to qualification of voter

79.   No objection shall be raised to the qualification of any voter except at the meeting or adjourned meeting at which the vote objected to is given or tendered, and every vote not disallowed at the meeting shall be valid for all purposes. Any such objection made in due time shall be referred to the Chairman of the meeting whose decision shall be final and conclusive.

Votes on a poll

80.   On a poll votes may be given either personally or by proxy. On a poll a member entitled to more than one vote need not use all his votes or cast all the votes in the same way.

Proxy need not be a member etc.

82.   A proxy need not be a member of the Company. A member may appoint more than one proxy to attend on the same occasion.

83.   The instrument appointing a proxy and, if required by the Board, the power of attorney or other authority (if any) under which it is signed, or a notarially certified copy of such power or authority, shall be deposited at the Office (or at such other place

in the United Kingdom specified in the notice convening the meeting or the notice of adjournment thereof or in any document sent with either of such notices) not less than forty-eight hours before the time appointed for holding the meeting or adjourned meeting, or in the case of a poll not less than twenty-four hours before the time appointed for the taking of the poll at which the person named in the instrument proposes to vote, and in default the instrument of proxy shall not be treated as valid.

Form of proxy

84.   An instrument of proxy may be in any common form or in such other form as the Board may approve.

Content of proxy

85.   The proxy shall be deemed to include the right to demand, or join in demanding, a poll, and shall include power to vote for or against any proposal and generally to act at the meeting for the member giving the proxy. An instrument appointing a proxy, whether in common form or not shall, unless the contrary is stated thereon, be valid as well for any adjournment of the meeting as for the for the meeting to which it relates.

Despatch of proxies

86.   Instruments of proxy shall be sent to all members of the Company in respect of any meeting of the Company at which a resolution is to be proposed and on which such members are entitled to vote, and such instrument shall be so worded that the members may vote either for or against the resolution or resolutions to be proposed at the meeting to which the same relates. The accidental omission to send or the non-receipt of an instrument of proxy shall not invalidate the proceedings at any such meeting.

Non-revocation of proxy in certain circumstances

87.   A vote given in accordance with the terms of an instrument of proxy shall be valid, notwithstanding the previous death or insanity of the principal or revocation of the proxy, or of the authority under which the proxy was executed, or the transfer of the share in respect of which the proxy is given, provided that no intimation in writing of such death, insanity, revocation or transfer shall have been received by the Company at the Office (or other place in the United Kingdom specified pursuant to Article 83) before the commencement of the meetings or adjourned meeting at which the proxy is used.

Corporation as a member

88.   Any corporation which is a member of the Company may by resolution of its directors or other governing body authorise such person as it thinks fit to act as its representative at any meeting of the Company, and any person so authorised shall be entitled to exercise the same powers on behalf of the corporation which he represents as that corporation could exercise if it were an individual member of the Company, but

such representative may be required to produce evidence of such authorisation on admission or at any time during the meeting or in connection with the exercise of any right in respect of such meeting, including without limitation participation in a poll on any resolution. Any such authorisation in writing purporting to be signed by an officer of or other person duly authorised for the purpose by the said corporation shall be conclusive evidence of the authority of the representative to act on behalf of the corporation.

89.   No instrument appointing a proxy shall be valid after the expiration of twelve months from the date named in it as the date of its execution, except at an adjourned meeting or on a poll demanded at a meeting or an adjourned meeting in a case where the meeting was originally held within twelve months from such date.

DIRECTORS

Number of Directors

90.   Unless and until otherwise determined by the Company in General Meeting, the Directors shall not be less than five nor more than twenty in number, but within these limits the Company may from time to time in General Meeting increase or reduce the maximum or minimum number of Directors.

Fees of Directors

91.   The Directors shall be paid fees for their services of such sums (not exceeding in aggregate £200,000 per annum or such larger amount as the Company may by ordinary resolution decide) as the Board or a committee authorised by the Board may from time to time determine, and such sums shall be divided among them in such proportions and manner as the Board or such committee may determine or in default equally. Any Director holding office for part of a year shall be entitled to a proportionate part of his fees. In addition to such fees the Board or such committee may make to any Director such expense allowance as may seem to the Board or such committee to be fair and reasonable to meet travelling, hotel, entertainment and other expenses which the Director may properly incur whilst engaged in the business of the Company.

Extra remuneration of Directors

92.   Any Director who holds any executive office (including for this purpose the office of Chairman, Deputy Chairman or Vice Chairman whether or not such office is held in an executive capacity) or who otherwise performs services which in the opinion of the Board or a committee authorised by the Board are outside the scope of the ordinary duties of a Director, may be paid such remuneration by way of salary, commission, percentage of profits or otherwise as the Board or such committee may determine in addition to any fee payable to him for his services as a Director pursuant to Article 91.

Share qualification

93.   A Director shall not be required to hold any share qualification. A Director who is not a member shall nevertheless be entitled to attend and speak at General Meetings.

Vacation of office of Director

94.   The office of a Director shall be vacated in any of the following events, namely:

(A)   if he shall become prohibited by law from acting as a Director; or

(B)   if he shall resign by notice in writing under his hand left at or sent to the Office or if he shall tender his resignation and the Directors resolve to accept the same; or

(C)   if he shall have a bankruptcy order made against him or shall compound or make any arrangement with his creditors generally; or

(D)   if in England or elsewhere an order shall be made by any court claiming jurisdiction in that behalf on the ground (however formulated) of mental disorder for his detention or for the appointment of a guardian or for the appointment of a receiver or other person (by whatever name called) to exercise powers with respect to his property or affairs; or

(E)   if he be absent from meetings of the Directors for six consecutive months without leave and his alternate Director (if any) shall not during such periods have attended in his stead, and the Board shall resolve that his office be vacated; or

(F)   if he be requested in writing by all his co-Directors to resign but so that if he holds an executive office which thereby automatically determines such removal shall be deemed an act of the Company and shall have effect without prejudice to any claim by either party against the other for breach of any contract of service between him and the Company.

Director not disqualified by age

95.   No person shall be disqualified from being appointed a Director in accordance with these Articles by reason of having attained the age of seventy years or any other age, nor shall special notice or other special formality be required on that account. No Director shall vacate his office by reason only of his age.

Power of a Director to hold other offices and contract with the Company

96.   (A)   A Director may hold any other office or place of profit with the Company in conjunction with his office of Director for such period and on such terms as to remuneration or otherwise as the Board may determine, and he or any firm in which he is interested may act in a professional capacity for the Company and he or such firm shall be entitled to remuneration (by way of salary, commission, fee, participation in profits or otherwise) for such services as if he were not a Director. Provided that nothing herein contained shall authorise a Director or any such firm to act as Auditor to the Company or any company controlled by the Company.

(B)   Subject to the provisions of the Companies Acts no Director shall be disqualified by his office from contracting with the Company or with any company in which the Company is interested either with regard to his tenure of any such other office or place of profit referred to in paragraph (A) of this Article or as vendor, purchaser, or otherwise, nor subject to the Companies Acts, shall any such contract, or any contract or arrangement entered into by or on behalf of the Company or any company in which the Company is interested, in which any Director is directly or indirectly interested be liable to be avoided nor shall any Director so contracting or being so interested be liable to account to the Company for any profit realised by any such contract or arrangement by reason of such Director holding that office, or of the fiduciary relation thereby established. Provided that no Director shall be liable to the Company in respect of any profit made by him or loss suffered by the Company as a result of such contract or arrangement if he shows that at the time the contract or arrangement was entered into he did not know of his interest therein.

(C)   A Director shall not vote in respect of any contract or arrangement or any other proposal in which he is interested and if he shall do so his vote shall not be counted, nor shall he be counted in the quorum present at the meeting, but these prohibitions shall not apply to:

(i)   to any arrangement for giving any Director any security or indemnity in respect of money lent by him to, or obligations undertaken by him for the benefit of, the Company or any of its subsidiaries; or

(ii)   to any contract to subscribe for or purchase shares debentures or other securities of the Company pursuant to an offer or invitation to members or debenture holders of the Company, or any class of them or to the public or any section of the public; or

(iii)   to any contract to underwrite, sub-underwrite or guarantee the subscription of any shares or debentures of the Company; or

(iv)   to any contract or arrangement with any other company in which he is interested only as a director, officer or creditor of the company or as a holder of shares or other securities provided that he is not the holder (other than as a bare trustee) of or beneficially interested in one per cent or more of the issued shares of any class of such company or of any third company through which his interest is derived or of the voting rights available to members of the relevant company (any such interest being deemed for this purpose to be a material interest in all circumstances); or

(v)   to any arrangement for giving by the Company of any security to a third party in respect of a debt or obligation of the Company or any of its subsidiaries for which the Director himself has assumed responsibility in whole or in part under a guarantee or indemnity or by the deposit of a security; or

(vi)   to any proposal concerning the adoption modification or operation of a superannuation fund or retirement benefits scheme or employee's share scheme under which he may benefit and which has been approved by or is subject to and conditional upon approval by the Board of the Inland Revenue for taxation purposes; or

(vii)   to any arrangement for the benefit of employees of the Company or of any of its subsidiaries under which the Director benefits in a similar manner to employees and does not accord to any Director as such any privilege or advantage not   generally accorded to employees to which such arrangement relates; or

(viii)   to any arrangement for purchasing or maintaining for the benefit of any Directors or for persons including Directors any insurance which the Company is empowered by Article 114 to purchase and maintain or any other insurance which the Company is empowered to purchase and maintain for the benefit of Directors or for persons including Directors.

(D)   The prohibitions contained in the foregoing paragraph of this Article may at any time be suspended or relaxed to any extent, and either generally or in respect of any particular contract, arrangement or transaction by the Company in General Meeting.

(E)   A general notice given to the Board by a Director to the effect that he is a member of or beneficially interested in a specified firm or company and is to be regarded as interested in any contracts or arrangements which may be made with that firm or company after the date of such notice shall be sufficient declaration of interest under this Article, provided that no such notice shall be of effect unless either it is given at a meeting of the Board or the Director takes reasonable steps to secure that it is brought up and read at the next meeting of the Board after it is given.

(F)   Where proposals are under consideration concerning the appointment (including fixing or varying the terms of appointment) of two or more Directors to offices or employments with the Company or any company in which the Company is interested, such proposals may be divided and considered in relation to each Director separately and in such cases each of the Directors concerned (if not debarred from voting by reason of being the holder or beneficially interested in one per cent or more of the issued shares of any class of the relevant company in which the Company is interested or of any third company through which his interest is derived or of the voting rights available to members of the relevant company) shall be entitled to vote (and be counted in the quorum) in respect of each resolution except that concerning his own appointment.

(G)   If any question shall arise at any meeting as to the materiality of a Director's interest or as to the entitlement of any Director to vote and such question is not resolved by his voluntarily agreeing to abstain from voting, such question shall be referred to the Chairman of the meeting and his ruling in relation to any Director (other than himself) shall be final and conclusive except in the case where the nature or extent of the interest of the Director concerned has not been fairly disclosed. In the case of any question in relation to the Chairman, such question shall be referred to and decided by the Directors present at the meeting (other than the Chairman), whose decision shall be final and conclusive.

EXECUTIVE DIRECTORS

Appointment of Executive Directors

97.   (A)   The Board may from time to time appoint one or more of their body to be the holder of any executive office (including, where considered appropriate, the office of Chairman, Deputy Chairman, Vice Chairman, Group Chief Executive or Group Managing Director) on such terms and (subject to the provisions of the Companies Acts) for such period as they think fit.

(B)   The appointment of a Director appointed to any executive office shall be subject to determination in accordance with the provisions of Article 105 or if he ceases from any cause to be a Director, but without prejudice to any claim he may have for damages for breach of contract of service between him and the Company.

Powers of Chairman and Executive Directors

98.   The Board may entrust to or confer upon the Chairman of the Board and upon a Director holding any such executive office as aforesaid any of the powers exercisable by them as Directors upon such terms and conditions and with such restrictions as they think fit and may from time to time revoke, withdraw, alter or vary all or any of such powers.

ROTATION OF DIRECTORS

Retirement of Directors

99.   At the Annual General Meeting in every year one-third of the Directors for the time being subject to retirement by rotation, or, if their number is not three or a multiple of three the number nearest to but not greater than one-third, shall retire from office. A Director retiring at a meeting shall retain office until the close or adjournment of the meeting.

Selection of Directors to retire

100.   The Directors to retire in every year shall be those who have been longest in office since their last election or appointment, but as between persons who became or were last elected Directors on the same day those to retire shall (unless they otherwise agree among themselves) be determined by lot. The Directors to retire in every year shall be determined by the composition of the Board at the date of the notice convening the Annual General Meeting. A retiring Director shall be eligible for re-election.

Filling vacated office

101.   The Company at the meeting at which a Director retires in the manner aforesaid may fill up the vacated office, by electing a person thereto, and in default the retiring Director shall, if offering himself for re-election, be deemed to have been re-elected, unless at such meeting it is expressly resolved not to fill up such vacated office, or unless a resolution for the re-election of such Director shall have been put to the meeting and lost.

Notice of intention to appoint Directors

102.   No person other than a Director retiring at the meeting shall, unless recommended by the Directors, be eligible for election to the office of Director at any General Meeting unless not less than seven nor more than forty-two clear days before the day appointed for the meeting there shall have been left at the Office notice in writing addressed to the Secretary (signed by some member other than the person to

be proposed) duly qualified to be present and vote at the meeting for which such notice is given of his intention to propose such person for election, and also notice in writing signed by the person to be proposed of his willingness to be elected.

Increase and reduction in number of Directors

103.   The Company in General Meeting may from time to time increase or reduce the number of Directors, and may also alter their qualification and determine in what rotation such increased or reduced number is to go out of office and may appoint any person to be a Director either to fill a casual vacancy or as an additional Director.

Power to fill casual vacancies

104.   The Board shall have power at any time, and from time to time, to appoint any person to be a Director, either to fill a casual vacancy or as an addition to the existing Board, but so that the total number of Directors shall not at any time exceed the maximum number fixed by or in accordance with these Articles. Any Director so appointed shall hold office only until the next following Annual General Meeting, and shall then be eligible for re-election. No Director who retires under this Article shall be taken into account in determining who are to retire by rotation at such meeting.

Removal of Directors

105.   The Company may by Ordinary Resolution remove any Director before the expiration of his period of office, notwithstanding any provision of these Articles or of any agreement between the Company and such Director, but without prejudice to any claim he may have for damages for breach of any such agreement. The Company may by like resolution appoint another person in place of a Director so removed from office and any person so appointed shall be subject to retirement by rotation at the same time as if he had become a Director on the day on which the Director in whose place he is appointed was last elected a Director. In default of such appointment the vacancy so arising may be filled by the Directors as a casual vacancy.

POWERS OF DIRECTORS

General powers of Directors

106.   The business of the Company shall be managed by the Board which may exercise all such powers of the Company as are not, by the Companies Acts or by these Articles required to be exercised by the Company in General Meeting, subject nevertheless to these Articles, to the provisions of the Companies Acts and to such regulations, being not inconsistent with the aforesaid regulations or provisions, as may be prescribed by extraordinary or special resolution, but no regulation so made by the Company shall invalidate any prior act of the Board which would have been valid if such regulation had not been made. The general powers given by this Article shall not be limited or restricted by any special authority or power given to the Board by any other Article.

Subsidiary companies

107.   The Board may arrange that any branch of the business carried on by the Company or any other business in which the Company may be interested shall be carried on by or through one or more subsidiary companies, and they may on behalf of the Company make such arrangements as they think advisable for taking the profits or bearing the losses of any branch or business so carried on or for financing, assisting or subsidising any such subsidiary company or guaranteeing its contracts, obligations or liabilities, and they may appoint, remove and re-appoint any persons (whether members of their own body or not) to act as Directors, Executive Directors or Managers of any such company or any other company in which the Company may be interested, and may determine the remuneration (whether by way of salary, commission on profits or otherwise) of any person so appointed and any Directors of the Company may retain any remuneration so payable to them.

Local boards

108.   The Board may establish any local boards or agencies for managing any of the affairs of the Company, either in the United Kingdom or elsewhere, and may appoint any persons to be members of such local boards or any managers or agents, and may fix their remuneration, and may delegate to any local board, manager or agent any of the powers, authorities and discretions vested in the Board, with power to sub-delegate, and may authorise the members of any local boards, or any of them, to fill any vacancies therein, and to act notwithstanding vacancies, and any such appointment or delegation may be made upon such terms and subject to such conditions as the Board may think fit, and the Board may remove any person so appointed, and may annul or vary any such delegation, but no person dealing in good faith and without notice of any annulment or variation shall be affected thereby.

Attorneys

109.   The Board may from time to time and at any time by power of attorney or otherwise appoint any company, firm or person or any fluctuating body of persons, whether nominated directly or indirectly by the Board, to be the agent of the Company for such purposes and with such powers, authorities and discretions (not exceeding those vested in or exercisable by the Board under these Articles) and for such period and subject to such conditions as they may think fit, and any such power of attorney may contain such provisions for the protection and convenience of persons dealing with any such agent as the Board may think fit and may also authorise any such agent to delegate all or any of the powers, authorities and discretions vested in him.

Local registers

110.   Subject to any provisions of the Companies Acts the Company may keep an overseas or local register in any place, and the Board may make and vary such regulations as it may think fit respecting the keeping of any such register.

Power to borrow and give security

111.   (A)   Subject as provided in this Article, the Board may exercise all the powers of the Company to borrow money, and to mortgage or charge its undertaking property and assets (present and future) and uncalled capital, to issue debentures, debenture stock, and other securities whether outright or as collateral security for any debt, liability or obligation of the Company or of any third party.

(B)   The Board shall restrict the borrowings of the Company and exercise all rights exercisable by the Company in relation to subsidiary companies so as to secure (as regards subsidiary companies so far as by such exercise it can secure) that the aggregate amount for the time being remaining undischarged of all moneys borrowed by the Group (which expression in this Article means and includes the Company and its subsidiary companies for the time being) and for the time being owing to persons outside the Group shall not at any time, without the previous sanction of a Special Resolution of the Company in General Meeting, exceed an amount equal to twice the share capital and consolidated reserves.

(C)   [Definitions for the purposes of paragraphs (A) and (B)]

(D)   A certificate or report by the Auditors as to the amount of the share capital and consolidated reserves or of any moneys borrowed or to the effect that the limit imposed by this Article has not been or will not be exceeded at any particular time or times shall be conclusive evidence of that amount or fact.

(E)   No debt incurred or security given in respect of moneys borrowed in excess of the limit hereby imposed shall be invalid or ineffectual, except in the case of express notice at the time when the debt was incurred or security given that the limit hereby imposed had been or would thereby be exceeded.

Provisions for employees

112.   The Board may by resolution exercise any power conferred by the Companies Acts to make provision for the benefit of persons employed or formerly employed by the Company or any of its subsidiaries in connection with the cessation or the transfer to any person of the whole or part of the undertaking of the Company or that subsidiary.

Power to give pensions

113.   Without restricting the generality of its powers the Board may give or award pensions, annuities, gratuities and superannuation or other allowances or benefits to any persons who are or have at any time been Directors of or employed by or in the service of the Company or of any company which is a subsidiary and to the wives, widows, children and other relatives and dependants of any such persons and may set up, establish, support and maintain pension, superannuation and other funds or schemes (whether contributory or non-contributory) for the benefit of any such persons.

Power to purchase liability insurance

114. Without prejudice to the provisions of Article 165 the Board shall have power

to purchase and maintain insurance for the benefit of any persons who are or were at any time Directors, officer or employees of the Company, or of any other company in which the Company has any interest whether direct or indirect or which is in any way allied to or associated with the Company, or of any subsidiary of the Company or of any such other company, or who are or were at any time trustees of any pension fund in which any employees of the Company or of any such other company or subsidiary are interested, including (without prejudice to the generality of the foregoing) insurance against any liability incurred by such persons in respect of any act or omission in the actual or purported execution or discharge of their powers or otherwise in relation to their duties, powers or offices in relation to the Company or any such other company, subsidiary or pension fund.

Holding of concurrent office
115.   A Director of the Company may be or become a Director or other officer of, or otherwise interested in, any company promoted by the Company or in which the Company may be interested as a shareholder or otherwise, and no such Director shall be accountable for any remuneration or other benefits received by him as a director or officer of, or from his interest in such other company. The Board may also exercise the voting power conferred by the shares in any other company held or owned by the Company in such manner in all respects as it thinks fit including the exercise in favour of any resolution appointing it or any of its number directors or other officers of such other company or voting or providing for the payment of remuneration to the directors or officers of such other company. Any rights in the manner aforesaid notwithstanding that he may be or be about to become a director or officer of such other company and as such or in any other manner is or may be interested in the exercise of such voting rights in the manner aforesaid.

Signature of cheques and bills
116.   All cheques, promissory notes, drafts, bills of exchange, and other negotiable instruments, and all receipts for moneys paid to the Company, shall be signed, drawn, accepted, endorsed, or otherwise executed, as the case may be, in such manner as the Board shall from time to time by resolution determine.

PROCEEDINGS OF DIRECTORS

Board meetings
117.   (A)   The Directors may meet together for the dispatch of business, adjourn and otherwise regulate their meetings as they think fit. Questions arising at any meeting shall be determined by a majority of votes. In case of an equality of votes the Chairman shall have a second or casting vote. A Director may, and the secretary on the requisition of a Director shall, at any time summon a meeting of the Board.
(B)   Notice of a meeting of the Board shall be deemed to be properly given to a Director if it is given to him personally or by word of mouth or sent in writing to him

at his last known address or any other address given by him to the Company for this purpose. A Director absent or intending to be absent from the United Kingdom may request the Board that notices of meetings of the Board shall during his absence be sent in writing to him at an address given by him to the Company for this purpose, but such notices need not be given any earlier than notices given to Directors not so absent and if no request is made to the Board it shall not be necessary to give notice of a meeting to any Director who is for the time being absent from the United Kingdom. A Director may waive notice of any meeting either prospectively or retrospectively.

Authority for one Director to vote for absent Director
118.   A Director unable to attend any meeting of the Board may at any time by writing under his hand and deposited at the Office, or delivered at a meeting of the Board, authorise any other Director to vote for him at that meeting and in that event the Director so authorised shall have a vote for each Director by whom he is so authorised in addition to his own vote.

Quorum
119.   The quorum necessary for the transaction of business of the Board may be fixed from time to time by the Board and unless so fixed at any other number shall be two. For the purposes of these Articles any Director who is able (directly or by telephonic communication) to speak and be heard by each of the other Directors present or deemed to be present at any meeting of the Board, shall be deemed to be present in person at such meeting and shall be entitled to vote or be counted in the quorum accordingly. Such meeting shall be deemed to take place where the largest group of those participating is assembled, or, if there is no such group, where the chairman of the meeting then is, and the word 'meeting' shall be construed accordingly.

Proceedings in case of vacancies
120.   The continuing Directors may act notwithstanding any vacancies in the Board, but if and so long as the number of Directors is reduced below the minimum number fixed by or in accordance with these Articles, the continuing Directors or Director may act for the purpose of filling up vacancies on the Board or of summoning General Meetings of the Company, but not for any other purpose. If there be no Directors or Director able or willing to act, then any two shareholders may summon a general meeting of shareholders for the purpose of appointing Directors.

Chairman, Deputy Chairman and Vice Chairman
121.   The Board may elect a Chairman, Deputy Chairman and Vice Chairman of its meetings and determine the period for which he is to hold office. If no such Chairman, Deputy Chairman or Vice Chairman shall have been appointed, or if at any meeting the Chairman, Deputy Chairman or Vice Chairman be not present within five minutes after the time appointed for holding the same, the Directors present may choose one of their number to be Chairman of the meeting.

Resolution in writing

122.   A resolution in writing signed by all the Directors for the time being in the United Kingdom shall be as effective as a resolution passed at a meeting of the Board duly convened and held, and may consist of several documents in like form each signed by one of more of the Directors.

Powers of Meeting at which a quorum is present

123.   A meeting of the Directors for the time being, at which a quorum is present, shall be competent to exercise all powers and discretions for the time being exercisable by the Board.

Power to appoint Committees

124.   (A)   The Board may delegate any of its powers, duties and discretions to committees consisting of such Directors or persons in the employment of the Company or of any subsidiary of the Company as it thinks fit. Any committee so formed shall in the exercise of the powers duties and discretions so delegated conform to any regulations that may be imposed on it by the Board. If any such regulations confer voting rights upon members of the committee who are not Directors, such members shall be less than half the total number of members of the committee and no resolution of the committee shall be effective unless a majority of the members of the committee present throughout the meeting are Directors. Any such committee may be given a distinguishing title by the Board and the title may include the word 'Board' with a descriptive prefix. A member of such committee who is not a Director shall not by virtue of his membership be or have the power in any respect to act as a Director (notwithstanding that the designation of his membership of or office in such committee may include the word 'Director') nor shall he be entitled to receive notice of or attend or vote at a meeting of the Board.

(B)   The meetings and proceedings of any such committee consisting of two or more members shall be governed by the provisions of these Articles regulating the meetings and proceedings of the Board, so far as the same are applicable and are not superseded by any regulations made by the Board under paragraph (A) of this Article.

(C)   The power to delegate contained in this Article shall be effective in relation to the powers, duties and discretions of the Board generally whether or not express reference is made in these Articles to powers, duties or discretions being exercised by the Board or by a committee authorised by the Board.

Validity of acts of Directors and Committees

125.   All acts done by a meeting of a committee of the Board consistently with the powers, duties and discretions conferred upon it shall as regards all person dealing in good faith with the Company be as valid as if done by the Board and all acts done by any meeting of the Board, or of a committee of the Board, or by a person acting as a Director or member of a committee shall as regards all persons dealing in good faith with the Company, notwithstanding that there was some defect in the appointment of any such Director or such committee or person acting as aforesaid, or (in the case of

Directors) that they or any of them were disqualified or had vacated office or were not entitled to vote, be as valid as if every such person had been duly appointed, and was qualified and had continued to be a Director or member of such committee and had been entitled to vote (as the case may be).

DEPARTMENTAL, DIVISIONAL OR LOCAL DIRECTORS

Departmental, Divisional or Local Directors

126.   The Board may from time to time appoint any person to be a Departmental, Divisional or Local Director and define, limit or restrict his powers and duties and determine his remuneration and the designation of his office and may at any time remove such person from such office. A Departmental, Divisional or Local Director (notwithstanding that the designation of his office may include the word 'Director') shall not by virtue of such office be or have power in any respect to act as a Director of the Company nor be entitled to receive notice of or attend and vote at meetings of Directors nor be deemed to be a Director for any of the purposes of these Articles.

SECRETARY

Appointment of Secretary

127.   The Board shall appoint a Secretary and may appoint one or more Deputy Secretaries or Assistant Secretaries each of whom, if more than one, shall for the purpose of these Articles be deemed to be the Secretary.

THE SEAL

Formalities for affixing Seal

128.   The Board shall determine from time to time the device of the Seal and provide for its safe custody. The Seal shall only be used by the authority of the Board or of a committee of the Board authorised by the Board in that behalf. Every instrument to which the Seal shall be affixed shall be signed by a Director and shall be countersigned by the Secretary or a second Director or such other person appointed by the Board for that purpose, save as except that a certificate or other document of title in respect of any share, stock or Debenture created or issued by the Company given under the Seal need not be signed.

Official Seals

129.   The Company may exercise the powers conferred by the Companies Acts with regard to having official seals and such powers shall be vested in the Board.

Signed instruments

130.   Where the Companies Acts so permit, any instrument signed by a Director and the Secretary or any two Directors and expressed to be executed by the Company shall have the same effect as if executed under the Seal.

AUTHENTICATION OF DOCUMENTS

Power to authenticate documents

131.   Any Director or Secretary or any person appointed by the Board for the purpose shall have the power to authenticate any documents affecting the constitution of the Company (including the Memorandum and Articles of Association) and any resolutions passed by the Company, the Board or a committee of the Board, and any books, records, documents and accounts relating to the business of the Company, and to certify copies thereof or extracts therefrom as true copies or extracts; and where any books, records, documents or accounts are elsewhere than at the Office the local manager or other officer of the Company having the custody thereof shall be deemed to be a person appointed by the Board as aforesaid.

Certified copies

132.   A document purporting to be a copy of a resolution of the Board or an extract from the minutes of a meeting of the Board or of a committee of the Board which is certified as such in accordance with the provisions of the last preceding Article shall be conclusive evidence in favour of persons dealing with the Company upon faith thereof that such resolution had been duly passed or, as the case may be, that such extract is a true and accurate record of a duly constituted meeting of the Board or of a committee of the Board as the case may be.

ALTERNATE DIRECTORS

133.   (A)   Any Director may at any time appoint any person approved by the Board to be an alternate Director of the Company, and may at any time remove an alternate Director so appointed by him from office. An alternate Director so appointed shall not be entitled to receive any remuneration from the Company, nor be required to hold any qualification, but shall otherwise be subject to the provisions of these Articles with regard to Directors. An alternate Director shall (subject to his giving to the Company an address within the United Kingdom at which notices may be served upon him) be entitled to receive notices of all meetings of the Board, and to attend and vote as a Director at any such meeting at which the director appointing him is not personally present and subject as provided in these Articles, be counted in the quorum at any such meeting at which the Director appointing him is not personally present and generally to perform all the functions of his appointor as a Director in the absence of such appointor except that an alternate Director shall not be entitled to appoint an alternate.

(B)   An alternate Director shall alone be responsible to the Company for his acts and defaults and shall not be deemed to be the agent of or for the Director appointing him. An alternate Director may be paid expenses and shall be entitled to be indemnified by the Company to the same extent mutatis mutandis as if he were a Director.

(C)   An alternate Director shall ipso facto cease to be an alternate Director if his appointor ceases to be a Director; provided that if any Director retires by rotation but is re-elected by the meeting at which his retirement took effect, any appointment made by him pursuant to this Article which was in force immediately prior to his retirement shall continue after his re-election as if he had not so retired. All appointments and removals of alternate Directors shall be effected in writing under the hand of the Director making or revoking such appointment and delivered to the Office.

NOTICES

158.   Any notice or document may be served by the Company on any member either personally or by sending it through the post in a prepaid letter addressed to such member at his registered address as appearing in the Register. In respect of joint holdings all notices shall be given to that one of the joint holders whose name stands first in the Register and notice so given shall be sufficient notice to all the joint holders.

Service on members resident abroad
159.   Any member described in the Register by an address not within the United Kingdom who shall from time to time give to the Company an address within the United Kingdom at which notices may be served upon him shall be entitled to have notices served upon him at such address, but save as aforesaid, no member other than a registered member described in the Register by an address within the United Kingdom shall be entitled to receive any notice from the Company.

Notice by advertisement
160.   Any notice required to be given by the Company to the members or any of them, and not expressly provided for by or pursuant to these Articles shall be sufficiently given if given by advertisement inserted once in at least one leading national newspaper.

Proof of service of notices
161.   Any notice or other document, if sent by post, shall be deemed to have been served or delivered at the expiration of twenty four hours (or, where second class mail is employed, forty eight hours) after the time when the letter containing the same is posted, and in proving such service or delivery it shall be sufficient to prove that the letter containing the notice or document was properly addressed, stamped and posted. Any notice or other document delivered or left at the registered address otherwise than by post shall be deemed to have been served or delivered on the day it was so delivered or left. A notice to be given or served by advertisement shall be deemed to have been served before noon on the day on which the advertisement appears.

Service on successor to dead or bankrupt member
162.   A person entitled to a share in consequence of the death or bankruptcy of a member upon supplying to the Company such evidence as the Board may reasonably require to show his title to the share, and upon supplying also an address within the

United Kingdom for the service of notices, shall be entitled to have served upon him at such address any notice or document to which the member but for his death or bankruptcy would be entitled, and such service shall for all purposes be deemed a sufficient service of such notice or document on all persons interested (whether jointly with or claiming through or under him) in the share. Save as aforesaid any notice or document delivered or sent by post to or left at the registered address of any member in pursuance of these Articles shall, notwithstanding that such member be then dead or bankrupt, and whether or not the Company have notice of his death or bankruptcy be deemed to have been duly served in respect of any share registered in the name of such member as sole or joint holder.

Convening of Meetings by advertisement

163.   If at any time by reason of suspension or curtailment of postal services within the United Kingdom the Company is unable effectively to convene a General Meeting by notices sent through the post, a General Meeting may be convened by a notice advertised on the same date in at least two leading daily newspapers with appropriate circulation, one of which at least shall be a leading daily newspaper published in London; and such notice shall be deemed to have been duly served on all members entitled thereto before noon on the day when the advertisement appears. In any such case the Company shall send confirmatory copies of the notices by post if at least seven days prior to the meeting the posting of notices to addresses throughout the United Kingdom again becomes practicable.

INDEMNITY

165.   Subject to the provisions of the Companies Acts, every Director, Auditor, Secretary or other officer of the Company shall be indemnified by the Company against all costs, charges, losses, expenses and liabilities incurred by him in the execution and discharge of his duties or in relation thereto and against any liability incurred by him in defending any proceedings whether civil or criminal in which judgment is given in his favour or in which he is acquitted or which are otherwise disposed of without a finding or admission of material breach of duty on his part or in connection with any application under the Companies Acts in which relief is granted to him by the Court.

Matters requiring shareholder approval under the Companies Act 1985 and the Insolvency Act 1986 and type of resolution required

Nature of resolution	Type of resolution	Companies Act 1985
Change of situation of registered office to Wales in memorandum of association	Special	s. 2(2)
Alteration of objects in memorandum of association	Special	s. 4(1)
Alteration of articles of association	Special	s. 9(1)
Alteration of conditions in memorandum which could lawfully be contained in the articles	Special	s. 17(1)
Change of company name	Special	s. 28(1)
Ratification of (and relief for) action by directors which is outside the capacity of the company	Special	s. 35(3)
Re-registration of private company as public	Special	s. 43(1)
Re-registration of unlimited company as public	Special	s. 48(2)
Re-registration of unlimited company as limited	Special	s. 51
Re-registration of public company as private	Special	s. 53(1)
Authority to directors to allot shares	Ordinary	s 80
To extend the period for which the general meeting may authorise the directors to allot shares under s. 80 of CA 1985	Elective	s. 80A
Disapplication of pre-emption rights	Special	s. 95
Transfer to public company of non-cash asset in initial period	Ordinary	s. 104
Resolution that uncalled share capital shall not be called up except in a winding up	Special	s. 120
Alteration of share capital	Ordinary	s. 121
Variation of class rights (not attached by memorandum) for which the articles make no alternative provision with respect to variation	Extra-ordinary	s. 125(2)
Reduction of share capital	Special	s. 135

Nature of resolution	Type of resolution	Companies Act 1985
Financial assistance by private company for acquisition of own shares	Special	s. 155
Resolution authorising terms of off-market purchase of own shares	Special	s. 164
Purchase of own shares under contingent purchase contract	Special	s. 165(2)
Authority for market purchase of own shares	Ordinary	s. 166
Assignment or release of company's right to purchase own shares	Special	s. 167
Purchase of own shares (payment out of capital of private company)	Special	s. 173
Resolution of dormant company not to appoint auditors	Special	s. 250
To dispense with the laying of accounts and reports before general meetings	Elective	s. 252
Removal of a director	Ordinary	s. 303
Approval of payment for loss of office to director	Ordinary	ss. 312 & 313
Resolution making liability of directors unlimited	Special	s. 307
Approval of assignment of office by a director	Special	s. 308
Director's contract of more than 5 years	Ordinary	s. 319
To dispense with holding annual general meetings	Elective	s. 366A
To reduce the majority required to authorise short notice of meetings	Elective	ss. 369(4) & 378(3)
Resolution to revoke elective resolution	Ordinary	s. 379A
Appointment of auditors by company in general meeting	Ordinary	ss. 385 & 385A
To dispense with the annual appointment of auditors	Elective	s. 386
Resolution to fix remuneration of auditors	Ordinary	s. 390A
Removal of auditors	Ordinary	s. 391
Making provision for employees on cessation or transfer of business	Ordinary	s. 719
	Insolvency Act 1986	
Resolution to wind up voluntarily	Special	s. 84(1)
Voluntary winding up of a company that cannot continue its business by reason of its liabilities	Extra-ordinary	s. 84(1)
Authorise liquidator to transfer assets of company to new company in exchange for securities in the new company	Special	s. 110(3)
Members' voluntary winding up, to sanction liquidator's proposals for a compromise with the company's creditors	Extra-ordinary	s. 165(2)
Resolution to be wound up by court	Special	s. 122(1)
	85 Table A	
Directions to directors	Special	reg. 70
Distribution by a liquidator of surplus assets in kind instead of realising them in cash.	Extra-ordinary	reg. 117

Entitlements under 1985 Table A to receive notice and accounts and to attend and vote

Member, representative or officer		Entitled to			
		Receive notice	Receive accounts	Attend meetings	Vote at meetings
Members	Voting shares	Yes (reg. 38)	Yes (s. 238)	Yes	Yes (reg. 54)
	Non-voting shares	Yes (reg. 38)	Yes (s. 238)	Note 1	Note 1
	Preference shares	Yes (reg. 38)	Yes (s. 238)	Note 1	No
Joint holders	First named	Yes (reg. 38)	Yes (s. 238)	Yes	Yes (reg. 55)
	Second, third or fourth named	No (reg. 112)	No (s. 238)	Yes	See reg. 55
Members overseas (no UK address)		No (reg. 112)	Yes (s. 238)	Yes	Yes (reg. 54)
Personal representative of deceased member		Yes (reg. 38)	Yes (s. 238)	No (reg. 31)	No (reg. 31)
Personal representative of bankrupt member		Yes (reg. 38)	Yes (s. 238)	No (reg. 31)	No (reg. 31)
Receiver in mental disorder		Send to member	Send to member	Yes (reg. 56)	Yes (reg. 56)
Member with calls unpaid		Yes (reg. 38)	Yes (s.238)	Yes	No (reg. 57)
Debenture holder		Note 1	Yes (s. 238)	Note 1	No
Auditors		Yes (reg. 38)	Yes (ss. 238 238 & 390)	Yes (s. 390)	No
Directors who are not members		Yes (reg. 38)	Yes (s. 238 & reg. 38)	Yes (reg. 44)	No

Note 1: Not covered in Table A. Will depend on articles or terms of issue.

Specimen briefing document for AGM

1. Location

The Company's AGM will take place at [Venue], [Address]
The areas being used are as follows:

Registration	Foyer, ground floor
Cloakroom	Foyer, ground floor
Shareholders' catering	[Room 1], third floor
Customer Enquiries	[Room 1], third floor
Shareholder Enquiries	[Room 1], third floor
Exhibition	[Room 2], third floor
Board members' lounge	[Room 3], third floor
Registrars' room	[Room 4], third floor
Organisers' office	[Room 5], third floor
Press office	[Room 6], third floor
Investor relations office	[Room 7], third floor
Researchers' room	[Room 8], third floor
AGM	[Room 9 and Room 2], third floor
Lunch	[Room 10], second floor

2. Car parking

Chauffeurs bringing directors and their guests to the AGM may drive onto the forecourt of the [venue]. If chauffeurs remain with their vehicles, they may wait on the forecourt but otherwise they must leave the area for the duration of the AGM.

There are no car parking facilities for [Company] staff or shareholders on site, but there are car parks within walking distance at [Locations].

3.   Timetable

Thursday 4 August 1994
Delivery and installation of stage set, display stands, question and answer system and exhibition panels throughout the morning.

1400	[Company] staff arrive for familiarisation tours and briefing
1430	Registrars' equipment delivery and installation
1600	Lighting check
1630	[Company] researchers arrive for briefing with Q & A personnel in the [Room 8]
1700	[Company] directors arrive for rehearsals

Friday 5 August 1994

0800	Chairman's rehearsal
0830	[Company] staff arrive
0845	Security briefing
0930	All staff at their posts
0945	All public areas to be ready
1000	Doors open
1030	All public areas to be ready
1055	Board escorted onto stage
1100	AGM commences
1300–1330	AGM ends
1330	Lunch commences
1400	Displays dismantled and removed according to agreed delivery schedule
1800	All [Company] equipment to be removed from the building

4.   Security procedures

In the event of an emergency, the security personnel at [Venue] will take all necessary action. If a suspicious object is discovered or if there is any other security or safety problem, please contact the organisers' office in [Room 5] immediately. The organisers can then take steps to contact all the relevant authorities.

5.   First aid procedures

First aid staff from St John's Ambulance Brigade will be in attendance at the Meeting and there is a fully equipped first aid room on site. In the event of an emergency, please contact the St John's Ambulance Brigade representative in [Room 2] direct or contact the organisers' office in [Room 5].

6. Guidelines for [Company] registration personnel

Registration is the point at which it is established whether people have the right to attend the meeting and also the means whereby shareholder attendance numbers are obtained.

[Company] personnel are to follow the procedures set out below:

(a) Shareholders should bring with them their admission card sent to them with the Company's annual report. (Samples will be provided to [Company] personnel involved.)

(b) Shareholders producing such cards should be asked to hand you the card in return for which you should give them a yellow shareholder (voting) card and a folder containing the Chairman's welcome letter and notice for the meeting. Shareholders are also to be provided with a self-adhesive badge. It is imperative that you obtain their admission card *before* handing them a shareholder badge card and folder. Thereafter shareholders are free to make their way to the lifts for the exhibition and catering area and meeting room which are all on the third floor.

(c) Shareholders who wish to bring a guest into the meeting with them can do so but the guest is to be given a shareholder guest badge together with a pink guest card (which is non-voting), and a folder.

(d) Where two people are joint shareholders and both wish to attend, only the first named may have a yellow voting card, the second must be given a pink guest card and folder. Although the second shareholder is not technically a guest, this is the only practical way of preventing a double vote against a single holding.

(e) Staff shareholders who only hold free and matching shares are not entitled to attend the meeting and any staff producing any blue card should be referred to [Registrars] personnel.

(f) Institutional shareholders or corporate bodies are entitled to appoint a corporate representative to attend the meeting and vote on their behalf. Such corporate representatives should produce a letter of authorisation on their company letter heading to this effect. Such letters should be signed by their company secretary or director and strictly speaking should also bear their company's seal, but the latter is not always applied. If you consider this letter to be authentic hand the representative a shareholder badge, a yellow shareholder voting card and folder. If you are in any doubt refer the individual to [Registrars] personnel.

(g) Shareholders without admission cards or anyone who says they are a proxy, should be referred to the desks' staff by [Registrars] personnel.

(h) Likewise, there are separate registration procedures for the press and guests of the company who should be referred to the appropriate desk.

(i) Under no circumstances should anyone who does not have any means of identification be admitted. If in any doubt, refer to [Name] of [Registrars] who will contact security if necessary.

(j) Please retain all admission cards as these will be 'wand' read by [Registrars] personnel during the meeting to enable an accurate count of shareholders attending.

7.   Guidelines for [Registrars] Verification Personnel

Verification is the area which handles shareholders who cannot be admitted to the meeting directly through registration. Most of these will be shareholders who have forgotten their admission cards but there may also be proxies.

The clerical procedures are as follows:

(a) A person claiming to be a shareholder who has forgotten his voting card should be asked his name, address and number of shares. These details should be compared to the details on the computer and if the details agree, the shareholder should be asked to sign the attendance record and given a yellow shareholder voting card.

(b) A person claiming to be a proxy should be asked his name and that of the shareholder he represents. These details should be compared to the list of proxies provided and if the details agree the proxy should be asked to sign the attendance record and given a blue proxy card. Any proxy who is not on the list may not be admitted, except as a guest under certain circumstances.

(c) There will be separate registration procedures for people who are guests of the company or members of the press, and these people should be referred to the appropriate staffed desk by [Company] personnel.

(d) Employees who hold free and matching shares or share options are not shareholders and may only be admitted to the meeting if they have stock as well. If such staff are insisting on admission it is suggested that you contact [Name] and [Company]'s security adviser, who collectively will determine the appropriate course of action.

(e) At the end of the meeting the admission cards and signatures can be counted to establish how many people attended the meeting.

8.   Guidelines for press registration

The [Company]'s press officer will brief the [Company] staff on the press desk as to the procedures to be adopted.

9.   Guidelines for visitors' registration

[Company] staff on this desk will be provided with guest lists before the meeting. These lists will provide the names of the guests and their status, that is shareholder or guest, so that these staff may issue the appropriate cards, that is yellow or pink and folders.

10.   Displays

There will be a series of small displays at the back of the main auditorium for shareholders' general interest before and after the AGM. The displays cover the main businesses such as [. . .].

[Company] personnel acting as stewards are to encourage shareholders to visit the display stands and models in the main auditorium. The doors to the main auditorium will be open at 1000 and a PA announcement will inform shareholders that the exhibition area is open.

11.   Customer and shareholder enquiries

There will be a customer enquiry desk situated in [Room 1] staffed by [Company] personnel who will be pleased to answer queries on [. . .].

Shareholders with enquiries relating to their shareholding should be directed to the shareholder enquiry desk situated [. . .]. This desk will be staffed by [Registrars] personnel and [Company] personnel. The company's statutory registers will be available for inspection by shareholders at this desk.

12.   Question points

There will be four question points, two in [Room 1] and two in the auditorium, for any shareholder wishing to raise a question. All questions should be registered in advance of the meeting as far as possible – details of this will be given to shareholders on their arrival. Included in the shareholders' folders will be a shareholder question card. The question card is for those shareholders who would prefer to receive a written answer – or if there is insufficient time for their question to be asked at the Meeting.

A number of questions that shareholders may have can be answered either at the customer enquiry desk or the shareholder enquiry desk and personnel at the question points should direct them as necessary.

13.   Question and answer management system

The system consists of purpose-designed software running on a network of IBM compatible PCs. The configuration of the system consists of four question registration points, each with a computer and printer, two PCs and printers processing the answers to the questions and two further PCs outputting the next question (preview) or the 'on air' question (current). The system is split into four parts:

- front of house question registration points, two in [Room 1] and two in the auditorium;
- the research area behind the scenes;
- outputting information to the platform; and
- on stage equipment.

At each registration point there is a computer and printer. There will be two personnel, a professional computer operator and a member of [Company] staff. The company employee is the first to meet the questioner. They make sure that he/she is entitled to ask a question (i.e. is a shareholder holding a yellow voting card). Proxies and visitors (i.e. those with blue and pink cards are not permitted to ask questions). They should have sufficient procedural knowledge to be able to allocate the question to the correct resolution by reference to the Notice of Meeting.

Shareholders may need assistance to compose their questions and therefore [Company] staff may wish to encourage questioners to draft questions on the pads provided at each point.

The question is then dictated to the computer operator. It is allocated a unique number which relates to the resolution to which it applies. Once the question has been entered, a print-out of the question is provided for the questioner to keep. A badge is also generated with all the essential information on it (i.e. question number, resolution number and the question point in the auditorium from which it is to be asked).

The badge is marked with a colour sticker and worn by the questioner to aid his or her identification as the questioner by [Company] personnel and [Event Organisers] staff marshalling questioners within the auditorium.

As the question is printed out for the questioner it is simultaneously networked to the research area, stored on the file server, and printed out on two part paper. In the research area there would be a number of senior company representatives with their own co-ordinator. One copy of the question goes to the co-ordinator who will then decide which researcher will answer it and pass it on. The other copy is filed as a control by the question controller backstage in [Room 8].

Once the question has been answered, hopefully with bullet points provided by the researchers, it is collected by either of two computer operators who add the answers to the questions. Once the answer has been added the page is re-stored on the file server and printed out again, locally, on two part paper. One copy is given to the question controller and the other held as a paper back-up.

The PCs and operators output to the stage. They will output the questions in the order called by the question controller. One PC is dedicated to previewing the next question, the other outputs the current question. At any time additional information can be added to the displayed page to cope with supplementary or non pre-registered questions. Any alterations made on the screen will be reflected instantly on the on-stage monitors.

On the platform the Chairman will have one monitor dedicated to the current question and one dedicated to the next question, or preview. Executive directors will have one monitor each with a switch to select 'next' or 'on-air' and non-executive directors will have one switchable monitor between two.

14. Entrance to the auditorium

[Company] personnel acting as stewards will monitor the admission of people entering the auditorium. Shareholders and their guests should have lapel stickers and have yellow or pink cards. Proxies should have a badge and blue card. Other personnel entering the auditorium should be wearing badges: either [Company] personnel, or [Registrars] personnel or representatives from the press or organisers.

15.   Seating arrangements

Seating for guests will be in the front row of the two seating blocks. Seating for questioners is in the back row of the two seating blocks, adjacent to the question points. Shareholders with pre-registered questions will be identified with badges and staff marshalling this area should seat questioners next to question point A or B in the auditorium as per the instruction on the badge. The question points are identified by overhead signs.

An area of the right side of the auditorium has been reserved for shareholders with wheelchairs and a signed area has been fitted with an induction loop system for the hard of hearing. This section will be clearly signed. Chairs will also be allocated for those accompanying the disabled.

Other shareholders may sit where they choose but if possible should be encouraged to sit near the front so that late arrivals sit towards the back. No special arrangements have been made for the press.

16.   Annual general meeting

The meeting will commence at 1100. Prior to this background music will be played in the auditorium from 1000. A short opening sequence of slides will be shown during this period. Once the meeting has commenced, [Company] personnel may take their seats in the reserved area at the rear of the auditorium.

The finishing time of the meeting cannot be ascertained, but the anticipated time is between 1300 and 1330. At this time, **all** exhibition, registration and customer/shareholder enquiry personnel should resume their positions until the last shareholder leaves the building.

17.   Counting of votes by a show of hands

[Registrars] personnel will be responsible for recording and counting the show of hands (that is, by shareholders raising their yellow cards) if it is not clear whether the resolution has been carried or not. [Name] of [Registrars] will be positioned near one of the Question Points in the auditorium so as to communicate with the Chairman.

18.   Poll

[Registrars] personnel are responsible for conducting a poll should the event occur. Again, [Name] of [Registrars] will be strategically placed near one of the question points so as to be able to communicate with the Chairman as to the validity of the poll request. The detailed procedure on the conduct of a poll will be dealt with by the Company Secretary at the Meeting. Ballot boxes and poll cards will be stored under lock and key in the registrars' office and only brought out by [Registrars] personnel in the event of a poll.

19.   Organisers' staff

The [Company] AGM is organised by the [Venue] and [Event Organisers]. As well as technical crew, stewards, caterers and security staff, the following people will be on duty throughout the day:

[Name]	event director	[Event Organisers]
[Name]	question controller	[Event Organisers]
[Name]	senior producer	[Venue]
[Name]	producer	[Venue]
[Name]	centre co-ordinator	[Venue]
[Name]	head of security	[Venue]

In the event of any queries or problems, please go to the organisers' office in room 3/10 on the third floor. They are both linked to the other members of the crew by walkie-talkie and can issue instructions as required.

20.   Communications

The general telephone number for the [Venue] is [Tel. No.]. To contact representatives of the [Venue] or [Event Organisers], the direct lines to the [Company] AGM organisers' office are as follows:

[Tel. No.] telephone   [Tel. No.] facsimile

To contact [Company] staff, the direct lines to the investor relations office are as follows:

[Tel. No.] telephone   [Tel. No.] facsimile

21.   Catering

21.1   *Shareholders' Catering Arrangements*

Shareholders will be served tea, coffee, orange juice or mineral water in [Room 1] before and after the AGM. The catering service will operate from 1000 to 1100 and 1300 to 1400.

21.2   *Board Members' Catering*

Light refreshments will be served in [Room 3] before and after the AGM.

21.3   *Lunch*

Lunch will be served to invited guests in [Room 10] from 1330 as a seated buffet.

Appendices

[Location Map of [Venue]]
[Plan of Registration Area (Room 1) and the Auditorium (Room 2 and Room 10)]

Specimen briefing document for AGM

Notices of meetings

34 – (1)   For the purposes of determining which perons are entitled to attend or vote at a meeting, and how many votes such persons may cast, the participating issuer may specify in the notice of the meeting a time, not more than 48 hours before the time fixed for the meeting, by which a person must be entered on the relevant register of securities in order to have the right to attend or vote at the meeting.

(2)   Changes to entries on the relevant register of securities after the time specified by virtue of paragraph (1) shall be disregarded in determining the rights of any person to attend or vote at the meeting, notwithstanding any provisions in any enactment, articles of association or other instrument to the contrary.

(3)   For the purposes of serving notices of meetings, whether under section 370(2) of the 1985 Act, any other enactment, a provision in the articles of association or any other instrument, a participating issuer may determine that persons entitled to receive such notices are those persons entered on the relevant register of securities at the close of business on a day determined by him.

(4)   The day determined by a participating issuer under paragraph (3) may not be more than 21 days before the day that the notices of the meeting are sent.

Index